DAVE'S TALES

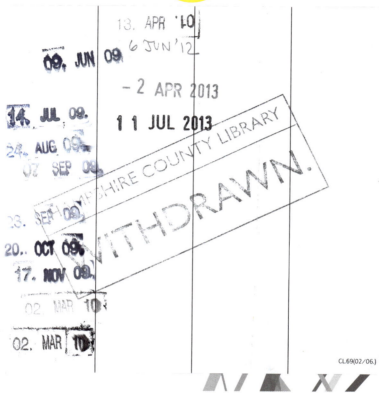
CL.69(02/06.)

Please return or renew this item by the last date shown.
You can renew online at www.hants.gov.uk/library
Or by phoning 0845 603 5631

Hampshire
County Council

DAVE'S TALES

From the 1930s to the 1990s

David Franklin

Book Guild Publishing
Sussex, England

First published in Great Britain in 2008 by
The Book Guild Ltd
Pavilion View
19 New Road
BN1 1UF

Typesetting in Times by
Keyboard Services, Luton, Bedfordshire

Printed and bound in Great Britain by
CPI Antony Rowe

A catalogue record for this book is available from
The British Library

ISBN 978 1 84624 193 2

Contents

Tale 1

Heil Hitler – Goodbye

The earliest of my tales relate to a yellowing dog-eared Brownie box-camera photo of myself standing in front of the Café Haus Kranzler in Berlin, hanging on to a dog's lead at the end of which Tony, a black dachshund, was straining at the leash.

The young David Fraenkel was only three years old but I was dressed in naval gear from navy-blue shorts, navy-blue jacket to navy-blue cap and the cap tally read 'Kriegs Marine'.

Almost twenty-five years later, very Ordinary Seaman David Franklin stood outside Victoria Barracks, halfway between the piers at Portsmouth and Southsea. I wore navy-blue 18-inch bell bottoms, a navy jersey, gleaming white dickie front and my cap tally read 'HMS *Victory*'.

I was born in Berlin in 1924 and my parents, older brother and I lived in a flat in the western suburb of Charlottenburg. The birth certificate lists my father's and mother's name but states the certificate is only valid for baptism. As my family are Jewish and I was koshered at birth, this would have caused a major problem with our rabbi and my family. They, like many Jewish families, were very liberal in their religious beliefs and were assimilated Germans. As most of them had lived there for generations, the men had carried their patriotism to the Western Front in World War I and the widows and mothers of the twelve thousand men who had fallen in the war wore the Kaiser's medals with pride. My father displayed his six mounted Iron Crosses at dinner parties after the guests were on their third schnapps.

I cannot remember any of this but the details come from diaries, photographs, official documents, school reports and newspaper cuttings. Retrograde amnesia is usually the result of severe concussion and the consequent memory loss can range from minutes to hours depending on the severity of the injury. However, it can also be caused by self-inflicted memory loss as a way of suppressing unpleasant memories and, in effect, is a brain safety mechanism. One of the most serious recorded cases of amnesia was the result of herpes simplex suffered by the conductor Clive Wearing, when a freak dose of this wreaked havoc with the lobes of his brain. However, he can now read music again and his life has become a ceaseless reawakening of the past twenty years.

The sparse reawakening of my nine-year memory loss is fortunately limited only to very few events of this period.

The lakes around Berlin are covered with woodland and, on weekends, we and many Berliners picnicked around the Wannsee. The brown-shirted jackbooted SA thugs had training camps in these forests and could make life for the picnicking weekenders a living hell. At night after drowning litres of beer, they used their leather truncheons on anyone within skull-smashing distance and so, week by week, fewer families visited these picnic grounds.

Joe, the janitor at my father's factory, was built like a Finnish Suomi fighter and he and his girlfriend, Josy, had a wooden bungalow by the lakeside. Because of the marauding SA gangs, he had put a four metre mesh-wire fence around the perimeter of his property and for added protection always took a Dobermann dog with them over the weekend. Dobermann are ferocious and almost uncontrollable and their short black-brown fur makes them look even more murderous. They stand about eighty centimetres high and their head with its huge jaw is the size of a baby's head. Some police forces will not use them because they can be so unpredictable.

I was about nine years old when Joe asked my father if I would like to spend the weekend with them by the lake and the excitement of swimming and sunbathing made me jump at the suggestion. Joe had a battered Model T Ford, which Josy and I climbed into on a Friday night. On arrival at the cottage she told me not to get out of the car until Joe had firmly secured Wolfy, the Dobermann. Snarling and growling like a wild animal, Wolfy arrived on a very short iron chain which Joe had great problems holding on to. I sat in the car until Wolfy was under control and we drove to the cottage and walked slowly up to it. On arrival, Wolfy was locked into a broom cupboard and Josy went to the kitchen and came back with a sliced loaf of black rye bread. She handed me two pieces, then removed a roll of tape from the first-aid kit, cut four

2

strips of the tape, placed one piece under each of my armpits and proceeded to tape the bread to the side of my body and arms. Joe then took me to my bunk and told me not to take any notice of strange noises in the night but if I felt scared I should wake them.

In the middle of the night I heard the drunken SA men rattling the iron fence, got out of the bunk, walked up to the window and saw five of them forming a human pyramid to climb up and over the fence. Joe came out with a Luger and told the thugs to get down from the fence. This resulted in them shaking it violently and screaming obscenities at Josy. When the thug at the top of the pyramid reached the top of the fence, he jumped over it shouting and screaming at us. I was transfixed and feared for my life as the other SA men came rushing at us with torched truncheons. Joe went over to the broom cupboard where Wolfy was not only straining at the chain, but was also throwing himself against the door and, with a final push, burst out like a rocket being shot out of a cannon, snarling and baring his long white teeth like a crocodile.

He hurtled across the garden and, on reaching the fence, arched his back like a giant taut spring, stretched out his front legs, straightened his back and, with a mighty leap, sailed over the fence with a metre to spare.

He sank his fangs into the first thug, who screamed with terror. Wolfy was tearing him apart limb from bloody limb and the torn pieces of flesh and blood were turning the sandy soil into a muddy dark-brown stinking morass. How Joe managed to pull Wolfy off the bloody body, I'll never know, but I could not watch any longer. Josy and Joe took me back to my bunk, gave me some hot milk and gently stroked me back to sleep.

In the morning, Josy came in with a cup of hot cocoa and told me they had a pleasant surprise for me. I looked up at her like a grateful puppy. She wouldn't tell me what the surprise was but when we sat down at breakfast, Joe came over and asked me to lift my arms. He removed the taped pieces of bread and called Wolfy in and made him sit hunchbacked next to my knee and I could feel the warmth of his head against my leg and almost died with fear. Joe took my hand and said, 'Don't move, I am going to put the two pieces of bread on top of Wolfy's jaw.' Then turning to Wolfy, he ordered, 'Brot.'

Wolfy tossed the two pieces of bread into the air, opened his gigantic jaws and the bread disappeared like minced lettuce leaves. He swallowed hard and came over to me like a loving puppy, waggled the stub of his tail, nudged my knee and gently, very gently, rested his huge jaw on it. I was petrified.

Joe stroked the dog's head and ears, and turning to me, said: 'You'll be all right now. The sweat from under your arm has been soaked up by the bread and Wolfy will be your faithful guardian for life.'

And he turned out to be the faithful guardian of my memory for years. Almost everything else from this time has gone; I can hardly remember names, faces or places. The flat we lived in, the school I went to or where it was are all blank, but the Dobermann has stuck in my memory, and although it is almost seventy years ago the memory of that night at the Wannsee still sends shivers down my spine.

But there are other memories, occasional chinks of pleasure or horror – mostly horror. The sounds of marching jackbooted thugs, the sight of hundreds of blood-red swirling flags with the hooked cross inside the white circle. These still haunt me today.

By the time Hitler became Chancellor on 30th January 1933, his street gangs had already seized control of the State and the gutter had come to power. The evil genius of Dr Paul Joseph Goebbels had control of the entire media, the written and printed word, all the radio networks and the cinema. The UFA film studio at Babelsberg, near the Wannsee immediately set about making Nazi epics portraying the tall, flaxen-haired, blue-eyed Aryan supermen who were going to conquer the world and make the Third Reich last a thousand years.

One of the films was *Hitler Youth Quex*, which glorified a 21-year-old brutal Berlin SA leader, Horst Wessel, who lived with and pimped for Erna Jännike, a prostitute in a Berlin slum.

One day they received a visit from another pimp, Ali Höhler, who had been Miss Jännike's procurer and had just emerged from prison. After some shouting they both pulled out guns and Höhler shot Wessel dead.

As Höhler was a communist, Goebbels immediately used this as an INFAMOUS ACT OF ANTI-NAZI TERRORISM. A special three stanza marching song, 'Hold the flag high', became the unofficial German National Anthem from the 1930s onwards. The *Quex* film was released throughout Germany and classes IV, V, VI and VII were ordered to see it on a Saturday afternoon in December

1933. The boys were waiting outside the SPLENDID cinema in Charlottenburg and suddenly a motorcade of four sleek black drop head Mercedes pulled up beside the steps leading up to the foyer of the cinema.

The glistening polished chrome of the spike wheels, the V-shape wedge-sharp radiator and the occupying SS men in their black uniforms with the silver skull and cross bones badges made them all look like scorpions from hell.

The cars had hardly stopped before the three SS occupants of the first car grabbed the top of the half-doors, pulled themselves up and leapt up, out and over onto the pavement. Mercedes two and three followed suit, then the fourth car pulled up slowly to the curb and stopped. The SS man next to the driver and his mate in the rear jumped out and waited on the pavement for the passenger in the rear seat.

He was very small, and had jet-black hair, flattened sleekly across his skull and his complexion had a grey pallor. As he pulled himself forward his hand grabbed the top of the half door and one foot appeared which he placed on the pavement. He now launched himself forward and the other leg came into view searching for the pavement. With one almighty tug he pulled himself forward and the rest of the leg came into view. The black trouser leg revealed a black clubfoot at its extremity. One of the SS men came forward to help him hobble to the pavement, up the steps and into the cinema, his open full-length black leather coat trailing behind him.

The boys had watched all this in stony silence and just one word started to ripple through their ranks like the icy sea on a cold winters day: '...Goebbels ... Goebbels ... Goebbels'. And I can still see that clubfoot today.

Once inside the cinema we settled comfortably into the too-big seats and the brilliant brainwashing of the film quickly enthralled all of us, whether we were the tender age of seven or a hardened fourteen. Some, perhaps, were more susceptible than others. Many at school had brothers and fathers who had been unemployed since the 1929 Crash – the fault of course, of greedy Jewish bankers. Some of their fathers were small shopkeepers who had been ruined by the big powerful stores, like Hertie, which were in Jewish hands but most of all, the glorious German army had not lost the first world war but the Jewish speculators and Bolsheviks had stabbed the German army in the back.

5

The German navy had finished the Royal Navy at Jutland and Baron von Richthofen had command of the air over the trenches. The stab in the back and the Bolsheviks were responsible for eight million unemployed and only the SA and the Hitler Youth could restore Germany to its former glory.

All this misery was sliced into film even down to the new technique of two or three frames, which the eye could not detect, but the brain registered the pictures.

Whenever the word 'Jew' was mentioned, two or three frames of the film, imperceptible to the eye but registered by the brain, showed rats in the sewer, and the wealthy swilling food and wine were intersliced with starving shoeless children in the streets. The entire film was a brilliant montage of reality twisted, turned and manipulated to fit the giant lies propagated by the Nazis.

The communist street gangs were portrayed as monsters and the outnumbered HJ were German heroes fighting for the lives of their mothers and sisters.

I was mesmerised by the marching, the flags flying and the deep-throated singing of the Storm Troopers. My pulse started racing when the innocent young Quex was butchered by the horrible communist gang. He died peacefully in the arms of his best mate and his bloody body slipped slowly to the ground and then floated upwards to the sky towards the one true god: Adolf Hitler.

After watching ninety minutes of this we were all eager candidates for the Hitler Youth. Many signed up in the foyer of the cinema and when I returned home, my mother and father asked me about the film. I told them about its content and finished up by asking when they would let me join the Hitler Youth. A stony silence was the immediate reply but later that night my mother tried to explain to me why that was not possible. I remember that I cried all night as I, too, wanted to do something for the Fatherland. After all, Dad had received six Iron Crosses from the Kaiser and Hitler was going to save us and all of Germany.

Just why or how my Dad had received his Iron Crosses both he or Mum were reluctant to tell me. They never talked about Dad's four years in France and Belgium fighting for the Kaiser whilst Mum was at home, all alone, for those four long years.

As I discovered many years later, perhaps the reason for Mum's silence was that during this time she was working voluntarily for the Red Cross in Berlin. It was run very efficiently by a woman whose husband was also fighting on the Western Front. He and Dad never met but Mum and the Red Cross lady started a lesbian relationship. When only Dad returned from the front in 1918, Mum set about finding a new husband for the Red Cross lady. Her find was a young, virile and undamaged soldier who fitted the bill perfectly. Well, actually he fitted two bills.

My Mum arranged the honeymoon for the young couple and chose Lugano, with its shimmering lake, beautiful mountains and very good hotels. I never found out what the young couple's comments were when Mum joined them at the beginning of week three.

Mum was the most organised and organising woman I have ever known. She not only worked with Dad in the family business of manufacturing ladies' coats and raincoats, but her private life would fit beautifully into a 21C Boon & Porter paperback. Mum's Dad had one of the leading pharmacies in Berlin and the oldest of her three sisters was married. The oldest offspring was a son who had been killed on the first day of World War I. Their religious beliefs were very liberal but in one area they still observed the old Jewish custom of daughters marrying in age order; that is, the oldest first and the youngest last. Mum was the last in line, and when a young Ernest Delby asked my grandad for my mum's hand, he was told that the old custom of 'youngest last' had to be observed and as Mum had two older unmarried sisters, the answer, reluctantly, was a sad but firm 'no'. So – Ernest Delby upped sticks and joined a bank in London.

One year later suitor number two, my Dad, asked Grandad the same question and was given an identical reply. Mum's response was simple – 'I either marry or leave the house' – and she got a bag out and started to pack. Grandad capitulated and Mum married Dad on the 6th July 1913. Retrograde amnesia or not, I'll never forget the date: 6.7.13.

One year later Dad went off to war but meanwhile young Ernest was interned in London, as he was classified an 'enemy alien'. After the war he was released and returned to Berlin in 1921. On his very first day back at work he went for his coffee break and ran into Mum who was also having a cuppa. He told her what had happened to him over the past years and than asked about her fate over the same period.

'Better still, why don't we have dinner tonight and chew over old times,' he said.

Mum gave him an old-fashioned look adding: 'That would be lovely, but I am married, have a baby son and I don't know what my husband would say.' What Dad did say when Mum told him over dinner was: 'Go on, it'll be nice ... the three of us can chat about old pre war times.'

'Uncle Ernest' did join them for dinner and stayed for life, which is how the ménage à trois was born and lasted for almost sixty years.

And so the dachshund in that yellowing dog-eared Brownie box-camera shot of myself, aged three, belonged to Uncle Ernest, who allowed me to take Tony for 'walkies' on Saturday mornings.

On Saturday nights Mum and Dad went to see a show or film. If it was the Opera, Mum would be in her finest reeking of perfume, while Dad smelled of cigar smoke. They would wake me on Sunday morning and tell me all about the latest Dietrich film or how that English singer, Eva Turner, had been fantastic at the Staatsoper.

But during the week they were both at work before I got ready for school and I hardly ever saw them in the evening after they came home.

During the daytime my brother and I were looked after by our pretty young 'Brunhilde' of a maid. Her care for us, was only interrupted with monotonous regularity by the results of her adventures with the young guardsmen from the nearby barracks. Mum always said she was attracted by their uniforms ... on and off. When my brother entered Berlin in September 1945 as a British Army sergeant he tried to discover what had happened to our dear 'Brunhilde'. He was horrified to discover she had been raped by a group of Cossacks after the Russians conquered Berlin in May 1945. After half the regiment had finished raping her, she was strung up on a lamp-post and left as a warning to any non-cooperative German woman.

My school reports from the Herder Gymnasium only list two 'good' subjects: music and mathematics. French was 'sufficient', but 'English' was not listed, neither written nor oral, as it was not in my curriculum. Mum always insisted it wasn't necessary and even if I did need it, it was easy to learn because, as she pointed out, a Pole, at an older age than I, had mastered it and become one of the leading writers in the language.

Joseph Conrad wrote the 20th-century haunting masterpiece 'Heart of Darkness' and coincidentally a few years later I came out of Wolfy's darkness and started remembering events with clarity.

8

In 1936 Josef Goebbels pulled off one of the most impressive events of the Nazi era, engineered with Teutonic precision, which was intended to impress upon the world the triumph of the German spirit over Bolshevik and Jewish world domination. The Berlin Olympics were a showpiece of law, order and Aryan supremacy, and the idea of a torch relay from the original Olympic site in Greece to Berlin was readily adopted by Goebbels and the Nazi hierarchy, who saw classical Greece as an Aryan forerunner to their modern Reich. During the Games, the German teams were winning medal after medal and Hitler was present to demonstrate to the world that his Aryan race theory was now a proven fact. Hitler's statement that the sporting contest should 'help knit the bonds of peace between nations' would soon ring hollow.

One of my classmate's fathers had a catering contract for the participating athletes in the Olympic village. He managed to get us two seats for the 100-metre men's final on 3rd August and, to us, it was like winning the lottery. We watched with anticipation as the athletes warmed up and got to their starting blocks; a deathly hush descended over the stadium. Next to the blonde competitors were two Americans and both were black.

Everyone held their breath as the athletes shot out of their blocks, all eyes turning towards Hitler as he watched the two black runners pulling away from the master race. When Jesse Owens crossed the winning line, he had not only won but the 10.2 seconds time was a world record. The stadium erupted and Hitler's race theory crumbled into the Olympic dust as he presented the gold medal to the winner who was American and as black as non-Aryan coal.

The excitement of the Olympics was quickly forgotten, however, when on my return home, my Mum told me that Dad had been taken away by the Gestapo that morning. The resourceful Mrs Fraenkel, however, was not going to be beaten by that vermin. She went to Dad's desk drawer and took out the Iron Crosses from the cigar box and took a cab to our office. Mum and Dad had been preparing for this eventuality and had been pushing their export sales to the UK. Not because they especially liked Mr Baldwin, but because they knew Hitler was short of foreign currency and would not want to see any loss in that direction. In the office she gathered all the documentary evidence she could and took it with her to the Gestapo headquarters. Initially they laughed at her but she pushed to see the man at the top, and when she did, even he was concerned that if Dad wasn't released, a large chunk of sterling would not be coming into the Reichsbank and the 'high-ups' would be less than happyy. Happily Dad was released the next day and Uncle Ernest caught the next ferry to Harwich to start up Delby Coats in London.

My parents now told me officially that we were off to the UK in the autumn and that this term was going to be my last at the Herder Gymnasium. My school report laconically states: 'Reason for leaving: Going to England.' The frantic departure preparations started and continued non-stop. The Nazi clampdown on taking furniture was not yet in force but the amount of your own money that you could take with you was strictly limited. Enterprising as ever, Mum had gone to the news kiosk and bought a copy of the latest *Völkischer Beobachter*, the official Nazi newspaper, and when I came home with a football, which I planned to take with me, I was told not to clean it. Mum wrapped it carefully in the crushed pages of VB, asked me to strip off my sweaty football gear and proceeded to pack everything into my little weather beaten pressed cardboard football case.

She paused when she came to the football, went over to the kitchen drawer, pulled out a small thin sharp knife and proceeded to carefully undo the laces of the leather ball. When she had opened a fist-sized hole, she went over to a holdall which she had brought from the office and emptied it. It was stashed full of bricklike, rubber-banded wads of 100-mark notes. A happy smile spread across her face as she turned to me: 'I think this should keep you in ice creams for a few days.' I just gasped as she packed the notes into the football, and, for extra security, wrapped it up in the latest copy of the *Völkischer Beobachter*, the official Nazi newspaper.

As departure day drew nearer I grew more apprehensive about the unknown future which would start in September. The dreaded day came and we caught the train to Cuxhafen with our own personal luggage, the furniture was being shipped over by the carrier who was handling the company's exports. There was no problem at customs and the burly customs and sinister black-uniformed SS guards permitted themselves a wry smile when they opened my little football case and saw the wrapped football inside the *Völkischer Beobachter*.

Wolfy must have numbed their brains, as a Jewish family leaving the Nazi paradise would hardly read this rag of sinister misinformation.

Once aboard the Hamburg-America ship *Bremen*, we settled into our two cabins, one for Mum and Dad, and one for me and my brother. I had the top bunk whilst my brother took the lower one. Mum popped in later to tuck us in and quietly said to me: 'Tomorrow you start a new life and you must promise to learn English fast. And for a start here are your first two words, which you will use a lot: "Yes" and "No" but be careful not to say the first one too often, it may land you in trouble.' She kissed me goodnight and left the cabin. Almost twenty-five years later, the identical advice was given to me by a burly old sailor who ran our mess deck with a rod of iron. It was my first day of basic training, and when he came to the words '...it may land you in trouble,' he winked at me and added: '...especially if you are in the showers and a stoker behind you has just dropped the soap and asked you to bend over and pick it up.'

It was a glorious morning when we sailed up the Solent and saw the shimmering Isle of Wight on our port beam. Minutes later Portsmouth came into view with dozens of warships at anchor in the harbour.

Just before Southampton docks we were joined by three little tugs who were going to shepherd us alongside. The gangway was secured and the passengers began to disembark. I shuffled gingerly down the wooden angled gangway and halfway down looked back at the ship from stem to stern and shuddered: that bloody swastika flag was fluttering from her stern. I momentarily stumbled. A firm hand grabbed my arm and I looked into the green eyes of a chirpy, freckled face of a kid about eighteen. His woollen cloth cap was resting on a shock of ginger curls and his green checked shirt had its sleeves rolled up above the elbow. A metal badge with the initials 'SR' was pinned to his sleeveless green knitted cardigan. There was not a black uniform with skull-and-crossbone badge or swastika in sight.

A broad grin stretched across his young face as he furrowed his forehead, raised his ginger eyebrows questioningly and quipped: 'OK ... son?' I just nodded which he acknowledged by clenching his fist, thumb firmly extended skywards.

As I watched the tugs guiding the *Bremen* back out to sea, I could see their little stern flags fluttering in the breeze. They were the red dusters, the red flags flown by British-registered ships, with the Union flag stuck firmly in the top corner next to the flagstaff.

11

Suddenly I felt free from the Nazi curse and if this was to be my new friendly home, Britain was going to be great and the sooner I bought a German/English dictionary, the better.

Tale 2

Refugee from Nazi Persecution to Enemy Alien

Mum radiated enthusiasm and bubbling energy. She stood only five foot five in her sheer silk stockings but her sky-blue eyes were like a shining magnet to all around her. Men just fell at her feet and she twisted everyone around her little finger as easily as she rolled those silk stockings down her shapely legs. She was a bundle of dynamite and determination which she had displayed to her Dad when overruling his decision of non-marriage to Dad. And that was in 1913 when she was only 23 years old. Men were there to be told what to do and to be loved. Her bursting into Gestapo headquarters and ordering them what to do seems unimaginable but Mum pulled it off, no problem. She was the eternal optimist and, even when all seemed lost, she would find the tiniest reason for being hopeful. All our friends used to say jokingly that she would always be looking for that chink of blue in the sky even when it was raining cats and dogs from the blackest of clouds.

It was Mum who coordinated Uncle Ernest's efforts to establish a bridgehead in London and he carried out her wishes with enthusiasm and efficiency. He and Charles, his younger brother, were born in Nienburg, northern Germany.

Charles left home at an early age and remained the typical bachelor throughout his life. His female conquests stretched from Vienna to Budapest, Paris to London; selling to female buyers in the textile trade enlarged his stock of the available opposite sex by leaps and bounds. When World War I broke out he was in Vienna and joined the Austrian army. They were working in conjunction with a German regiment taking part in the occupation of Brussels. He arranged a move to a special police unit which had the organisation of the brothels under its control and Charles had to visit the prostitutes regularly in the course of duty to check

13

that their finances and health checks were in order. He carried out both areas of inspection with due diligence which cemented his relationship with the girls, the doctors and the clients. This sexual paradise came to an end in 1918 when the war ended and, much to his disappointment, he had to leave. However, this four-year apprenticeship also taught him French, Italian and English – the brothels attracted all nationalities. He was twenty-eight years old and the world was his oyster and he had no need of a scraper to detach the oysters from their shells. He looked like the French actor Maurice Chevalier who immortalised the song 'Zank 'eaven for leedel gels', which was also Charles's signature tune. Only Charles wasn't particular about their size; little, medium or large, he loved them all. In the years before World War II he was selling into the ladies rag trade in the UK; fine silks from St Gallen in Switzerland, luxuriously soft cashmere from Hawick in Scotland, minor couture collections from Paris. There just weren't enough days in the week for him to seduce and conquer all the willing and expectant ladies who were queuing up to be admired, flattered and lavishly entertained by my Uncle Charles.

When Mum, Dad and Uncle Ernest's ménage was in full swing in Berlin, Mum ran her two men with a sugar-coated rod of iron. *She* ordered and *they* jumped through her hoop. Mum quite correctly assumed that in the years prior to Uncle Ernest's return to Berlin he had made a lot of friends in the London banking world. One of these, Mr Joseph, started a small merchant bank in London in 1919 and Leopold Joseph and Sons were the first private bank specialising in foreign currency dealings. Uncle Ernest was fascinated by the stiff-upper-lip banking fraternity, but his major problem was his very Jewish surname and he spoke to one of his stiff-upper-lip friends about it.

Tom Avery was the epitome of a retired colonial army colonel: ruddy complexion, a shock of white hair with matching thick white moustache, six foot two inches out of his jodhpurs and a booming voice straight off the parade ground at Sandhurst. On hearing that Uncle Ernest was thinking of having visiting cards printed he shook his head disapprovingly. Ernest's and Charles's family surname was Israel and Tom Avery felt this was a distinctive disadvantage when dealing with the staid English business establishment. 'No, no, no...,' he said, shaking his head of white hair. 'You must sound as terribly British as you already look with your rolled umbrella and bowler hat. With a name like Israel they'll tell you to go back to your barrow in Brick Lane.' Over a very pleasant, thinly carved pink roast beef lunch at Simpson's in The Strand, Tom Avery approached the problem like planning the next attack against the rebels in the Punjab. 'Forget Israel; it's a very nice name but nothing as pukka as Harrods or Fortnum & Mason. What was your mother's family name?' he asked Ernest, who felt his ship had been holed in the bows and the stern. 'Friedländer,' he murmured, sinking fast whilst Tom ordered another double Grant's whisky.

Taking his sip from the refilled glass Tom continued: 'We'll have to accept the fact that all your ancestors appear to be firmly stuck in Middle Europe.' There was a long pause. '...So what's your grandparents surname?' Poor Uncle Ernest didn't think there was enough room for him to crawl under the table but almost inaudibly mumbled, 'Elb.'

For one second Tom Avery lost his cool but immediately remembered what his CO had said to him all those years ago when all his men were being cut down by the marauding tribesmen: 'Steady on, old boy...' He reached for the glass, took a huge gulp, draining it totally, and swiftly ordered another from the waiter with the black sleeveless waistcoat and long white apron reaching down to his toes.

'What have we got...' Another long pause. 'Let's start with Elb.' He took a deep breath.

They tucked into their delicious smoked salmon with thinly buttered brown bread on the side. As the maître d' approached their table, he bowed from the waist, looked at Tom and froze. He hadn't seen his face since the Punjab days.

'How nice to see you here, Sir. I must have missed you on your last trip just after the King died.'

Tom was momentarily taken aback but smiled broadly when he recognised his RSM of many years gone by. 'Pleased to see you as well, Thompson. Might even see you sooner than we think again if young David marries that Simpson woman. She's chased so many wealthy men over the years they now call her the lady in much seduced circumstances. It's him and the throne she's after, take my word for it.' And in a moment the two had resurrected the old informal service relationship which had served them so well over the years.

15

Thompson smiled at Tom Avery, raised his eyebrows and asked: 'Salmon on form, was it, Sir? Shall I call the carver over for you?' He waved his hand towards the kitchen and a trolley appeared as swiftly as a 12-inch-gun salute on the parade ground.

The carver manoeuvred the trolley next to their table, swung the silver half-dome open and the delicious smell of a huge side of beef wafted over them.

'Fat or lean, Sir, red or well done?' Thompson queried.

Uncle Ernest stared at the procedure and added meekly. 'I'll just have the same, thank you.'

'Gravy, Sir?' asked the carver as Tom nodded and the reddish-brown liquid around the beef was spooned up and delicately dribbled over the beef. After the carver and maître d' had departed and Tom had rewarded their open palms with a shilling, they dug into the feast in front of them.

'Let us continue our search of your name,' said Tom, wiping drops of gravy from his chin. 'Many English names end with a "y", like mine, and I think if we add a "y" to our "elb" we've made a good start with "Elby". Let's go through the alphabet to find a suitable letter to stick in front. Aelby sounds like some kind of fish. Belby is too much of a tongue twister. Celby sounds like some godforsaken village in Leicester. Delby ... hang on ... I think we've got it.' And he sank back triumphantly just as if he had won the winner at Ascot.

Ernest was very pleased with his new name and breathed a sigh of relief. Not for long.

Tom was now in full flow. Item 2 and 3 needed planning and completion. The name change needed to be registered and a visit to the Trade Name Registration was also required to register the company name, too. He was relentless.

Tom next pressed Uncle Ernest on the quantity of required company directors. Uncle Ernest sheepishly asked the minimum number required for registration.

'You're as thick as two planks and they're not fine-honed,' said Tom disgustedly. 'You already have three for starters ... but they are all non-Brits so if you think you need a genuine Brit, would you like me on the board? If all the directors are non-British, they have to disclose their nationality and it might look a bit odd if there are only German nationals on the Board. Some dickhead might assume it's a Nazi set-up.'

Uncle Ernest gawped at him. 'Would *you* like to become a director?'

For once Tom dropped his stiff-upper-lip composure and allowed himself the faintest of smiles. 'I really thought you'd never ask' he said stretching his hand across to Uncle Ernest and squeezing it like a vice. 'Take me back to the Army and Navy and we'll meet tomorrow morning to get Delby Coats afloat. I'll make all the arrangements.'

Uncle Ernest looked at him like a grateful puppy that had just found his basket.

As Mum had planned and hoped, the bridgehead was now established and awaited the arrival of our family in London.

I couldn't get that chirpy eighteen-year-old SR porter out of my head and all the way to London he was there in my thoughts, friendly in his cheerful green attire. Just like the trees and fields which all seemed to be in the same lush green palette.

In the train Mum looked at me and smiled and asked if I was happy and I nodded, furiously burbling on about all the greenery and the small houses. In Berlin there was nothing but big blocks of flats, asphalted streets, cheerless uniforms and those bloody, bloody flags.

When we got to Waterloo the carriages were swarming with un-uniformed porters who were all whistling the same tune. Mum had hoped I would pick up English easily and her belief was based on my having a musical ear. Any tune or accent, my ear picked it and stored it and I was up and away like a parrot. We walked to the head of the train but saw no engine. I asked Mum why and she gave me the logical answer that there were no "puff-puffs" pulling it on Southern Railway because they were all electric.

'Why?' became my major question. Why is everything green? Why don't porters wear uniforms? Why were there no uniforms anywhere? Why did the police wear domed helmets and why weren't their chinstraps under their chins? And why was everybody so quiet and pleasant and nobody was shouting at you? Why ... why ... why? Mum had received a crash course in English culture from Uncle Ernest in the form of little brown envelopes each marked with the relevant subject matter. 'Money' told us about farthings, halfpennies, pennies, sixpences, shillings and half crowns, and that there were twelve pence to the shilling, twenty shillings to the pound. Why?? 'Taking a taxi' included how Mum could put her

17

pretty English to good use.'What to look out for on trip' gave instructions about which side of the train we should sit on so that when the train left Waterloo we would be able to see the Houses of Parliament and Big Ben. The Thames, the instructions told us, we would cross twice before we reached Richmond... Why? Why? Mum nearly lost her patience before explaining that the Thames curled like a snake through the green countryside.

Outside Richmond station Mum accordingly practised her English with a friendly cabbie whose knowledge extended professionally to our destination. Once inside the taxi, Mum opened the 'Richmond Bridge Mansions' envelope, which described our new home as being next to the bridge at Richmond. She told the cabbie, but he shook his head. 'Which end of the bridge?' he asked impatiently. Mum again said 'Richmond', at which point he would have torn his hair out had he not been so very thin on top. In desperation, Mum showed him the address. Looking at Mum in a very strange way, he said, 'Lady, it ain't in Richmond; the other side's East Twickenham, in'it.'

Tom Avery and Uncle Ernest felt that the location of a flat between two of the best non-boarding schools was the best choice as they did not know which either one us would be able to go to. Richmond was equidistant between St Pauls in Hammersmith and Hampton Grammar and Tom had found out that, scholastically, they were the top of London's educational tree.

Both my brother and I managed to get into Hampton Grammar. Although his English was not bad, my own was non-existent. As Dad's English was pretty ropey, Mum decided to come to both interviews with the respective headmasters. St Pauls did not fancy having a non-English speaking pupil in class but 'Bossy' Mason at Hampton was enthusiastic. Whether it was the challenge of having non English-speaking pupils or the fact that we were refugees I shall never know, but if it had not been for him and Bill Steffens, the maths master, my life and my business career would never have blossomed. They both bent over backwards to get me interested in the English language even to the point of spending a few hours per day in Hampton's prep school, Denmead, in Wensleydale Road. Mr and Mrs James almost became my private English tutors and every minute of 'break' time was spent by them teaching English to this almost deaf mute from Berlin.

Alfred Siddel Mason OBE was a brilliant Headmaster with about sixteen subject masters under him and to us he was 'Bossy'. He was a tall gaunt figure and his thin silvery hair made him look older than his age. At assembly in the morning we shook in our boots and he was strict about everything, especially language. Once, however, when a health scare was being whipped up by the tabloids, he quietly announced at assembly that 'we must take special care to always wash our hands ... after taking a shit.' Sadly, the days of pocket tape recorders had not yet arrived but the story circulated for years.

F.E. Steffens had joined the school as a junior boy in 1918, left as a school captain in 1926 and returned later as a schoolmaster. He had a habit of standing at the back of the class, which enabled him to see whose head was beginning to droop to one side, and then would be on to his victim like a fox pouncing on a rabbit. I had a third mentor, 'Jammy' James, who was a specialist in grammar and played the school organ. He and his wife devoted pretty much every minute of breaktime to teaching me English.

Whatever I asked any one of the three mentors 'Why,' the reply was instant. I once remember asking 'Jammy' if Shakespeare could be funny and the next time we had an English lesson he called me to the front of the class and thrust the Swan Shakespeare *Comedies* under my nose and sternly commanded, 'Read it!'

English grammar presented no problems whatsoever because nouns only had one gender. There were two in French and three in German, so very few 'whys'. However, my biggest problem was pronunciation. 'Ease', 'breeze' and 'seize' were all pronounced the same way yet were spelled differently. When it came to 'Worcester' or 'Cholmondeley', even Mr James could give me no logical answer. Generally speaking, I picked English up easily, though the boys in 2C ribbed me murderously, especially when it came to my name. Although Fraenkel was not a tongue-twister it was immediately bastardised into 'Freddy'. Years later, my matelot mess-mates chose the direct path and called me 'Dave', which soon degenerated into 'Doive' if they hailed from within the sound of Bow bells.

Hampton School will be 450 years old in 2007 and was founded from the will of Robert Hammond in the days of Bloody Queen Mary. When I first attended in 1937 it was situated near the water reservoir on Upper Sunbury Road. A new school was being built on Hanworth Road in 1938. There is some dispute about its actual foundation date but it's Rampant Lion Crest is scrolled AD 1556,

19

below it stating PRAESTAT OPES SAPIENTIA, which makes me settle for 1556. After all, I will not see the 2056 anniversary.

Two of my best-remembered clangers were dropped when I had to read out aloud in class. Usually my classmates hung on my every 'th', which initially gave me a problem until I was told to practise putting my tongue between my teeth and blowing hard. In this particular instance I came to a bit about 'flowers blooming in the garden', which I paraphrased as 'blooming flowers'. 'Jammy' cleared his throat and quietly pointed out that 'blooming' was not in general usage as it suggested a mild swear. The other mild clanger occurred when I was again fronting the class reading out a piece about lighthouses. It rambled on about the 'eternal night-light' being a lifeline to sailors out at sea and shining a safe passage to their home port. The class was dropping off nicely until I came to the bit about the beam being like a beacon, which I pronounced as 'bacon' ... neither salted nor koshered.

My closest friend was my House and class Captain, who later achieved the ultimate of becoming School Captain. He led from the front scholastically and on the sports field. I'll never forget the time when we were sunning ourselves in the cricket field in 1939. We looked up at the blue sky and spun wishes of what we were going to do once we had left school. I had no plans short of wanting to be better than him in English. The butterflies were lazily dancing around us and Mike caught one and, as if gently disrobing a young virgin, pulled its wings off and placed them in a glass jar he had handy.

'I'm going to be a surgeon,' Mike Brudenell said. Later Mike would become one of Britain's leading obstetricians and gynae-cologists and I have followed his rise to royal fame and fortune with admiration and pleasure.

I never attained such dizzy heights. 'Steffs' set me on the 'figures' road which built the foundation for my international trading business. 'Two and two make four, but never fool yourself.' This was his advice that would assure my survival through currency crises and devaluations.

My journey to school on my first day was tortuous. Had Uncle Ernest known that going to Hampton Grammar meant a bus ride to Teddington, a train ride to Strawberry Hill, where I had to change for Hampton, he and Mum would surely not have exposed me to the hidden dangers that this meant for a very innocent twelve-year-old. The Southern Rail carriages were made up of single compartments, with doors on the platform sides. On quiet mornings there was a maximum of two or three passengers per compartment and the time between stations was five to ten minutes. One of my seniors at school was a fat, sloppy and generally repulsive slob who did not believe in washing, on principle! He towered above me in height and as soon as he discovered me in an empty compartment, he pounced. I was much too naive to even guess what he actually wanted to do, but the minute the train left the station, he jumped on me. Off came his stinking trousers and yellowing underpants and the smell became overpowering. Fortunately, the railway stations were too close to each other for matters to reach an explosive conclusion. It was just a question of groping. My knowledge of sex was zero. My Dad never spoke to me about it; Mum thought the birds-and-bees business was taboo; and Billy, my brother, was far too busy chasing the girls at the Hammersmith Palais de Danse to pass on his experience

Billy, however, did supply me with the name of the song the porters had whistled down at Southampton. I heard it often on our Telefunken radio (this, incidentally, had survived the trip after a new three-pin plug had been fitted as our German two pin did not fit the English three holer).

'I'll have a nice cup of tea in the morning' was sung, whistled dance band played morning, noon and night although we did not have a nice cup of tea with our tea as we were still drinking coffee.

My solution to the revolting groper situation resulted in the very first financial transaction of my new life. I calculated the total cost of the bus and train fares and went to Halfords in Twickenham to look for a cheap bike. They displayed second-hand ones outside the shop and I went there after a Saturday's rugby match at Twickers. The milling and slightly drunk fans thronged the pavements and, fortunately for me, one of the unsteady spectators had touched a bike with his size eight boots and knocked it over, providing me with a 'rugby-special-knocked-down-price', slightly scratched Triumph three-speed Stormey Archer gear bike. Mum was very impressed when I put the financial proposal arrangement to her. Train and bus fare costs for a five to six-day week plus a haggled 2 per cent interest rate against the cost of a three-year never-never loan to me.

What I did not appreciate at the time was the fact that I was a total virgin and had 'it' happened with that slob of a boy, sex would have been revolting to me for life and I shudder to think what I would have missed. Let's face it, if Uncle Charles had not taught me all the enjoyable 57 varieties of sexual pleasure, my life would have been all the poorer and very dull.

On the very first day of the bike run to Hampton I collected Bryan Walsh from the Cresswell Road bus garage where his Dad was a London Transport No. 73 bus driver. The family lived next door to the garage and as I dismounted I saw all the buses parked in the garage and gawped. They were all red. In Berlin they were yellow... Why? Bryan explained that all buses in London were red and so were the trolley buses and suddenly he looked guilty.

'Sorry, I should have told you about the trolleybuses; they're like the buses but have a cable arrangement on top to the overhead electric lines which feed the power to the bus. They're really trams but not on rails.' I just shook my head in disbelief until en route to school I saw the Fulwell trolleybus depot with its 'Diddlers'.

My transport queries were endless. 'But why does all the traffic drive on the wrong side of the road?' Bryan could not give me an answer but just said, 'Watch it when you step off the pavement or they'll have you!' Another thing that puzzled me were the names on the side of the buses, of which I found no trace in my *Concise Oxford Dictionary*. Bovril, Heinz, Hovis and Oxo were nowhere in that bible of the English language. *Why?!*

In addition to my circle of English teachers was a friend of Mum and Dad's who had an office in the attic above the firm's workroom in Wardour Street in Soho. Mum and Dad were still speaking German to each other when they met Geoffrey Child on the Wardour Street stairs. When Geoffrey interrupted in broad German they were totally taken aback and he explained that he had been to Berlin University and picked up a thick Berlin accent in the two years of his stay. His fluent French came from another two-year stay at the Sorbonne and his two little rooms in Wardour Street housed a mini-recording studio, which apart from the languages, was his major hobby. Mum was puzzled about his income but soon discovered that Geoffrey was 'comfortable' as he had an allowance from his family. His father had been a property lawyer to Boots the Chemists and after World War I had searched for new shop properties in the UK. Whenever he found one for Boots he bought another for himself, and by 1938 his and Boot's property portfolio was distinctly healthy. Big enough to have paid for Geoffrey to have gone to Rugby and thence to Berlin and Paris. Geoffrey's ear was not just musical but virtually symphonic and he picked any language up in hours. When he discovered my hunger for English he became private tutor number four and introduced my ear to Shakespeare and took me to every play in the West End.

During 1937/38 season the Old Vic featured a 28-year-old Laurence Olivier who, over sixteen months, played a Freudian Hamlet, a succulent Toby Belch, a glowering Macbeth and a satanic Iago. I was, it seemed, less surprised than the rest of the audience when Olivier startled them by kissing Ralph Richardson's Othello full on the mouth. At Christmas 1937, Geoffrey gave me my first English diary and made me promise to keep a record of all important events on a daily basis. Geoffrey came for dinner at least once a month and the first hour became the 'Geoffrey hour' for me. I showed him all the entries in the diary and he then told me which plays he had booked for the following weeks.

In Richmond I saw the films with my brother, Bryan and the other local Hamptonians and the entries read like 'What's On' the silver screen. 'Carefree' at the Ritz followed three pages later by 'Thunder Afloat' at Richmond Bridge and 'Shipyard Sally' at the Royalty totalled six visits in January up to and including Saturday 17th.

Time and the English lessons flew by. My interest in football made a visit to the 'Royalty' a must. 'The Arsenal Stadium Mystery' was a 'who-done-it' with footballers as the centrepiece and their weekly wages were £5 a week, if they were lucky.

One of Geoffrey's visits particularly sticks in my memory. Geoffrey came for dinner on 11th November 1938 and when I opened the door to him he asked to see Mum and Dad. They followed him into the sitting room but suggested I did not come in to join then just yet. Geoffrey knew all our family background details and turned to Mum with a grave face. 'You told me that you still have sisters in Berlin?' Mum nodded, remembering how both she and Dad had pleaded with Auntie Else and Martha to come with us to London. They were both in their early sixties, shared the flat in which they were born, and could not make the break. Anyway, they spoke no English and were sure no one would do anything to them because their brother had received the Iron Cross posthumously on the first day of World War I. Geoffrey seemed to have friends everywhere and on his stay in Berlin he had made a lot of friends with whom he was still in contact. They knew he had Jewish friends in London and asked Geoffrey to find out if his London friends had heard anything from friends or their relations in Berlin. Mum's sisters fitted the bill and he asked Mum if she wanted him to find out if the two aunties were OK.

Apparently all hell against the Jews had broken loose in Germany since the 9th November when, on Kristallnacht, Goebbels, had begun a national three-day terror campaign. Over a thousand synagogues were torched, some 7,500 Jewish shops were looted and vandalised, and over 30,000 Jewish men were dragged out of their beds and packed off to concentration camps (KZs). Geoffrey's friend at the British Embassy would try and get some news about Mum's sisters and perhaps get them out of that hell. Mum gave Geoffrey the sisters' address and within forty-eight hours Mum had the good news that they were OK though they were still refusing to leave their flat.

Goebbels, meanwhile, was getting concerned about the bad publicity Kristallnacht and the KZs were getting in the foreign press (orchestrated, of course, by the Jewish world conspiracy) and decided to build a model KZ to which he would then invite the press. During the war he asked the Red Cross to inspect the camp, complete with filmed UFA evidence. He also promoted it to the remaining old Jewish men, widows and spinsters who were living on their savings and pensions. In return for handing every mark over they were given a signed contract which said:

'The State agrees, for the rest of one's life, to cover board and food expenses in the old-age home; to have one's washing done; to provide medical treatment and medication. However, the State reserves the right to move the accommodation elsewhere...'

In Auntie Else and Martha's case this turned out to be the gas ovens. At the end of the war, Mum had two postcards returned through the Red Cross. They had been sent from Theresienstadt and forwarded to Mum and stated 'Gone away.'

When Uncle Ernest was told about the systematic terror campaign he contacted his brother Charles to up tents from Vienna, leave his loves and join him in London. Three days later Ernest went to Croydon Airport and Charles stepped out of the Imperial Airways plane which had transported him and his broad smile to safety and further amorous conquests. Apart from having found our flat at Richmond Bridge Mansions, Ernest discovered 'Madingley', a splendid B&B boarding house for himself which was only a hundred yards along Willoughby Road from our flat.

The B&B was a highly recommended establishment and boasted a first-class cellar with an enormous collection of fine French, Italian and German wines. They also stored a large collection of fine tinned vegetables such as asparagus and petit pois as well as smooth pâté which was imported directly from Strasbourg.

Both Richmond Bridge Mansions and Madingley had vast gardens which stretched about fifty yards down to the Thames. However, because of the unpredictable spring tides, a four-foot high wall had been built to shield all the properties against the rising waters. In February 1939 an exceptional spring tide rose over the wall and when we awoke in the morning and looked down on the lawn, we had a first-class view over a lake with bushes and trees sticking out of it like miniature islands. The Madingley lawns had a similar view but no damage appeared to have been done to the building. Sadly, the water had flooded the cellar, and hundreds of tins and dozens of bottles were now floating aimlessly in the muddy water – and all without their labels. The only bonus was that the stock lasted well into the rationing period, although every night was gastronomic equivalent of the tombola, trying to guess what the contents of the tins and bottles might be.

After the terror of the Kristallnacht, Uncle Ernest's friend Tom Avery asked him to meet him at Simpson's. After coffee and mints Tom turned to Uncle Ernest with a serious look on his face.

'I think the balloon has gone up with Adolf. I am told in the highest quarters that we'll be at war before the Aussies come over to win the Ashes later in the year. You had your basinful of interment last time around in 1914. Now, your name's already got the Union flag written all over it but you must apply for a deed-poll change of name and naturalisation immediately. It's a two-edged decision, as you may be called up for military service, but at least you won't be locked up as an enemy alien for the second time.' Tom seemed to know all the best people in the right places and he contacted Tim Rogers in the Home Office Naturalisation Department.

'After that,' Tom continued, 'get the deed-poll change of name papers and fill them in. Come over on Thursday, bring two passport photos and it will be done. You can take me over to my favourite watering and eating hole and when we come back, everything should be finished.'

Suddenly Tom paused and knitted his thick white eyebrows which seemed to be growing into one thick white bushy strip. 'Hang on a minute...' Another long pause. 'You've made me a director and you are one as well... So as far as the greedy taxman is concerned one director is taking out another to discuss business matters...' A large smile stretched from one corner of a bushy lip to the other. 'It's a very legitimate business expense and an allowable tax-free perk ... I think your family friends would call it "strictly kosher".'

Tim Rogers came up trumps and Uncle Ernest had his nationality and Status of 'Aliens Act 1914 Certificate of naturalization' certificate in his hands by the end of the week. Tom's solicitor friend in Lincoln Inn Fields had his special courier, a fifteen-year-old telegram boy from Newman Street, on standby for any extra casual job. The lad picked up the completed deed-poll change-of-name forms from Jeffrey Tooth, biked them to Tim at Somerset House, who attached a personal note which read: 'Thanks for the docs. Don't forget to put change-of-name notice in the *London Gazette* and make sure you keep a copy.'

This very British Ernest Delby had now completed his transformation and when Ernest phoned Tom to tell him the good news, he urged Ernest to immediately get Charles, his brother, to repeat the exercise.

'Those docs confirming your new status, plus the rolled umbrella and your new bowler from "Locks", will provide you with splendid camouflage with your prospective pukka clients. Please don't thank me for greasing the sticky wheels of the Establishment. Remember that if you scratch somebody's back, they'll happily return the compliment. However never intentionally piss on them ... it always blows back on you. Back scratching is the lifeblood of the nation and we all do it. Freemasons, trade unionists, football friends and especially past and present service chums. I hope old Toothy didn't make you break the bank?'

Ernest was happy to confirm that A & G Tooth's bill had only come to £7.14.9, including the deed Poll, office copies and statutory documents.

He sauntered happily across Waterloo Bridge to the station, up the few stairs and into the Concourse. The Richmond train was expected to leave in fifteen minutes and it was a 'fast', only one stop at Clapham Junction. He reckoned he'd be home for 'tea and fancies' by six o'clock to tell Mum and Dad the good news. He walked over to the ticket office and the newsstand boy was shouting: 'EXTRA ... EXTRA ... read all about it!' and bought himself a copy of the *Star*' Banner-headlined across the page was 'Hitler marches into Czechoslovakia' and Ernest froze. The piece continued:

'This morning, Monday the thirteenth of March 1939, units of the German Army crossed into Czechoslovakia and entered the town of Moravska-Ostrava...' Before he could continue, Ernest heard the departure whistle for his Richmond train. He rushed to the barrier and just made the last carriage with seconds to spare. At Richmond, he caught the 73 bus to Cresswell Road and walked the few metres to our flat. Mum was not crying but just looked stone cold and Dad looked glum. Mum suddenly pecked up, gave a large smile and saw her 'blue' through the cloud.

'What a good thing we're all here and safe,' she said cheerily and embraced Dad and Ernest in a warm hug whilst Billy and I just stared.

At school we had all talked about the possible 'war' in a very abstract way, but many of the teachers had seen World War I in active terms and, to them, another one was not glamorous at all. The cynics among them had scorned Chamberlain's visit last September to see Hitler. Was it just a ploy to get Britain ready for war? 'Peace in our time... More like one year if you ask me!' Steffs was heard to say from the staff room.

Their fears were confirmed when four Army trucks arrived at the end of the summer holiday and started to unload four machine guns, which they then placed at the four corners of our enormous rectangular playing field.

The next day another truck arrived and a small Army platoon started to assemble sandbags and the guns for possible use against the enemy aircraft. For once, the sixth-formers turned their attention away from the girls at the Lady Eleanor Holles School, which was adjacent to our sports field. The girl sixth-formers were very happy to get the attention of the young soldiers, who to me, appeared to be speaking in a foreign language, but they also attracted a large audience from the Hampton Grammar boys whose language they understood perfectly. I gawped and my ear strained to hear the

27

strange sounds coming from the mouths of the soldiers. ''Allo mite ... allrite then?... Got nuffink to do?' accompanied by leering grins. Fortunately the remarks they made about the girls from next door were incomprehensible to me. At assembly the next morning, Bossy explained to us that the Army had placed the four 'nests' to protect us from the possible might of the Luftwaffe should the Stukas dare enter Hampton Grammar airspace.

Just before the school broke up for the summer holiday, Geoffrey Child came over to Richmond to tell us he had volunteered to join the Army Intelligence Corps, which was only too happy to get the services of someone who had as many languages at his fingertips as he had toes. He tousled my hair and smiled at me. 'Don't worry, when I'm on leave I'll still take you to the theatre ... if they're open. I'll keep in touch and if I see any nasty Nazis I'll tell them to keep away from Richmond. Oh yes I'll also tell them that I love the Jews and there's a family in London who are ten times as good and much kinder than Goebbels.'

Mum tried to wipe away the small tear that ran slowly down her cheek leaving a streaky mascara trail.

We and the rest of the nation were glued to our radio on Sunday the 3rd of September. At 11:15 the weary voice of Neville Chamberlain crackled over Mum, Dad, Billy and myself. ED, as we had now renamed Uncle Ernest, was at Madingley still awaiting his gas mask which had been misdelivered.

'I am speaking to you from the cabinet room of number ten Downing Street. This morning, the British Ambassador in Berlin handed the German Government a final note...' Meanwhile the Stukas peeled off and dived down on the civilians in Warsaw, blowing women and children into small pieces. '...Unless we heard from them by eleven o'clock that they were prepared to withdraw their troops from Poland...' The Gestapo were rounding up and shooting the Jews they had already captured in the first three days. '...A state of war would exist between us...'

Mum rushed to the kitchen, picked up our four gas masks and ordered us to put them on.

'...No such communication has been received and consequently this country is at war with Germany.'

Before we could object the sirens started to wail, frightening the seagulls and birds in the garden. We all wandered around aimlessly with our gas masks on, sweating profusely, wondering what would

28

happen next and then rushed to the window to look for the imminent arrival of the Stukas. After seeing nothing but seagulls settling down peacefully on the Thames, Dad quietly took his gas mask off and calmed us down as the all-clear 'steady' note sounded, 'Idiots,' he grunted. Quite correctly, he realised that some over zealous spotter had mistaken our aircraft for the Germans.

No one knew what to do next and the months to Xmas were officially labelled the period of the 'phoney war'. It was a quiet time for everyone except the poor Poles who were having their last breath crushed out of them. Stalin had previously carved up Poland with Hitler and the Russians occupied the half of Poland that Hitler had generously handed to Stalin. We recorded the developments of the war on a map on our bedroom wall. As 1940 approached the map was replaced by pictures of Spitfires, Hurricanes and any aircraft silhouette we could lay our hands on.

There was a flutter of excitement when we were all issued with identity cards. As they were a muddy brown colour and had no photograph, the very first black-market operation was created by HM Government. Billy looked older than his eighteen years and used to go into Soho to watch the IDs being flogged over the bar counters. The reason was quite logical – no photo, no proof of identity – and he used to laugh his head off when a small weedy-looking black-haired Jewish boy flogged his card to a brawny red-haired Scotsman who did not fancy being called up into the Seaforth Highlanders. The Military Police took no notice, even if the ginger face and bushy red eyebrows did not fit the face of someone called Levy.

In February 1940 a letter arrived from Geoffrey from 'somewhere in France'. He was enjoying the wine and the food was *magnifique*. He was now attached to a French tank division as a liaison interpreter and his immediate CO was a huge chap who towered above everybody in size, manner and efficiency. Geoffrey said Colonel de Gaulle had lots of fire under his belly, which proved to be a brilliant assessment as he was the only one who would win a tank battle against the Germans Panzers a few months later. He also showed his steel by persuading many of his countrymen to fight on after France surrendered to the Germans on 16th June 1940. Geoffrey's love affair with André Citroën's Traction Avant motorcar was also rekindled. He had been among the first to take a shine to this eccentric front-wheel-drive car while at the Sorbonne before the war.

29

In 1940, when the German's broke through and pushed us to Dunkirk Geoffrey and the other 330,000 waited patiently to be evacuated by the 800 'little boats' which were picking them off the very shallow beaches. Most boats did not get right up to the beach, so those waiting to be rescued either had to swim or wade towards their rescuers. Geoffrey waited four days before being taken off but had prepared himself to at least have liquid refreshment at his lips. This was in the shape of numerous bottles of wine left on their luncheon tables by the fleeing farmers, which Geoffrey had pushed into the large pockets of his British Army greatcoat. When he finally got close to the rescuers he had to make the dreadful decision of either swimming the remaining yards to his rescuers or remaining on the beach. The weight of the greatcoat with the bottles dragged him down and after a few strokes he very reluctantly took off the coat with the bottles and swam the last few yards towards a Royal Navy minelayer. He was totally exhausted when they pulled him aboard and as soon as he hit the deck dropped off. The next thing he knew was that a young sailor was kicking him unceremoniously with the loving words: 'Ya can't kip 'ere, mate; them Messerschmidts are havin' a go at us!'

Geoffrey saw the logic of his remarks when three of the fighters dived down, levelled out and started to spray them with machine guns. Bullets flew all around, pinging off the metalwork of the ship.

'Told ya, didn't I?' grinned the sailor with a triumphant smirk on his face. Feeling sorry for the exhausted Geoffrey, he stretched out his hand and helped Geoffrey to his feet. 'C'mon, I'll take ya below and you can kip there, if you can find a space.' He helped Geoffrey down the ladder and pointed him towards a large locker. 'I'll give you a shake when we get to Southampton.'

Four hours later Geoffrey awoke, sat up and gawped. He had been sleeping on top of about four dozen mines which were ready for dropping overboard.

'Good kip, mate?' questioned the sailor, who was standing on the top rung of the ladder leading to the stores deck.

As Geoffrey stumbled ashore from the mine layer, the sailor waved him a goodbye and pointed to a cluster of buildings and shouted, 'Look for the Regulating Office.'

Geoffrey and the other soldiers who had been aboard made their way towards the buildings. But they never made it. They had arrived in the middle of an air raid and its cluster of bombs. The next thing Geoffrey saw was the smiling face of a young nurse in Southampton hospital.

'How are you feeling, Sir; you seem in quite good shape. I think you are very lucky.'

Geoffrey didn't have the strength to argue and left the hospital a month later, slightly the worse for wear but quite chirpy.

He was given some convalescent leave which he spent with some friends on a farm at Totton, a few miles outside Southampton. Their place was a magnet for all and sundry who implemented their meagre weekly ration of sugar, cream and butter by exchanging petrol coupons which were like gold from Fort Knox. Over dinner they asked Geoffrey about France and Hitler; and did he think we had a ghost of a chance of winning the war? Geoffrey showed his sangfroid. 'If we lose the war,' he told them, 'Hitler will be here and we lose everything. If we *win*, all the goods we have will be worth more than money...' He then went on to outline his plan. 'Because of the petrol rationing,' he began, 'cars are at present worthless. Now if the cars are in good nick, we should buy them up and keep them in barns and straw, oil them up and when the war ends, flog 'em.' The proposition met with approval, and the very next day he, his hosts and fellow guests put out a few feelers and soon had a gaggle of Citroën Light Fifteens in their barns. Geoffrey became a four-wheel sleeping partner and the investment turned out to be much more lucrative than the Government War Bonds.

My diary entries for 1940 included 'best' songs for 1939 and I transferred 'St Louis Blues', and 'Hold Tight' over to the first page for the New Year. Swing music played by Artie Shaw, Benny Goodman and the Dorsey Brothers was high on the best-seller list, and Bryan and I made the record shop Benstead's and Milo's, the ice-cream parlour in George Street, our regular stops on the one Saturday shopping day per month. Apart from carrying our gas masks in the small cardboard boxes, life seemed to go on and Flanagan & Allan were still singing 'Underneath the Arches' with monotonous regularity. To us, 'Satchmo' growling 'It's a wonderful world' through the trumpet solo was much more exciting. In fact, the 'phoney war' had turned into the 'phoney peace'. But all this changed on 9th April 1940 when Hitler invaded Norway and Denmark. Unperturbed, I went to the Dominion in Tottenham Court

Road and saw *Ninotchka* and *Angels wash their Faces*, with the Movietone News and the Wurlitzer organ wedged in between, and all for 1/9 (about 9p in today's money).

The consequent army and naval losses as a result of military cock-ups caused a government crises, and on the 10th May I noted in my diary: 'Neville Chamberlain gone and a Mr W.S. Churchill is now the Prime Minister.' Why I continued a daily report of the military disasters that followed I have no idea but every day I entered them: 'Rotterdam captured' (14th May), 'Holland capitulates' (15th May), 'Situation Grave' (17th May). And so the bad news was continuously noted on the following pages, but I still went to see *Contraband* in Richmond on the 22nd May.

Throughout the week we had seen hundreds of little boats being towed downstream. They were like dozens of little puppies being taken for a walk on Sunday mornings in Richmond Park, and the stream of boats was endless: small private yachts, rowing boats, tiny barges ... even small Mears pleasure steamers. It looked as if everything that could float was being towed downstream to the Thames Estuary. On the 31st May we heard that in excess of 330,000 of the British Army had been evacuated from the beaches of Dunkirk.

At this point the Home Office went into senile decline and reclassified the German refugees who had escaped the Nazis from 'refugees from Nazi persecution' to 'enemy aliens' and, in order to save the British people and country from this new enemy threat, HM Government decided to intern them. In June 1940 all males over the age of seventeen were taken away by the police and thrown into hastily assembled camps at racecourses and barbed wire assembly points throughout the UK. Kempton Park and Lingfield Racecourses were now mini concentration camps, and the Isle of Man was considered safe and far enough away for the refugees not to topple King and country.

The knock on the door for Dad and Billy came at 6:30 on the morning of Thursday, 17th June 1940. The two Met coppers were firm but vaguely pleasant, allowing them to pack their suitcases with personal belongings. Mum was unbelievably calm and tried all her contacts including Tom, but this produced no clues as to where the two had been taken to. On Monday morning, 1st July, I was preparing myself to bike to Hampton to start my exams. Just as I was leaving the phone rang and, true to form, one of

Tom's contacts had found out that both Dad and Billy were at Lingfield Racecourse internment camp. Mum immediately phoned ED, who came over to offer moral support. He brought Uncle Charles with him, which immediately brought on Mum's 'blue-sky' optimism.

'What a good thing Tom persuaded you both to be naturalised last year,' she said and planted big wet kisses on their four cheeks. I don't know whether I did not fully comprehend the situation but my diary records: 'going to the Ritz cinema on 6th July with Bryan to see *Arouse and Beware*. To this I laconically added: 'First film without "Billy".'

On Friday 19th July Bryan and I went to the Ritz to see *The Invisible Man Returns*. But he did NOT! Because Billy was one of those selected on that Monday morning to be shipped on an eight-week sail to Australia to safeguard Brits from 'enemy action' from within the state. In the event, he was in the company of the cream of the European intelligentsia, ranging from the founders of the Amadeus Quartet to Sigmund Freud's grandson Walter Freud. In fact, the list of the 2000 *Dunera* internees reads like a 'who's who' of scientists, scholars, painters and musicians. To add insult to injury, their guardians aboard the *Dunera* the Army Pioneers Corps, were members of the lower echelons of the criminal fraternity, many of whom, including the officers, deserved to be and were later court-martialled. They treated the prisoners like animals and it is fortunate that no one was killed or seriously maimed for life. On arrival in Sydney the Aussies had prepared fixed bayonets and machine guns to welcome the party of 'dangerous Nazi prisoners'. Learning the truth they reacted with fury and dismay, immediately instigating an enquiry and inviting the somewhat traumatised 'prisoners' either to join the Australian Army or be shipped back to the UK to join the British one.

However, the worst case of official bumbledom was the fate and treatment of the Italian British community, many of whom had made Britain and the ice-cream parlours their real and spiritual home since the 1920s. As Mussolini had also joined Hitler and declared war on us on 11th June, their reclassification from 'friendly alien' was also changed to 'enemy alien' and they, too, were interned. Many were shipped to Canada aboard the *Arondora Star* and these people were packed like sardines below deck. En route across the Atlantic, a German U-boat torpedoed her and thousands of the Italians were drowned, locked below deck like rats in a watery trap.

Mum's blue-sky optimism was usually a combination of hope and 'fingers firmly crossed – it will be all right variety.' Three years before, in the *Bremen*'s cabin as we sailed towards the UK, she had asked me to promise her to learn English quickly. Her promises were fulfilled in the assembly hall at Hampton Grammar at 19.00hrs on 11th June 1940 when Air Vice-Marshal Sir David Munro KCB MA LLD handed out the prizes and the boys sang 'Let us now praise famous men', which may have sounded a little premature to those attending the ceremony. When my name was called, I shuddered and walked up and onto the school stage, passing Bossy, Jammy and Steffs on the way up to the Air Vice-Marshal, who presented me with three bound volumes of the Swan Shakespeare covering Comedies, Histories and Tragedies. I had been awarded the English First Prize! I looked back at the three sets of smiling faces and I felt that they, really, should have been the recipients of the three volumes.

Steffs had taught me to be methodical and to always plan everything in advance. Remembering his army days he quoted the infantry's motto to never forget the 'six Ps' – 'Perfect planning prevents piss-poor performances' – and following this advice I had diligently recorded every daily air raid in my diary – to the nearest minute. The raids started to build up from the beginning of September 1940 and reached a crescendo on the 15th, when I recorded: 'Bombs in Creswell Road near garage and the number of air-raid warnings sounded is now seven, the most of any day.' However, the most unique of all entries in my diary is on the 18th September when I recorded the events on my way to school. I lived the furthest from the school and collected others on the way. They usually numbered five to six other cyclists, and on this day we were almost at the entrance to the school field and the manned machine-gun nests.

No one had taken any notice of the air-raid wails, although there had been warnings at 07.30, 08.00 and 09.30, but we were blissfully cycling along when we heard the sound of aircraft engines and stopped to look skywards. As the sound got nearer, the first came into view and a fierce argument started as to it being a Hurricane or Spitfire, as all the various identification of the silhouettes on our bedroom charts were quoted. 'No, it's a Spit … look at the wings... No it can't be ... it's definitely a Hurricane...' The argument got quite fierce until they dived on us with all guns firing. 'Told you it was a Messerschmidt!' was not greeted with much cheering but at assembly the next morning Bossy Mason added his elegant sarcastic touch: 'In future, will pupils observe the air raid warnings and take cover and avoid damage to themselves or others.'

The papers made a habit of listing the air-raids with almost perverse pleasure. They reported that the number of 'alerts' in London in 1940 had reached 44 days or 56 hours. There were 400 day and night warnings from a few minutes to an 'all night' alert, which lasted just over fourteen hours, the longest record. On many days the greater part of the twenty-four hours had been on alert.

On the 1st September I recorded another visit to the cinema. Bryan was not able to come, as his family were clearing up the mess from the bomb that had hit the house five doors away, so Mum volunteered to come with me instead. I shall never know if the irony of the film's title struck her. It was *My Two Husbands*.

However, what I do know now is that the 15th September was the turning point in the Battle of Britain. Reichmarschall Hermann Goering had thrown everything against the RAF and lost. The Luftwaffe had flattened Poland, Denmark, Norway, Belgium, Holland and France and were confidently predicted to 'rub out' the RAF without any problems. Their three to one superiority in the air meant that nothing was going to stop them.

When we watched the white vapour trails against the deep-blue sky we had no idea that Britain's fate was in the very hands of a few young men, some of whom had held prayer books at assembly next to us at Hampton Grammar only a few weeks before. No one could have expressed the sentiment better than Winston Churchill who, in the House of Commons on the 20th August 1940, before those young men had won the battle said: 'Never in the field of human conflict was so much owed by so many to so few.'

Nearly all of us were too young to be accepted into the RAF to join the fight but wanted to do something to help our ex-school mates, so when HM Government started the Air Training Corps Mr Crocker at Hampton had more volunteers than places. There was no Iron Cross urge to drive me into the arms of the ATC, but I, too, wanted to help in a small way and joined in October 1940. Training was mainly discipline, map reading, Morse code and

35

aircraft recognition – auxiliary services vaguely connected with the training we would receive when we reached the glamour status of pilot, which we were all seeking. Dad was still shell-shocked after his 'enemy alien' treatment but was very pleased that I had joined the cause so I could reverse the shock and bolster his as well as my own ego. He and Mr Crocker were even more shocked when the Air Ministry kicked me out after six months because they could not have an 'enemy alien' in their ranks.

It is a general belief that two shocks at the same time are easier to handle than two over a period of time. I can personally vouch for the accuracy of this theory. I was called into Bossy's study in early December and when I entered the room he shot out of his chair and rushed up to me, squeezed my hand and ushered me into a chair opposite him on the other side of the desk. A very large smile spread across his usually stern face and I immediately thought this was the softening up process for bad news about bombs at Richmond Bridge Mansions having wiped out all my family. Instead he handed me a letter from the Home Office and when I had finished reading it he permitted himself a small smile. 'I have shown Mr James my reply and he feels my mild sarcasm is fully justified. We do not teach Greek here but he feels that "sarkasmos" – to gnash one's teeth – is very much in order.' I started to read the letter.

> The Grammar School.
> Hampton on Thames.
> 6th December 40.

To whom it may concern,

David Fraenkel becomes sixteen on the 8th of this month and must, I believe, obtain a permit to use a bicycle and must appear before an alien tribunal. As his Head Master I should like to put forward certain points.

I cannot imagine that any harm to this country would be caused by Fraenkel having a cycle while at school. The journey from his home to this School is very awkward for all but motorists and cyclists. Some 400 of our boys cycle to this School for similar reasons.

As regards the question of internment I very much hope

that will not be considered necessary. Fraenkel's behaviour and industry while here have been excellent and I have never had any reason to suppose that he or his family were anything but loyal to this Country. The boy is within 18 months of taking the General School Examination and I hope he will be allowed to complete his education by staying here and working for it.

signed A.S. Mason
Head Master.

I handed the letter back to Bossy and he leant back with a very satisfied look on his face. In the event I was not sent to the Tower to be interned, I kept riding my bike and passed my GCE with flying colours.

However, there seemed no end to my misdemeanours against the rules and regulations, I was subjected to. In one instance, I was charged under the Enemy Alien: Subject to 'Art. 1 Aliens Movement Restriction Order 1940', which restricted 'enemy aliens' to their place of residence between 12 and and 6 a.m. I was found out in the street at seven minutes after midnight and Tom Avery felt it would hardly warrant engaging silk to fight a seven minute lateness. In the event I was charged 'at the Courthouse in Paradise Road,' cost five pounds and bound over for twelve months.

Tom refused to accept reimbursement for his help and felt it was worth every penny to have witnessed officialdom at work. He did ask where I had been and I sheepishly had to admit that I had been drinking with friends 'up West'.

'Idiots, they could have had you for causing an affray by a minor. Better make sure you keep your nose clean from next year onwards.'

He patted me on the back and took me up to Richmond Hill and the Roebuck, proceeded to get me totally drunk and we finally got a cab back to Richmond Bridge Mansions. He did add, with a hint of disappointment, that a lad of my age should have had a slightly racier explanation for the late seven minutes.

'I think you should have a chat with Ernest's brother, Charles. I'm sure he could give you a starter course. After all, he's almost family, or should that be "mishpoche"?'

At the end of 1940 Goering switched the bombers away from day raids to night bombing. We had no shelter at the flat, and some bright spark suggested we slept below the arches of Richmond Bridge and took some blankets and pillows there for the night. In theory this was a brilliant and safe way to survive the bombs, but nobody had explained to us that the Thames was tidal below and up to Teddington. During our first night there, the water rose and fell every four hours with a 'still' tide in between, which made us and the rats move up and down with the tide. Next morning, wet and miserable, we all decided that the risk of being bombed in bed was preferable to being wet and rat-gnarled.

Although the diary Geoffrey had given me was only a pocket diary it had a page a day and fifteen lines per page. Normally this was quite sufficient to record the daily events, but as the air raids got heavier after the Battle of Britain, the air raids I recorded filled an increasing number of lines. As the day raids turned into night raids 'no day alarms' became more frequent until the 23rd August 1940 when the numbers increased by night.

There was a lull from the 3rd October until the middle of November but all hell broke loose throughout November. Early December had 'No night or day raid' and even the 29th December night raid 'only started at 18.15hrs.'

However, no Londoner was aware that this was to be London's Armageddon. The firestorm that was unleashed by Goering was the heaviest of the war, with 24,000 incendiary bombs and 120 tons of high explosives dropped on the City and the surrounding docks. The heroes, like the RAF pilots before them, were the firemen and rescue workmen and no one who experienced the firestorm will ever forget them.

Around 20.00hrs Bryan came around and told me that Dad was stopped from taking the No.73 out as those drivers who had managed to get back from their runs said it was hell 'up West'. Although there had been no 'all clear' siren, Bryan and I decided to go up on the roof at the flats and when we got there we could not believe our eyes. Richmond is fifteen miles from the City as the crow flies and Goering's eagles had been worse than the Black Death. In the distance we saw a huge deep-red glow, which seemed to cover the whole horizon in a huge red arc. Flames were shooting in and out of it and as the bombs dropped we could hear the whistle, crunch and thud as they landed. They were blowing the City to kingdom come and Bryan and I were numbed into disbelief and the only word that passed our lips was the occasional 'Coooorr!' We were mesmerised by the horror which was unfolding before our very eyes and only thought of those poor Londoners who were caught in this inferno.

Tale 3

From Boyhood to Manhood

There was not much of a celebration on Mum's birthday on New Year's Eve 1940. The shock of the firestorm of two days earlier had put paid to that and, for once, there was no 'blue sky' anywhere. Gloom, doom and disaster was the order of every day and for me one of the worst things was the lack of sleep. An air-raid warning sounded every night, playing havoc with getting up and getting to school on time.

There were fewer boys at assembly every morning and Bossy was at his wit's end. However, he soon found a way to soften this blow by announcing that if the 'Raid Alert' sirens went off after 10.00 p.m. and lasted for an hour, we could delay our arrival for assembly by one hour, after 11.15 by two hours, after 11.55 by three hours, after 12.30 by four hours and was a brilliant idea.

My family could sleep like dogs throughout anything. The 'Blue-Sky Dept' came to an arrangement with our neighbours to put a slip through the door to tell us when the 'All clear' had sounded and we could then adjust our rise-and-shine pattern. I remember Mum coming in one morning to ask if I had heard the bomb which demolished the house opposite our flat. As she walked towards my bed she screamed, tearing me out of a deep sleep.

'Look at all the glass on your bed,' she exclaimed. She pointed to the top of my duvet which was covered with shining bits of glass – the remains of the window by the side of my bed. I told her I had heard nothing.

My diary entry was a one-liner: 'Glass on bed.'

At the beginning of 1941 the bombs had sent many Londoners away from their homes and into the bombless countryside. Those who could afford it or had relations outside the UK sold their properties or leases, and many houses and flats became vacant.

Prices dropped as fast as the bombs and anyone who could get some money, and felt Old Churchill might actually pull us through and win, took the plunge and bought into flats and houses. One had very little to lose as it was a 50/50 situation. If Hitler won we'd all be dead, and if Winnie won we'd be sitting on a goldmine. This was precisely what Dad, ED and Uncle Charles did. Dad bought a beautiful mid-1930s (non-vacant possession), four-bedroom, three-bathroom house, with front and back garden, on the edge of Sheen Common. ED bought a flat just off Willoughby Road in East Twickenham and Charles a flat in Chelsea, which being so central, catered to all tastes. The locals' name for it was Chelsea Closets.

Tom had given ED an update on my virginal status, which he duly passed on to Charles which resulted in my going to 'starting college', which was situated at 779 Chelsea Cloisters in Chelsea. Charles knew I was into swing and had thoughtfully gone to HMV to buy the latest recording of 'Moonlight Serenade', beautifully played by Glenn Miller. He bought some tinned salmon at Harrods and home-made bread at Grodzinski's and selected some not too intoxicating liquid to keep me wide awake but pleasantly animated. After about an hour there was a ring at the door and Charles ushered in Grace Thompson who had recently become Dad's secretary.

Uncle Charles had immediately spotted that her talents were not only confined to the Olympia typewriter. Charles watched me like a hawk and when he felt that I was ripe and ready for plucking guided me to the bathroom.

'You must always be spotlessly clean otherwise it takes away all the pleasure,' he told me, and I suddenly remembered my disgust in the Southern Railway train compartment. Charles washed me down with some beautifully smelling soap and I started to float towards cloud 69. I was standing upright as he washed me in the bath, soaping every part of my body. I suddenly remembered what Mum had told me years ago about Lot's wife looking back and turning to stone and warning me that if I saw anything naughty I, too, would turn to stone. I now felt it had started.

Charles had learnt his craft in the Brussels brothels and knew exactly what would satisfy my young, smooth and innocent little body. He gave Mrs T. his findings and she was gentle, caring and very understanding knowing that I had never experienced any of

41

the 57 varieties. After she had taken me through perhaps nine of the different varieties, Charles called a halt, pointing out that we had all night to fully explore all the rest. He went out to the bathroom and returned with two thick cotton dressing gowns and beckoned us to the sitting room to a low sofa table with three crystal glasses next to an opened champagne bottle. I was in seventh heaven and told Uncle Charles. He shook his head and suggested it was not complete until one has been to the sixty-ninth heaven and proceeded to demonstrate this with Mrs T. I stayed all night and never counted how many times I went down for the count but felt like Joe Louis after a boxing fight, totally exhausted but deliciously happy. Charles smiled at me and told me that in life there are three very pleasant experiences, food, wine and sex, but last longest in that order. He also informed me that generally if you have a bed, you have no girl, and if you have a girl, you have no bed. He grabbed my hand and led me back to the bedroom and grinned all over his face. 'But at the moment you are lucky enough to have both.'

On Saturday 10th February I went to the pictures with Bryan to see *Thunder Afloat*, which must have fired my hopes of joining the one organisation which had not yet been informed of my 'enemy alien' status. I seemed to have exhausted most of the services except the RN who now sent a very curt note which said 'not accepted' and in order to forestall any further disappointment I joined 'Fire Watching' at school. This entailed attendance on a basis of a three-quarters duty rosta per week, but to this day I have never discovered why we should have watched the fire after reporting it. We had only one bucket of water and one with sand.

When rationing of eggs, cheese, jam and clothing was added to tea, sugar, cream, butter, meat and petrol, Mum's 'blue sky' turned dark blue. Clothing could only be purchased with coupons and all manufacturers had to produce evidence of the quantities of clothing they manufactured and were given the appropriate number of coupons as a 'float' to enable them to buy cloth. As business was pretty slack during the first year of the war, the float turned into a golden 'lake'.

Having achieved a marketable commodity the trading opportunity of this float knew no bounds. Mum's activities became a *La Ronde* without the sex: clothing coupons to the butcher's wife = more meat = grocer's for more eggs = eggs to the cake shop = cakes =

to petrol station = more petrol to go to the country for more eggs, and so on, and the circle increased weekly.

At school, Wednesday was a half-day and I always visited my parents in Wardour Street in London's Soho. That area had always been famous as the Red Light district and after my initial training with Uncle Charles, I began to take more interest of the ladies who traded in the streets and doorways of this area. After a few weeks of visiting the firm, the girls got to know my face and I their bodies, particularly the clouds of perfume that wafted around them. They appeared to be puzzled by my young age and wondered if I was either a pimp's 'runner' or some delinquent perverted youth.

"Allo love... late today, ain't you?... Hot, inn't?' they greeted, followed by a raising of the eyebrows and/or a tongue appearing between their lips. If there was a football match on they would be rushing around arranging their after-match tricks, and our conversation used to be shorter and much more to the point: 'No time today ... I'm knackered already... Me feet are killin' me ... up and down those stairs all day...' After acquiring all this knowledge, I felt I could have easily have become a pimp's runner.

My visits to the 'University of Life' at 779 Chelsea Cloisters, meanwhile, were proving to be not only pleasurable but physically highly satisfying. Uncle Charles had already instructed me in the rudiments. Now he added: 'Of course there are many ways to skin a rabbit. If you have neither bed nor girl you can always resort to the "five finger exercise" and then proceeded to instruct me in this solitary way of sexual satisfaction. 'But if you do it in your bed always have a tissue ready in case Mum looks at the yellow stain on the sheets. She'll tell you to stop or you'll go blind. Don't believe a word of it, I'm fifty-five years old and I can still see well enough to tell a woman from a man even if it's with the help of my hand or tongue. But whatever you do in your sex life don't believe a word you see on that silver screen at the "Dominion". Boy meets girl, they fall in love, get married, have kids and live happily ever after. Not in my experience, they don't. None of my married friends are deliriously happy or celibate and you or I will be hard put to think of one.' I looked at Charles, thought for a moment and then blurted out: 'What about my Mum and Dad?' and for once Charles was speechless.

One of Charles's non-bedding friends at the Cloisters was a

charming lady called Georgie, short for Georgina. She was a two-ringer WRNS on Louis Mountbatten's staff when he was Commander-in-Chief in the Mediterranean after Hitler had conquered Yugoslavia and Greece in the spring of 41. An attack on Crete seemed imminent and Lord Louis called a meeting of the top brass of the Army, Navy and Air Force, who all assured him that there was no way that the Germans could capture Crete. The RAF would destroy the Luftwaffe before it got to the island; the Royal Navy would sink any German or Italian ships before they could get near Crete and the Army, under and with the help of General Freyberg's New Zealanders, would destroy any Germans if they managed to land. In the event, and with the help of the two German parachute divisions, the island fell in days and after its loss a post-mortem inquest was held in Cairo.

As it promised to be a somewhat tense meeting, Georgie was requested to be Mountbatten's aide-de-camp as she was also perfect in shorthand and Lord Louis had now christened her his 'Ada Camp'. 'Icy' was Georgie's description of the meeting. The three heads of departments blamed each other and all and sundry for the Crete disaster, and after about an hour of listening to the bickering, of which Georgie was taking verbatim notes, Lord Louis got redder and redder in the face and Georgie thought he was going to explode when he slammed his fists on the table and roared: 'If we'd had enough planes, if we'd had more troops in the north of the island ... and more MTBs to attack the landing crafts ... if ... if ... if!' He momentarily seemed to forget Georgie's presence. '... If ... if this, if that ... if my mother had had balls ... she would have been my father.' And with that stormed out of the meeting.

My own 'blue sky' came through the clouds when there was a knock on our front door. I answered the postman's knock who handed me a large pack of envelopes held together with a rubber band. 'You gotta gal in Australia?' he queried pushing a thick bunch of identically sized letters into my hands. I couldn't wait to open them; and there were about twenty dating back to August 1940 from Billy. Mum came rushing up and we went to the kitchen to open these and read their contents. Mum was shaking her head after she had opened about half of them. 'When we write back we must tell him to number them to see if there are any missing. I've got one here which refers to something we have not received,' she cried, with a gentle stamp of the foot. Billy wrote that he loved the climate and the company he was in. The London intelligentia and musical circle of ex-*Dunera* prisoners were a new and exciting world to him and he hoped that they would also decide to come back to London with him. Rumour had it that this was going to be in the summer or autumn, but meanwhile the tuition in piano and wind instruments given him by the violist Peter Schidlof would make the reading of music as easy as eating pie ... or kangaroo, which was quite 'tasty,' he added in the letter.

After April Billy's letters arrived with monotonous regularity and, much to Mum's satisfaction, they were all dated and numbered. As the months went by I was asked to play telephone Cupid and resurrect the various loves he had left behind in London.

'Phone, don't write... We don't want any broken promises or court cases,' he instructed, so I started a small exercise book with names, phone numbers and contact dates:. Petra from Chelsea, Yvonne from Streatham, Winnie from Edinburgh, Sarah from Hampstead and Eva from Swiss Cottage. The list was endless and every time he wrote he remembered another amour which I dutifully followed up by phone.

Billy arrived back just before Xmas 1941. He and many others had joined the Pioneer Corps at Catterick Camp in Yorkshire.

When he phoned me from the North, he said that during his train journey he had hardly recognised England's green and pleasant land. Liverpool docks looked like huge mountains of bricks and the train journey across to Yorkshire was horrific. 'Nothing but misery and rubble,' he almost cried, 'and when we got to...' at which point the censor cut him off. He came through again a few minutes later and corrected himself by telling me and the anonymous censor that he was 'somewhere in the North of England'.

Three nights later after his signing-on and completing the clerical formalities, he and two of his friends went to the nearest local to drown their sorrows in a pint. He had got his Xmas leave but did not know what day or time he was due into Kings Cross. 'Don't bother to meet me. I'll get a bus to Tottenham Court Road and change to a number 73. It'll only be an hour.' Had he known what the German bombers had done to the City, East and West End, he would not have been so foolishly optimistic.

A little of Kings Cross station had survived and the last half-mile track into the station was a mess of twisted rails, craters of bombs and blocks of cement. As for the Oxford Street bus journey, he hardly recognised any landmarks of eighteen months ago. Half the shops in Tottenham Court Road were just burnt-out shells and Oxford Circus was only just recognisable by a battered sign hanging on one solitary hook which made 'Jay's' just visible. Mum's favourite store, John Lewis, was a scorched wreck the ruins of whose façade bore only the legend '... wis Ltd'.

Three hours after arriving in London he staggered into the flat and inspected all the windows. He could not comprehend that we had not been subjected to the destruction of fifteen miles away as apart from the air-raid sirens, only a few bombs had fallen in Richmond. After all the checking on the entries in the exercise book, he drifted gently off in the large armchair; even Mum, with a large cup of coffee, could not waken him.

'Come on, off to bed!' (what she actually said with a friendly clapping of the hands was, 'Bettchen, Bettchen gehen!') and Billy obediently slouched off to bed.

Next morning he was standing over my bed.

'C'mon, lazy bones,' he said, shaking me. 'There's a lot to do. I've arranged to meet Hymie Kirschbaum at the Regent Palace at 15.00hrs. He's never been to London and I've promised to show him the fleshpots of Hampstead, Swiss Cottage and Chelsea. He'll have a hell of a job as he's not exactly Adonis. Five foot five in his socks which he hardly ever changes, fat as a sauerkraut barrel and thick horn-rimmed glasses. Do you get the drift? Do you think there's anyone for him in your notebook, Davie boy?'

Thinking of my newly acquired degree at the 'Closets' I shook my head negatively. 'But if finding a partner is going to be difficult, why are we meeting?' I queried.

Billy smirked. 'You remember your name-change tale with Tom Avery?' I nodded. 'The War Office have suddenly regained their brains and thought about all that motley crew who are now HM soldiers in khaki. There is a possibility that we will actually fight the Germans and if we get captured and Gerry looks at our ID, someone whose name is Hymie Kirschbaum is not going to live long if the Gestapo catch him. I told him the Toothy name-change story and was going to ask you to fix an appointment for a name change. That's for him, you and me. Perhaps we can get a wholesale rate for three?'

Hymie duly arrived and I immediately felt that Billy's description of the little Jewish boy was, if anything, not kosher enough. Billy ordered tea all around at a small table in the lounge and when the waiter came up with an empty tray, raised his eyebrows and asked, 'Yeeees?' 'Tea for three, please' answered Billy, to which the waiter smiled benignly. 'Makes a change from tea for two, Sir?'

Minutes later another waiter was sidling through the lounge looking and calling for a customer who was wanted on the telephone. As he came towards us with an almost empty tray with a small piece of paper on it, he turned his head from left to right calling the name of the wanted person '... Mr ... ill, please ... chill, please ... Churchhill ... Mr Churchill, please.'

Hymie remembered the new name he had chosen for himself and got to his feet, straightened himself to almost five foot five inches and in a loud voice asked:

'Mister Cherchill ... vot inishal?'

Billy and I could not contain ourselves. 'Why did you choose Churchill, Hymie?'

'My name is Kirschbaum and *Kirche* is church and I also think it's a nice name and he's a lovely fella but I think Hymie doesn't really go with it. What do you think, Davie boy?' he asked, turning to me.

I thought for a moment. 'Churchill is great but what about his forenames – Winston, Spencer?' Hymie was jubilant. 'Spencer!' he trumpeted. 'Just like Marks and Spencer,' and Billy buried his head in shame.

After the formalities were completed at Lincoln's Inn Fields, Franklin, Franklin and Churchill appeared in the *London* Gazette and Mum proudly showed this to all and sundry. If she had told them the cost alone of advertising them in the *Gazette*, they would not have been so impressed. When I told Bryan, he said I should have chosen another forename, like Benjamin, after the great American, but added: 'On second thoughts, though, you can always slay Goliath, can't you?... As long as he's taller than you ... and that won't be difficult ... but as Uncle Charles told you when you thought you were overdoing it at No. 779, it won't make you blind and it might even make you grow. But you must tell me what you would like for your birthday in December when you are going to be sweet seventeen. We'll have to arrange a super party for you, and if Billy can arrange leave, we'll have a tombola for all the girls in that exercise book of names you kept for him. If they all come at the same time we could have a daisy chain. Anything special you want, Dave?'

'Go on, surprise me with a 78 from Benstead's. You can start looking at the *Melody Maker* from now on and see which is the Swing Seller in the Big Band section.'

True to his word, Bryan sent his Mum down to the shop on Saturday 6th December and she collected a recording of Tommy Dorsey's latest hit with their new singer 'Blue Eyes' Frank Sinatra singing the vocal in half-unison with the singing non-playing musicians.

Bryan also prepared a complete analysis of the three-minute record. No doubt the review notes nicked from the *MM* helped, but it was very descriptive: 'Sinatra's vocal soars into the upper regions and mingles playfully with the members of the band downing their instruments and singing the chorus. He then hands the music over to the trumpeter Ziggy Elman and Buddy Rich, the drummer. They climb up the scales intertwining each other like two athletes climbing a gigantic wooden wall fixtures..' 'Just like us in the gym at Hampton on the wooden wall bars,' added Bryan with a nod.

He gave it to me on the Sunday with a grin: 'Sorry, I can't make tomorrow, but it could be just the one for your mum as well. It's called "Blue Skies".' He walked over to the radiogram with it, lifted the wooden lid, pulled the record out of the paper sleeve, placed it on the turntable, lifted the needle holder arm to start the record and looked at his watch.

'Just in time to hear the news,' he said and turned the radio on.

'Here is the news at nine o'clock on Sunday 7th December. The news has just been given that Japanese aircraft have raided the American naval base at Hawaii. The announcement was made by President Roosevelt in a brief statement from Washington.'

Bryan turned the radio off, carefully lifted the needle arm up and across the shellac, dropped it gently on to the record and awaited the first bar of the Dorsey sound.

When the words 'Blue Skies' came out of the 'gram, I walked over to Mum, planted a big wet kiss on her powdered cheek, smiled at her and said: 'I do hope so; it would be a nice "blue-sky" birthday present!'

Tale 4

The GIs at Eisenhower Platz

Transferring last year's important notes to the 1942 diary, I listed 'brought forward' cash: as £6.0.1, followed by the second most important event recorded: 'saw 52 films' and 'Second New Year's Eve without Billy'.

The air raids had stopped in September as the Luftwaffe had transferred to the East to pulverise the Russians. However, we were all weary and tired as the two years had totally exhausted everybody and the food rations had got smaller and smaller. Although Mum managed to see a bit of blue sky at least once a week, we and the other 50 million in Britain did not share her optimism.

The strangest item missing from my diary was the non-entry on the 7th December 1941. Although everyone had heard the sixty-second radio announcement about the Japanese attack on Hawaii I had no idea where this was. When I spoke to the boys at school on Monday 8th, they said as far as they were concerned it was 'somewhere down there' and pointed vaguely at the large globe we used for geography. They spun it 180 degrees and pointed to an area somewhere between the west coast of America and Australia. The tall deep-voiced Trusler ventured a 'Cooor, that's where all those lovely Polynesian girls with long dark hair dance with their hula grass skirts ... and they're barefooted on the white sand, next to the deep-blue sea, coooooor.' And then he did a poor young man's imitation of 'Alloha.'

None of us or the rest of the population knew that it was also the Headquarters of the US Pacific Fleet whose ships were anchored at Pearl Harbor. Nor did we realise that President Franklin Delano Roosevelt's 'Date which will live in infamy' would be the day which changed the European war to the beginning of World War II.

49

Geoffrey's telephone call in February cheered Mum up no end. Especially when he asked her if he could borrow Billy's bed on the odd occasion when he had a '48-hour' leave. 'I'm only about an hour from Euston and it would be very handy to have a temp "home from home".' Mum was over the moon and prepared Billy's bed and when Geoffrey walked through the door at 4 Richmond Bridge Mansions it was hugs all round. Mum pushed him away, brought her open palms to her face and, pointing at him, exclaimed: 'Look at our Geoff...'

Geoffrey squirmed. He hated being called by the shortened version and Mum corrected herself immediately.

'Look!' she exclaimed, 'he's got two pips...'

It was my turn to correct her:

'He's a first lieutenant, Mum.' This was about as far as my army rank identification went. 'What's the badge?' I asked.

This brought a one-word reply: 'Intelligence.' Mum did her Yiddischer mama act of open palms against both cheeks.

'I always knew our...' She stopped herself. ... 'Geoffrey was intelligent.'

'Where have you come from?' she pressed.

He shook his head and murmured, 'Sorry I can't tell you; it's a secret.'

Mum was crestfallen, adding: 'But you can tell Mama.'

He looked at her seriously. 'Sorry no, really I can't.'

Making one final snatch at that blue sky she said triumphantly: 'I promise not to tell anybody, cross my heart.'

A large grin spread across Geoffrey's face. 'Wot, your little Jewish heart, wis a cross on it?'

Mum dismissed the mild repartee and gave up.

She put out her hand, opened the palm and stretched the arm towards Geoffrey, 'C'mon, Bettchen, Bettchen gehen,' and pulled him towards my and Billy's bedroom and showed him Billy's bed.

Mum must have bribed Taffs in Wardour Street with some extra petrol coupons to get four slices of veal, but Geoffrey complimented her on the delicious *Wiener Schnitzel*, which Geoffrey loved. 'You never know,' he said, wiping the breadcrumbs from his chin, 'perhaps my Army travels will take me to Vienna.'

'Anywhere special you want to go tonight?' he asked me in the morning and I shook my head negatively. 'Tell you what, do you remember one of those letters I wrote you two years ago from France when I was attached to a French army unit which was commanded by that huge chap Colonel De Gaulle?' I nodded.

'As you probably know he's over here now and is the General commanding the Frenchmen who escaped before France capitulated. All the airmen, soldiers and sailors who got away and now fight the Nazis are called the "Free French" and wear the Cross of Lorraine Badge on their sleeves, and they and de Gaulle have adopted a pub in Soho as their unofficial Free French London headquarters. We'll go there and I'll show you the official de Gaulle call to arms which he broadcast on BBC which started off with the war cry. "Citoyens..." It's framed as a picture hanging next to the bar. I'll introduce you to Gaston and his Dad if he's around. Gaston Berlemont and his large Walrus moustache *are* the Yorkminster.'

'Funny name for a French pub, isn't it?' I said, scratching my head.

Geoffrey smiled and nodded his head. 'I've always told Gaston to change the name, something like 'Bonjour' or perhaps 'Frenchies' or the 'French House'.'

We pushed our way into the packed bar in the early evening after I had dragged Geoffrey into HMV to buy Tommy Dorsey's 'Opus One'. Geoffrey shuddered with disgust; swing was definitely not his forté. Gaston spotted Geoffrey the minute he appeared, looked at me and turned to Geoffrey: 'Très jeune?' Geoffrey replied 'Ta geule,' which, I had heard, was the French for 'shut up'.

After a lengthy conversation of which I did not understand a single word, we pushed our way right into the pub, which was now like a ship's messdeck, with more bodies being pushed into hammocks by the second. I was not used to absynthe or two pints of lager and around ten o'clock I asked Geoffrey for the location of the loo. He pointed me in the right direction and I walked into the tiled smallish area. There were two empty urinals; and the third was occupied by a French sailor who turned round as I stood next to him. He was about twenty-five years old and looked like one of those suntanned French legionaries from *Beau Geste*. As I stood alongside him and started to relieve myself, he looked at me, smiled and said, 'Petit filet mignon,' and raised his eyebrows. Charles had never instructed me to go down this road before and initially had no idea what he wanted or what I should do.

51

Charles had told me about never being too old as long as you can use your hands or tongue, and this, despite his young age, the matelot now confirmed and practiced to the letter. When he had finished and looked pleasantly satisfied, I looked at him, nodded and said 'Merci beaucaup,' to which he replied, 'Mon plaisir,' and today I can still see that little red woollen pompom on top of his *beret de marin* bouncing backwards and forwards with wild abandon. When I reappeared at the bar, Geoffrey asked if I was OK and nodded. 'I was not going to be the first one to introduce you to the vice versa and, being family, rest assured I will never try it on you.' And he kept that promise until the day he died, forty years later.

Geoffrey was recalled after four days' leave but when he returned he asked me if I wanted to see more fleshpots, to which I replied that I wasn't sure about the 'pots'. 'Right,' he said, 'we'll go to that most famous of Fitzrovian pubs The Fitzroy, just the other side of Oxford Street. It's been the haunt of artists and writers, and has been the magnet of sexual excess and alcohol for generations.'

Geoffrey hadn't mentioned the walls and ceiling, which were covered with cap tallies and naval ribbons, there was even one from a U-boat. We managed to get a quiet, cramped corner to stand up in and he looked at me and said.

'Too much for you or is it all right?'

I just nodded, changed the subject and turned to him.

'I know you didn't want to tell us what you do after you get on that train at Euston but is it really that hush-hush?'

Geoffrey nodded. 'You know I'm pretty good with languages and all the work I do is translations. There are many of us working on this and since last December the Americans have joined the circus. I can't tell you where it is or its name but at the moment our lot are pretty cross with the Japs because they nicked our idea at Pearl Harbor. Do you remember the Navy's destruction of the Italian Fleet with a few ancient Swordfish at Taranto?'

Last year, after our old Stringbags caused havoc with the cream of the Italian navy, the Japanese Embassy in Rome sent two of their naval attachés to have a look of what we Brits had done with twenty-one old B1 Planes strung together with vertical wire, for the loss of two chaps killed and two captured. One of the Jap Lieutenant commanders, Takeshi Naito, had been Naval attaché in Berlin. He and Commander Fuchida stayed in Kagoshima overnight, where they talked at length about our attack at Taranto. This was duly passed to Admiral Yamamoto, the brilliant architect of the attack on Pearl Harbor.

'You'll probably remember that I have a recording studio on the top floor in Wardour Street and every record I sell gets a royalty paid on it. Do you think that as the Royal Navy was the originator of destroying ships at anchor and the Japs nicked the idea for Pearl Harbor, the RN should be paid royalties by the Japs?' He grinned and punched my shoulder.

'I'll have to ask Tommy Flowers when I get back to Bletchley...' And he let out the only curse I had ever heard him utter. 'You didn't hear that last word, did you?'

I grinned at him 'oh Bletchley? No, of course I didn't.'

I never heard Geoffrey mention the word again until the early 1970s when the entire story of the codebreakers at Bletchley Park was released. Before then I had only met a few service friends of his from the 'The Park', and throughout 1942, the nationality mix of its personnel was swollen by the arrival of 'The Yanks', a word they hated, especially if they hailed from south of the Mason-Dixon Line which had divided the States during the Civil War.

The trickle of the GIs to Britain became a torrent during the year. The US military had realised that looking after the welfare of their troops made them better fighting machines, just like Napoleon knew that an army marches on its stomach. Washington, DC created a separate Entertainment Unit from the stars of the Hollywood screen and the musicians from the bandstands of the dance halls. The first of these to arrive in Britain was the sixteen-piece No. 1 United States Army Dance Band, who were but one part of the total band of nearly seventy musicians. Apart from the dancing activities of the GIs their major interest was of the horizontal type with the so called 'Piccadilly Commandos'. This operated from the 'top trade' Burlington Gardens area to the more down-market variety around Piccadilly, Glasshouse and Maddox streets. To us Brits, GIs were 'overpaid, oversexed and over here'. I can personally vouch for this by the info passed to me by the ladies in Wardour Street. However, the remark made to me as a seventeen-year-old by a GI adds to the evidence. 'Got any gum, chum?' to which he pulled out a pack of Wrigley's chewing gum, pushed it in my direction, then added: 'You got a sister, Mister?'

The looming matriculation exams played havoc with my social

life and Uncle Charles insisted I cease my lessons of life until I had my 'matric', which I managed to achieve in the summer. As soon as I had it in my hand Mum and Dad gave hugs and kisses all round. Number 779 Chelsea Cloisters followed suit, horizontally, vertically in the shower, out of the shower and every possible way from the Heinz varieties.

At one point I told Charles of the extra-curriculum activities which I had experienced in Soho. He wasn't in the least taken aback and just shook his head. 'But I told you, like good food and drink, sex is pleasurable in many ways. To have a full life, you must eat drink and be merry. You can always discard or say no to something you have not enjoyed and from the way you described the cementing of the Entente Cordiale you seem to have enjoyed it. All I can add is to say *encore*. You've got a thing about smells so I suggest you steer clear of animal worship and with your delicate skin I would not recommend whips and chains.'

He got up from the sofa, went outside to a big cupboard and brought in a large box which contained photos and items of the two subjects he had just mentioned. He handed me the box and I inspected its contents, handed the box back, shook my head and said, 'I think you're right... Still, if the worst, comes to the worst I can always change my mind.'

Charles nodded approval. 'You stick to what you have enjoyed and remember anyone can be right-handed or left-handed at some time or other. There's nothing wrong in being ambidextrous. Equally, I have learned there's not much wrong in being ambisextrous either.'

I looked at him like a grateful puppy and made to leave the flat. Charles got up and pushed me down on the three-seater settee and plonked himself in the middle of the cushioned seat.

'Come and sit here,' he commanded, patting the empty seat next to him. I walked over to the vacant space and sat beside him, knees touching.

'If you think I have any ideas like that French sailor at the "Yorkminister", forget it. The lecture I have just given you about being ambisextrous is based on my very long experience of life, but as long as you keep it to yourself, I'll tell you some more. As you probably observed and experienced, this block of flats is not called Chelsea Closets for nothing and sex is available morning, noon and night and I have followed that procedure to the letter. I have no objection to any of it. As your French sailor would say, "Chacun à son goût".

'However, if I did feel that you were my *petit filet mignon* I would, as the French sailor's counterpart, a RN sailor, would say, "one does not piss on one's own doorstep".

'You are "sort of family" through the ménage-à-trois connection, and as no one in your family seems to have made a man of you I felt it was my duty to fill in all the missing gaps.' He moved his hand over to my thigh and squeezed it gently.

'Good tuition?' he questioned. I nodded and he moved his hand swiftly away and leant back against the cushion with a satisfied sigh. 'End of discussion. Anything else?' But before I could answer there was a ring at the door.

I shot off the settee and made for the flat door, saying, 'OK, I'll get it!' opened the door and could not believe my eyes. Broadly smiling at me was a poor woman's imitation of 'Down Argentine Way' – Carmen Miranda, without fruit. Her hair was piled high, South American blotched make-up, shiny rayon stockings, sexy boots with very high heels and a mink coat which covered her entire body from neck to toe. She took one look at me, glanced into the room and saw Charles coming up behind me.

'Oooh!' she exclaimed with the hand-up-to-face surprised expression. 'Charles, darling, I didn't know that you fancied crisp young chicken,' she said, squeezing my cheek. I didn't like the squeeze but the waft of the heavy perfume was, I admit, vaguely down my street – at least more down than up. She smiled at me with a pleading look. 'You got any rubbers, love. I've just run out and my first trick is due in half an hour.'

Charles had always taught me to be prepared for any eventuality and I searched my hip pocket for two of the London Rubber Company products and pressed them into her expectant hands. She smacked a very wet kiss on my cheek, turned around and disappeared down the corridor to number 783.

I walked back into the room behind Charles and we sat down. Charles was grinning from ear to ear and started to unfold the history of the occupant of number 783, who had been at the Closets since June '40. It would have been better, he told me, if she had stayed on the beaches at Dunkirk. After all, the 330,000 could have left her behind so she would have had to do with the members of the Armed Forces of the Reich. Since the arrival of the US forces in UK she had found a brilliant method for her operation, which now switched to a continuous 24-hour routine.

Immediately after breakfast having made the bed and checked that the utensils required were ready for action, she would start the first shift going up and down in the lift. She was very expensively dressed with her full-length fake mink trailing to the lift floor. If a prospective punter, now preferably an American officer with at least three golden bars on his shoulders, entered the lift and pressed the down button, she would smile sweetly at him, await the reaction and open her mink coat. As she did not have on a stitch of clothing under the mink, the only delay was caused by a possible haggling over the price.

I smiled at Charles when he had finished the tale and was about to reply but Charles forestalled me.

'I can vouch, from personal experience, that it's not worth sixpence. Your French sailor friend is bound to be better than No. 783. I know for a fact that her tongue is like a piece of sandpaper ... and well worn at that. But is there anything more you want to tell? I'm a very good listener and it wouldn't be the first time I've led you into paradise.' He squeezed my knee, gripped it and pushed it firmly away.

'I don't really know how to begin,' I said hesitantly. 'Looking back on my years I suppose it started in Berlin of which I remember almost nothing, and to lose twelve years of memories is taunting. Only the worst Nazi moments and a few good ones remain. And when we came here in '37, my entire life was spent learning English. I had some terrific help from the headmaster and two masters who put me on the English road, and there's Tom Avery, Ernest's friend, and Geoffrey Child who perfected that side of life.

'But there seems to have been nothing apart from studying until now and Mum and Dad are always busy working and Billy is never home. Uncle Ernest is great but I don't see him half as much as you ... You're like father, teacher and friend all rolled into one.

'And then there's the sex bit. As you discovered I was a virgin until the time that I should have been sowing my oats with the girls at the school next door but when you're shy and five foot four and have no English, it gets a bit difficult. Around the time I was fifteen I had a great crush on a dark-haired beauty called Katie next door at Lady Eleanor Holles's, but that ebbed away when she married Len Smith, one of my classmates, but I never even dared tell him about it.

'The pictures of love and marriage portrayed on the silver screen you are very cynical of. You will probably agree with the *Oxford Dictionary* definition which is on the shelf behind us. "Warm affection", "fondness", "likeness" is probably what we agree with' and Charles nodded. 'Paternal benevolence' Charles shook his head at and added angrily. 'Look at your lot' which he almost spat out 'They don't care a...' and just stopped himself before descending to the vernacular of the Lower Deck, of either the French or Royal Navy.

'Sorry about that,' he added quietly. 'I'll agree with "Warm Affection" bit and if you feel you want that in your life, grab it when you find it and, take it from me .. it doesn't matter what colour, size, age or sex it is.

'If you want to be really confused, get the "Oxford" in and turn it to "love ... (games)" no score, nothing at all,' which I had heard when they announced the tennis match proceedings.

'But if you want to be even more confused go and quote the scoring of points "love all" or in cricket when someone "bowls a maiden over" or is caught at "silly mid-on"... Oh I give up, and if we had Grace here now we'd just get on with it,' I blurted out.

'That really is my biggest problem. She is my number one in the sex register and frankly, everything that has followed has been Woolworths standard. She is experienced and kind which comes with age. You and all the others I have always listened to are all older and I just love ... and I mean love ... experience with kindness which I can't get from young people.

'Here's to experience from those people,' and Charles stopped me.

'Want to go out and have a drink?' he added and I nodded.

We left the flat, took the lift, which mercifully was empty, walked out into Sloane Street and hailed a cab. Charles got in first and I looked back at him and asked: 'Where to?'

He shrugged his shoulders, pointed to the cabbie and he looked at me.

'Drop us at Piccadilly Circus,' and I fell back into the rear seat next to Charles.

'Wise choice! It's equidistant from all the fleshpots you and I know,' he said, adding: 'It will certainly give us a wide choice whichever way you look at it – up or down.'

At the bottom end of Bond Street, the cabbie turned into Piccadilly and asked, 'Which part of the Circus?'

Charles leant forward and replied, 'Near Lillywhite's.'

'You're lucky, Guv, it's still there, might as well take a last look, if you ask me.' He pushed down the meter as he pulled up to the side entrance in Lower Regent Street.

Charles handed him a ten shilling note, nodding 'Keep the change', and pushed me out and into the street. We walked one block and turned left after the side entrance of Lillywhite's, Charles led the way to the next corner, walked down some steps and pushed open a door. I followed him obediently and we were hit by a smell which was neither beery nor the pungent tobacco pong of most pubs.

'Different?' asked Charles and I nodded. 'It's the smell of rum, and should you ever get an "accepted letter" from their Lords of the Admiralty, you will find out that all sailors over the age of nineteen receive a ration of rum every day at noon.'

'What about those under nineteen?' I asked.

'They are labelled as UA – under age – and if they have some friends aboard, they call their "oppos" they may get a sip from them if they ask "sippers" nicely. I may not know as much useful information as Tom Avery but I feel sure that if you ask him nicely he will always come up with the answer. What about Geoffrey? But hang on, let me get the specials, and they are very special. You got the smell, didn't you? This place, the "Captain's Cabin" serves a rum and orange with it, either hot or cold and if you like you can have another one ... or two ... or as many as you like. We can always catch up on anything else you fancy later.'

Two rum specials – hot – appeared as fast as Charles could say the last word and we chin-chinned.

'Tasty, isn't it,' I confirmed licking the last drop of rum off my lips, and Charles immediately ordered another round.

As he pushed the second glass over to me, he suddenly turned to me in a concerned tone of voice. 'It's your matric year this summer, isn't it, and I should not really lead you astray. ED has told me that you are working at your exam as if there's no tomorrow...'

'It's June to be precise,' I interrupted and Charles nodded. 'That's precisely why I asked about Geoffrey and perhaps Tom Avery. I'm sure they could answer some of your questions on some of the exam papers.'

'Thanks very much. I'll ask ED to contact Tom Avery and I'm sure he'll come up to town for a couple days but what about Geoffrey? Do you think he could help you scholastically?'

I scratched my head. 'The problem with him is that he's very friendly but secretive and I don't really want to pester him if he is so buttoned up.'

Charles frowned and asked, 'Secretive like what?'

'Well I don't even know what he does in the Army.'

Charles roared with laughter. 'To coin a phrase, ... you didn't know there's a war on? You might just as well send a telegram to Reichmarschall Goering and tell him Geoffrey's location and get his Stukas to bomb it...' He looked around to see if there was anyone within listening distance. 'So what do you know about him... You've told me he's is a linguist and he's in Intelligence. Which means if the War Office has recovered its composure after Norway, Dunkirk and those idiotic mistakes over locking up Europe's finest scientists, mathematicians and others they will have made use of Geoffrey's languages.

'When he comes to see your family he stays days rather than months?' I nodded. 'And you say he comes from Euston and he says his work is about an hour away. So that's somewhere in the Home Counties. I'll listen around the bar at the Closets. We've got all sorts of odd people staying there... Hang on, there's two typical boffins, teacher types, mathematicians who come at very odd times. When I have a drink in the bar with them next time, I'll ask; they're always talking about having met other blokes from Hut 8 or 11 and add a different language words, behind the number like "German, you see, it's really child's play if you put two and two together".'

I gawped and looked at Charles, 'What did you say just now?'

'What do you mean?' Charles looked blank.

'You said it's easy, like child's play, but did you know that Geoffrey's name is Child?'

'Ouch,' and he slapped me on the shoulder and said, 'Next time you meet with him, ask if by coincidence, he knows those two in the bar at the Closets, one is Gordon Priest and I can't think of the other. But they are all Oxford or Cambridge ex-dons, so next time you see Geoffrey just slip the words Hut 6 or 8 and then ask when are you next off to Bletchley? You never know, he might just forget himself, regardless of being in the hush-hush Intelligence.

'But you don't want to learn that stuff anyway. All you want now are answers to certain questions on your exams ... a bit like you a couple of years ago when you were asking "why?" all the time. I'll get ED to contact Tom Avery and we can fix up a meeting for more exam cramming. ED can give him your phone number and I'm sure Tom will phone you.'

The first six months of 1942 were almost totally taken up by study, study and study. There were a few chinks of horizontal 'blue sky' but my main aim was to pass the matric. I poured my heart out to Uncle Charles and he passed these pourings on to ED who in turn contacted Tom Avery down at Cliftonville. Billy meanwhile, was making up for Australian lost horizontal time and every spare non-Army minute was taken up by working his way through that notebook which listed every pre-Australia contact. He must have gone through that book from page to page and top to bottom line, and then started all over again. He did offer me a few cast-offs but Uncle Charles's invitations were much more to the point and more enjoyable. If the six months up to matric had not been so time-consuming, I may have bothered more but, as Charles told me when I tackled him on this subject, 'I really don't know why you're in such a hurry. You're seventeen years old... Lots of years ahead of you... What's all the mad dash for? Nice and easy does it.'

Nice and easy did not describe the pace of the numbers of GIs arriving in the UK throughout 1942. From a slow trickle after Pearl Harbor, it reached a flood by the end of the year. In Mayfair many houses were requisitioned by the US Forces and they renamed Grosvenor Square 'Eisenhower Platz' after the Commander-in-Chief, 'Ike', of SHAEF, the newly created Supreme Headquarters of the Allied Expeditionary Force. Packards, Studebakers and many of the other US-made cars made that area look like the streets of Detroit or Manhattan.

At 99 Park Street, the six floors were stacked full with members of the US Army Band. They were all professional musicians who split into groups of military, ceremonial and dance-band sections at night-time. I and Bryan had been following the jazz groups like bees round a honeypot and when the *Melody Maker* listed the locations of the various ventures, we started to follow them to Rainbow Corner and other places of worship.

As we were the direct route into sisters and mothers we got to know many of the GIs. We were the pot to eager bees in search of honey in return for Lucky Strikes, Hershey Bars and every form of direct entertainment. Apart from the money flowing out of the pockets of the beautifully pressed uniforms of the GIs, unobtainable rationed luxuries such as nylon stockings and rations of food kept flowing from the Post Exchanges (PXs) to the hungry British mouths and their empty pockets.

Having once satisfied their carnal desires, the occupants of 99 Park Street asked Bryan and I if there were any non-sex clubs that we could point them to when they were off-duty and where they could join into jam sessions with their British counterparts. Mr Feldman, a tailoring friend of Dad's had just opened a converted cellar at 100 Oxford Street and the No.2 Swing Club opened its premises there on Saturday and Sunday nights. He had three sons, Monty, Robert and Victor, the last at least ten years younger than his brothers. Robert played the clarinet and Monty the accordeon, while Victor was a drummer prodigy.

When Bryan and I pointed the members of 99 Park Street to 100 Oxford Street they could not believe their eyes and ears and after the initial shock rechristened young Victor the 'young Krupa' after the flamboyant drummer of Benny Goodman and Tommy Dorsey fame. We helped them by sitting at the table collecting the entrance money, which had the additional advantage of sitting down and listening to the jam session for free. Both he and I became club members in December 1942 and I still cherish membership card No.709. It was free, so I saved the annual membership fee of five shillings.

News of 'swing' sensation spread like wildfire and within weeks every up-and-coming British musicians such as Kenny Baker, Vic Lewis, Jack Parnell, Ralph Sharon and George Shearing, sat in on the jam sessions with the Americans. All the big names from the US continent joined in on these and I still have a signed picture of young Victor at the drums with Glenn Miller's drummer, Ray McKinley.

Apart from the Miller Band the other big name was Artie Shaw. He had joined the US Navy and formed that organisation's official band which toured the Far East. When they returned stateside, Shaw left the band and Sam Donahue, the leader of the sax section, took over. Once over here they joined the day-and-night circus and

I took a photo of them playing a lunchtime concert in Lincolns Inn Fields but I don't think Mr Tooth was present to hear them.

Not surprisingly there was little time or space to record every detail except the almost weekly comment of 'jamboree ... with ... TERRIFIC!' If my mouth had been a soup plate, I would have needed a very large spoon to empty it and the Feldmans became a close part of our family. Victor eventually went to the States and made a name for himself in the jazz world.

For about two years my second home was 99 Park Street. It was very difficult to get home on time after the club closed and I did not want a repeat of the seven-minute-past-midnight episode. Frank Vićari, the drummer of the Army Band, suggested I had some 'dog tags' embossed with my name and blood group to allow me to stay at night. These were thin metal-stencilled domino-sized tags. The following week I was presented with the tags and suffered the equivalent of a 'Crossing the Line' ceremony.

To the accompaniment of loud cheers I was stripped and pushed into the shower. Two of the GIs got two scrubbers and commenced to scrub me down 'to remove the smell from that stinkin' fuckin' limey cocksucker' which fortunately for me, I did not understand completely. I could hardly await the outcome of the torment after Frank put his nose under my armpits and powdered me down from neck to toe and then proceeded to empty a bottle of aftershave over me. 'That's great, you now smell like a whorehouse,' he said as he ceremoniously draped the two tags around my neck and to loud cheers gave me a vicious slap on my bottom. 'There you go ... you are no longer a stinkin' fu..li.cór.'

The tags enabled me to join them at the unrationed PX in Eisenhower Platz every Sunday morning for two eggs, sunny side up, three rashers of bacon, three sausages and deep-fried bread. Coffee in the mugs two or three times. Afterwards I removed my dog tags and GI fatigues and handed them back. Then the GIs escorted me to the No.73 bus stop in Park Lane. The final touch at the bus stop was watching the girls on 'early shift' in the doorway of the Dorchester, whose side door was just wide enough for two girls. Whilst one kept a lookout for the cruising large American staff cars, the other was watching for the local constabulary, who, if the girls couldn't come up with the food bribes for the missus, would arrest them.

I was in the doorway waiting for the No.73 when a big Buick

came crawling down Park Lane scoop-netting for the two-or three-star occupants in the back seat. The driver spotted the ladies as fast as they had spotted him and one, in the too-high heels, clattered across the pavement towards the slowing car. When it stopped, the window was wound down, the girl pushed her head through the open window and a short discussion of the Sunday rate took place. Her bottom straightened and she turned around to give a report to her friend who was standing beside me as if she were waiting for the greyhound race results at Hackney Stadium.

'He'll give us bacon and two eggs in Wimbledon, but no money.'

It was a rationed food offer supplement neither could afford to miss and the lady next to me clattered over to her friend, the car door opened and they proceeded southwards at a very rapid rate. I reported this back to 99 Park Street and had to give a detailed description to almost the entire occupants of that establishment and could not understand why the ladies had not been round to 99 Park Street.

All the musicians practised their musical scales every day, all day, and walking past the house on a nice open-window day was like walking past the Albert Hall an hour before the concert when the flutes, clarinets, saxophones (Alto and tenor), trumpets, trombones and cymbals were all practising their scales: up and down etc, etc.

How all these activities were crammed into one year I cannot understand when there were so many other things to take care of. A saxophone was purchased for Billy with the help of a musician friend from the 100 Club – Douggie Robinson, one of the elite in the alto sax field. Monty Feldman was on hand with the purchase of an accordeon, so Billy's wants were taken care of in the musical department. On 26th December the 100 Club held a huge end-of-year jam session which I simply recorded in the diary as 'TERRIFIC', and Mum and I finished the year by going to the Ritz Cinema in Richmond to see *Birth of the Blues.*'

However, none of this could have happened without Tom Avery, ED's friend in Cliftonville. Uncle Charles had passed my outpourings on earlier in the year to ED, who had dutifully reported them to Tom. One Sunday morning earlier in the year the telephone rang at breakfast time. I followed the 'procedure on answering the phone' as laid down by Tom:

'Paper and pen must always be at the ready BEFORE you lift the receiver so you are not caught with your pants down and don't have to say to a client "'ang on, I'll just get some paper" and let the poor chap wait. He'll know he's working with an distinguished set of dimwits.' I lifted the receiver, paper and pen at the ready.

'It's Tom, Tom Avery here. Is David there, please?'

Somewhat taken aback at being asked for as 'David' I just said 'Yes', and he said he wanted to come up to London to see if he could help with any preparations for the matric. I was surprised but delighted as I felt he knew everything and everybody who could help me across that hurdle.

He came up every week and I met him at Waterloo and from there we lunched at the Hungarian Czardas in Dean Street as Tom felt that Simpson's would be a little overpowering. Furthermore, he had known Mr Weisz since before the war because he had needed a little help ... and so the reminiscing began. On the third visit I plucked up enough courage to thank Tom and asked him why me? His serious face turned even more sombre.

'Because, David, when I was very young, my family were killed in a car accident. As I had no friends but a very good education, I volunteered for the Army and worked my way up and up. The Winchester schooling helped but I discovered at an early age that you need friends in life and the Army became my real family. As I rose through the hierarchy, I followed the old principle of "Always be nice to people on the way up. You never know, you might need them on the way down."

'And throughout my life I've followed that route. When I was out East, a lot of the other ranks were near breaking point because of the long period away from home and families, and it always gave me satisfaction when I and the other officers could sort out the personal problems in the ranks. When Ernest told me about you and your family under those inhuman swine in Germany I just had to help by getting you into Hampton Grammar and I'm over the moon to see the progress you have made in the last three years.

'All I can add is that if you carry on like this, I'll be very proud of you!' He suddenly smiled and added: 'In fact, I am very proud of you now, David.' He offered me his hand and clasped mine, squeezing it very hard. 'And call me Tom in future.'

For me that conversation marked the end of my childhood and the beginning of my manhood.

My diaries up to 1942 had been a collection of war miseries and defeats, but now the war was turning in our favour and the

Allies were winning their first victories against Hitler's armed forces. The Russians and the deep snow had brought the mighty Wehrmacht to a halt at the gates of Moscow; at Stalingrad they annihilated General Paulus's 6th Army; in the Battle of Egypt the British 8th Army defeated General Rommel's Afrika Korps and the Americans landed in North Africa. Sensing a future victory, Winston Churchill said at the Mansion House: 'This is not the end. It is not even the beginning of the end. But perhaps, the end of the beginning.'

At the height of the Blitz in 1940, Dad, ED and Charles had bought property on a purely hunch basis. ED's and Charles flats were with vacant possession but 91 Christchurch Road was not. Either it was fate or sheer good luck but the owners decided to sell the freehold at the moment when not only Winston Churchill, but teenagers like myself, felt that the beginning of the end of the war was not in the too-distant future. Dad was able to buy the freehold at the beginning of January and we moved into 'Balcomie', in Christchurch Road, in April when my own 'blue sky' was in the ascendancy. Sadly not for long.

I had foolishly assumed that my seven-minute affair in January had been forgotten, but when a summons arrived in late February 'to appear before the Court of Summary Jurisdiction' I went to panic stations and in desperation turned to Tom. He seemed my only hope of escape.

'Escape?' said Tom. 'You can't escape from facts and in all situations you must accept them. In your case you have contravened Article 1 Aliens (Movement Restrictions) Order 1940, but they can't put you in front of a firing squad for that. What me must do is follow the Senior Service's advice and perform "damage control" or mitigation. They have to do this because if a ship gets holed below the waterline, it sinks and only DC may save it. So what DC can we do in your case?' He scratched that enormous beehive of white hair.

'As I told you earlier we won't waste money on getting "silk" to possibly reduce the misdemeanour,' and he chuckled, 'seven minutes down to what? No, we must play the Establishments own game, which is something we always practiced in the Army. The people involved here are you, the keen but totally correct PC at Richmond Station who applied the law, his sergeant who processed the report and the various civil servants who have gone through the motion.

'The young copper got brownie points by upping his offences score and ditto the sergeant. As for all the pen-pushers in between, they have proven to the powers-that-be that they require additional staff as they are grossly overworked. The only chink in this formidable wall of bureaucracy is to play on their feelings of guilt. I signed all those bloody permits for your family to come and live here and remember that your official Home Office status then was "Refugee from Nazi Persecution". So you agree to the misdemeanour, but tell them that when you saw the copper in his uniform you panicked because of the Gestapo and just couldn't think straight and gave him some wrong answers which you are extremely sorry about. If it starts to go pear-shaped ... squeeze out a few tears... That's always a good standby, believe me. I know, being a magistrate myself down in Margate. There's always the religious angle, too. Find out who the local rabbi is... Bet you don't know ... you never go to synagogue do you? If any one like that gets in the way of the grinding police mill they run a mile... It's way out of their procedure and means more paperwork.'

Tom was spot on as always and the PC met Rabbi Ginsberg, who did the wailing-wall act with the local cops. 'Anything else?' he grinned and joined me in Court where fortunately I did not even have to go as far as the tears bit. I eventually got to feel quite sorry for PC 724 V as Charles Wing was only doing his duty and in turn was now being crucified by the Beak.

After that episode I felt that 1943 was going to be my year and now nothing could go wrong.

I walked Tom to Richmond Station and he gripped my hand firmly and started to grin from ear to ear.

'Glad to have been of help. If you have any more problems, just give me a call. Charles has promised to set up a bridge foursome at the Cloisters ... and, you can take that smile off your face.' He looked me straight in the eyes. 'Yes, it IS bridge. I've heard all about your extra-curricular lessons at the Cloisters. Goodbye for now.' He waved, gave me a big warm smile, turned on his heels and disappeared in the direction of Richmond Station.

On 1st June his sister phoned and told us he had been killed in a daytime raid in Cliftonville.

Tale 5

Midnight Mass

We were all shattered by the news and I was totally gutted at losing my friend. Whether it was Wolfy's ghost or just fate, but at the same time Britain was being swamped by an avalanche of arrivals from the New World. The colour of England's green and pleasant land was now matched by the GIs uniforms and their equipment, which mirrored the one colour that had so impressed me on arrival in Southampton. The jeeps were green and the GIs in their fatigues were of a similar green camouflage. The netting which hid the fake guns stored under it was green. They had been built to fool the German aircraft into the existence of a big Allied Army which even had it's own fake radio network.

All these preparations were for the enormous build-up for the invasion which Winston Churchill and President Roosevelt had agreed to launch sometime in 1944. Tens of thousands of well-dressed, gum-chewing and fat-walletted GIs descended on the war-weary under-rationed Brits whose husbands, sons and brothers were fighting in the deserts of North Africa, the jungles of Malaya and Burma. London was the focal point for entertainment and many GIs made for the city, though it was not for sightseeing. They were happily endorsing the foundations of the Western capitalist system – 'If you've got the money, we've got the goods' – and it was not surprising that the poor male Brits didn't get a look-in, though some did, including me.

Because of the large influx of GIs many new music and entertainment ventures opened in the West End: the Portman Hall, the Criterion Theatre, the Town Hall in Wembley, the Queensberry Club, and the Old London Casino in Old Compton Street were turned into vast palaces of entertainment. Even the BBC's underground studio, the Paris, in Lower Regent Street became a 'live' broadcasting

67

venue. Tommy Handley and the popular ITMA show broadcasts from the Paris and the RAF's 'Squadronaires' performed jointly with all or some of the bands of the US Army and US Navy. To me, the film I saw at the Dominion became reality. It's title was *This Demi-Paradise*. I was swallowed up in this whirlpool of activity and there was barely time to decide whether 779 Chelsea Cloisters or the sexless Park Street had prime position. In the end Park Street won because of the endless amounts of food available. There were the additional plus supplies from Frank Vićari, George Kieffer, Sammie Anzello and Emile Oulliber showering Ma-dame not only with lots of hugs and kisses but enormous amounts of food from the PX. In the end she used to give them wanted lists to complement and not over supply the stock of eggs, butter, spam tins and Lucky Strikes ('bricks' of 200 packed in 20s) which were worth more than their weight in pounds, shillings or pence.

There were very few bombs in 1943 as the V1s or V2s were not even a speck on the horizon. I asked young George Kieffer if any new phrases had been added to the foreplay conversation of 'you got any gum, chum ... you gotta sister, mister' and the only one he could come up with was based on the fact that the British male used no talcum powder or aftershave whereas, as I had discovered, the GIs used them liberally. George used to dowse himself with the two items and told me it helped enormously when the 'gals' snuggled up. 'Oh you do smell looovely,' they cooed, to which the standard reply from the Southerner was:

''Corse I do, maaaaam. All over.' And he would then gently push her head to the lower regions of his powdered, perfumed, smooth and hairless young body.

Most members of the No. 1 United States Army band came from New Orleans, or 'Nu Orlns' as the 'fellers' called it. They were all first-generation Americans whose parents hailed from France, Italy and other European countries. Their ID religion mainly stated 'Roman Catholic', which was required information if they were killed in battle. When it came to the battle of the sexes the marital status stateside was conveniently forgotten. Or so Frank Vićari, who was the father of a two-year-old boy, explained to me at Xmas 1943.

Being RC was as important to him as my absence of synagogue going. He knew of my official faith but asked if I would like to join them at Midnight Mass on Xmas Eve. As Uncle Charles had persuaded me to try everything in life once I was quite keen to see this very ancient procedure. As six of us wanted to go, Frank had haggled with the driver of one of the very large Packard 'Big Brass' staff cars to provide transport to Westminster Cathedral. The driver got a very good deal as the exchange for the deal were two gals ... well actually 'two great dames', one for the trip to the cathedral and the second for the return journey. I was certainly impressed by the beautiful service and efficiency of the proceedings and on the return journey I asked Frank if he went to church often.

'Hell, no ... it depends how many times I have sinned in the week ... I sorta bunch it up, saves going to confession more often.' But I did not report this to Mum. She would not have believed that her six-foot smooth-faced dark-haired innocent Frank could do that when the picture of his little boy back in 'Nu Orlns' was in the wallet nestling in his hip pockets and was proudly on show to all and sundry.

As we walked out of Westminster Cathedral, the streets were deserted except for the Packard waiting patiently for its occupants. The driver, who had already cashed in on the exchange for the one trip, took one look at us and started singing 'I'm Confessin' That I Love You' without the last four words, grinned and raised his eyebrows. 'Where to fellas?'

Before he could be stopped by the others Frank said, '99 Park Street.'

'No shit' was the surprised response from the driver, but he probably looked at me and felt Frank should not lead someone so young astray after Midnight Mass. Not that this seemed to make a difference when we got to Park Street ten minutes later. George got my camp bed ready and Frank unscrewed a bottle of Kentucky Rye whiskey. George brought over three tumblers and filled them to the brim.

'It's kinda early but here's down the hatch ... Merry Xmas!' and George gulped the tumbler in one big schlurp and turned to me as I had taken only a little sip.

'C'mon, maaaaan ... you gotta down that double fast.' He watched me as I made an effort not to let the whiskey run out of the side of my mouth. As soon as I had drained the glass, Frank refilled it, and again and I don't remember much except Frank pushing me horizontal on the camp bed and turning to George said: 'Leave, Daveyboy alone now and don't give him a midnight kiss. He'll be so goddam scared he won't sleep a wink all night.'

The next thing I remember in the morning was Frank pushing another glass into my hand and grinning from ear to ear urging me on: 'Mornin', maaaan! MERRY XMAS!'

I have never had another Xmas like that again ... not even another Midnight Mass.

Tale 6

The Fellers From 'Nu Orlns'

The news of my matric was of no interest to any one at Park Street. 'Mat what?' was the usual response, along with very blank looks, as the word did not appear on any of their music sheets or those of the US Navy bands. George's comment was in tune with the others except that it descended to the very low level of 'Some godam' Limey shit language.' Fortunately I did not report the exact words to Mum as she would not only have been deeply shocked but her 'pure blue image of those lovely boys' would have been severely tarnished.

After passing my matric I left school and worked in the firm at Wardour Street while waiting for a call into the armed forces, it was almost like wanting to go to the toilet but having a block of nature I had tried the ATC, the RN and even volunteered for a new RN unit which was being set up under the sea off the French coast to monitor German ship movements. It was mini-sub radio base and the small boats were sending details and monitoring the radio signals back to the UK based stations.

In the event, the news that I was still an enemy alien reached the home bases faster than the radio signals and I was slung out within six weeks. Geoffrey was fuming as he had been instrumental in getting me screened and passed as 'safe'. After this final blow I just gave up and awaited events. The comments in my diary are worse than the rather descriptive words the GIs had used at my initiation ceremony with the metal dog tags.

I now threw myself into the 99 Park Street, 779 Chelsea Cloisters and Mum's catering 'Balcomie activities'.

The previous owner of the home had thoughtfully built a large air-raid shelter in the garden which resembled a grass-covered igloo. It slept eight people, which expanded the sleeping arrangements

71

of the house from twelve to twenty. When it was a 'no bed / full house situation' Mum was in her element, but I doubt if it ever extended into the sexual area. I do remember one Sunday morning when Geoffrey appeared for breakfast, put his arm around Mum's shoulder and was perplexed by the number of different uniformed males arriving for a good breakfast nosh. The uniforms were all colours of the Allied rainbow. Smooth khaki American, RAF blue from the Brits, a few khaki-clad Brits with the SHAEF shoulder flash, a sprinkle of Free French and an occasional Pole or Czech, as the very nosy occupant from No. 783 discovered when one of the Free Poles gave her a cheque.

Geoffrey pressed Mum's shoulder, surveyed this hotpotch of nationalities and proclaimed in a loud voice: 'From now on I will call you "Ma-dame",' pronouncing the word in the long, stretched-out French way. The name stuck with her until the day she died.

I asked him later in the morning why he had chosen this rather strange description for dear Mum, but he simply shrugged his shoulders, adding: 'Well, coming in here in the mornings and seeing all the different uniforms, it's like walking into a Bovril...' and he paused for a minute

'I think I'll be adding another spoonful of the stuff in the not too distant future. We have had quite a number of new arrivals in the past few weeks...'

I interrupted him. 'Where from, Geoff...?' I knew he would explode.

'I've told you before ... my name is Geoffrey. And in addition, you should know that "Careless talk costs lives". It says so on all the posters ... unless of course you've forgotten how to read ... and for your information ... they are all from somewhere west of Liverpool.'

Go on, I thought to myself, I can play your bloody game and blurted out, 'Oh well, it's either in the Irish Sea or Ireland...'

Geoffrey capitulated and congratulated me on not having fallen asleep during Geography at Hampton Grammar.

On his next visit Geoffrey presented Captain Kurt Zimansky to Madame and she was over her blue moon. He was as tall as General de Gaulle but oozed a US Midwestern charm which wrapped itself around Madame like a well-aimed lasso. He was seconded to the Circus, being fluent in German, Polish and Russian because of his ancestry (Madame insisted he must have been at least the son of a count or baron) but the Circus also used his many other talents as he was a brilliant mathematician from Middletown University.

Geoffrey and I had to introduce him to all the 'London, England' sightseeing wonders but when I asked Geoffrey about possible visits to the Fitzroy or Yorkminster he shook his head, 'I haven't broached the subject as yet. All I know he is married and has a four-year-old back in Iowa ... although minor problems like that have never stopped me in the past.' The Tower, Buck House, Whitehall, Downing Street were dutifully ticked off, but when Geoffrey coyly told him and me that he had been upgraded to Captain, Kurt slapped Geoffrey on the back and ordered another scotch for him at the Army and Navy bar in Pall Mall.

Geoffrey still dressed like an impoverished undergraduate at the Sorbonne. He wore a jacket, if forced into one, and his elbow-holed sweaters and shirts had seen better and very much younger days. His CO and fellow officers said he had to get himself a decent uniform and whilst he was at it, get a British Army 'Warm' overcoat of substance. Geoffrey thought my knowledge of the ragtrade might point him in the right direction but I told him I would have to make enquiries regarding supplies to the menswear retail trade. My female buyers contacts pointed me in the Regent Street, Bond Street direction and all agreed that tailoring and high class menswear were synonymous with Gieves of Bond Street and I passed this information on to Geoffrey who was nodding his head like a toy dummy. 'Ah yes ...' he said, 'that's the company that made Jeeves famous as *the* butler in the Establishment.' For once ... just once, I got the better of Geoffrey.

Having done my research and visited the shop in Bond Street they very kindly presented me with two A4 sheets of the firm's history and the fact that they had no connection whatsoever with the fictitious character. 'Gieves and Hawkes were founded in 1771 and 1785 ...' I trumpeted, 'and I have had two copies typed out for you and Kurt to bring you up to date on their long tailoring history. As you can see G & H stand for the best in men's tailoring; their first Royal Warrant was granted in the reign of George III in 1809. You'll then have to explain the "Royal Warrant" bit to Kurt. If *you* don't know it I would be delighted to tell you ...' I felt that sort of paid back the bit about me and 'Geoff' and the location of Ireland. In the event, I explained the Royal Warrant over double Pimm's at the Army and Navy. 'For future information the correct pronunciation of Gieves is with a hard "G" not as in "gin", but hard as in "give" and whilst you're at it, "giss" us another round ... all round.' I felt that this was game, set and match ...for once ... just bloody once!

As we drowned our third Pimm's, Kurt became fascinated by the Royal Warrant recital. '... And all that still goes on today? You're kiddin'?' he queried incredulously.

'Sure does...' I replied in my best imitation of a 'Nu Orlns' accent.

'There's the RW association and you have to produce documentary evidence that you have supplied a member of the Royal Household for a number of years. If they agree to the goods having been supplied, they will give you permission to use the warrant on your notepaper or outside the shop. All sorts of suppliers get it. Car manufacturers, shirtmakers, dressmakers, food suppliers, in fact anyone or anything that has been supplied then helps your sales no end.'

It did occur to me that if the London Rubber Company supplied their goods to the Palace, had they got a Royal Warrant?

Kurt Zimansky became a fully paid non-Royal Warrant supplier/member to 'Balcomie' and after every stay received a complete list of requests in the way of rationed items which were required and Madame made up as 'GB' lists. GB stood for the German words *grosse Bitte* – 'Big Request' and this naming of a GB list has survived Madame, Dad, ED and Uncle Charles until today.

In fact, Madame had almost got to the stage where she could have opened her own PX. All the 'GB' suppliers were more like multi-coloured liquorice all sorts than the universal brown Bovril colour.

Another addition to my mother's entourage was, Frank Vićari from the 'sub station' at 99 Park Street, a six foot five giant with jet-black hair and a permanent smile which stretched, like a 'smiley' face, from ear to ear. His charm oozed like the red wine from Calabria where his parents hailed from. He started playing the drums at the age of eleven and his enormous hands had been strengthened by the continual practice of holding the drumsticks and were the size of two enormous pancakes stuffed with tomatoes and mortadella cheese.

George Kieffer was the nineteen-year-old baby of the band and his strong lips and brilliant breath control produced the sweetest alto sax sound you have ever heard. His name and thick blond curly hair could have made him a role model for a typical Aryan superman except for the fact he was only five feet five inches tall.

Joe Brace, the bass player from New York, had played with the Louis Prima Band and their fellow members had been called up by Uncle Sam to entertain the US forces, like the Glenn Miller and Sam Donahue bands after them. They were all professional musicians who read and played every type of music from 'Moonlight Sonata' to 'Moonlight Serenade'. Although I always had to endure the 'goddam Limey' insults they never tagged a label to their 'bonded' mates. The reason was that they were virtually all first-generation Americans and it would have been akin to a 'Kraut' calling an 'Eyetie' black. But they all fitted into Madame's file of 'newly acquired' men as smoothly as the tightly packed song sheets on their bandstands.

Madame's New Year's Eve birthday was an unusually quiet affair. There was a war on and Geoffrey and Kurt were Bletchley-bound. The occupants from 99 Park Street were either on duty in Trafalgar Square or Parliament Square, and, at night, split into the various dance bands and trios to entertain the New Year's Eve revellers. Billy was stuck at Catterick. Anyway, that was his story and I don't know whether it was with the lonely sheep on Ilkley Moor or the two-legged variety from the camp followers. All the same, Madame, Dad, ED, Uncle Charles and I had the new neighbours at 'Balcomie', the Purcells, who saw the New Year in with us. Madame and I agreed 1943 had been a 'demi-paradise', as we clinked our glasses to a healthy, happy and prosperous 1944.

Tale 7

Wartime Work of National Importance

When I transferred last year's diary addresses to the New Year's, the 'A' section produced a small tear. 'Tiempaka' in Holly Lane, Cliftonville, Kent was just a wonderful memory and I could hear Tom say: 'C'mon, David, everything in life has two sides to it and you must remember all the plusses you've had through our friendship.' I could not even begin to think of all the things he had taught me. 'Facts are facts and never kid yourself otherwise your dear Mum's "blue sky" will blind you and taint your judgement.'

Turning the diary pages of 1943 to December I noticed a strange pattern of change of people since the previous year. Many of the school contact names had disappeared. Bossy, Jammy and Steffs were not listed and the only schoolboy name that cropped up throughout the year was Brudy who appeared twenty-eight times. The last entry, on 27th December relates: 'Brudy here for tea, went to the 100 Club, stayed for night and had long walk in morning.' It was at this point he asked me a big favour. 'I know my name is Brudenell and all of you call me "Brudy" but PLEASE, in the new year can you and all the others change it to Mike?' I couldn't really foresee any problems with that and he compromised by calling me 'David' instead of 'Freddy' in future, and I suggested 'Dave' to which he replied with 'I'll see'.

Mike started on his mercurial career by going to King's College Hospital on Denmark Hill which being so close to each other cemented our future contact. I did not help him with delivering his very first baby but I was kept up to date when he filled me in after our weekly squash matches at King's.

He qualified MB BS (London) but his rise to the top of the profession could fill two books as the clients husbands ranged from 'Who's Who' to Debrett which was not the case with any of the other school contact names who did not even make it to the 'Addresses'. All the replacements were either American, European or British musicians.

I was very contented and far too busy to worry about next week, let alone next year, and there appeared to be no specks of trouble on the horizon. Fortunately they did not appear until the following June. The larder was overfull. Madame was in her element as she had the maximum number of beds filled. Dad was constantly going to Manchester to do business, although I never did find out why or what kind of business it was. Billy never seemed to have reached the end of the list of females and my physical desires in that direction were never totally exhausted. My mental pleasures were catered for by the '100 Club' and its consequent spin offs as they grew in quantity by the week. There seemed to be no end to the increasing number of US entertainment ventures that were opening. This was not surprising as thousands of GIs were now arriving aboard the *Queen Mary* and *Queen Elizabeth* every month. In fact the boys at No.99 were getting so crammed together that they moved to a larger house at 31 Green Street.

On Monday 3rd January Madame met the postman just as he was about to put two letters through the letter box and she pushed them into my hand, glancing at the senders. One was a plain envelope with a 'Passed by censor' stamp which seemed like a 'thank you' from Geoffrey. The other she just stared at and it was addressed to me with a block-lettered sentence across the top. She smiled, her face breaking into a large 'blue-sky' look.

'Look who it's from,' she gushed excitedly. ' "On His Majesty's Service" *and* it's addressed to you!'

I do believe she imagined that George VI had actually put pen to paper to write to me personally.

'Go on!' she urged and handed me a knife. 'Open it.'

I slit the smallish buff envelope open and removed a pre-printed folded brown piece of paper from it. Apart from my name and address it quoted a few facts which were not totally unknown to me: 'it has come to my attention that you have passed your eighteenth birthday and we have no record of you having registered for National Service. Consequently we request you to attend this office for an interview on Monday 17th February at 09.00hrs.' It then went on to give a contact number in case of any problems with possible reasons for non-attendance. The sender's address was not Buckingham Palace but the Labour Exchange at Chiswick in West London, which partially blocked Madame's blue sky. I knew that officialdom's wheels ground very slowly from dear Tom's tales, but as I was now approaching my twentieth birthday, two years' delay was quite a long time. Ah well, Tom had always said, officialdom and solicitors know nothing is so urgent that waiting another year or two does not increase its urgency.

I showed the letter to Geoffrey the following week and he dismissed it with a very logical comment: 'Just wait and see.' In the meantime, he approached me with his own *grosse Bitte* – GB: would Dad agree to his keeping his car in our garage so he could use it when in London in return for me using it when he was away. It was really like one of the Wardour Street girls asking me if I wanted a freebie and Dad agreed immediately, although he did ask Geoffrey who would insure the car. Geoffrey said he would, and neither Dad nor I could believe our luck. Our neighbours, the Purcells, were duly impressed when they saw the Citroën. The 1939 Traction Avant was one of Ronnie's favourites and Joyce and the two girls loved the silver-grey look. Their friend Louis Klemantaski was equally interested as he had been very involved in the motor-racing fraternity and had spent all his spare time with them just before the war.

Another Geoffrey GB was in the form of a telephone call and was a sort of cry for help. He was a very shy person by nature, and after the 'you must get a decent uniform suggestion' he had finally succumbed and asked me to make an appointment for him in Bond Street. This was hardly insurmountable and he and Kurt came up in the first week of February, Kurt being there to give additional moral support to Geoffrey who had told him that even in his Rugby days he had been scared to go to the tailors alone as they always wanted to take his inside-leg measurements when he bought a tie. G & H were a tremendous success, not only with Geoffrey who was measured for a major's uniform, but with Major Zimansky who bought some spare uniform buttons and a tie which he was not measured for. However, the very attentive salesman gave Kurt a pre-printed sheet of paper and requested him to fill in his details regarding APO mail reference. 'You can always telegram us on "Uniforms Portsmouth" for any special service requests,' he added.

Special Melton British Army 'Warm' and uniform for Geoffrey

completed the whole picture and Kurt was even handed the identical sheets of G & H history which they had kindly given to me as a history starter. Kurt was greatly impressed as we walked the few yards down Regent Street and Geoffrey was not only relieved to have had Kurt's support but was also pleased that he had received almost 'Warrant Holder' attention. We caught a taxi from Regent Street to Waterloo where the cabbie dropped me. 'See you on the 14th,' said Geoffrey who had promised to go with me to the appointment at the Labour Exchange. I waved back to the taxi as it sped to Euston to drop the two passengers to catch their train to 'somewhere in the Home Counties'.

Remembering all the training dear Tom had given me, I had kept a slim file with copies of all the letters of my fruitless attempts to help the war effort. As per Tom's instructions they were all in alphabetical order with all replies and/or rejection slips. I had sentimentally marked the file 'TA'.

The special instruction section by Tom listed clothing as 'sober with quiet' tie. At 7 a.m., on the 7th February, Geoffrey phoned to say that he couldn't make it. 'There's a panic on in the office.' I set off at eight. 'Always be early for an appointment and have a pee in case you get stage fright' was another piece of Tom's advice. 'Check everything you want to have with you as evidence and remember the six Ps.' I was twenty minutes early and waited, waited and waited. At twenty past ten a gentleman aged about forty-five appeared, introduced himself and apologised for being late.

Now that's a good start, I said to myself. This meant the chap 'owed me one'. Sadly, the interviewer had not read Tom's 'Instructions' and set off towards his office as if there was a fire in the building.

'Sit down, please; I'm running a bit late.' He kept looking at his watch at five-minute intervals as if there was no afternoon. I put my file on the desk in front of me and he looked at it as if it had been contaminated by some poisonous substance.

'We have your details and do not require additional material to assess your case' was his dismissal of my unseen docs.

'This may be due to your having changed your name,' he added as if I had been a master spy wanting to escape capture by a brigade of guards.

'In your case,' he continued as if I had already been judged and found guilty, 'we feel, under the circumstance, a best purpose would be served if you undertook a crash course as a centre lathe turner and after sixteen weeks' training were drafted to an engineering establishment to produce essential items for the war effort.'

My brain was reaching for the blue sky at a very fast rate of knots. We were in West London. Not far away in Kingston were Hawkers who were the biggest factory producing aircraft and I could already see myself producing a record number of extra Hurricanes to finish off the Luftwaffe.

When he had looked at his watch for the tenth time, he finally signed the fifth chit, handed me the bunch, adding: 'You will be informed where and when to report at the Hounslow Training centre and when you pass out sometime in June, you will be allocated a place in an essential war effort place of employment.'

He got up, allowed himself the smallest of smiles and ushered me out of the room. No doubt he was on his way to a cup of tea or a rapid slash before the next appointment.

If this had been the overture to an exciting opera, it did not live up to Geoffrey, Madame, Dad's, or my imagination. A centre lathe was as familiar to me as the back of a truck, a ten-tonner. The basic technique of turning a piece of metal into a 20mm-diameter did not require a brain of Einsteinian calibre and why it needed a sixteen-week course to master this art was beyond my comprehension. The only interesting thing were the people who were being trained for this master class. Here was I, a well-educated little Jewish bloke, rubbing shoulders with deserters from the Forces, including a foul-mouthed Canadian sailor who had already deserted for the fourth time. However, I found his language interesting as his entire vocabulary appeared to consist of words only starting with the letters A, B, C, D and F, which referred to many parts of the human anatomy and were all interchangeable as nouns, pronouns and verbs.

All the same, the sixteen weeks were most informative and shed some light on a life which I never knew existed. In a perverse sort of a way it was like being introduced to the different varieties I had sampled at 779 Chelsea Cloisters – without sex. After the instructions we had to do our share of fire watching and I kept my fingers crossed that when my first 'turn' came up for night duty, my partner would not be the Canadian. Sadly, my prayers were not answered or perhaps my fingers had not been crossed sufficiently. Around two o'clock in the morning he announced that he 'had to go for a slash' and disappeared and reappeared with legs crossed commenting, 'All the goddam bogs are locked', and walked across to the fire which was burning brightly in the fireplace to keep us warm. He dropped his pants, aimed for the burning logs and extinguished all three logs with one mighty arc. 'Geez, that's better,' he announced triumphantly, adding, 'Go on ... you go ... one of the logs is still smouldering ... as easy as bowling over the clubs in a bowling alley.' I was not in the mood to discuss the matter and was greatly relieved to see him pull his trousers up and on.

The sixteen weeks were over in a flash and on leaving I received a certificate stating I was now a 'qualified centre lathe turner' and would receive my allocated place of work in due course.

Surprisingly, three weeks later I was instructed to report for work at the Belmont Engineering Company in Chiswick. The actual name was Belmont Garage and it could not even live up to that splendid description. Before starting I cycled over on a Sunday morning to orientate myself regarding its location. I really need not have bothered as it was a cross between a 'satanic mill' and a discarded 'Steptoe and Son' shed. The two iron gates were securely held together with a rusty chain from which hung a rusty unusable lock, and when I arrived on Monday morning to report for work, the gates were not prized open until 9.30. A pleasant youngish man introduced himself as Frankie, the foreman, or 'anything you cares to call us', adding that the 'Gaffer' hardly ever comes anyhow.

'Little fella like you will be in the shithouse before you can reach for the toilet paper. Only there ain't none. Bet the Gaffer ain't even got nothing for you to do. So you'd better join the union or you won't get no pay.'

This was the helpful advice he gave me from day one and I was allocated no job with the result that I received no wages on Friday.

'Told ya,' commented Frankie and handed me a form to join the Barnes Branch of the Amalgamated Engineering Union, which was founded in 1920 and had survived longer than the Belmont Engineering Company.

Brother Franklin had never been near a union and now discovered that the more members they had, the more problems their brothers faced, and they could then enforce their rules and regulations or, in my case, fight for my wages and rights. I became a 5ATRA union member on the 20th October 1944 and with two lawyers, three County Court appearances for non-receipt of wages and harassment procedures, I was finally allowed to leave this non-demi-paradise in May 1945. Final costs being obtained by Messrs Tooth from Lincoln's Inn Fields. However, I did have the dubious distinction of appearing in the *Daily Worker* and the *New Propeller*, the official organ of the Engineering and Allied Trades Shop Stewards National Council, who reported the case in their February and April issues. Both detailed this sordid case and commented that Kingston District AEU council was 'following this long drawn-out case from August 1944 to April 1945 with great interest and were determined to get justice for our Brother.' It was heart-warming for me to have this support from the bosom of brotherly solidarity. Looking back on this I found it most instructive and my only regret was that dear Tom was unable to witness officialdom in action, or should it be inaction?

When I reported the eight-month fiasco to Ronnie Purcell, our next-door neighbour, he just shook his head in disbelief. Dr R.H. Purcell CB was a lecturer in Physical Chemistry at Imperial College next to the Albert Hall in London. In the first weeks of the war there were a number of mysterious explosions in the Thames estuary between Tower Bridge and the mouth of the estuary. The Port of London Authority contacted the Navy, who called in their minesweepers but no mines were found. The explosions continued and a few days later some kids who were playing on the Essex foreshore saw an object lying on the shingle. It was shaped like a giant metal beehive and was about two feet in diameter and six feet long but neither looked like a mine nor had the telltale marks of the exploding horns. The cops had never seen anything like this before and prudently contacted HMS *Vernon* who sent a special team from their mine and torpedo department to go and 'have a look'. Lieutenant Commander John Ouvry and his team of experts hauled the trophy ashore at Shoeburyness on 23rd November 1939 and rendered it safe and wrote a new chapter in the war weaponary section as they had defused the first German magnetic mine of World War II.

The Purcell's were our neighbours in Christchurch Road. Ronnie was about forty years old when we met him and was the quietest, reserved and most gentle person you could ever hope to meet. His hobby was glass-blowing and I grasped every opportunity to watch him in this most delicate of hobbies. Ronnie was a perfectionist and to see him warm up the glass bulbs, heat them up over a Bunsen burner, stretch them and mould them gently into shape like a loving sculptor was miraculous to watch and photograph, which I was thrilled and delighted to do.

We had brought a 1935 Retina II over from Berlin and the indoor lab shots turned out a treat. Ronnie was surprised that no one had ever instructed me how to get the best out of it and he introduced me to his friend Louis Klemantaski, who was a regular visitor in Christchurch Road. As a result he made me into a budding professional photographer, a career which I would have loved to pursue had there been a David Bailey or Anthony Armstrong-Jones around to make millions flow through the camera shutters. All that was on offer were stiff studio photos of babies, marriages and family groups, which were not enough to make a fortune with and which was why Louis was the highest-earning person in the field. He specialised in one area which suited his talents perfectly – motor-car racing – and it paid well.

He was the greatest exponent of this art and his racetrack images were captured inches away from the racing cars. He was born in 1912 in Harbin, Manchuria, of a Dutch father and Russian mother. The family business in Harbin had an agency for Willys-Overland cars and Louis came to England by the Trans-Siberian Railway at the age of sixteen. At King's College London he met Ronnie and Joyce Purcell and they became friends for life. He had a lifelong passion for motor cars and raced them pre-war at Brooklands. Ronnie and he met professionally during the 'magnetic mine incident', after which they worked together on many experimental naval projects, which had to be photographed as they were, untested, in case the experiments went badly wrong. One of those tests was the Panjandrum spinning wheel, which fired rockets in all directions as it spun towards the enemy. On one test it spun badly out of control, and turned back to the starting point scattering everyone, including Louis, in all directions.

He was a very dapper, distinguished-looking figure who always wore a bow tie which set off his trim imperial goatee beard. When he came to 'Balcomie' and saw I had a separate bathroom he immediately suggested I turn it into a mini darkroom. This started me off on a crash Klemantaski photo course. He taught me all the right angles based on his racetrack experience and after about three months let me loose on Sunday race meetings all over the UK. If

83

there were two meetings of different places, I would shoot the minor event and he would take the cream. After a while we would swap to give me more experience and I got a hell of a kick when my shots had the 'Photograph by Louis Klemantaski' byline under the right-hand bottom corner. They were taken after 1945 when Billy was spending his Army Sergeant time in Berlin.

Louis had instructed Billy to 'get' a Leica of correct age and production number with a special lens. The price was negotiable with 'sticks' of cigarettes, which I was able to get through my PX contacts on Eisenhower Platz in London. My Leica was my oyster, and had the age of celebrity photogapher come around twenty years earlier I may not have married royalty but my bank balance would have been much healthier. But the monetary side to Louis's friendship never entered the equation. He was my photographic Svengali and I was an enthralled member of the Klemantaksi photographic masterclass. He knew my limiations but was also aware that I was pretty good at some shots with high-angled dimensions. Or, as he used to put it: 'You must always reach for the sky...' But I was really more interested in getting a good shot featured in the top magazines and at exhibitions.

Tom Avery had taught me that backscratching was the foundation of British life, and his opinion was now confirmed when I scratched the journalistic and photographic areas of business. The first door Louis kicked open for me was in 1951 when Britain was still suffering from the post-war blues. Wolfy must have carried Madame's thoughts with him to the South Bank, as the new Festival Hall South Bank Chairman Karsten Witt described the modern buildings as 'blue-sky' thinking. The Hall, of course, has survived to this day, although the 'Skylon' and 'Dome of Discovery' did not, which Louis noted and therefore suggested I photograph them (for Franklin posterity and pocket).

'Do a night shot and it'll look stunning in black and white.' I followed his advice and they became some of my exhibition shots for many years.

On 2nd June 1953 Her Majesty arrived in the state coach at Westminster Abbey to be crowned Queen Elizabeth II. 'Don't bother to even try and get near her with your Leica,' said Louis. 'Every photographer from here to Timbuktu will try as well. Go down The Mall a few days before HM has opened the floodlighting on the arches and coronets surmounted by lions which hang above the traffic. A time-exposure nightshot should be brilliant against the black sky. I'll get a colour film which should make the "floating" coronets sparkle.' As always, Svengali was spot on and my shot appeared with my own byline in the *Illustrated London News* on the Anniversary Royal Issue in July 1993 and Louis and I were over our royal moons.

In 1958, just after Pucky and Billy had moved into their new house in Uplands Close, Louis phoned me and mentioned that one of his magazine friends had just heard of a new-type 'perfect suburban house' and as I knew the area could I do some interior and exterior shots for *Modern Woman*. This should come under the 'ask a silly question' section but I was delighted to oblige as long as Louis lent me a Leica wide-angle lens. This was not insurmountable as it screwed into my Leica and a two-page spread duly appeared in the October issue of the magazine. Louis was delighted to have been of help. Molly Castle, the Home Editor, was grateful to Louis for the prompt service and Louis apologised profusely for not getting it bylined, neither Klemantaski nor Franklin.

In the early 1990s when Louis heard that the Imperial War Museum was preparing an exhibition entitled 'From the Bomb to the Beatles', arranged for four of my photographs to be on show. I had finally put pen to paper and had my first novel published and this tied in very nicely with the exhibition and resulted in subsequent book signings of *Shoot the Model* at James Thin in Portsmouth.

But way back in 1944, my page-a-day diary was now getting overfull and I only just managed to get a one-liner in for 6th June which was 'INVASION'. I had heard 'Ike' on the radio that morning telling us that: 'A landing was made this morning by members of the AEF ... and the hour of liberation is arriving.' In fact, June 6th became almost as chronologically significant as the birth of Christ as every passing day became known as 'D+', followed by the number of days after the first landing.

Before the main exodus in 1945 Madame arranged a huge 'get together-cum-farewell' in the garden. There were so many bodies around the house that she had to push them out into the garden where I photographed from an upstairs window as I had no wide-angle lens to get them all onto one frame in the garden. The party was a mixture of sexes, ages and nationalities, which made the entire *entente* more *cordiale*. On the female side I was surprised that there were so many amours from Billy's exercise book in attendance but all of them found someone to help them into and out of their different coloured skirts. In fact, this party totally justified Geoffrey's descriptive name of Madame in action except there was no money changing hands. In any case, the hands were far too busy holding onto what they considered to be 'cash in hand'.

Throughout 1944 I was as happy as a 'Star and Stripes' boy until the night of 12th June when I recorded 'strange noises in the night' in my diary. These continued throughout the day and were the first pilotless flying bombs which Hitler had christened 'weapons of retribution' – *Vergeltungswaffen* – which were known to us as the hated 'V-Bomb', or V1. The 'strange noises' which I noted in my diary were the throbbing noises of a motorbike-like sound which woof-woof-woofed until the V1 was over its target and then stopped, making the bomb plunge down onto the public below. We always had air-raid warnings and were perfectly safe until the engine cut out.

About two weeks later Geoffrey had arranged to meet me in the bar on the platform at Victoria overground called 'The Hole in the Wall'. We were all happily drowning our pints when the air-raid siren wailed. No one took the blindest notice as the 'woof-woof' V1 sound was still wailing. When it suddenly stopped overhead, everyone put their pints on the bar and fell flat on the floor. After a few seconds we heard the explosion which meant we could continue to drown our sorrows and everyone got up off the floor, brushed their trousers and gulped down the remainder from their beer glasses. At this moment Geoffrey walked into the bar as cool as a cucumber and looked at his wristwatch.

'Oh, they're a bit late today. That one was due at 14.20hrs.' Which is what Bletchley had told him. A sailor who had just brushed the last dust of his bell-bottoms nodded approval.

'Yeah, mate, old Adolf is adrift to fuck. Still, gi's us more drinking time, don't it.'

Bletchley had been plotting all V1s since day one and had found a number of ways of saving the lives of some Londoners. As the distances from France to London were pre-set, the British 'XX' system was sending false information to Gerry as to the explosive positioning of the bombs. They let the Germans know that the 14.20 was five kilometres short of target, so the Germans advanced the giros to cut out further north, thus saving a few thousand Londoners. The other method was the Mosquito pilots fitting explosives to their wingtips, flying alongside the bomb and gradually tipping their wings with the explosives at the bomb and detonating it. Nevertheless, the carnage caused by the V1s was horrific.

The V2s were even more terrifying, as you never heard them coming at all. Wernheer von Braun, whom the US Forces would purloin after 1945, designed the first V2 at Peenemunde on the Baltic and after many mishaps finally came up with a perfect death machine. Thousands of slave labourers died in Germany making these monsters of death, and the only good thing about them was that at least you didn't know that you were about to be blown to kingdom come in seconds.

The V2 was identical to Braun's 'Apollo' moon rocket, except the pointed head of the rocket was full of explosives. The first one landed in London at Staveley Road in Chiswick on the 8th September 1944 – a night that Geoffrey happened to be staying with us. Next morning I had gone to buy the paper with him and when we returned to 'Balcomie' Madame was at 'blue sky' battle stations.

'Someone phoned for you, Geoffrey. I told them you were out but they said they'd ring back.'

Ten minutes later they did and after a few words Geoffrey put the phone down. Anticipating a fishing expedition, he looked at Madame and, smiling sweetly, turned to her: 'Get David to get the car. We'll be out for about an hour and when we come back I might … just might tell you where we have been.'

He looked at me, told me to get the car and the A–Z atlas of London.

He walked out of the door before Madame could ask 'Why?', joined me in the car, where I handed the A–Z to him. He turned to the index looking for Staveley Road, found it on the noted page, opened it and handed it to me.

'You know the area around here. Does it ring a bell?

I saw Chertsey Bridge and nodded. 'It's about five minutes from the roundabout.'

We crossed the bridge and turned left on the other side, where we were stopped next to a police barrier by a copper who had the 'ya can't come 'ere' look on him.

Bletchley had told Geoffrey to put on his best uniform, and have his ID card at the ready, so when Geoffrey saw the PC he immediately used his 'superior officer procedure' and in a firm but pleasant voice waved the ID card at him. The copper was duly impressed, and Geoffrey gave him a small but pleasant smile, adding: 'Thank you very much, officer. Are you in charge here?'

This was straight out of Tom's book under the heading 'flattery will get you everywhere', and the PC bowed and scraped and pointed his finger 'dead ahead'. I edged the car towards the side of a small yacht basin which had a huge crater by its side and looked like an inverted tip of Mount Vesuvius. It must have been twenty feet deep and thirty feet in circumference and had destroyed five houses. Another copper came up and asked surlily if he could help us. Geoffrey nodded a 'thank you but no thank you'. Geoffrey got out to take a closer look. He looked splendid in his new G & H outfit and had even remembered to bring the badge of officer recognition: the short stick.

I stayed in the car, having no impressive formal identification except a normal ID card without photo. I didn't think a 100 Club membership card would impress the copper. Eventually, Geoffrey came back scratching his head mumbling something about not being deliriously happy with his findings. I turned the car around and we left like Queen Mary driving through the Castle Gate at Windsor, Geoffrey giving a gracious wave to the copper at Staveley Road.

'What are you going to tell Madame?' I asked.

He grinned. 'Can't tell her we've been to see the ducks, can we? If you hear any more bangs, I'll tell her, but at the moment you and I have got to stay shtum.'

Sadly, nearly more than a thousand V2s were dropped and the Ministry of (mis)Information had to drop the 'exploding gasometer' fibs with thousands of bodies being buried. The Brits in southern England were only saved by the advancing Allies as they captured the V1 and V2 bases on the Continent.

Apart from the carnage to the Americans at Omaha Beach, the invasion had been very successful, and when Billy met Geoffrey at 'Balcomie' in July, he instructed Billy how not to get his letters stopped by the censor. 'Never give a place name but think of something associated with the place. For example, Paris equals Folies Bergère or Brussels equals sprouts, and,' he added, 'I don't think you'll be in Berlin by Xmas.' As usual Geoffrey was 'right on' and when we received Billy's first letter it was headed Sgt.

H.M. Franklin 13051482, Intelligence Control Staff HQ, BAOR and started off by saying he had enjoyed the sprouts very much last night. Knowing that he hated that soggy veg it was obvious they were still stuck in Belgium's capital. When I told Uncle Charles his face lit up and he slapped his thigh, exclaiming:

'I'll have to dig out that address we used to queue up at where everything was provided for, even down to the donkeys. Perhaps one of the girls' daughters is still working there ... though it must be twenty-six years ago, at least.' He sighed a deep long sigh then grinned at me. 'Just as well it isn't you. You confirmed to me some time ago that the only animals you tolerated were dogs, especially dachshunds. That little black one Uncle Ernest had in Berlin, did Tony have a smooth tongue or rough? You don't remember of course; you were too young!'

As the number of different uniforms visiting 'Balcomie' decreased, visits from the Purcells increased. Ronnie particularly reminded me of a younger Tom as he was so down to earth and was always helpful and understanding. When he had his status changed from being 'seconded' to the RN to becoming a permanent fixture, he had to visit research establishments around the UK. Teddington was a day trip but Poole in Dorset needed longer, overnight trips, and if hindsight had had 20/20 vision, he would have been warned of the problems associated with this change of lifestyle.

The two girls were growing up and wanted to spend more time with Daddy but Joyce liked London and eventually the girls moved down to Lytchett Mattravers with Daddy. The inevitable break occurred and Ronnie had to find an au pair for the girls down in Dorset. With the help of the RN he was introduced to a charming late-twenties French lady who had escaped from France. She moved in with the Purcells and Ronnie and Pierette lived happily ever after. Throughout the next twenty years we almost became 'family' and the French national holiday, 'Quatorze Juillet', became an annual event with them. Early evening we would meet at the Yorkminster and, when we were all pleasantly absinthe-tiddly, we would return to their flat in Notting Hill Gate, where Pierette always produced the most delicious *crêpes Suzette* with far too much brandy.

Ronnie always teased me about the 'enemy alien bit' and over the years he had followed my unsuccessful route into ANY service with great interest and disbelief.

After one of our 14th July meetings Pierette told us that Ronnie was now Chief Royal Navy Scientific Adviser and it was time he chatted to somebody about opening a door or two for this keen but by now not so young alien.

Totally out of the blue, I received a Royal Navy blue letter saying entering as an officer entry was not possible as there were no vacancies but if I wanted to join the Lower Deck there may be a vacancy for me.

As this was just after the Korean War had started in the early 1950s it was a pleasant surprise although posters everywhere were requesting ex-sailors to return as 'There is an opening for you in the Navy'.

They must have overlooked my status as I had tried to be a sailor a great number of times but there had never been an opening for me. However, I felt it was not in my interest to dampen their enthusiasm and joined the RNVR in 1952 and Madame was all over her Navy Blue Sky. But much had happened in the five years since the end of World War II in 1945.

Tale 8

VE Day

Geoffrey had quite correctly told Billy he would not be in Berlin by Xmas 1944. However, in the first few months of 1945 the 'Thousand-Year Reich' was falling apart. The Russians were closing in on Berlin from the east; Ike was slicing through Germany with his armies from the west, and it was only a question of time before the Nazi nightmare would end. We could tell that it would not be long, as our own representatives of the Allied armies stopped visiting 'Balcomie'. As I waved them all goodbye I felt like I was going to my own funeral.

The Nazi nightmare came to an end on Monday 30th April 1945 in the Berlin bunker. With a Wagnerian sense for Grand Guignol, Hitler had shot himself and Eva Braun, his 'new' wife, had taken poison. The time was half past three in the afternoon and it was ten days after Hitler's fifty-sixth birthday. On 7th May Germany surrendered and VE – Victory in Europe – Day was officially declared to be the eighth.

On the afternoon of Sunday 6th May, Ronnie Purcell came round with a sort of GB. He had been preparing some celebratory items for VE Day and wondered if I would care to join him as a carrier-cum-photographer to 'let 'em off'. He had made some perfectly safe but very noisy firecrackers to celebrate the occasion and wondered if I could assist him. Needless to say I jumped at the chance to let off a lot of bangs made by one of the top experts in the land.

'When you moved into 'Balcomie', did you ditch your gas masks, and if you didn't do you still have the little brown cardboard boxes they nestled in?'

I nodded and felt sure we had them stowed away in the loft and went upstairs to look for them. 'Would you like this as well

91

for your research?' I asked Ronnie on my return, thrusting a somewhat rusty burnt-out incendiary bomb under his nose.

'Good God!' he exclaimed. 'How do you know it's safe?'

'Thought you might be able to tell me. Can't ask anyone better than a top-of-the-pile scientist, can I?'

Ronnie ignored the remark with the contempt it deserved and started removing the six gas masks from their dusty boxes, smiling benignly.

'Absolutely perfect,' he said, lovingly removing the dust from the boxes. 'I've made a mixture of red/white/blue thunderbolts which should scare the backsides which will be rolling around the grass in Hyde Park, Green Park and St James's. They'll fit beautifully in the boxes. I'll pick you up on VE Day and don't forget to bring a couple of 'fast' films for the shots you are going to take when it gets dark. Cheerio for now and we'll liaise on Monday 7th.' He waved and returned next door.

We did Buck House first as the entire 'tiarared lot' were going to be there, which is the way Ronnie described HM the King, the Queen, Winnie Churchill and Princesses Elizabeth and Margaret, who both looked suitably dressed in their army uniforms. Louis had not lent me a telephoto lens, so my own shots were not saleable, but once darkness fell, the copulating couples were quite well portrayed as Ronnie let off the fireworks. Not good enough to be flogged but certainly good enough to be bylined as 'VE' – 'Victory Exposed.'

In London Billy finished his leave and returned to Brussels to celebrate his twenty-fourth birthday. Geoffrey bade us farewell and gave Madame a double bear-hug. Kurt Zimansky gave us hearty handshakes all round and made me promise to see 'm all in Iowa if I came stateside. The 8th June was farewell day at 31 Green Street and I was showered with presents but thankfully had no 'farewell' initiation scrubbed off me. The final presents were pressed into my hands by Frank – some V-Discs, which were the treasured possession of all Brits who could play twelve-inch 78 rpm records for six minutes.

When Japan attacked Pearl Harbor on 7th December 1941, the US had one of the smallest numbers of soldiers, sailors and airmen under colours. This increased to hundreds of thousands within months and Uncle Sam formed the Armed Forces Radio Service which supplied all the forces with radios, records and record players.

In a gesture of patriotic fervour, the Musicians Union called all their members out on strike, which resulted in no pieces of music recorded being played or broadcast on the air. After eighteen months the music-starved troops persuaded Uncle Sam to put the screws on the union and give them an ultimatum: either lift the strike or we'll break it. They eventually came to a compromise which allowed music to be recorded without pay and Uncle Sam produced the V-Discs, on which no royalties were paid to the artists and which were not on sale to the general public. In return, the US government promised to destroy all records left at the end of the war. As in excess of 15 million were produced, it is not surprising that around 1 million were unaccounted for by the end of World War II. I was the proud possessor of six of those V-Discs, but the one I cherished most was Tommy Dorsey's 'Blue Skies' – the six-minute twelve-inch version.

On 8th June at 05.30hrs I was present at Green Street when they and all the instruments, music stands and duffle bags had been stowed away in six green trucks. At 09.23hrs this mini army left by train, from Waterloo, platform 12, and they all hung out of windows and gave a mighty cheer to Dave, that fu— lim— co— bastard. At 09.25hrs I photographed the platform clock and the platform, which was now totally deserted.

The only remaining transatlantic army musician was George Anderson, the lead trumpeter from the Canadian Army Band of Bob Farnon's, and he departed to Toronto on 9th October. Had Geoffrey not been on his way to the schnitzel pots of Vienna he would have had to have rename Madame. After all: no customers – no Bovril.

Tale 9

Two Cupids at 'Balcomie'

When I stood lonely and forlorn on the platform at Waterloo Station, at 09.25hrs on 8th June 1945, it seemed as if Wolfy had finally deserted me. Whether it was fate or just luck but the years 1946–8 turned out to be the years that Wolfy became not only my guide but became the Franklin family's cupid.

When the war finally finished in May 1945 there were millions of people churning around Europe looking for any family members or relations – not just the Holocaust survivors but the refugees who had been driven from their homes fleeing the Germans and Russians. On Saturdays *The Times* carried pages and pages of 'Looking for anyone who knew...' adverts, with relevant names, places and box numbers. Although Madame had lost her sisters in the Holocaust she was also wondering what had happened to her many friends left behind in Berlin. It was *de rigueur* for her to scan these columns every Saturday morning after breakfast and one name she found made her sit up.

ED had worked in a small Berlin bank when he returned after World War I and one of the partner's names was Angress. The advert was 'Looking for anyone who knew Mr Angress, my late husband, at a bank in Berlin in 1933'. Madame ringed this and when she saw ED on Sunday showed it to him and he nodded vigorously.

'Of course I knew Mr Angress. He was married and had three sons.' Madame wrote down the details, went to her typewriter and started typing a letter to the box number. ED looked up in puzzlement and Madame stopped for one second.

'Well, you can't just sit there and do nothing... Might as well not read the paper in the first place!'

Within fourteen days ED received a reply from a Mrs Angress

94

with an Amsterdam address which gave a heart-rending résumé of the Angress's family saga since 1933. When Hitler became Chancellor anyone who could possibly be a problem or be of influence was packed off to concentration camps or murdered, which included not only Jews but anyone who could present a problem to the Nazis, such as trade unionists, Freemasons, communists, high-up civil servants and many police officials who hated the Nazi rabble.

Mr Angress had been a partner in a small private bank which was a potential threat to the Nazi funding machine and early in April 1933 Mr Angress received a phone call from one of his friends in the police who told him that there was a warrant out for the arrest of the five members of the Angress family. The police inspector stressed the importance of the number five as, true to Prussian efficiency, all border posts on Germany's frontiers had received notice for the arrest of a five-person Angress family.

'What you must do is split the family up and let each member cross into Switzerland, Belgium, Holland, France and Luxemburg and no one will stop you. Get five passports immediately and all should go well. You never know, the two of us could have a schnapps together after the war, whenever Adolf decides to start it. Farewell and the best of luck and when they're safely joined up in there new homes get the five to send me postcards from the five places. I have never had one of Manneken Pis in Brussels ... That should confirm their safe arrival. Good luck and bye-bye.'

There was no hitch in this splendid plan and they all met up together in Amsterdam six weeks later. They now planned to go on to Brazil as Dad Angress had banking connections there but they all needed entry visas with immunisation certificates. These they all possessed, except the youngest boy who had not had the jabs because of his young age; Daddy Angress could hardly write to the Nazis to give him this certificate.

They waited patiently but in 1940 Hitler launched his Blitzkrieg and Amsterdam was among the first cities to see the hated SS and one of the first victims was poor Mr Angress who was immediately eliminated. The eldest boy managed to escape to the United States but Mrs Henny Angress was hidden underground by a kind Dutch family who protected her and the other two boys throughout the whole war.

When the war finished, the oldest one, who had volunteered to join a US parachute regiment, entered Amsterdam in 1945 and went to the house where he had last seen his mum and brothers in 1940. He was wearing GI battle fatigue and had a sub-machine gun slung over his shoulder. The door was opened by his mother, who was scared to death by the sight of a steel-helmeted soldier with a machine gun. He, however, recognised her immediately and removed his helmet, and they fell into each other's arms sobbing and touching each other's faces with disbelief and delight. The other two sons had heard the furore and fell into their brother's arms. One of the sons married the daughter of the Dutch family who had hidden the family and the other one joined his brother back in the States.

As soon as she had read the last page of the saga, Madame told ED to write and suggest a meeting in Amsterdam. Henny wrote back and the following month ED visited for the weekend – which soon turned into regular weekly meetings. Eventualy Madame put a straight question to ED: 'How long are you going to keep this up? Ask her to come over to London, and if she likes your flat at Queens Keep and us, for goodness' sake ask her to marry you.' ED could not really fault Madame's logic and flew over to see Henny, and in February 1947, when the snow was still on the ground in the garden, there was a very small wedding reception at 'Balcomie' attended by the newly-weds, Madame, Dad, Uncle Charles and I. In the evening we went to London's longest-running film at Marble Arch, *Caesar and Cleopatra*, which proudly proclaimed that it was 'Now in the 8th month' which was just below the word 'Cleopatra.' Henny loved the film and fortunately had not seen the notice about the 8th month.

Having been the planner of Billy's amours for over three years I had not been aware of any of his future matrimonial plans, nor had he aired these to me on his last leave from his Berlin Army HQ. The effect on me by his very personal letter in August was a little like Ronnie Purcell's exploding firecrackers on VE day. None of the letters to me had ever been of a delicate nature and when he was on leave in London the personal side of his liaisons had never been disclosed to me. I knew far more details of the physical and personal affairs at Park and Green Street and never asked any questions or was given a hint of who or what Billy was planning next, horizontally speaking.

The firecracker I received from Billy was posted in Berlin on 29th August 1946. In effect, it was a maxi GB in the form of a consultation with his grown-up brother. The seven-page tightly typed letter was really a cry for help. He had met a girl whom he felt was the right one for him *for life*! She was pretty, intelligent, hard-working and was hoping she'd meet us all at 'Balcomie' as soon as possible.

There was only one small problem, which was the GB bit. She was German and not Jewish, and Billy wanted me to P-L-E-A-S-E break the news to Madame and Dad as neither were passionately fond of the Germans, from whom they had managed to get away only by the skin of their teeth. There was a PS which said: 'Don't talk to Uncle Charles about it as his conception of life is a different one from mine.' Which was absolutely correct but I immediately phoned 779 all the same to arrange a meeting. There was no long discussion on the phone: 'If you've got a problem, grab a cab and come over now,' Charles ordered. Half an hour later, he plonked me down on the settee, gave me a brandy and told me to take a sip.

'Now, what's all this about? Do you need a doctor because you've caught the boat up?'

I shook my head violently.

'Girl trouble? Boy trouble?'

But I kept shaking my head and started telling him about the letter, which I now handed to him.

When he had finished the seventh page he leant back, took a gulp from his glass and said: 'Dear old Tom would have said "Damage Control"... So Billy's got the "I'm in love bug" ... Well good luck to him ... ask him if she's preggers and if not...' Long pause. 'He says in the letter they've been shacking up together for sixteen months. Go to Madame and tell her it seems that Billy appears to have found his partner for life. It doesn't really matter who she is but Madame should suggest they live together in Berlin for another six months... He can "sign on" in the Army in Berlin ... it's much cheaper that way ... and if it still works let him come back to "Balcomie" next year and they can get spliced for Easter.'

I thought that Tom would have been pleased with the procedure and clear DC thinking. Charles picked up the letter again and turned to the page about not wanting to marry an English girl and coughed heavily.

'I suppose because you've got all those Shakespeare volumes

and you've always mixed with the Brits, plus the help from Tom and Geoffrey Child, effectively, you are much more of a Brit than Billy ever could have been. In fact, one could suppose you were found in a laundry basket on HMS *Victory*'s gundeck ... but definitely the "Lower Deck". Go home and make an appointment to have Madame on your own and tell her the happy news ... more blue skies to celebrate next year and a guaranteed enlarged Franklin brood on the way. Go on ... drink up... Do you require an immediate wash down in the bathroom or can it wait?'

It certainly did wait and when I saw Madame she immediately agreed to the DC proposal and got me to write a reply to Billy outlining Charles's very practical proposal adding that they should not come and marry in the UK before Billy was naturalised and then he can get the bride to come to Britain to marry her British husband. It had not taken Madame a minute to get back to action and battle stations and all her attention was now on the preparations to change the two rooms which had been on constant standby for all the married or single members of Allied Expeditionary Forces for the past two years.

Easter 1947 was awaited with pleasant anticipation and Mr and Mrs Delby were the overture to the opera that commenced in February with the arrival of Henny. It was a very simple registry-office affair and ED and bride caught the honeymoon train to Bournemouth. Madame and Dad had spent many pleasant weeks at the Imperial Hotel overlooking the front and sea and Madame had booked a suite for the happy couple for two weeks. On their return, Henny told me she had thoroughly enjoyed the breathtaking view, the wedding suite and the splendid hotel. However, she was a little taken aback when, on the second Saturday, ED had risen a little early, showered and put on his best suit and made to go to breakfast. Henny sat up in bed and asked what all the rush was for, and he waved her a little smile and said: 'I'm going to the station to meet Madame ... she's going to join us for week two.'

Fortunately, Wolfy was in total Franklin control on 19th April, which was wedding reception day at 'Balcomie' between 15.00 and 18.00hrs. The darkroom at 'Balcomie' was out of bounds for anyone apart from Louis and myself who had montaged a 'Billy and Pucky picture' for the occasion. The artwork was a cross between *Vogue* and *Auto Car* but sadly not in colour. All the same, the layout and photographs were 'in house' productions so no one received any royalties or became Warrant Holders Associate members and the Leica 11 with its Summar 1 = 5cm lens was a perfect present from Billy to me with a 'thanks' for the help with Madame and Dad!

Pucky was welcomed into the bosom of the family and her young and effervescent charm bubbled over us like a freshly opened bottle of German champagne. This is not surprising as her maiden name was Henkel, the German bubbly. She picked up English as fast as drowning the last drops out of the glass and, through my rag trade connections, I got her into the leading mannequin academy in London's rag trade land.

'Lucy Clayton' was synonymous with THE model agency of the '60s and '70s and there were now many corks pulled out of the Henkel bottles.

Pucky loved all the hullabaloo. Her accent was there but not readily locatable, which added a certain air of mystery to the whole glamour package. I photographed her many times in fashion shoots which did not earn me any shekels but saved our company lots of money. I had the added advantage of receiving a photographer's freelance badge which helped my Klemantaski weekend status no end.

Madame's sky was cloudless blue week after week and Billy seemed to be settling down in the factory in Wardour Street. The exercise books had all been destroyed and I shudder to think what would have happened had they been around and Pucky had found one. It would have been the War of the Roses all over again but certainly without flowers or petals but plenty of thorns. In fact, now, everything in the garden was blooming lovely...

The Americans and Canadians had returned home and even Geoffrey said farewell and flew off to Vienna to join the Control Commission which appeared to have been expressedly created for him. He got his major's pay, was billeted in a first-class hotel which was conveniently located in the I District just off the Ring, with all the Viennese culture within his grasp: the Opera, the Burgtheater, the Staatsoper, the Volksoper and all the museums you could hope to visit in months. He was like a fish in a huge pond and loved every second of it, especially the thin, succulent, crisp Wiener Schnitzels which hung over the rims of the plates.

Having had the small recording studio in Wardour Street, he started researching and finding rare and unobtainable pressings of new artists whose names were totally unknown in Britain. Ljuba Welitsch was a tremendous singer from the depths of the Balkans. She was quite small in stature but oozed tremendous charm which bubbled quietly like a small dormant volcano waiting to erupt. On our many visits to Vienna at later dates we always had to take her a special hair shampoo, which, she swore, kept her hair flaming red. At that time she was married to a six-foot Adonis of a policeman who had picked her up when she was speeding in her car to get to the opera fast. He flagged her down in his little VW police car, the White Mouse, and asked for her licence. She took one look at him and made sure he wrote down the address correctly. Later that night she had a very good look at him in bed and decided that her Karl's surname was incorrect. Schmalvogel, in very down-market, rough German, can mean a 'tiny chopper'. Sadly they divorced later, which was not really surprising as it was strange to meet them in the bar at the Sacher Hotel after the opera when he was in his copper's attire and she had slipped into something loose and glittery after being on stage in *La Traviata*.

Geoffrey's list of acquaintances was like a directory of the glitterati, and on another of our business visits we were invited to meet the Director of the Staatsoper, who gave us a grand tour with comments at each corner of the place. 'This is where Hitler sat on his first night in Vienna in 1938,' said Ernest Schneider, and went on to drop names as magnificent as the giant crystal chandeliers that hung in the opera bar and sparkled like glittering fountains to everyone looking up at it from the Hotel Sacher across the road.

Even in the Sacher Bar you could sample that most famous of all sweets speciality, the Sacher Torte, a delicious own recipe chocolate tart famous all over the world for over 150 years which must be heavily laden with whipped cream to help it down.

Vienna's olde-world charm just got hold of us and on all our business visits we were always drawn back to its leisurely, and very enjoyable, relaxing atmosphere. It came as no surprise that, when Geoffrey reached the end of his military contract, he stayed on and worked for the Viennese office of the BBC. Even when his BBC tour ended he stayed on, but, as at Bletchley, we never found what he actually did. He went to Russia a lot but never on a direct route. It was always by bus to Riga or Bucharest and on by train and we all concluded that he was practising his Russian, which he now spoke fluently. The most famous visit he told us about was the time the Russians overran Hungary in 1956, when he only managed to get out of the country by the skin of his teeth, on the last train out of Budapest dressed as a train driver.

He did tell us quite a lot about the chaos that was now the rubble and orderless community of around 80 million people. All state employees and civil servants had to be party members and it followed that many were only Nazi's in name.

In order for the Allies to re-establish some kind of order they were faced with the task of trying to sort out ex-Nazis from the silent majority. The Americans and Brits established de-nazifaction units and broke them down into professions and trades. Once 'cleared', two million received a *PERSIL SCHEIN*. There was a lot of heart searching to decide whether Wilhelm Furtwaengler was a Nazi or not. He had conducted concerts in front of Hitler but had he not, he would have ended up in a KZ and there were millions like him with identical dilemmas.

The UFA film studios were totally controlled by Dr Goebbels and those who worked there or the starlets under him had to be Nazi members which was the case in 1945 when the state fell apart. In Berlin, Billy had had his own share of the glitz. While there, he had worked in a 'de-nazifaction unit' and had the unenviable job of sorting out ex-Nazis from the silent majorty.

Billy's opposite number with the US Forces was Elli Silman, who had been a film agent at the Universal Film AG (UFA), the principal German film company before 1933. When the Japs attacked Pearl Harbor she left her Hollywood agency, joined the US Forces and returned to Berlin at the end of the war.

She was in her late thirties and looked stunning in her custom-made uniform and was always on the personal lookout for agency material of both sexes. Her first find was a young teenage German actress who was a 50s' version of Marlene Dietrich. She was elegantly slim, with flaxen hair and ultramarine almost transparent hazy blue-green eyes – Hildegard Knef qualified as being the most sultry blonde of the 1950s and 60s. The East German film people had snapped her up just after the war had finished and she made two brilliant films with the communists at Babelsberg, immediately creating sensations in *The Murderers Are Amongst Us* and *Film Without Title*.

Elli immediately put Knef on her wish list, and as soon as the Allies took over UFA, Elli was there and, although still in the Army, signed her up as the first client of her new agency. David O'Selznick had just completed *Gone with the Wind* and as Elli knew him from her pre-war Hollywood days got Hilde to sign for Hollywood. The only fly in the ointment was her nationality which, only months after the war, would not have impressed Hollywood. This resulted in Elli playing commercial cupid and her eyes fell on a very young US Army officer by the name of Kurt Hirsch. It was a very good match on paper: he was young and handsome and she was young and stunningly beautiful. However, his parents did not go a bundle on this very pretty war bride as they were a staunch Jewish family from New York.

Billy kept us up to date on all these details as he worked closely with Elli and also had to keep her supplied with strapping young and very willing British Army males. Elli had a similar motto to the Royal Navy 'UA' definition of youngsters who were not old enough to draw their rum ration, being under the age of nineteen. Elli's motto was 'USA – Under 25 Sex Adventures', although she did stretch the age limit upwards under duress.

Billy just made the age limit but he did not want to ruin his newly found love-for-life. Nevertheless, he was a willing researcher among his very eager room-mates and friends who were happy and eager to submit. They were bowled over by this stunning, not so young, but very experienced female from Hollywood and all her starlets. They were not the only ones to be intoxicated by Elli. She came to London with Billy on a number of occasions and Madame was confident that 'Balcomie' would soon become Sunset Boulevard mark 2.

Wolfy had nothing to do with 'The Royal Wedding' between Princess Elizabeth and the dashing Naval Officer Phillip Mountbatten on the 20th November. Buck House was lit up and the whole nation celebrated the glorious event. This time Ronnie had not prepared any fireworks to document the copulating couples in the parks which I sadly noticed when they were conspicuous by their absence.

Xmas was a very quiet 'Balcomie' affair after all, the two newly wed couples were happily locked in each others arms and all they got from Madame was a loving goodnight kiss and a 'Happy New Year' wish.

The year 1948 started with a Billy 'GB' to me as to his function in the company. He had settled in well but disliked any travel and consequent absence from the marital nest. The 'GB' to me was the request that I take over the sales side totally. I foresaw no problems with this arrangement as it kept me in close touch with our customers – literally. As dear Charles had implanted his wisdom to me that it takes all sorts to enjoy life I raised no objection to Billy's proposal and at the same time decided to make an in-depth research into the company's sales, which were falling.

The problem as I saw it was that the products we were selling were stuck in a time warp. We manufactured a raincoat which was 100 per cent waterproof but also air-circulation proof and very hot and heavy to wear. During the war, experiments had been made into making material not waterproof but simply showerproof and I felt that this would make our products far more comfortable to wear. The big manufacturers were already going down this road, but I nonetheless met with stubborn resistance from my family. Sales continued to drop. One of our clients, Associated Merchandising Corporation, had established buying offices in every major European city and I spoke to a few buyers at AMC who suggested I did a fast fact-finding trip in the US to get their views and then put these ideas to the family. 'How much?' was the immediate cost response and I had prepared myself for this pertinent question and made a 'Tom' plan of a reply.

All my wartime GI friends hailed from many of the major US cities, so I could marry their 'Hope to see you when you come stateside' offer to a GB from me for accommodation. The reply from all of them said 'When and how long' and within two weeks I had a route mapped out with red marks for 'Accommodation-AOK', which somehow reminded me of my original aircraft silhouettes and of wartime Europe. The plan included visits to Washington, New Orleans, San Francisco, Chicago and Toronto, but sadly there was not one of the GIs who had contacts in the Cunard White Star Line, so there was no saving crossing the Atlantic. The final bonus in this plan was when Elli asked if Hildegard and her new spouse Kurt could be housed at 'Balcomie' for three days as the studio paid hotel accommodation was not available without filming which, at present, put London off the map.

Consequently, after a very pleasant stay at 'Balcomie' they invited me to stay in Hollywood with them. I accepted with pleasure and was now able to add Los Angeles to my route list. I set off aboard RMS *Queen Mary* at the beginning of April. Madame had organised a black tie do at 'Balcomie' and the forty or so guests looked splendid in their attire. Elli outshone all the ladies in her silk dress, pearls and the six-foot thick white fox stole casually draped over her shoulders. Some party ... some send-off!

AMC had prepared an itinerary complete with contact names and phone numbers and I was set to 'go and research'.

I bade a fond farewell to all at 'Balcomie' on my last but one night, as Charles felt I should have a rousing farewell at 779 and he voluntarily gave up his place in bed and slept on two armchairs. He also went through a long list of items to take with me. 'Don't ask me,' he finally said, 'whether you should or shouldn't do this or that. Just have a good time and don't catch the boat up.'

Tale 10

New York and New Orleans

In the morning I caught a cab to Waterloo and trained to Southampton, keeping a lookout for my ginger SR porter who by now had probably retired to the Emerald Isle. Once aboard the *Queen* I settled in but sadly only for one night as we hit the worst gale recorded that year. Force 9 even in a ship that size is not a pleasant experience and we were all pleased to see Pier 90 in New York after a seven-hour delay. A yellow-cab drive to the hotel was uneventful except that the cabbie's cousin had been to London during the war and my Limey accent sent him off on a long trail of the 'wonnerful English people who took the Blitz so well'. Thankfully we arrived at the hotel within ten minutes and I got a long 'Limey fella' farewell.

There was a letter from AMC awaiting my arrival and I started on the 'contact trail' the next morning. I had been around the GIs for a long time and found them, like the ladies in the offices, almost over-friendly but soon discovered that this was their normal modus operandi. The standard joke around their offices was that visiting Brits mistook their very informal and pleasant office procedure as genuine friendship, which could send one's optimism to unchartered 'blue' heights. I learnt something of the sort that very night in the hotel bar.

I had bought a ticket for a brilliant play with James Stewart, who was terrific in 'Harvey', the invisible 6 foot rabbit whom he was continually talking to. As I came out of the theatre the heavens opened, but as it was only four blocks back to 50th Street and the hotel, I walked and arrived soaked. The barman spotted me, dragged the wet coat off my back and sat me down on a stool at the bar.

'What'll it be, fella?' asked the barman.

Wanting something to warm me up, I turned to him: 'Could I have a whisky please?'

A large grin spread across his face. 'Sure ... why not? Do ya want a Kinsey straight or on the rocks?'

I had always been under the impression we Brits spoke the same language but now realised we could be divided by it and just gawped at him. Having just read Professor Kinsey's report on sexual behaviour in males, I felt that his question had nothing to do with sex but 'rocks'??

He looked as puzzled as I felt and helpfully added, 'Rocks ... ice ... rocks ... ice ...' and my English penny dropped as fast as a dime and I recovered my composure.

'Sorry ... no thanks, but I'll have a large beer to chase it down afterwards ... Any kind,' I added.

He poured the whisky into one glass and lovingly emptied the beer bottle slowly into another.

Before either he or I could make any comments, a well-dressed gent in his mid-thirties looked at him, turned to me, shook his head like a wet poodle coming out of the Hudson River and uttered one word: 'Boilermaker.'

The barman patiently explained to me that this expression for a whisky chased by a beer was more familiar to the dockers around the Westside at Pier 90 than in an excellent hotel in the 90s on the Eastside.

'Where you from?' asked the gent, turning to me.

'London,' I replied.

'Ontario or England?' questioned the gent.

'England,' I said and the barman hit the bar counter with his fist and stretched his hand out. 'Glad to know you ... My second cousin was with the 3rd Armoured Brigade before they got slaughtered on Omaha Beach ... Had a great time in Canner Berry before D-Day. Have a drink on me,' he added, triumphantly filling up another whisky glass.

After the consumption of many more boilermakers the gent looked at his watch and turned to the barman.

'D'ya know when the Astor turns out? My wife has gone to that new movie *Mr Blandings Builds His Dream House*.' Then he turned to me. 'Let's go upstairs and have a nightcap with her when she returns.' He slipped off his barstool, waved at me and I looked at the barman. I had been warned about carrying money on me and about talking to strangers and looked questioningly at the barman but he reassuringly gave me a discreet thumbs-up sign.

I followed him into the lift, he pressed the button, the doors slid shut and we were transported silently to the 41st floor. He led the way along the corridor and stopped at an unnumbered door, opened it with his own key, entered the room and switched on the light. We were in a very spacious sitting room and as he closed the door I noticed a very small discreet card with 'House Manager' on it.

'Make yourself at home,' he said, and glanced at his watch. We moved into an adjacent room, which had a large double bed and a bathroom en suite. 'One of the comforts of the job,' he said, patting the large bed. The next thing I remember was being pushed onto the bed, my clothes being peeled off me and from then onwards I started to float towards my own 'Blandings Dream House'.

In the middle of the night I searched for the missing wife on his side of the bed but was told that she had probably got mislaid en route. My only comment was: 'That should read "laid", shouldn't it?'

'Probably,' was his only reply.

In the morning I heard him showering and minutes later he appeared, towel around his waist, walked over to the bed and stretched out his hand.

'My name is Tom ... and thanks for introducing me to my first Limey.' A big grin spread across his face. 'Are they all as nice a squeeze as you?' I just shrugged my shoulders.

He walked over to the wardrobe, pulled out his jacket and searched for a card and handed it to me. 'You've got the phone number and the room number. If the Big Apple gets too lonely one night, gi's a call and the wife and I will make you very welcome. I gotta go, I'm on mornin' shift at seven.'

He walked out, giving me a little wave. I placed his card in my wallet and wondered how welcome the wife would make me.

The next day the business side of the city proved very pleasant but very unproductive. They were all oozing charm and showed great interest but when it got down to the buying side and actually writing an order for goods they seemed to get writer's cramp. Bergdorf Goodman, Bonwit Teller, Macy's, Saks Fifth Avenue and the other members of the New York cream of retailers just 'looooved' the collection, adding that I should 'show us summin' nu next time you're in the BA'. It all seemed to confirm my fears about the saleability of our merchandise. As for returning to the Big Apple without a single order ... well, that seemed off the cards. My blue sky was decidedly grey.

When I got back to the hotel in the late afternoon I felt the need of a drink, though not necessarily a boilermaker.

'Mr Franklin ... gotta note for ya,' shouted the barman as I was about to take the lift.

He handed me a half-folded piece of paper which I opened and read two short lines of handwriting addressed to 'The Limey'.

'Come upstairs to the 41st and have a drink with us' it read and was signed with just one letter, 'T'.

I got the elevator to the 41st floor, retraced my steps to the House Manager's room and knocked on the door, which opened slowly. I entered the room, which seemed deserted, and walked towards the bedroom door which was slightly ajar. I pushed it open, entered the room and I was gobsmacked.

Lying on top of the bed was an American version of the Grace Thomson of eight years ago who had opened all the doors to my virginal dreams. This lady was stark naked. Her smooth white skin was like alabaster and her long black hair hung loosely across and down her body, encircling her beautifully shaped breasts. As I approached her she lifted her right arm lazily, beckoned me over and held out her hand.

'Nice to meet you,' she drooled. 'My name is Tina, in case you wondered what the "T" stood for.' She patted the bed beside her and asked if I would like to shower first.

Suddenly I could smell the results of my abortive walking trips around the various offices. 'Sorry!' I mumbled as she grabbed my head and brutally kissed me on the mouth.

'Never apologise unless you're drunk or had too much of it and are no good to man, woman or beast.'

She pointed me to the bathroom, which resembled a mixture of a barber's, perfume shop, and doctor's surgery. Along one wall was a one-piece mirror above the sunk-in marble wash basin. A white marble shelf above it was filled with cream tubs, talcum powder and bottles, while in a small cabinet discreetly hidden behind the door were packs of Durexes and small Vaseline jars mingled with some thin medical rubber gloves. Over the side of the bath were two large soft white towels with two matching pairs of thick slippers and on top of the towels nestled two oval-shaped, beautifully perfumed bars of soap.

I suddenly remembered my initiation at 99 Park Street and felt I really did smell like a Bovril.

Tina had been patiently awaiting my return, and after what seemed like hours we finally both came to a deserved rest, which was only broken by Tina wanting a Lucky Strike, which I graciously helped to light for her. Everything else she had managed beautifully on her own. As she lent back with a contented look on her face, she sighed and asked how old I was.

'Why, does it make a difference?' I replied.

'Gawd ... no ... but where did you learn all this stuff?'

'In Limey-land,' I grinned back at her. 'But tell me, why do you call us Limeys?'

'Well, it's not a long story but some time ago between Columbus finding the US of A and your ménage-a-trois Lord Nelson, the Brits ruled the seven seas but had a scurvy problem which was due to an over supply of salt meat and too few fresh vegetables. When they came here they ate and squeezed a lot of limes which cured it. Q-E-D ... Brits ... Limeys ... so to make sure I don't get the scurvy ... you gotta have a load of juice for me ... you little Limey bastard.'

New York was the only city without Park Street contacts and as I now also had more time on my hands, I put the Leica to good use. The *Atlas* statue with the metal frame globe behind it at the Rockerfeller Centre provided me with my first Royal Photographic Society exhibit mention, which, to be very honest, was now worth more to me than business or sex. The older I got the more I agreed with Uncle Charles's dictum abou sex, food and drink.

Washington business results were also zilch and after three days I trained down to New Orleans, which cheered me up no end. Frank and five-year-old Frankie were at the station and the first words junior said were: 'Say summin', Limey', and apart from me singing 'God Save the King' I couldn't think of anything else. In any case, Frank would have wanted it in any key but 'F'.

His wife Louise was all over me for 'lookin' after Frank and keepin' him out of trouble in London, England'. 'And thank your Ma for me, I'm sure that without you and her my Frank could never have stayed on the straight and narrow.' Fortunately Frank was in the kitchen when this eulogy on Frank's abstinence was delivered to me; otherwise I could have confirmed to her that his paths had always been very straight if not necessarily narrow.

Louise lent me her battered '37 Chevy and young Frankie became my guide for the next two weeks, drowning himself in expressions like 'good heavens, you don't say' which he initially dismissed as 'baloney' ... 'you can't do both...' but after one week he could have passed for a Limey and I for someone from Nu Orlns.

He also enlightened me that the reason for the temperature being in the hundreds was that they were in the same latitude as Cairo and 'it's mighty hot there'.

Time flew by and Frank gave me a night tour of New Orleans' nightspots including Antoine's, that most famous of restaurants whose wrought-iron balconies were a feature of the French quarter, the Vieux Carré. I was unaware that there really was a tramcar line called 'Desire' and the 'Streetcar Named Desire' shot became another frame for the Leica. Sadly the tramcar also introduced me to my first experience of the two-coloured nature of American society. Although I had mixed with the GIs in London, colour and race never reared their ugly heads and I was totally unaware that the armed forces still had a strict colour ban. Although the war had been over when I visited the USA, the 'No coloreds' ban was still strictly in force throughout the Southern States and one couldn't get more south than Louisiana. The very first time I fulfilled my desire and got on the streetcar 'Desire' in Bourbon Street, I sat down on the first seat near the rear platform. I was almost lynched, as that section was for 'coloreds only', and I was noisily evicted from the tram. After that I carefully looked out for the signs outside barber shops, restaurants and indeed any establishment serving either the white or black community, but never both in the same room or even in the toilets.

It was a colossal shock to me. After all, we were supposed to have fought World War II for freedom and democracy, and here I found that this kind of behaviour was the norm three years after Dr Goebbels had committed suicide with his family after pushing this vile race theory down the throats of millions of people.

After two weeks of wonderful Vićari hospitality, Southern-fried chicken, fresh oysters like eating a packet of crisps served at a bar counter and an exchange of very happy memories, Frank Senior and Junior took me to the station and the Sunset train on 21st May. Frank drove down to the harbour and I had my last cup of coffee at Morning Call – 'New Orleans's most famous Coffee Drinking Place'. Vićari Senior and Junior walked me to the carriage destined for Houston, San Antonio, El Paso and Los Angeles. The black, white-jacketed porters shouted 'Aaaall aboard' and blew their whistles as Frank stretched out his two hands.

'T'was great havin' ya, Dave. Come again soon...' And before I could thank him young Frankie planted a big wet kiss on my cheek.

A little tear appeared and rolled slowly down his pale cheek.

'I'll miss you, maaan, you'll come again soon ...promise?' A little sob gurgled out and he stared at me with his big dark-brown eyes and added: 'I love my Limey!' He hugged me and threw his arms around my neck as if never to let go.

Tale 11

Flickering Lights and Top o' The Mark

The Southern hospitality had overwhelmed me and I now thought over the events of the past two months since first seeing the Statue of Liberty in New York Harbour. I remembered Tom's army advice about the '6 Ps' and decided to plan my life for the rest of the year. My suspicions about selling beautifully manufactured raincoats that were good enough for a queen continued to be confirmed and were compounded by the distinct lack of rain. In fact it was as if I were trying to sell sand to the Arabs, and I hadn't even gotten to Los Angeles. When the train left Houston, it turned inland towards San Antonio, El Paso and Tuscon. They looked as if they hadn't had rain since the days of Noah's Flood.

But I was off to the dream factories of Los Angeles and was looking forward to meeting Hildegarde once more.

I had bidden Hildegarde and Kurt goodbye at 'Balcomie' barely two months ago and they had volunteered to reciprocate their hospitality in LA.

Hildegarde was born in Berlin before the war as Hilde Knef but even as a young teenager she looked like a supernatural Elf. Slim, with wispy blonde hair and almost green eyes she looked like a sculptured goddess from a greek temple and due to her extraordinary beauty and immense talent she was the embodiment of stunning and desirable sexual adventures which eventually turned her life in to a Greek tragedy.

Sex symbol she was from the age of 15 and during the war fell deeply in love with a German producer Ewald von Demandowsky, who put her in uniform and she fought beside him to defend the freight yards from the Russians at Schmargendorf near Berlin.

When the war ended her youth and incredible beauty destined her as a starlet at Babelsberg, first with the Russians and then the UFA.

112

Hilde was hardly a name that would capture a thousand eyes so she used the complete version of that name which was Hildegarde. Even in London Knef was unpronounceable to the film viewers so she dropped the K and became Neff.

She was the most magnetic person I have ever met in my life and her looks were unsurpassed. She had a biting humour and could ensnare any male or female at the snap of a finger. She was like a figure destined to become the leading character in a Greek tragedy. The Bible's old saying that 'the love of money is the root of all evil' did not wholly apply to Hildegarde. Her tragedy included the love of fame, which she achieved in her early teens and twenties. The two Babelsberg films made her the shining star in all German-speaking countries and after going to Hollywood she would partner Gregory Peck in *The Snows of Kilimanjaro* and James Mason in *The Man Between*, which she jokingly substituted with 'the man in between'.

On 19th August 1953, *The Sinner* was gala premiered at the Cameo Poly at Oxford Circus in London and caused a sensation. The film critic Robert Ottaway wrote that 'Hildegarde radiates the kind of appeal that makes the censor sharpen his scissors' and mentioned that she spoke with a low pitched growl which earned her many record contracts. One of her LPs was fittingly titled 'Illusions'.

Whenever she was in London I was mentally ensnared by her and admittedly was tempted to have a five-finger exercise session.

She always giggled when she later heard about my naval adventures and at one time gave me a pack of very sultry photographs of herself in the almost nude.

She signed them all 'To keep you warm when you get to the Far East' and they turned out to be my biggest rum wagon 'sippers' from the lads in the Navy who stuck the photos on the inside of their locker doors.

Not surprisingly her marriage to Kurt Hirsch would eventually be dissolved. She had an uncanny knack of sleeping with the wrong men – they were either divorced with three kids or married. Once I met her at Heathrow to take her to the Savoy to escape the paparazzi. She went straight to the Gents and changed into jeans and sweater and tucked her hair under a beret. 'Darling!' she cooed, 'How wonderful to meet you!' and we made an unmolested escape to my car.

When we got to the Savoy and went up to her room she noticed a vase with at least fifty roses on the bay-window table. She rushed over, expecting them to be an arrival present from her current amour, a married surgeon. She tore open the small envelope expectantly, read it and cursed, tore it up, grabbed the roses and the vase and threw them out of the bay window. They landed with a mighty crash six floors below on the pavement. I walked up behind her to comfort her but she pushed me back, cursing under her breath: 'They're not from him; they're from the f——g studio.'

Stunning to look at, charming to meet, but somewhat difficult to live with was my dear Hilde.

Over a period of years she made many films, recorded masses of records and eventually married David Cameron, an English coloured actor, and moved to Germany to live with him.

In May 1948 when I got out of that station in Los Angeles she rushed up to me, hugs and kisses and masses of 'darlings' and she and Kurt dragged me to the car. For a week I was on a dreamlike roller-coaster of fame, films and concerts, whose performers ranged from Frank Sinatra to Van Johnson, from Mickey Rooney to Jimmy Durante. Even Lena Horne was on the list of the LA Press Club and when they took me to the Hollywood Palladium the glamour of Hollywood ensnared me. I was even toured around the Paramount Studios.

I spent a fantastic dream existence with Hildegarde under the palm trees, swimming through the Pacific waves at Malibu Beach and generally pretending hard I was not madly attracted to her. Hugging in their pool was extremely bad for my blood pressure, especially when she commented on my physical prowess in my lower regions: 'Oh dear, we'll have to put that down.'

Underneath all the glitz, however, the 'Hollywood star system' had taken its toll on Hildegarde. She, like most of the 'new' stars, had been signed up by a studio only to prevent her from being poached by a competitor and she, with many actors and actresses, was just 'resting'. For someone like Hildegarde, waiting for a script every day, day after day, was like being on ice and to her it was a slow melting death and the inevitable tragedy destroyed her marriage and her whole life. For me, the flickering of make-believe tinsel town disappeared after three weeks. I bade Hildegarde and Kurt farewell on 21st June at Union Station and boarded 'Daylight', the train for San Francisco. On board, I found comfortable chairs and two-seater armchairs in a special section of the diner on the train. The white-jacketed black waiters were at everyone's beck and call and I came to the conclusion that, sooner or later, I would come down to earth with a bump, which was after the second drink. That nagging thought in the back of my brain about how much all this was costing, and why was I trying to sell rubberised raincoats in a place with sunshine all day, every day, 365 days in the year, suddenly broke out with a vengeance. I came to the conclusion that I must have caught sunstroke before I even set foot in the US. Never mind, I said to myself, you've had a fantastic time and kept costs to a minimum. I drowned the last drop from the glass on the small circular table by my left hand and very accidentally touched a soft hand next to the glass. I had been so deep in thought that I hadn't noticed the well-dressed, mid-thirties lady sitting next to me on the two-seater.

'I'm sorry,' I said giving her a small smile.

'Oh ... you're very welcome,' she said in a way that reminded me of days gone by in London's Soho. I had to stop myself from asking how much the rate was and just smiled back benignly. Ignoring my non-interest she moved towards me, and her leg started gently to rub mine.

I moved as far to the right as I could but reached the armrest of the two-seater. She smiled triumphantly at me and her hand started to move up my leg. Uncle Charles had advised me that you should never pay for it as there are millions willing do it for free. But, as the point of the conversation had now decidedly reached the commercial arena, I looked at her, raised my eyebrows and popped the question. 'How much?'

'What the hell do you take me for?' came the inevitable burst of indignation.

I brushed this aside: 'Oh, I think we've established what you are and we're now discussing the price.'

This rather floored her and I waited ... and waited.

Never having paid for it before either in the UK let alone the USA, I had no yardstick to measure the cost by and I was just interested in the amount.

There was the additional physical problem of where the transaction was going to take place. The preliminaries in the lift at Chelsea were always concluded in her flat but the question was where and how was the operation going to take place on the 'Daylight' train and/or in daylight as the train was not due into San Francisco until 21.55hrs.

I seemed to be back on the 'why' trail and suddenly realised that the whole transaction was going to be in dollars and I did not even know what the equivalent exchange rate was in Pounds Sterling.

I was still awaiting the magical dollar rate when she suddenly seemed to recover her composure and shot out:

'Twenty dollars the whole way or ten dollars for a blowjob,' she eventually stated.

I started calculating. We had been on the train about two hours and there were another seven to go. The whole trip was around 470 miles so we had gone about a third of the way. The ticket had cost $7.50 one way from LA to San Francisco, so the train cost for the remainder worked out around $5, which I tried to explain to her but she had not had the 'Steffs' training which I had been privileged to and her answer was simply physical and verbal.

She stuck out her tongue adding: 'Fuckin' wise guy', sat back and started brooding.

I looked her straight in the eye and quietly said: 'I'll compromise and pay you $5, but where is all this going to take place?'

She calmed down and shot out: 'In the boys' room of course.' This I felt was fairly logical but very cramped.

Every hour, on the hour either one of us would go to the toilets, male and female, but we could never find a vacant one. Hours later, and not exhausted by any other physical exercise, we were approaching the 'Golden Gate City' and both felt it was pointless to pursue our proposition. I pulled out a $5-dollar bill and gave it to her. She fell around my neck and kissed me squarely on the mouth, whispering: 'You're a fuckin' gent, you are. Don't forget to go to the Top o' the Mark; it offers the best view over the whole of San Francisco and the bay from the bar. Give Jack the barman a kiss from me; he's a Limey barman at the Mark Hopkins Hotel. My name is Flo, short for Florence not Floosy, as he always says.' She waved me a quick bye-bye.

After passing through Salinas, the train wound its way through the mountains to San José and dropped down to San Francisco Bay. The lights at the other end flickered across the water and the Oakland Bay Bridge with its own twinkling lights reflected like

116

white snakes across the bay. Minutes later we arrived at the station and I collected my luggage around me. Before I could even look for a porter a voice behind me chirped 'Help ya, fella?' and I turned around and saw the American twin of my Southampton days grinning at me. Ginger, around seventeen years old and a cheeky grin hid guaranteed availability of anything on offer for cash.

'Cab to the Plaza Hotel, please?' I requested and Ginger departed like a greyhound towards the cab rank, hailed a cab, opened the door and thrust his open palm towards me. 'Anything I can get you at the Plaza? Any girls... Any boys? Twosomes, threesomes, gi's your name and call me on this number' and he pushed a card with a phone number typed on it into my hand.

I pressed a silver dollar into his open palm and he grinned back at me. 'Gi's a call any time day or night, I'll be ready for ya,' he called and disappeared in the direction of his next prospective client.

Ten minutes later the cab pulled up outside the hotel which was a six-storey concrete block in the main square and before the cab had come to a halt, the door was pulled open and I blinked. I thought I had left Ginge behind at the station but this, down to the friendly grin, could be his Doppelgänger.

When I checked in at the desk, the porter banged the little bell on it, turned to me and assured me that the bellhop would be along with all my luggage in a minute. 'Go up to the room and he'll be right up and don't over-tip him; he might get the wrong idea.' As I had no idea what the right amount of tip was and was not quite sure what the right or wrong idea was, I was no wiser. I took pot luck and selected a dollar when the bellhop brought my luggage to the room.

'Thaaank you, Surr,' he bowed. 'First time in San Francisco?' he asked pleasantly and I nodded. 'Never call it Frisco ... the locals hate their city being called that. But if it's your first visit to the Golden City, you gotta see Telegraph Hill...' He pushed me towards the window and pointed to the streets below which seemed to trail like a giant roller-coaster up, down to and from the hill.

'If you're goin' to get a Hertz car, watch it when you're parkin'. Never side onto the curb otherwise the brakes won't hold it...' He pointed to all the cars in the street which ended at Coit Tower at the top of Telegraph Hill and were all parked at right angles to the steep street.

117

'If you like Chink food you're in the right place here, 'Corse SF is the largest Oriental settlement outside of the Oriental world. That's what all the menus say, so I guess it must be true. As for the best view of the Bay and the Bridge, go to the Mark Hopkins Hotel and take the elevator up to the bar on the top floor. It's called The Top o' the Mark and if you're in SF and ain't bin there, you ain't seen nuttin'. You can even see Alcatraz from there; that's for those who didn't make it to the Madison Dolores. Their food ain't quite the standard of Fisherman's Wharf but it don't smell half as bad. Have a good day!' He glanced at his wristwatch. 'Have a good night as well...' he added, shutting the room door quietly behind him.

Within seconds he knocked on the door and reappeared.

'Pardon me,' he spluttered, 'the Golden Bridge ain't golden, it's red.' He hesitated for a moment and my dime suddenly dropped. I hadn't given him a large enough tip and searched for another silver dollar as his Baedeker tour had been worth every dollar, nickel and dime.

I was absolutely exhausted and went straight to bed. Next morning I got up, went to the window, looked out and there was Wolfy.

The streets were wet and it seemed to be drizzling. I showered, dressed and went to breakfast, which was doughnuts, syrup, fresh orange juice and toast and coffee and suddenly Madame's blue sky had reappeared. Before leaving the hotel I spoke to the bellhop who greeted me with great respect and I commented on my surprise and delight on seeing the rain. 'Rain?' he quizzed, 'Hell no, we ain't got no rain here, that's the fog we get every mornin' and before noon it dries up and it's like goin' to a sauna.' And I felt as if Wolfy had disappeared forever.

However, undaunted by this information, I went off to see or try and see the main store buyers, but after visiting five without any positive response I decided to return to the Plaza for a nap. I awoke around six and made for the Mark Hopkins Hotel and took the elevator to the bar. It had a large semicircular plate-glass window overlooking the Bay and I could see many of the steep streets which tumbled down to the water from Telegraph Hill.

In the centre of the room was the half-circular bar and behind it was a thirtyish tall barman who was immaculate in his white jacket, which seemed to have come straight out of the laundry. There were only three people at the bar, one of whom was talking to Jack, the barman. The other two were around my age: one was tallish but very heavily built and the other was about six inches taller than me, slim, with flaxen hair and a very pale complexion. I grabbed the barstool next to the slim, fair-haired one and as I sat down he looked at me and just stared.

'What'll it be?' asked the barman, looking at me.

'You're Jack?' I quizzed and he nodded with a puzzled look on his face. I enlightened him and told him 'Flo' sent him her best wishes.

A big grin started to stretch across his face which he accompanied with 'Oh, 'er?' and my language radar started to ping. That accent! It had to be somewhere from near the Elephant and Castle.

'Ow d'ya know?' the barman asked.

'Take's one to tell one,' I shrugged and he stretched out his hand.

'Glad to know you... What's your name?'

I grabbed his hand. 'It's Dave, glad to know you, Jack.'

The fair-haired chap who had been staring at me suddenly started to sway, grabbed a paper napkin, put it to his face, got off the barstool and rushed to the Gents.

His friend came over to apologise, adding, 'He'll be all right in a minute.' Then, turning to me, he asked if my name was Dave and I nodded.

'Thing is, me and my buddy are up here on a seventy-two-hour pass from San Diego and we've got to be back on board our flat-top in a couple of days. He's had a bit of a rough time. He's only twenty-three years old and his Mam died when he was born. His Dad was a farm labourer on a ranch near Saugus in the Joaquin Valley. When Jimmy was fifteen his Dad was crushed by a tractor which overturned and Jimmy walked to San Diego to join the US Navy. He looked older than his age and as it was just after Pearl where so many sailors had gotten killed by the Japs they didn't ask too many questions. He met a buddy aboard the *Yorktown*, after she was patched up and they were both aboard her during the battle of the Coral Sea in May '42.

'The ship escaped everything the Japs could throw at her but she was hit by a single bomb which penetrated four decks and killed sixty-four sailors. Jimmy was among the first to help in the carnage but all he could find of his buddy were the dog tags, and a stump of an arm with a hand on it and Jimmy still wears the ring he pulled off his buddy's bloody finger. His name was Dave and he looked a hell of a lot like you. I think when Jimmy saw you he thought he'd seen a ghost...'

Jimmy returned at that moment and grinned at me. 'I'll be fine now but why don't we go back to the motel and have a drink?'

I bade Jack the barman goodbye and promised to return.

The three of us left the bar, walked to the car and Dick drove the three miles back to the motel. Jimmy led the way into the room, stopped and grabbed my shoulder. Pleadingly, he looked me in the eyes, barely whispering: 'You'll stay, Dave, won't you...?'

''Corse I will, Jimmy, if you want.'

He just nodded and turned to Dick to ask him if he could take the settee.

'Sure,' he nodded. 'You'll be OK with Dave in the double, he ain't my barrel size.' He went to the cupboard, grabbed a bottle of rye and three glasses.

After I'd told them some of my tales Dick suggested we got some shut-eye and I stripped before getting into the double bed. Jimmy followed me minutes later, also stripped and lay alongside of me and never said a word. Suddenly he rolled towards me and his arm encircled my chest. His head came to rest on it, his breathing moved into a regular smooth rhythm, and he fell fast asleep. He mumbled a few 'Daves' and never moved an inch in the night.

In the morning he turned towards me and just smiled and said: 'Thanks, Dave ... you helped me kinda get through the night.' He searched for my hand and squeezed it very gently.

That day they did the Baedeker tour with me, and Jimmy seemed to get happier by the hour. We had three hearty hamburgers with fries for lunch and the three Cokes washed them down nicely. The remaining Baedeker sites were ticked off by the early afternoon and we staggered into the Golden Pheasant for a very pleasant Sino-American meal.

After Dick had paid the bill his eyebrows shot up and he asked, 'Top o' the Mark?', and fifteen minutes later we were ordering our first drinks from Jack.

The friendly welcome was followed by a 'What'll you have?' and I asked Dick and Jimmy if they'd like to try a real English drink.

'I know it's after the meal now but to be a real Limey you gotta have a sherry. Are you on?'

Jimmy nodded, and Dick just shook his shoulders and said, 'Why not?'

'Medium or dry?' asked Jack the barman, who produced two bottles of the sherry as he explained what sherry was.

'Don't drink no damn cherry brandy!' added Dick helpfully.

Jack the barman straightened up and in his haughtiest of voices said: 'No, no, Sir, it has nothing to do with cherries and, actually it's pronounced with an *sh* . . .'

Jimmy broke into the explanatory session and blurted out, 'So it's with a soft *sh* like in "shit", is it?'

Dick was getting impatient and added to the rising temperature by raising his voice: 'Where's the goddam drinks?'

Jack produced four sherry glasses and poured two 'sippers' into each glass with equal portions of sweet and dry. He pushed then towards Dick and Jimmy who both tasted the pale first and then gave a thumbs-up sign.

'That pale one's great! What about the dark one?' they both asked. They tried it.

'No way!' was the unanimous comment. 'Too damn sweet for me but you can fill up the other.'

They did not chase them with beer but downed a few whiskies within the hour whilst I kept on looking at my watch.

'I know, I know,' said Dick, 'you gotta get up early tomorrow and so do we, but let's go back to the motel and have a last "glad to have met you" drink.'

'OK,' I replied, 'but you'll have to run me back before midnight.'

At eleven I removed Jimmy's arm from across my chest and lowered his head onto the pillow. I crept quietly out of the room, closed the door behind me and glanced back at Jimmy who looked as peaceful as a newborn baby. His left arm was lying on top of the duvet and on the small finger of his left hand was a very narrow simple golden ring which was badly scarred.

Dick ran me back to the Plaza and shook my hand. 'It's been great meetin' you, Dave. Gi's your address in London and we'll keep in touch. If not before, we'll send you a card at Xmas.'

There were no cards or letters in '49, but in '50 Jimmy had gone ashore in San Diego and had just disappeared. In 1951 I received an air mail postmarked Tokyo, which bought me up to date on his naval movements. He was now in the Pacific Fleet and they had joined with our lot and been to Kure in Japan on exercises.

'Your flat-tops are smaller than ours but they have steel decks and I think if the *Yorktown* had not had those wooden decks we used perhaps Jimmy's buddy would still be alive now. I met one of your sailors ashore who was from HMS *Unicorn*, but your fellas do like their "Tigers". Couldn't get enough pints down this fella I got talkin' to, told me he came from Eastbourne on the English coast which he said is only about seventy miles from London. He seemed a helluva great guy but very quiet and only liked real music, like classics. I asked him if he wanted some of those wartime V-Discs which we still had aboard, but he said no thanks.

'Funny thing is his Christian name was Jimmy as well and the surname was like that Limey drink you made me drink at the Top o' the Mark. That sherry's a bit too sweet for me but I remember the label on the bottle said: "Harvey's Bristol Cream".'

Tale 12

Back to the East Coast

The next morning I caught a cab to the railroad station and caught the San Francisco No. 28 Overland train which left from track 10 at 12.30hrs and I sat back in the comfortable reclining chair and closed my eyes. Geographically I was now on my return trip, and Tom Avery's ghost was prodding me to establish the facts and to list the results of the trip so far.

Out of the dozens of retail store buyers I had spoken to, no one seemed to bend over backwards to buy from us. As already related, I actually didn't mind which way they bent over as long as they put pen to paper. The only exception was the lady at Bonwit Teller way back in New York who felt the goodies from us might suit their elderly ladies but they would only review the situation in spring '49.

'Can you give me all the skedules as to price and stock availability?' she had asked and I didn't know whether to kiss her or say 'you're kidding'. 'Landed, of course, and in dollars,' she added hastily, as I tried to hide my ignorance. I knew that in Wardour Street the request would be met with equal dismay and I made a mental note to ask our shippers about it on my return.

Those were clearly the facts but what about the 'fact-finding' bit. On the pleasure front I had received confirmation of Uncle Charles's theory that there are many ways of skinning a rabbit and I had discovered that they were all *pleasurable* ways, with the exception of those animals and chains he had warned me against – I certainly had heeded his warning. What I was totally unprepared for was the vastness and size of everything in America. It seemed to me to be a huge arsenal of men, machines and raw materials from livestock to manufactured goods and cars. The only book I had read on that subject was an economic study of the US by

Admiral Yamamoto who had spent many years at Harvard in the US. Before planning the attack on Pearl Harbor he wrote that if they attacked the Americans, it had to be a total knockout blow. As he discovered to his horror after the attack, the carriers had sailed that Sunday morning and returned later to haunt him at Midway Island, which became the turning point of the war. 'We have awakened the sleeping giant and wounded him,' he is said to have commented after the Tora! Tora! Tora! attack, 'but have not killed him.'

With poetic, if not gentlemanly, justice, the White House sanctioned the assassination of the Admiral, who was in the habit of visiting his troops as they advanced across the Pacific Islands. American Intelligence intercepted a Japanese signal informing New Guinea of the expected arrival of Yamamoto at Bougainville on 16th April 1943 to inspect front line troops. Four Lightning fighters awaited the arrival of the Admiral's plane and at 09.33 the American welcoming party glimpsed the light reflecting off the Admiral's plane. They broke radio silence with a whisper and said: 'Bogeys at eleven o'clock. High,' and two minutes later the Admiral's plane and all its occupants joined their holy ancestors.

Our company's products were never going to wake any giants (sleeping or awake), so I started to wrack my brains how, instead, I could wake up the good, starved, rationed British public with products from ... *anywhere*! By the time we reached Chicago in the late afternoon my mind was made up. 'Look around, boy, and see if there's anything you've missed' was a dreadful joke Charles had once told me about a rapist and I was determined to look and search for anything I had missed, as long it was legal.

My brooding thoughts had stopped me from taking any notice of the scenery we had passed through. I remembered nothing of land or the cities we had passed through but was brought back from my semi-slumber when the train slowed down and stopped in the 'Windy City': 'Chicago ... this is Chicago ... anyone wanting to detrain, please leave by the side doors which will be opening right away.' I duly made my way to the side doors which had been opened by the black, white coated porters who seemed to be distributed uniformly throughout the US. This should not have come as a surprise to me, they were all employed by the same company.

'Wake up!' I said to myself and the helpful porter helped me with my luggage. I pressed a silver dollar into his hand and was overwhelmed with a mouthful of 'Thank you, Sirrrrrs'. I turned around and suddenly felt faint. He came back and grabbed my arm.

'You OK, Sir?' I nodded slowly. 'It's the smell ... what is it?'

He looked at me as if I had just stepped out of a moon spaceship.

'First time in the "Windy City"?' he questioned and I nodded.

'All the big slaughterhouses within 100 miles radius have their cattle butchered in the abattoirs on the edge of the city and as the temperature is around 110, it ain't really surprisin' that the Windy City stinks like shit,' he explained in a very matter-of-fact tone of voice. 'Have a nice day,' he added reassuringly.

My next two days were not exactly the highlight of the trip, but at this point I really couldn't care a shit if I never wrote another order in my life. Wolfy must have had 20/20 vision when the entire trip was being planned. The remaining ports of call were the two 'thank-yous' from Kurt Zimansky in Iowa and George Anderson from the Canadian Army band of Bob Farnon, now back in Toronto.

In Iowa I hardly recognised Kurt in his black professional gown and he was as quiet as a downed V1. His two boys were straight out of a Culver City Mickey Rooney movie and I had a repeat of my New Orleans experience from his wife: 'You were so wonderful to my Kurt.' I don't know if Geoffrey would have appreciated all the womanly hugging but fortunately he was thousands of miles away in Vienna. My next and last stop before setting sail in the *Queen Mary* was Toronto and this time there were only two hugs received from George's little girl, who could have stepped straight out of the flickering Shirley Temple shadows. She clung on to me when the spray of the Niagra Falls started to settle on her blonde curls like fine silver dust. I felt almost saintly, but I was unsure into which category the other kisses I had received en route would have pushed me.

I boarded the Cunarder and arrived gale-free in Southampton four days later. After all my experiences, some of which had not only shaken me but proved very enjoyable, a new language was added to my vocabulary which translated Braces as Suspenders, Pavements as Sidewalks, Lavatories as Washrooms, Goloshes as Rubbers and Pageboys as Bellhops.

Perhaps if I had lashed out two dollars instead of the one, I would have been stirred to discover their preferences and found out what the actual male or female going rate was.

125

Tale 13

Back to the UK – With a Bump

With Tom's guidance I had now prepared myself with a credit and debit balance sheet and hoped that the other members of the firm would take the facts on board and listen to my suggestions of what should be done in the way of damage control to stop the company ship from sinking without trace.

I need not have wasted my breath as Madame was convinced that the company would always find another bit of blue sky. Dad, as usual, stayed schtum and ED joined his stony silence. Billy, who had caught the incurable 'blue-sky' disease, was really only interested if there was sufficient 'petty cash' to go to the pictures every Friday night. I just listened in amazement and felt like being on the bridge of the *Titanic* without even one lifeboat. My only hope lay in talking to Uncle Charles whom I telephoned that night.

'Good trip?' he asked chirpily.

'Depends what you mean by good. I am in one piece, slightly bruised by non-business; the other thing I'll have to tell you about when I see you. Don't bother to call in Grace Thompson just yet. There won't be any time to tell you all my tales if she's there. Tomorrow night OK with you? It'll give me some time to unload and unwind. I'll bring all the remaining stock of unused items along ...'

He interrupted me. 'Why? Have you decided to be celibate?' he exclaimed in disbelief.

'No, no, no,' I protested, 'They all seemed to be so well prepared for all eventualities I didn't need them. I knew that the Boy Scout movement was big in the US but they seem to be prepared for everything all the time and in all places. See you tomorrow, bye-bye.'

Just before turning in for the night at 'Balcomie', Madame came in and sat next to me by my bedside. 'You look so much older,' she said touching my cheek fondly. 'You look a real man.' (If only she had known what I was going to say to her at our meeting the next day she would have been horrified at what her real man was going to tell them about the real world.) She held my hand and looked me straight in the eyes. 'I've got a little GB for you. When you set off to the States you budgeted and got some travellers cheques for the whole trip. I know you've been very careful but do you have any left?'

I got out of bed, went for my wallet, opened it and took the little American traveller's cheques folder out and thumbed through them like shuffling a pack of cards.

'I've only used half the amount,' I said proudly.

She made a grab at them, took them from me and smilingly said: 'They'll be lovely for Friday. We're a bit short in the petty cash this week.'

When I told Uncle Charles about that little GB, he nodded sadly. 'I didn't want to disillusion you about your mishpoche. They are a charming lot, but since I have started adding Delby Coats to my sales collection I have spent quite a lot of time in Wardour Street and you know what they say "What the eye doesn't see etc." and sadly I have now seen too much to make me happy.

'Before you tell me about the trip, I think you would be well advised to cut your business links with them, and I mean *money-wise*, or you'll never be able to sleep at night. I discovered flogging those coats was like trying to sell rubberised dead sheep so I have now got an agency to sell a ladies' couture collection from Vienna. Their stuff is like the couture ranges from Paris but one rung down price-wise and consequently many more stores can handle them in larger quantities. You've got to go to Scotland during the next few weeks, so why don't I join you in your car and you can come and have a look how I skin my rabbits.

'We can share the cost and we'll only use one lot of petrol coupons. Every time I flog one of those lovely snappy little numbers you can listen. You never know, you might be able to share the buyers as well. Strapping young fellow like you should be on top of things in no time.'

I was nodding hopefully thinking of all those red-haired Scottish maidens waiting to be taken by a strong, youthful versatile Sassenach. He didn't tell me that they were mainly pushy spinsters whose drops at the end of their noses appeared to be permanent fixtures.

However, before we set sail for north of the Border, Madame had arranged a 'welcome home' party for her last-born. Harrods were doing the smoked-salmon sandwiches, Fortnum's the canapés, and Selfridges the assorted mixed vols-au-vent. Billy had found a little man around the corner in Wardour Street who was still flogging assorted bottles of American whisky and rum which had been nicked before they were packed up at Eisenhower Platz.

Elli had flown over from her new office in Munich and brought a new starlet from Holland. As she found neither a film script nor a willing male for her I was requested to be duty stallion. Elli supplied a cheap weekend return to Amsterdam for me to keep the lady entertained over the next weekend, which simply resulted in me having a very weak end. I had never seen so many new faces. One of Billy's Army friends brought his new amour along who had also been gobbled at and up by Elli. Jane Griffiths was a raven-haired beauty with a haunting look and would star in many English films of the 60s and 70s, one of then being *The Million Pound Note* with Gregory Peck.

Louis Klemantaski made my day by booking three 'shoots' for me over the next months. The one that stirred me was the Grand Prix at Silverstone on Saturday 2nd October 1948. Early in the new year I was told to go to the weekend Hill Climb outside Eastbourne at Butts Lane and the cheering-up news was that all my published shots would be bylined with my own name. When they were published Louis presented me with one of the 6 × 4 prints of a Citroën Light Fifteen whose competitor number was 69 and Louis had handwritten on the back: 'It's a very good shot but how did you manage to get the competitor to stick your lucky number on his windscreen?'

The do was a great success and the only two men in uniforms were Geoffrey who had flown in especially from Vienna. He had run some very rare Mussorgsky Russian pressings to ground for the BBC and the Russians were delighted to receive twenty V-Discs in exchange for these treasures. The V-Discs were the residue of the box which the boys from Green Street had left behind for me in exchange for the treats they'd gotten in London town. The BBC were over their Russian sickle and rewarded Geoffrey handsomely for going to the trouble of not only finding them but also delivering them personally to their door. The other uniformed visitor was Mike, my medical friend, who was now attached to the BM hospital in Hannover but sadly did not yet have access to 'with compliments' flights from Greven.

Apart from the Dutch lady who I had to comfort the following weekend, Elli also had another Canadian young starlet in tow who ensnared me. She was a copy of Hildegarde and her hair was pulled back into a tight bun which gave her a hard face but me a certain stiffness to my anatomy. I have never or since met as fierce a man-eater as her. She had asked me for the location of the 'boys' room' at 'Balcomie' and I took her upstairs and pointed at the door. She opened it and pulled me in and shut the door behind us. I have heard of people having their clothes torn off them but I could not count the shirt or pants buttons on the floor fast enough as she ripped them off the garments. Her tongue was like three of Wolfie's and Tony's rolled into one and I wondered if I could ever satisfy her sexually, as she exhausted me physically without even satisfying my sex urge.

Afterwards she bounced downstairs embracing Dad as if she was already standing next to me at the altar and kissed him non-stop. As Charles had always said, it took all sorts and in all my young years I had always been told that you never look a gift horse in the mouth. But I'd certainly found one which I'd rather not have looked at, open or closed.

Tale 14

Highland Flings

Billy told me that he had been unable to spare the time to get up to Scotland in my absence. I had heard of a specialist organisation for travellers and UKCTA (United Kingdom Commercial Travellers Association) offered many attractive deals and addresses of simple but very pleasant and inexpensive accommodation. The B&Bs were spotlessly clean and always provided an almost homely atmosphere; one was surrounded by kindred spirits whose shoulders one could always cry on.

On the way up to Scotland, I stopped in a B&B in Carlisle. I had come up alone as Charles wasn't quite ready with his collection. There were ten other weary and dog-tired reps in the lounge after 'late supper', and we were all either nodding off or trying to read the papers before they slipped to the floor, when Mrs Johnson, the landlady, put her head around the door and apologised: 'Sorry to disturb you gents but there's a Mr Fraenkel wanted on the phone.'

I had been nodding off nicely when she sang the name out a second time and my brain subconsciously jerked me back to my pre-name change period. I got off my chair and quietly said that I was the wanted person, but then another gentleman rose and said that his name was Fraenkel. Now being wide awake, I approached him when he returned after taking the phone call and I apologised to him, explaining the mistake, and asked him to join me in a McEwen's. During the following hours, he told me the story of his life, which could have filled a magazine, but only one on sale from the top shelf.

He was born in Nuremberg after World War I and escaped to Genoa as a young boy where he stayed with his aunt who ran a brothel for seamen. From the age of fourteen he was trained in cleanliness, medical care and all the requirements for the efficient running of the establishment. When he was sixteen, and if the brothel was empty, the aunt sent him out scoop-netting in toilets for sailors who were well endowed to satisfy her girls and as he grew older developed a fetish in this area. Not that he had the slightest inclination to participate himself but he got a kick out of making sure that the girls had total satisfaction in joy through length.

He managed to escape to Scotland prior to World War II and was intrigued by the Scottish soldiers telling him that before they were allowed out of barracks they had to make sure they wore nothing under their sporrans and kilts. Freddy loved standing by the exit door as the soldiers walked across the mirrored floor and got quite a kick to see how well they were endowed. This fetish remained with him until he met his future wife, a WAAF, during World War II at the Lyons Corner House at Marble Arch in London in 1945. She was holding a letter in her hand and was crying her eyes out. She had met a Sergeant GI who had been at Omaha Beach, the Ardennes and the final push into the Third Reich, but had not got as much as a scratch on his body. He was on leave, and when they met at Rainbow Corner they fell in love and decided to get married. She would follow him stateside as soon as his unit was back in the US of A and she awaited a letter from him telling her when the date would be set. The letter she held in her hand was from the GI's mother telling her that her son had been shipped home aboard the *Queen Elizabeth*. When they arrived in New York, he walked down the gangway with his rifle and duffle bag, stumbled and crashed onto the concrete dockside. His helmet had fallen off and his head had been pulped into a bloody mess.

Rhoda was still crying her eyes out when Freddy moved alongside, trying to comfort her. They had some more tea, and later had a meal at Rainbow Corner. She gradually recovered and they went to the Cumberland around ten o'clock. She fell into Freddy's arms and sobbed all night but in the morning they talked and finally agreed that good sometimes comes out of evil. When she was demobbed she would join him in Edinburgh where he had started a business and made his home. They had a boy and girl and when he had stood up at the B&B it was Rhoda phoning him to ask when he would be home.

Mrs Thomson brought us another McEwen's but insisted we go to bed. Freddy asked if I had already booked accommodation in

131

Edinburgh. 'For tomorrow yes, but I only have three calls to make, one at R.W. Forsyth's and Romane & Patterson in Princes Street in the morning and the other in the afternoon at Fraser's on the other side of the bridge.' Freddy suggested I give a ring when the last call had been made and gave me his phone number.

The following day, when I walked out of the store around three thirty, I found a phone box and rang them. Rhoda answered the phone and joked about the name being a mistake and was surprised that I had not booked a hotel and was going to be all alone in Edinburgh. 'We've got a spare room with a small bed, it's tiny but Freddy told me you're no giant. Come over now. You can park outside; Warrender Park Road is never packed. See you in half an hour.'

They lived in a typical tall late-Victorian block of flats and the kitchen and living room covered the ground-floor area. Downstairs were the bedrooms and toilet and she showed me to a single bedroom and apologised for its small size. 'Never mind the size. I'll be quite comfortable and...' I began. She interrupted me: 'It'll be quite handy for you ... it's free!'

Freddy had told me about their kids but only Jacky, the boy, was there and when I asked about the four-year-old girl, Rhoda looked at her watch in a very unperturbed way, adding, 'Oh she's all right; she's coming home with her friend Janey.' At that moment Manuella rushed in, went downstairs, and ten minutes later she reappeared beautifully scrubbed, fit enough to be a sculptured figure on the Castle's ramparts. An hour later we were sitting around the dinner table and the kids told us all about their day's events.

We were into the coffee when the front door-bell rang and Freddy pushed back his chair and made for the door. He opened it and there was a lot of talk between him and a lady who was sobbing. After what seemed ages, Rhoda popped outside to see what was going on and Jacky, the little boy, and Manuella went to bed. Freddy eventually reappeared, grinning from ear to ear.

'That was Janey's mother from next door,' he said. 'Her daughter hasn't stopped crying since she came home from school. Apparently, on the way home she and Manuella were approached by a horrible old man in Warrender Park. He was awful, about sixty, in his old, torn raincoat and he came up to Janey and asked her if she would like to see his "John Willy", opened his raincoat and thrust it at her. She started screaming and has still not got over the shock. Janey's mother seemed surprised Manuella hasn't said anything about it.' Freddy turned to Rhoda, 'You go downstairs and ask her if anything strange happened at school or on her way home.'

When Rhoda put that question to Manuella she just looked at her mother and replied: 'Not really ... except there was that horrid dirty old man who came up to me and Janey in Warrender Park, opened his raincoat and zipped down his trousers. He got out this smelly wrinkled old "John Willy", turned to me and asked if I would like to hold it and I shuddered, took another look and told him, "No thank you very much; it's not very clean and, in any case, Daddy's is much bigger".'

'Now there's praise ... and from my own daughter as well,' giggled Freddy. 'I think we'll have to have a drink on that!' He walked over to the sideboard, opened the lower door, got out a bottle of Drambuie and three glasses.

They moved over to the lounger which was standing on the other side of the room and Rhoda patted the cushion next to her. 'Come and sit down here,' she said, turning to me.

Freddy got up and asked if I wanted to go to the boys' room. I nodded and followed him downstairs into a spacious toilet come bathroom. 'Me first, OK?' he said, and I nodded. When he had finished he turned to me, adding, 'All yours ... you never told me your Christian name?' and I replied, 'It's David, but you can call me Dave if you like.'

As I was having my 'relief of Mafeking', he was watching every move I made, right up to me pulling the zip up. 'That's quite presentable for a small chap like you, does it get bigger with age or time?'

I hadn't a clue where we were going as this had no similarity to any previous experience I had ever come across.

'Come on, let's go back and talk to Rhoda,' he finally said.

We returned to Rhoda who was sitting comfortably on the settee. Very comfortably, as she hadn't got a stitch of clothing on her. We walked over to her and Freddy put his hand over my zip, pulled it down and looked at Rhoda. 'I feel like Christopher Columbus tonight. I've discovered a big new continent and it's called David...' Very gently he pushed my face onto hers and after that I had the most exciting hours I had ever experienced in my entire life, including those spent at Chelsea Cloisters. But after all, they were all twosomes and my mathematical mind calculated threesomes should be 50 per cent better.

After two very hectic hours and three showers I coyly asked what the actual sleeping arrangements were going to be and Rhoda replied rather crossly: 'You're a very decisive little planner, but you can't sleep three on your single bed, so Freddy and I will have to introduce you to all the various alternatives we have been practising over all these years. As you've just had your third shower is there anything else you would prefer to not experience?'

I hurriedly blurted out the usual 'whips, chains and animals'.

'Oh dear,' said Freddy with sadness in his voice and opened a box with leather and heavy metal objects in it.

'Never mind, dear,' said Rhoda, closing the box. 'Do you know something about *ménages à trois* and *soixante-neuf*s?' I nodded. 'Well, that's a start,' and clapped her hands and after that slapped my bare bottom.

In the middle of the night I got up to get some fresh air, which Freddy noted. 'What's next?' he asked, 'Or do you want some shut-eye before you leave in the morning?'

'Oh, I thought you said he's got all week,' added Rhoda with disappointment in her voice.

I looked up at her. 'But I promise to come up to Scotland as long as you'll have me.'

Rhoda smiled at me adding: 'I'll endorse those words ... all of them ... literally.'

I then slept like a log, although there were very few logs available that night. The smell of freshly grilled bacon wafted into the room when I got up in the morning. The sizzling bacon led me into the kitchen where both were busy preparing a hearty Scottish breakfast, including freshly pressed orange juice, two boiled eggs and warm muffins and oatmeal crisps.

'Go on, sit down,' beckoned Freddy. 'Did you have a good night?' he asked, raising his eyebrows.

I looked at him. 'What the sleep or the other?'

Rhoda turned around from the Aga and smiled at me. 'Well, you can always make up for the sleep tonight.'

She placed the freshly cooked breakfast onto a plate, handed it to me and I suddenly sat up. 'I can't eat all your rations up in one go. Please, at least let me share some of the bits that are rationed.'

They looked at me in total amazement. 'You're not in London

now. We have what we call little "arrangements" with the grocer, baker but not the candlestick maker, and the rationing doesn't really effect us that much...' I already had visions of a long queue of tradesmen collecting their 'you scratch my back and I'll scratch yours' outside and in the bedroom.

'No,' said Freddy, shaking his head, 'we don't really have problems about food but the police are getting pretty hot on the petrol side. The farmers get "red" petrol in larger quantities but the cops are now spot-checking cars, looking at the colour of the petrol, and if it's red, and a private car, you're nicked. With a lot of persuasion you can ask a small garage owner to part with a few gallons for "favours".'

Rhoda started to grin. 'Yes, that young Scot outside Loanhead is quite a dishy wee lad; he unpins his kilt without much bother... What about you, David? Do you have much trouble?'

'It's so-so and I always carry four jerrycans hidden under some very old and smelly blankets in case the cops nose around. The smell helps to put them off.'

Freddy looked at me, went to his notebook and found the petrol provider's phone number and gave it to me.

'Cheers!' I wrote down the number. Suddenly the thought of how much extra it would cost sent my brain to panic stations.

Money meant possible loss of money which pushed my wandering brain to the insurance ... the car outside the flat ... the samples outside in the street ... and my alarm bells started ringing as if the Gathering of the Clans had got hold of me, the car, the samples and rolled them all down Castle Hill before they crashed into Princes Street below them.

I shot out of the chair, went for the car keys and opened the front door. Rhoda following on my footsteps.

'What on earth is the matter with you?'

'It's the car ... and it's got all my samples in it ...I forgot all about it last night...'

Freddy had joined us and walked outside of the front door and pointed triumphantly at the Citroën and I almost fell into his arms. Well, almost because I got the keys out, opened the car doors and undid the boot and breathed a sigh of relief. They were all in the car: the four suitcases in the back seat and one on the floor and the two smaller cases and holdall resting peacefully and intact in the boot.

'You're as white as a sheet!' said Rhoda.

'I feel like a very wet white sheet because my contents sample insurance will only cover me "if garaged".'

Rhoda suddenly collapsed into laughter and turned to me.

'Freddy told me last night your name is David, but not Goliath. What on earth have you got in all those cases. You should have the use of a Pickford's van.'

Freddy added, 'Come on, let's have a look at the treasures of one case.' He leant over and picked one up. 'Bloody hell, have you got the Coronation Stone in here ... and you've got three more of these? You'll get yourself a double hernia by the time you're forty-five.'

I interrupted him: 'What about a compromise, and make it thirty-five ... that's halfway to sixty-nine.'

'Oh, we're feeling better, are we?' Rhoda chipped in.

'Yes, thank you, but if Freddy could carry one inside I'll show you what I have to do to earn a few shekels.' Freddy picked up the case and we followed him like lambs into the house whilst I almost felt like a dead sheep trying to carry the other two.

I opened one on the settee and she gasped.

'Good heavens!' she exclaimed, 'They're all so tidy and ... just as if they've come from the cleaners.' The yellow cape I unfolded flowed into a volumous shape as if blown up by an invisible pump.

'So now you see why I have to fold them very carefully before stowing them away in the case,' I proudly explained.

Freddy started scratching his very bald head. 'Do you have to do this every time you see a customer and for every sample?' He sank back in the armchair and looked at me in despair.

'You said last night that business was piss-poor...'

Rhoda looked at him sternly and said, 'Freddy careful with your language!'

Freddy's response was explosive and far more descriptive than George Kieffer's had been in Park and Green Street.

'You're out of your fuckin' mind, David!'

His logic seemed to confirm my worst fears and I asked him what he was selling and whether he had to carry suitcases to hold the goods he was offering. He got off his chair, went downstairs and five minutes later reappeared with a very smart leather briefcase and gave it to me.

'I'll tell ya a wee story...' he began, and then reverted back to his German/Italian/Scottish mishmash of an accent. 'Like many refugees, I joined the Intelligence Army branch after '42 because of my languages. Sadly they did not supply the squaddies with brothels where I could have looked after them blindfolded. After El Alamein, the POW camps started to fill up with German and Italian prisoners and there came a point where they either drowned in the North Sea or were dispatched offshore. As the two *Queens* were shipping thousands of GIs eastwards, some very bright spark at the War Office felt the empty *Queens* could be employed usefully by shipping the POW westwards to be looked after by Uncle Sam. The brilliance of the MOD was now without parallel. They put me to very good use on the westward journey and I got to know a number of these German and Italian lads who were delirious when someone spoke to them in their own language.

'On the eastward run the GI contacts proved very useful for London and Liverpool retailers and specific establishments who fulfilled the desires of the sex hungry GIs. One of the German POWs was from Solingen, which was *the* steel city in Germany, and this bloke's father had a specialist factory manufacturing souvenirs for any area with a large influx of visitors like London, Stratford or any holiday resort that the public was willing to spend their souvenir money on.

'When I had a wee dram with a Seaforth Highlander aboard the *Queens* he casually mentioned and showed me a very tatty souvenir replica of the Forth Bridge, which I bought off him. When I showed it to my German POW friend from Solingen he was over the moon and when I came out in '45, domiciled myself in Edinburgh and became the biggest importer of Scottish souvenirs...'

'Hang on, you said you sold local souvenirs and now you say that your bloke in Solingen made them...' Freddy vigorously nodded his head. 'So you're flogging Scottish souvenirs to visitors which are made in Germany?'

Freddy was quite hurt and protested. 'They are *Scottish* souvenirs but I never pretend they're *made* in Scotland, and at half a crown a piece the buyers couldn't care a caper's toss. But, David, you know the rag trade retailers and, from what I see and hear when I go around, all the top end ones are eager for well-made goods from France and Italy because their colour sense is brilliant and the Brits are still knee-deep in rationing. The Germans were very lucky to have their country flattened three years ago. The finance came from the Yanks' Marshall Plan, which our idiotic politicians used to nationalise industries which always have been, and will always be, bankrupt. The Scots are the only ones still making brilliant merchandise which sells abroad, but I'm sure they all have selling agents that go up to Hawick or Peebles, but I'm sure you'll find some small manufacturers who'd love to work with a slick and very versatile salesman like you. Nottingham and Leicester are good for cheaper knitwear and...'

Rhoda cut in: '... And it's not half as heavy as your bloody backbreakers...'

Depressed and dejected I slept the night alone, counting sheep and finally knitting myself to sleep. The next thing I felt in the morning was Rhoda shaking me gently. 'Rise and shine ... and I intentionally didn't say "get up" because you have a 400-mile trip ahead of you to get home.'

I did not tell her that I was not looking forward to the conversation that I was going to have in Wardour Street at the end of the trip.

I had once been told that good comes out of evil but in my case it had come out of pleasurable and satisfying sex in Edinburgh.

Tale 15

Home Truths

The company meeting in Wardour Street the next day was all I had dreaded. My official status in the company was as a sometimes paid salesman and what the three directors, Madame, Dad and ED, decided went, although mainly down the drain. As usual, my business proposals were killed stone-dead and had the telephone not rung at this point, I would simply have walked out. I was twenty-three years old, owed no one any money and apart from the blood mishpoche connection had no connections with the rest of the Franklins.

Billy picked up the phone and a sort of glazed 'blue-sky' look came over his face. 'That's wonderful!' he gushed. 'You can get us two on Friday night... Yes, I'll bring some cash... Put some extra red pepper into the goulash. See you around seven thirty. Thanks again.' He replaced the receiver with a very satisfied look as if he had just won the Irish Sweepstakes. If only! 'Where were we?'

I exploded for the very first and last time in my life. Forgetting that Madame was a foot away from me I blurted out: 'I've just come back from two of the most depressing sales trips in my entire life and all you can think about is having a bloody good meal on Friday night at the Czardas. Who's going to pay for it anyway as you've already spent all the traveller's cheques?'

Billy nonchantly brushed aside my comment as if he were flicking a fly off the white tablecloth on the restaurant table.

'Next Friday is pay day and we can use the NI stamp money before we buy the NI stamps and stick 'em on the employee cards next month...'

At this point I did walk out, went to the outside office and asked Grace Thompson to ring Charles and warn him that I was on my way.

I was still fuming when he opened the door and gave me his warm smile. I rushed past him, almost knocking him over. 'Sorry about that...' Charles got hold of my shoulders, steered me to the settee and pushed me down on it.

'Now what's all this about?' he asked in a very quiet and calming voice.

I babbled out: 'They're all a shower of crooks and it comes as a bit of a shock when you find this out at my age...'

Charles kept on nodding approvingly. To calm me down, he adopted one of the same sales techniques he'd taught me – changing the subject. 'You've not told me any details, I mean *those* details, about what happened to you in all those forty-eight states and sixty-nine different positions you adopted over there.'

Charles's medicine worked like a charm and we continued to discuss these items over lunch in the Cloisters Restaurant on the ground floor. It was an extremely pleasant business-like eatery with prices half those of the Épicure or Czardas. At the end of my long Wardour Street saga I told him of my adventures north of the Border. He was particularly intrigued by Freddy's voyeurism, of which he had not had personal experience.

'Sorry I had to abort my trip with you, but when you plan your next one find out if any more persons can join them for a haggis meal.'

He was over the moon when I told him about my ideas about a possible change of products. 'I'll get in touch with Premingers, the couture collection people in Vienna, and I also have some past contacts with the Iklé's in St Gallen in Switzerland. I had some very pleasant adventures with their young daughter which came to a sad end with me being literally kicked out of her father's house when he realised that my intentions were strictly dishonourable.'

I shook his hand and felt I owed him a kiss as a thank-you but didn't want to rebuffed, as I felt sure I would have been.

'Keep me posted,' he said and pushed me out the door. Suddenly he grabbed my shoulders and planted a heavily aftershave-laden kiss on both my cheeks.

I nearly missed getting the right train at Sloane Square but was deep in thought at Hammersmith and finally caught the train to Richmond. I cursed myself for not remembering that we had moved to Sheen and walked the good mile to 'Balcomie'. I was dreading the return to a 'blue sky' land that had turned decidedly black and stormy. But in fact there was other bad news.

Madame welcomed me with a strange look on her face and gave me the keys to the garage, which housed Geoffrey's Citroën – the car I used as transport for all my trips. I opened the garage door and Madame pointed to a large pool of oil under the car.

'Oil!' I exclaimed weakly. Although I was a fully fledged certificated centre lathe turner, my knowledge of automechanics was about as comprehensive as Geoffrey's. It consisted of making sure it was full of petrol and checking the oil and tyres at least once a week.

I phoned S.E. Thomas & Co., off the High Road, only a stone's throw from Belmont Garage. I dialled the number and a very pleasant, young voice cheerily answered the phone.

'Good afternoon. Can I help you?' I thought I must have phoned the managing director at Citroën's by mistake.

'I do hope so...'

'...We do try our best, Sir. That's what we're here for.'

The voice turned out to belong to Phil Thomas, the boss's son. Before the war Citroën's had had a factory at Fulham but it had moved to Slough, where the government encouraged companies to relocate themselves. The majority of the staff did not want to move, including their chief engineer and technical electrician, who, instead, found a very small workshop in Chiswick and opened the tiniest best-run mini Citroën garage in the UK.

'There's a bit of oil under the engine and it won't start,' I continued, full of ignorance.

'So you can't drive it to us?' asked Phil. I apologised.

'No problem, Sir; we'll come over to you and hoist it up.'

I gave him the 'Balcomie' address and told him I looked forward to seeing their driver. Phil laughed, adding: 'Yes, until tomorrow. I look forward to meeting a new customer.'

On the nose at 8.30, Phil jumped off the truck with a huge smile on his face. He hoisted the car up and onto the trailer with a midget helper aged maximum thirteen years of age. He gave me a form to fill in which had been beautifully typed and asked me for details of payment and reference names in case of bouncing cheques. I thanked him for the prompt service and he again assured me that was always what Dad had taught him for months before he left school.

'Mind you, he'll miss me for the next two years. They caught up with me for National Service but it's the RAF so it'll be quite handy.' I looked blank. 'When the office down the road heard I was a fully qualified mechanic they put me down for the Catering Corps. But a few pints plus a few quid later I managed to get into the RAF over in Paris. It's very close to the Citroën factory, so I reckon I'll learn a few tricks about their DS series which will be launched before you can say André Citroën, brush up my French and ask all those French girls about *soixante-neuf* and have a *ménage à trois* and see if I, like the Citroën, can give them *Traction Avant.*'

The next day he phoned and gave me the bad news that cars, like people, got old and, as Geoffrey's was now in its eleventh year and on its last wheels, suggested we put down an order for a new Light 15. 'It will take 18 months anyhow because of the change-over from right-hand drive but Dad will lend you a car when you need one and work out how much we can give you on your old wreck. There's always bits on there we can cannibalise. Come over and sign the forms before I'm off to Paris. Cheerio, I might see you when I'm on leave.'

His Dad phoned me the next day, I went to Chiswick and there was no haggling. He and I came to a very pleasant agreement over the price of Geoffrey's clapped-out, semi-rusty treasure which had once been the pride of the French motor industry. But it was literally falling apart. When one did a right-hand turn, the left front door opened mysteriously as if touched by a magic Gallic hand. If Geoffrey was the passenger, he grabbed it before it could hit a pedestrian or a post by the side of the road. His standard comment to this was: 'Never mind, it'll be perfectly all right when Phil fixes it in Chiswick.' That it required bodywork and a respray he conveniently forgot. The door was sometimes securely held by a loop of a very strong piece of string, which blocked entry through the passenger door. The only way in was by getting through the driver's door and crawling over to the passenger seat.

A shrug of the shoulders accompanied by 'C'est la vie' was the standard dismissal which he brushed aside like the smooth gear-change through the 'H' gate on the dashboard. It held a 12" slightly bent chrome stick which, at its extremity had a black bulbous 3" diameter smooth billiard ball type object.

Being a French object of desire, I was certain that André Citroën had specifically designed the shape of the gear lever to accustom lady passengers to the feel of this bulbous object. When pushing the lever through and down the gate into top gear the lady passenger's knee was within feeling distance of the driver and she could move her leg to the right if she wanted to get into gear. Alternatively, she could move her leg to the left which was a clear signal to the driver to keep both his hands on the wheel or try again at the next gear change.

Tom had always told me that the faster nasty problems are solved the better it is for everyone concerned, so you can then get on with your life. 'Facts ... always face the facts ... there is no escape from facts.' So I decided to have a 779 'talk-in'. The other items could follow and in any case a rapid trip to Edinburgh could always solve that one. I could bottle the other things up or as Frank from New Orleans had told me he did not go to confession often but I sorta bunch 'em up.' And in any case, I could face the third question from Uncle Charles and ask myself 'what's all the mad rush for, after all my birthday was going to be in December when I would reach the ripe old age of twenty four and at present, I still had the use of not only my hands but also my tongue.'

My twenty-fourth birthday came and went, and Madame's birthday on New Year's Eve, too, was a happy family affair; at that moment there seemed no immediate danger from the bailiffs. Indeed, Billy and Pucky got their own flat in a modern apartment block on the Upper Richmond Road at Sheen. Courtlands was sufficiently close to 'Balcomie' to do a reverse PX supply chain, so the new flat was adequately stocked by Madame with every nosh requirement. Uncle Charles also predicted that within the foreseeable future this flat could also get to be too small if Pucky got larger, which appeared unlikely at the moment as she was not modelling maternity wear.

Uncle Charles pressed me to a meeting at 779. He felt I should come on sales training courses with him and we planned a complete month-by-month tour for 1949 through England and Scotland. I was impressed and I felt he must have been in on the D-Day planning in 1944 – excluding Omaha Beach, of course. I had never seen that side of him before as I had only ever seen him in action in the bathroom at No. 779.

He even had little notebooks which included not only the names, addresses and phone numbers of buyers but also their age, food likes and dislikes and, most importantly of all, the names of husbands, wives, boyfriends or girlfriends who would be rewarded

143

with small or large gifts after the orders had been written. Whether it was smoked salmon from Harrods, Dundee cake from Fortnum's or malt whisky from Jenner's in Edinburgh, Charles *never* disappointed and it was all done with a Maurice Chevalier-style charm which would have been envied by many Hollywood producers in Culver City.

Age had nothing to do with it, so I was able to mirror his teachings with ease and, if some of his female buyers had shut their order books, they could be, and were, serviced by my brain, tongue and hands. My new 1949 UKCTA diary was chock-a-block with pages of B&Bs in all major towns which were on our list and I began to find out that the only way I could remember the day was because of the place I was in – Eastbourne, so it had to be a Wednesday. But we got results, and after three months the money bags started to fill. Wolfy must have turned the rain taps on and at last people had to buy raincoats, and as we were the only surviving waterproof manufacturers, apart from Alligator's in Manchester, the liquidators were not in hot pursuit, not yet anyway.

Tale 16

The Terpsichorean Art

My three mentors at Hampton Grammar, Bossy, Jamie and Steffs, gave me a very comprehensive education which only excluded the oldest profession in the world: prostitution. That subject was taboo and only when some of us reached the age when not only our voices but also two small parts of our anatomy dropped did the subject raise it's head.

The second oldest we all knew and practised with great pleasure at different levels of efficiency. The terpsichorean art dates back three thousand years to the Greek maidens who first danced around their temples and marble monuments.

In the seventeenth and eighteenth century ball gowns and crinolines were swirling through vast ballrooms and in the nineteenth century Franz Lehar and the two Strauss's waltzes were delighting their dancers, not only in the Viennese vast and crystal-hung temples of dance but across the whole of the European continent. After World War I the invention of the wireless brought this type of music to all homes and it became the musical opium of the people. Dance halls became Palais de Danse and even today one of TV's most popular programmes is *Strictly Come Dancing*, hosted by Bruce Forsyth.

With this explosion of popular taste, many dancing schools sprang up worldwide and Madame's father's relatives joined this quadrille. His sister had two daughters who escaped to what was then Palestine and opened a School of Dancing in Haifa. After World War II it prospered and Inge and Hertha travelled far and wide to keep up with the latest international dance steps, even looking at the contortions of the jitterbug after the GIs had returned to the States.

Bubbly, warm-hearted Inge was married to an Israeli who was born in Palestine and could have been a stand-in for a pale-skinned

Omar Sharif. Before the birth of Israel, Emanuel had fought the Brits and later joined MOSSAD, the very secret Israeli secret service, as he spoke fluent English, German, French, Hebrew and Arabic. He travelled extensively throughout the Middle East and was made Israeli consul in Cyprus. Handsome he certainly was, which the ladies confirmed when he travelled without Inge. When meeting them together they seemed joined at the hip, but apart they each became their own 'man'.

Inge came to London in the early 1950s and Madame was immediately smitten by this distant relative. She wasn't the only one. I could not keep my eyes or hands off her and this elegant mid-thirties lady got under my skin, especially when we tangoed together, which was often and our arms and legs entwined with a passion I had never experienced before, on or off the dance floor. Neither she nor I ever mentioned Emanuel, the handsome Adonis of a distant husband.

Madame insisted I show Inge all the London sights and places of interest around London. I made no objections, especially when we had to see Stratford, Oxford and Cambridge, which meant overnight stops outside of London. How I managed to 'do' all these sights, and the nightly 'dos' as well, I can't think but I was in my twenties and virile; with someone like her it was not too difficult to keep one's concentration up and doing. No. 779 certainly did not get a look-in when Inge was in town, though she only visited twice a year to update herself on the latest dance moves; I could hardly be expected to be celibate ten months of the year but those two months were very pleasurable indeed, if a bit exhausting.

Her dancing lessons took place only on three days of the week so she came on many of my short trips with me but never to Edinburgh. When I returned from there she asked me for detailed descriptions of my nightly adventures. I didn't really mind telling her, but it seemed to me that during her two months I was closer to her than many a husband might be, including her own.

On one occasion, she coyly brought the conversation round to my Scottish escapades, I felt particularly reluctant to talk about it. She sat up in bed, unwound my legs from around her hips, stared at me with her blue-green eyes and blurted out: 'Why the f—k won't you tell me how you do it with them?' I felt as if I had been hit by an ice pick.

She continued on this pushy path until she was like Madame trying to squeeze the last drop of juice from a lemon.

'It's none of your f—ing business,' I shouted back brutally, which seemed to have no effect on her whatsoever.

She continued to seek out all the most salacious details, especially Freddy's rather bizarre preferences in the field of mixed male and female relations. I nearly hit her. Finally I could shut her up only by suggesting she come up with me to Scotland not only to try the haggis but to savour the flavour of 'mixed' spices.

Early in 1951 I got a warm embrace from Madame when she had opened an air mail date-stamped Haifa. Inge was coming on her regular top-up dance trip in February, but this time Emanuel was coming with her, too, to see the sights. When I met them I felt a complete shyster and could hardly shake his hand or return the warm bear-hug embrace he nearly crushed me with. We did all the sights and I was saved thinking about the completely bizarre situation I had got myself into when Wolfy appeared in the shape of a new Citroën Traction Avant in February. Inge found this grey beauty 'so comfortable' and Emanuel only had one complaint, which was the registration number of the car. 'The first three letters are great,' he said, pointing to the number plate, 'but from what I hear from my dear wife, the figures behind it need changing.' The number Croydon Registration Office had allocated to the Citroën was 'JOY 580'. A 'joy' she was and took me safely from Penzance to Port Talbot, Bedford to Birmingham and Eastleigh to Eastbourne. At that time there was a group of small stores in all the towns on the south coast and I always 'did' three Plummer Roddis in one go. After I had taken all my four suitcases and been up and down the lifts and/or stairs I felt it really was time to close the suitcases once and for all, walk along to the pier with them and throw them into the Channel.

In Eastbourne Miss Townsend had been most patient and pleasant, and when I had recovered from the shock of her not having had writer's cramp, she looked at me in sorrow and pity, said, 'I'll give you a hand folding all your shmattes,' and started to help me fill one case. When she had finished the last one she looked at the cases and commented: 'Oh dear ... it's a bit like the exodus of the children of Israel. I'll get someone to help.' Their young window-dresser, Gerry, appeared as if called by Wolfy, smiled at me, picked two up and asked where my car was. Like reaching the Holy Land after thirty days in the desert, I looked at him gratefully and I bade the lady goodbye, gave her the smallest of kisses, which was not reciprocated, and she softy said: 'See you in six months ... and don't be late on deliveries, cheerio.'

Downstairs at the car, Gerry stowed the suitcases away expertly.

'Have you got a place for tonight? There's a few on the Hastings Road. Always prepared?' he asked, when he noticed the UKCTA book on the windscreen shelf.

I nodded and he suddenly brightened up. 'Tell you what, once you've got a place, here's my home phone number. If you feel like a pint, I'm meeting an old friend from the Boys Club tonight. He's just come home from the Far East and as soon as he drops his kitbag and gas mask, we're going to meet at The Pier. Better still, if you can't make it immediately, we'll be there after twenty hundred hours.'

I stopped him. 'What were you in then?'

He smiled. 'The RAF, I was flown out there without it costing me a penny. All by kind permission of His Majesty, and the last time I met this bloke who I hope is going to join us tonight, we were in Colombo. His ship was just on the way home and we had a few "Tigers" together.'

I did find a B&B which was up to the UKCTA standard, and wandered down to The Pier around half past eight. It was quite empty but I spotted Gerry the minute I walked through the door. Facing him was a sailor who had just taken his cap off and when I sat down I noticed the cap tally which read 'HMS *Unicorn*'.

He got up, gave a very quiet smile, held out his hand and said: 'My name's Jim. What's yours?'

'David, but I prefer Dave.'

He said very little and when I eventually got him to say something Jim mentioned he hated jazz but his real love was classical music. He suddenly glanced at his watch and got up, placed his cap squarely on his head and excused himself.

'Sorry, but I'm knackered. I've been on that train from Guz all day and just before I left they gave me a draft chit to an air station in the Midlands. Don't know what it's like but perhaps it will live up to its name. It's HMS *Gamecock*!'

Tale 17

Eastbourne – Sussex

When the railway arrived in Terminus Road Eastbourne in 1849 the town had been nestling peacefully and gracefully in the shadows of the rolling South Downs for generations and its population had risen from around 3,000 in 1811 to 10,500 by the end of the nineteenth century.

Britain had an Empire on which the sun never set and the Royal Navy ruled the waves of the world's Seven Seas. Many of those in high positions in the Empire and the Services retired to Eastbourne to live in its grand houses along broad tree-lined roads. They settled into leisurely retirement in 'The Meads' and other distinguished places of residence. However, many of the town's younger generation did not have this privileged lifestyle and followed the path set out by the town's motto which was:

'Let us follow better things'.

Many chose this advice and joined the civil and the fighting services.

At the turn of the twentieth century, 'Seaweed's' (Jim Harvey's) Uncle Jim went to sea 'under sail' at the age of fifteen. He told young Jim all those wonderful tales about the magical Far East and its overpowering spices, which he blended with his own adventures and the things he had seen from Cairo to Colombo. Young Jim was drawn to the stories and when Jim's Dad added to all these tales by telling him his World War I experiences with the Army in Mesopotamia and India, young Jim searched every book he could lay his hands on from the school library and the town's public library.

Mum and Dad Harvey must have been psychic because they

149

gave baby Jim the middle name of Thackeray which caused much banter on all the messdecks from HMS *Patroller* to HMS *Perseus*, and HMS *Triumph* to HMS *Unicorn* and all the landlocked Naval Air stations which included the rather romantically titled establishment in Middle England named 'HMS Gamecock'. Jim and the entire ships companies treasured their cap tallies, which were more valuable than 'sippers'.

As soon as young Jim could walk Dad took him down to the seashore below Beachy Head and showed him how to catch crabs and small fish. They watched the boats with their different company stripes on their funnels sail through the Channel to all those romantic places Dad and Uncle Jim had told him about. If it rained, Dad taught Jim how to build his own radio set and bought the crystals to listen to the local fishermen chatting to each other and complain about the 'Froggies' nicking their catch of fish from their nets.

When World War I finished Jim's Dad earned his living by painting houses together with an old army pal, while his Mum helped with earnings by being 'downstairs' in a 'big house' whenever extra help was needed. They rented rooms in Salehurst Road and later the owner gave Jim's Dad a fixed mortgage which expired in 1965, but they had no money for luxuries. Young Jim helped out by doing the shopping for the neighbours and a paper round. He did very well at school and passed his exam to join the local grammar school but they could not afford to lose the money he would earn by not being at school.

Just after his sixteenth birthday he took a job in Hobson's timberyard which really was 'Hobson's choice'. His two loves were electricity and the Royal Navy. He went to night school to fulfil his love of the sparks and also joined the Eastbourne Youth Centre whose motto was:

'Youth today ... Leaders tomorrow'.

He passed his apprenticeship with sparkling colours which assured him the first rung of the motto's ladder. When he joined the RN they looked at his qualifications and pushed him on the 'sparks' ladder as he was a qualified electrician. He had been chief librarian at the Youth Club Youth Centre and with Uncle Jim's help knew almost more about naval routine than the PO who had a go at the raw recruits at Glendower, the first of many establishments Jim sparked through. Uncle Jim had taught him 'Jackspeak', the Lower

150

Deck's somewhat descriptive language, a few words of which I had heard from the rather elegant dictionary of the Canadian sailor in Chiswick.

So when Jim reached Glendower, he was already regarded as an 'old salt' by the rest of the very raw recruits whose average age was from a 'claimed' sixteen to those around eighteen who had been called up.

Jim was immediately made 'Killick' of the mess, which meant he was 'in charge' of sixteen very raw youths. His first job was to allocate names to them which everyone could easily remember and which were usually based on the geographical origin or local accent of the lad. If they came from Liverpool they were 'Scousers', 'Taffs' came from Wales, 'Geordies' from Newcastle and 'Brummies' from Birmingham. Strangely enough, Harveys were known as 'Tacks', although Jim was addressed by the exalted rank of 'hookey' or 'Killick' of the mess. As many Scotsmen were stokers, it was fatal if you called 'Jock' down to the engine room as all the stokers shouted back 'aye' in unison.

Jim's first problem was a timid pimply sixteen-year-old from Woolwich. Officially he had no father on his records and his mum's current bloke was only around to collect his money from the unemployment office on Fridays. He then got pissed with his mates and on coming home either went for Mum or, if she had managed to escape from his clutches to her bottle of meths, grabbed young Chris, tore down his trousers and raped him. Jim found the oldest of his bunch and allocated 'Brummie' Read to take young Chris under his wings which made him 'Brummies' official 'Winger'. Because Chris stank to high heaven, Jim told him to take 'Wings' to the showers for a good scrub and thought he had solved the problem. Chris screamed navy-blue murder when told he was being taken to the shower, as the only 'shower' he knew was his 'uncle's' mates, who were always talked of as 'a shower of fuckin' bastards'. With the help of 'Taff' Jones and 'Geordie' Johnson they eventually managed to drag Chris's clothes off him and push him into the cubicle. As the water gushed over Chris, they discovered the source of the odour, which now got stronger.

His loving mother had never informed the lad of the rudiments of hygiene including the most basic procedure of what to do when going to the toilet. She *had* told him to unbutton his trousers when he needed a slash, but had never demonstrated what he should do after 'sitting down', and consequently Chris always wiped himself from back to front.

Holding their noses with a couple of laundry clips they found inside the shower, the two helpers washed him clean. After this, they christened young Chris 'Chocballs', a name which stuck with him until he left the Navy twenty-one years later as a Chief Petty Officer.

However, Jim solved the first of these problems with the same nonchalance which he had displayed when I met the Harveys for the very first time in Eastbourne. The contrast between the Franklins and them was like the chalky Beachy Head to a Liptauer cheese. The Harveys were the most contented and happy family I had ever met, and Mum, Dad and young Joyce, Jim's younger sister, had welcomed me into their arms as if I had been the long lost member of the Harvey–Page circle. Uncle Jim came from the Page side, was six feet tall and looked like the sailor from the Players cigarette pack without a beard. After about 30 years' RN service, Chief Petty Officer Jim Page hung up his oilskin, sea boots and sou'wester and retired to his home town. However, he still hankered after his first love, the sea, and became the Pier Master in Eastbourne.

Back in Wardour Street, my wandering thoughts were rudely interrupted by Billy thrusting a phone at me. 'Someone on the phone for you. They asked for a Mr Franklin and when I asked what it was about, said it was something to do with the Plummer Roddis orders.'

I could already see the Delby Coats order sheets floating southwards towards Calais because the Controller had not passed them and reluctantly picked up the phone.

'Plummer Roddis here. Is that Mr Franklin?'

I just gave a very long 'Yeeeees', playing for time.

'It's Jerry here. I helped you down with those stones from the Parthenon. Sorry to disturb you but I've had my bit of Seaweed on the phone. He apologised for the rapid exit at The Pier but he was still shattered from that long trip from Devonport. He wanted to have your address and, I hope you don't mind, but I gave it to him.'

I was completely flummoxed as I had not given my address to anybody and said so to Jerry. 'Oh, we are getting forgetful, aren't we? ... I simply went upstairs, looked at your order sheets and found the phone number, your address and the telegram address in case of urgency. No great mystery really... He seemed to sink back exhausted.

I waited a few moments, wondering what on earth *he* was phoning me for. I asked him and I could visually see him hitting his forehead as the answer came back loud and clear.

'Oh I'm sorry... That phone call from Seaweed. He wanted your address as he may be coming up to London and wants a bed for the night. He's just heard that draft to *Gamecock* is off and has been replaced by another back to the Far East...'

I cut in: '...But he's just come back from there...'

Jerry blustered: 'Well, don't get on to me about it... tell Seaweed to get onto wherever it grows and sways lazily in the wind and I'm sure their Lords of the Admiralty can search for the answer in the in-tray ... if it hasn't sunk without trace already. Anyway ... you don't mind if I give him the phone number?'

I felt like telling him he could give him the telegram address if he wanted to; after all they did have electric machines on board to handle such modern messages.

'Thanks a lot,' said Gerry. 'Incidentally, what did you think of him?'

'Bit quiet but if he dries out and gets windswept I'll tell you. Thanks again and I might even take you up on that offer of the B&B next time I'm in Eastbourne.'

'Now that would be nice. There's always room for you at Clive Villas,' and before I could hang up he gave me his phone number.

Tale 18

The Lady from the Holy Land

I had no sooner replaced the phone in its cradle when it rang again and a somewhat surly Billy said: 'It's for you ... *again!*' I was a little shattered to hear Inge's voice happily chirping away wanting to speak to *her* David. I almost gasped, as I was under the impression that that particular chapter had been closed.

Emanuel, she informed me, had to break his journey to London and was stuck in Paris for two nights and could I put her up at 'Balcomie' for those nights. I felt under the circumstances her choice of words was unfortunate, but the minute she turned the lamp off on my bedside table I was sucked into the most explosive orgy I had ever experienced...

When I awoke in the morning I sat up in bed and could hear her showering next door in the bathroom. I looked around the room and shuddered – it looked like a bridal suite after a couple had consummated their wedding night. My clothes, while intertwined with hers, trailed from the door to the bed like a virgin-white ski trail in the snow, around both sides on the floor were a collection of Kleenexes, used and unused. Even the small Vaseline jars had their screw tops missing, which I eventually found looking rather forlorn under my side of the bed. I tried to put everything away tidily before Inge returned and removed the last items from the top of the bedside table, including the packet of Durexes. I froze. It had originally held four individual packets and there were *still* four packets in the box, all unopened.

Inge bounced back from the shower and playfully gave me a kiss, happily smiling. A smile was the last thing I could reciprocate and I could hardly wait to speak to Chelsea Cloisters.

When I did Charles went straight to the point and told me not to panic for at least one month.

154

'We can always reach a decision after month two.'

I protested and Charles just gave up, cursing himself for not completing his instructions how not to get someone pregnant and immediately got out a calendar to mark the relevant weeks with two red crosses. 'Phone her on those two dates and we can decide what to do.'

Helpfully I added by asking Charles if I should phone Michael, my 'gynae' friend.

'Are you out of your bloody mind. Surely you know he is virtually in tiara territory; his mentor John Peel is in and out of Buck House before you can say Durex. Even if the switchboard girls hear you mention that dreadful word abortion, Mike's whole career goes down the bedpan and you will be his friend for ... death. I'll talk to our permanent-duty filly; she's bound to know some backstreet Soho person who does these things. Leave it to me.' With a grin he added: 'Well, we can't just leave it, can we?' I didn't know where to crawl to. I couldn't even flush myself down the pan as it was next door.

One month went by and Inge phoned to say she'd have to wait for month two. When that came and went the growing item continued on its natural course, so Charles decided drastic action had to be taken and never having had an experience like this before I felt like the executioner-in-waiting.

Hot baths, lots of gins, plenty of exercise, even jitterbugging were tried, and perhaps one of those old wives' tales brought up to date with the GI jive finally produced the sad but requested result that none of us were deliriously happy with. Charles merely said, 'C'est la vie', which, as I pointed out to him, should have had the last word changed to 'mort'.

During all this upheaval, Inge had introduced me to a very sweet and innocent distant relation of hers from Hampstead. Leoni was a charming young maiden and why Inge felt I should inflict myself on such a sweet person I could not comprehend; I had just about been as close to the human sewer as you could think. At times I almost felt as guilty as when Emanuel had first grasped my hand, when instead he should have inflicted serious damage to my lower personal parts.

The other lady during this turmoil was the fiery black haired Steffi from Golders Green. Madame and Billy thought she was the perfect partner for me as Daddy owned the patent to a very good soft drink conglomerate who eventually sold out to a multinational. I'm sure Madame and Billy had visions of them taking us over but the soft drink would have rolled off our raincoats like water off a dead duck's back.

Chelsea and Scotland kept my house full in all positions and when JOY was not taking me to all points north, south, east and west, there seemed not enough hours in the day to even think about the straight and narrow.

Tale 19

Tales from the Seven Seas

In January I opened an airmail Seaweed letter from the Far East. It was a handwritten ten-page Cook's Tour of Malta, Port Said, Aden, Colombo, Singapore and Japan. I did not even know that Britannia still had so many possessions under her corset. The punchline was that he was expecting to have a pint of bitter onshore in the UK soon and hoped it would not upset my own 'schedule' too much to see him. Whether this was with a reference to Inge or Scotland I never did find out. What I *did* find out was that there was a distinct streak of literary talent hidden under that seaweed.

One of the tales he told me was an update on young Chris who now felt much more comfortable about life having been initiated into the mysteries of ablution. Being young and virile, he had a habit of carrying out the 'five-finger exercise' with regularity at night, every night, and sometimes twice on Sundays.

Hammocks are extremely comfortable to sleep in and are usually slung four to five feet above the deck. As they hang on hooks which hold the hammock level, they never move with the ship's motions, making them much more comfortable than bunks. In order to get into it at night, one had to grab a pipe above the hammock, haul oneself up and drop down into the snug, comfortable home for the night, which wrapped itself around you like a cosy blanket. However, the pipes above it were also snug resting places for cockroaches, who loved the warmth of the hot-water pipes. No sailor pulled himself up before running his hand across the pipe to brush the cockroaches off.

Young Chris had not been told to wipe the little animals off the pipe and on his first haul into the hammock, put his hand on the rail above him and grabbed a fistful of cockroaches. When he

157

screamed, one of his mates looked at the fistful of brown crushed animals, shook his head, punched Chris's shoulder and commented: 'Cor ... better than that last lot of brown stuff you had in your hand, Chocballs?'

When the Killick was informed of the five-finger exercise excesses, he called Chris into his tiny cabouche and applied the stick-and-carrot approach.

'Sit down,' Jim beckoned and Chris looked at him with his large blue eyes which had large black bags under them.

Jim surveyed him in a very fatherly manner and explained that it could impair your vision if you did 'it' too often. This seemed to have no effect at all, so Jim switched to the 'carrot' approach. 'Tell you what, Chris, if you can keep your hands off it one day, I'll arrange the four lads who sling their hammocks fore and aft and on the starboard and portside to give you sippers. If you cut down to one a week they'll give you double sippers. That'll give them a good night's sleep, because, at the moment, after 'lights out' that mick of yours starts to move and creak like a racehorse in the National. By the time it reaches Beechers Brook it's puffing like a brewery horse and it keeps the lads awake fore and aft, on the starboard and portside. Go on, try it, it's worth the extra sippers.'

The ship's padre had taken some of the lads to Hiroshima and they stared at that famous roofless structure of domed steel which was the spot where the bomb had dropped. Jim got into a deep conversation with the Padre about why God could have let this happen. Jim explained that he was agnostic, although he had to fall in on Sunday mornings on the flight deck with all the other lads who were just coming to after consuming too many pints and having visited the local places of horizontal entertainment too often. One thing led to another until the Padre looked very sternly at Jim and explained: 'But surely, Harvey...' There was a deep theological pause. '... You must believe ... mustn't you?'

In the letter Jim said he rather enjoyed his response, when he looked the Padre straight in the eyes and asked: 'Believe in what, Padre?'

'God, of course!' replied the Padre as if he was standing in the pulpit in Guzz.

'But which one, Padre? When we went ashore to Kochin in India, they told me there were sixteen different ones there. So which one should I believe in?'

158

Jim wrote: 'And do you know something? To date he hasn't finished counting.' But Jim always preferred to say very little and he didn't suffer fools easily; he'd rather not speak to them.

The next letter came from Tricomalee and was just a one-liner.

'Put the lager in the fridge; we'll open it at Easter. But don't bank on it . . .'

From Kriegsmarine *to HMS* Victory

When I had first seen the Houses of Parliament and Big Ben from the train way back in 1937, I had not noticed three little ships off the Embankment on the northern side of the Thames.

If you had asked any one of the millions of Londoner as to the identity, the answer would have equally have been one word: 'Dunno'.

HMS *President* was a converted sloop; HMS *Chrysanthemum* came from a similar stable, but HMS *Discovery* was the ship in which Scott had discovered the Antarctic.

When I walked across Waterloo Bridge on 16th September 1952 I asked a friendly copper where I could discover my prey which was listed on a small piece of paper in my hand. He looked at the RN crest, looked at the Portsmouth postmark and in the friendliest of manners pointed me back to Waterloo Station and said: 'I think *Chrysanthemum* is down at Pompey. Go back to the station and take a train but be careful you get out at Portsmouth Harbour Station, otherwise you'll have to walk a mile.'

I waited until he had departed and kept walking across Waterloo Bridge and when I got to The Strand I saw the goal of my search and walked down to the Embankment. When I got to HMS *Chrysanthemum* I saw the white ensign flutter from her stern. However, my path up the gangway was blocked by the firm but pleasant shape of a petty officer who eyed me up and down in a very suspicious manner.

'Can I help you?' he asked in a stern manner. I nodded. 'You gotta name, 'ave ya?'

Tom Avery had given me the procedure when addressing rank and I realised I had mentally under-identified the person I was talking to, 'Yes, Chief ... and the name is Franklin ... I am report-ing as per instructions and...'

At this point he grabbed the piece of paper, looked at it and before marching off said, 'Follow me, son. Just watch yourself when we go down the first ladder; we don't want to lose a little short-arse like you on day one, do we?' I followed him like a pack of hounds at the hunt, only it was he who was doing the hunting. And suddenly it hit me. When we reached the last rung of the ladder there was that mixture of smells of oil, cleaning gear, sweat and salt that would stick with me for the rest of my naval career.

We walked along a narrow passage way and he stood aside to let me pass. The smell of tobacco, sweat and gallons of beer enveloped me as I squeezed past him. He pointed ahead with his extended finger and said: 'Third on the starboard side and knock before you go in or he'll 'ave ya.'

There were no mishaps en route and when the occupant of the cabin returned my knock with a 'Come', I stepped into a tiny cabin rather like a large sit-down loo at Waterloo Station.

He looked up at me and seemed to be younger than myself. According to the *Seamanship Manual Volume 1*, however, I knew he must be an officer on the lowest rung of the commission ladder. I handed him all the papers in my possession, but to my surprise he had a file marked 'Franklin' in front of him. He opened it whilst I was still standing there and turned over page after page of notes. I felt as if M15, M16 and the Gestapo had been recording every detail of my lurid past. When he had finished turning the pages, he scratched his head for the ninth time and pronounced his verdict.

'Bit of a pig's ear, aren't you?' He turned back to the 'personal' sheet. 'Sorry about that; you're Jewish, aren't you?' A large grin spread across the Chief's face as he crossed himself. 'You're supposed to do two years' National Service but all the Service periods you've done and the training all add up to roughly twenty months. After those two years you must do five on the reserve so ... as we're getting clobbered in Korea and all the posters tell us that there's an opening for you in the Navy ... we'll compromise and make it five round years in the VR...'

Turning to the Chief he added: 'What about Franklin doing a joining routine and basic training down at Pompey and follow it up for a four week's A/B course ... Grammar school boy like him should walk it, so when he takes his Leading Hand lot down at

Pompey in two years' time he'll have saved the taxpayer seven weeks board and lodging. What about it Chief, talk to your Oppo at the Reg Office in Pompey; it's Chiefie Hawks, isn't it? And what you told me, he owes you one?' The Chief nodded his head and left the cabouche.

He returned minutes later with a thumbs-up gesture. 'No problem. Franklin can do the three in one go, keep him out of mischief for six months so he can start his five years in the VR in March.'

He went on: 'Do you remember Alfie Locks who was in the Reg Office in Pompey?' The officer nodded. 'Well, he's in the Reg Office in Guzz and they're at panic stations. One of the "Scribes" put a draft chit in the wrong tray and sent this bloke to the Far East by mistake and when he got there they put him straight back on a carrier which was coming back home to pay off. Someone is going to be in the rattle for that.'

'Glad it's not you, Chief,' grinned the officer and looked at me and added:

'Take him away then ... and don't drop him in the "ogging"; they say the Thames is polluted so that's one way we could get rid of him.

'DISMISS!' he shouted and we both fled as if we had been shot out of a 16-inch gun down at Portsmouth.

'Follow me, Franklin,' said Chiefie and he marched off at a rate of knots which would have made an MTB proud.

'Ladders ... up top ... down below ... waaatch it ... we don't want no arse-over-tit broken bones...' and I was on the Chief's instructional Jackspeakland roller-coaster and ended up in the canteen. 'Cup o' tea, son?' said the Chief, grinning at me. 'Don't take no notice of Junior; he's just throwing his weight around to get that second ring ... if he's not careful he'll have to watch how he gets it. When you've had your cuppa I'll show you the ropes, only we calls them "bends and hitches". Drink up!' This was my introduction to my years in the Puss.

Next day it was Portsmouth Harbour Railway Station where a two-ton truck awaited the arrival of the new recruits. We waited around half an hour until everyone climbed aboard and a marine drove us towards Southsea's Victoria Barracks. I was sitting at the tail end looking back and out and was greatly impressed by a very new and shiny pink Sunbeam Talbot drophead following us very closely. At the first set of green lights the marine driving our truck must have been mesmerised by a bird with very long legs and a very short skirt who was standing at the lights. When they changed to red the marine rammed his foot down on the brakes and the Sunbeam came to a screeching halt behind us and a little tinkle of glass clattered to the ground.

The driver of the car jumped out furiously, checked the damage to the Sunbeam and ran to the front of the truck, looked at the marine driver and, almost spitting blood, said: 'Look what you've done to my nice new car.'

The Marine wound down the window, stuck out his elbowed arm and said: 'You can kiss my arse...'

The Sunbeam driver took a close look at the marine and replied: 'This is no time for love ... I'm mad.'

The marine rammed the truck into gear, stamped his size-9 boot on the accelerator and we disappeared in a cloud of dust and ten minutes later arrived at Victoria Barracks. The journey from the Café Kranzler in Berlin when my cap tally read 'Kriegsmarine' had taken almost twenty-five years but now my cap tally read 'HMS *Victory*'.

There were sixteen of us in 'C' Mess on the third floor of 'Nelson' block whose walls were painted in a warming two-tone colour scheme. The lower half was a sickly green and the dirty yellow above it no doubt prepared us for 'roughers' in the Atlantic. I felt that next time a paint-job was done I would have to act as colour consultant to the RN. We were all kitted out with identical uniforms and kitbags; Jim had warned me to bring a sink plug as on the entire floor of 'C' Mess there were thirty-two bodies and just six sinks and they were all plugless. My own plug proved worth double its weight in 'sippers' when I bartered it out by the fifteen minutes.

The lads who were a little shy about their privacy had this knocked out of them on their first visit to the toilets. The 'heads' were door-less, which made everyone about equal in their communal nakedness. However, I must have inherited Madame's 'blue' streak because none of this troubled me in the slightest. Uncle Charles had always told me to try everything once and I was determined to discover this new planet as thoroughly as I had explored the United States. I actually quite liked the 'identity number' bit and felt a thrill when the first letter I received was addressed to O/D Franklin, David LD 9355 c/o Admiralty London. It was from

Seaweed and just had one line on it: 'Welcome aboard – just watch it in the showers'.

'By the right, quick march' and 'By the left, quick march' were now daily routines and we all had to take turns to practise giving commands. I made a complete cock-up on my first attempt of ordering sixteen very reluctant left-footed ordinary seamen around the barrack square. The PO just told me to scream at them as if they were shit, which he knew they were, motioning me 'get on with it, lad'. However, I had never done this before nor was my voice the right pitch or similar to the venom which the PO had perfected over the past twenty years. 'Remember,' he said, 'they will always follow your command and if you say "shit", they will.' I was marching them forward ... 'About turn ... halt ... by the right' ... and was already congratulating myself when the front-row three were approaching the end wall of the parade ground. When I tried to 'about turn' them, my voice dried up.

The PO screamed at me as the front row now had their noses against the first row of bricks. 'For fuck's sake, halt 'em.'

My voice didn't even croak and I saw the entire squad of sixteen pile on top of each other against the wall creating a very pretty human heap of a blue pyramid with the odd black boot sticking out at a very peculiar angle.

'Dismiss!' screamed the PO, which was followed by a bellowing 'Franklin ... come 'ere!' which could even be heard at the other side of the harbour and I wasn't sure if it was mine or the PO's throat that needed more attention.

When I got back to our mess they had elected 'Scouse' Murphy as spokesman on their behalf and he told me it was their unanimous decision that my punishment was not going to be a gang rape. 'Don't fancy that; it don't last long enough,' added Scouse. Instead each one would have my daily tot every day for the next sixteen days; 'UA' or not 'UA'.

There were no major mishaps after this and the various routines and courses were ticked off in a fairly satisfactory manner with the exception of the 'medical' at Haslar. We were all stripped down to our shorts or Y fronts as the very young two-ringer doctor pushed and prodded the various parts of our anatomy.

'Hop up there,' he said to Scouse, pointing at a plastic-covered high trolley.

'Pull 'em down,' said Doc, pointing to Scouse's Y-front. 'No son, take 'em right off and turn on your side facing the wall.'

Doc reached for a jar of Vaseline and inserted his thin rubber-gloved little finger. 'Pull your knees up.'

Scouse was watching him out of the corner of his eye and commented: 'Last time I had summin' like this done was in the 'orspital when a nice nurse pushed a needle into my bum and said: 'I'm just going to give you a little prick, it won't hurt at all...'

Doc gently pushed his finger up Scouse's anus and gave a very satisfied grunt. 'Clean as a whistle,' he murmured happily, withdrawing his finger and playfully slapped Scouse's bum. 'I don't think you'll have any problems with haemorrhoids... Next...'

Scouse asked me later what 'them' were.

'Piles, of course,' I replied.

'Why the bleedin' 'ell didn't he say so?' Shaking his head in disbelief. 'I thought he were lookin' for the Crown Jewels.'

When I got home on Xmas leave there were a few letters waiting for me. One was from Louis Klemantaski who wondered where I had got to. He thanked me for the help earlier in the year at Bo'ness and also being a standby for Le Mans, which unfortunately had not materialised. However, he commented that the six Aston Martins had done brilliantly and perhaps I'd be there in the future if I got any leave.

However, what worried me most was the state Dad was in. Over the past years he had not been very active physically. When I had last seen him he seemed to be chair-bound but with a cigar in his hand. He could not manage the stairs any longer and had moved into the spare room upstairs with his armchair and cigar. Geoffrey, who was now back permanently at Decca, had got him a giant new experimental TV projection set, which Dad was glued to all day and every night.

On my first night back he asked me to sit with him and it was the very first time that I could remember that we had had a heart-to-heart talk.

'Come and sit next to me,' he said, patting the chair next to his.

'As you are probably aware, Billy and Pucky want to start a family of their own and the local estate agents have sent me a brochure of properties that they have planning permission for. There is one quite close to here at the edge of Sheen Common and I have asked Billy to source out the possibility of buying the land and building a house on it. Planahome have drawn up some plans for the perfect suburban home and I'll show them to you later. They estimate the building costs to be around £4,250 and the plot is another £5,000, so for around £10,000 he would have a property which in twenty-five years' time should be worth around a quarter of a million.

'I have therefore made a codicil to my will that when "Balcomie" is sold the first £10,000 should go to you before the rest is split...' He smiled. 'Unless it's in fifty years, in which case you'll be sitting on half a million.'

Sadly Dad did not even see the end of the following year and died on the 7th February 1954. I came up on compassionate leave to bury him and received the death certificate as next of kin. Neither Madame nor Billy ever told me why I should have been that person. Nor did they take any notice of the codicil to the will when 'Balcomie' was sold two years later.

Tale 21

Stalin Is Dead

Seaweed, whom I had now rechristened 'Jim', was washed ashore to RNAS Culham in Oxfordshire and had visited Dad and 'Balcomie' during the last months of the year and suggested he and I should split our Easter leaves between Eastbourne and London. One of the 'rabbits' he had brought back for me from Japan was a travelling Shinto shrine which he swore was called 'Fukayuso', though as Geoffrey did not have Japanese in his repertoire of languages I never had Jim's story authenticated. It was a black lacquered 9^1/$_2$" high $\times$ 7^1/$_2$" deep cabinet with two vertically hinged doors. Inside was gold-covered and held a cross-legged figure sitting on six bags of rice. In each arm he cradled one lady, one white and the other pale-coloured, and he represented the God of Plenty. Enough money and women but I never did find out if Jim's title was correct. I renamed it 'NW' – 'Never Worse' – and over the years I think Wolfy must have joined 'Fukayuso' sitting on all those bags.

In the RN, everything was going to plan. The one-ringer had correctly predicted that my grammar-school training would make me sail 'full ahead'. At the end of February 1953 I finished my 'six months' and now proceeded to phase two of the five-year plan. However, I was rewarded with fourteen days' leave with an order 'to report back on board HMS *President* on 15th March 1953 at 17.00hrs'.

Six months without haggis and extras had to be resuscitated and there was no objection from Warrender Park Road. Even 181 Wardour Street were happy when I volunteered to make a few calls on their behalf – and without pay – in Edinburgh, Glasgow, Dumfries and Alnwick in the first week of March. Everything was quite kosher as the NI stamps were being looked after by the RN during my official leave and Wardour Street had a little extra petty cash.

I arrived in Warrender Park Road in the late afternoon on Thursday 5th March. The haggis and malt whisky slipped down smoothly and I hadn't realised how much I had missed the company. In the middle of the night Rhoda sat up like a stiff poker and shook me.

'Did Freddy tell you the story about that naval officer he met at the Festival Club during the Festival?'

I cringed, expecting to hear another one of their fascinating adventures, but at that time in the morning I really wanted to catch up on some sleep.

Rhoda persisted, adding: 'No ... no ... no, it wasn't like that at all. You must have read about the 1,500 pipers 'Gathering of the Clans' who had come to the 'frae a' the airts' when they marched sixteen abreast down Princes Street on the Festival Saturday?'

'How could I forget,' sighed Freddy. 'All those bagpipes being blown by those brawny kilted Highlanders, Islanders and Lowlanders.'

Rhoda exploded: 'It's not *that* I was going to tell David about.' Freddy, too, was now sitting up like a stiff bagpipe.

'That naval officer,' Rhoda continued, 'we met at the Festival Club was charming. Lieutenant Murray never stopped talking about having skied in the Scottish Kandahar last year and I told him that we had a friend who was in the RN – that's you – and although he hadn't done any skiing he would no doubt be interested in that wonderful sport. I remember asking him if he spoke German and he nodded. 'Tell me, have you ever wondered why we Brits pronounce the "k" in skiing the hard way and in German "ski" is pronounced "she fahren"? 'I hadn't,' replied Rhoda, 'but that means our friend David must start his "she fahren" immediately.' Lieutenant Murray nodded his head, pulled out his pen, grabbed a bit of paper and wrote down the address of the British Ski Club in Eaton Square in London and told me to tell *you* to give them my name. He's also in the RN Ski Club and suggested you join that as well.'

I thanked her. 'I'll do that when I get back to town. Thanks for the intro, but what about a little "skiing" right now?'

Friday the sixth was rest day as Rhoda had insisted on 'plenty of sleep' before my return trip to London, or 'The Smoke', as it was called in Jackspeak. After tea around five o'clock there was just a loving kiss without afters and I made my farewell with a promise of telling them when Her Majesty would allow me to return to the pleasures of the High and Lowlands. I switched on the ignition and JOY rose quietly to her required height. I pushed

168

the chrome gear lever and black knob through the gate and waved Rhoda and Freddy goodbye. I let the clutch in and JOY leapt forward like a snarling tiger; anyone looking at the car from the front could have mistaken it for just that. The two huge lidless wing-mounted headlights completed the menacing look, which had made the Bertoni-designed sleek black car the trademark for the long-running *Inspector Maigret* TV series which millions of Brits watched every week. To them, the Citroën was as French as a packet of Gauloises or the whiff of garlic. I glanced at my watch and calculated that with luck, no rain and no fog, I would reach London in the early hours of the morning.

Apart from trucks, the A1 was fairly quiet and I pointed JOY southwards towards Penicuik. Once over the top at Crawford, I saw the 'England South' signs and promised myself a mug of tea near Carlisle. The dark-brown liquid went down a treat and, before leaving, I checked my timing again and gave myself a satisfactory grunt. 'Keep this up and I'll be home in Madame's arms in non-kosher Sheen in time for a late bacon, eggs, sausages and tomatoes.'

Shap Fell was clouded in mist and on the other side hung a thick dark cotton-wool cloud. My two large headlights always gave two piercing steely beams but, in the swirling cloud, all you got was the reflection back off the beams. This wasn't a bit like a glamorous Maigret episode and I cursed myself for not accepting the ménage-à-trois warmth of the Edinburgh bed. 'A foggy day in London-town' had nothing on this and all the caffs were full with truckers who had given up the foggy ghost. It was now 'complete surrender' for me or 'carry on regardless', and at every caff I came to I promised myself to join the ranks of those who had surrendered. It was the usual toss-up with myself – 'I bet it will get better another few miles down the road' – but only when I got into Staffordshire did the fog get thinner. I took my courage in both hands and decided to cross over into Nottinghamshire and congratulated myself.

The fog lifted and I stopped at the first caff which was chock-a-block with truckers and had a cup of warming mud-like tea. As I returned to JOY, a truck and trailer pulled into the car park. I looked at the HGV driver who shook his head and pointed behind himself, commenting: 'You're not going south, mate, are ya? You're bloody barmy, it's even more of a peasouper down there.' I ignored him. got into JOY, switched on the engine and drove on to the

three-lane two-way A1 and ....
....
....
??

I had a banging noise in my head. I opened one eye and saw two blue figures standing by my bed ... *my* bed? ... where the hell was I? One of the coppers walked up to me and said: 'Oh ... he's awake, Serge. Shall I ask him what happened?'

Serge was not al all happy with the young PC.

'Didn't they teach at Hendon that, if you can, look at the chart at the bottom of the bed ... what does it say?'

Junior returned dutifully to the bed end, lifted the wooden board, scratched his head and gave it to the Sergeant. He looked at it, came up to my bed and in a very concerned voice said, 'Can you hear me, Sir?' I nodded.

'It says 'ere you've got severe concussion so it's not much good to ask you what happened.'

Being in a total daze I didn't know whether to nod or shake my head. When I did shake it I thought it was going to burst. My hands went up to steady myself and felt this huge bandage around my head which seemed to have been taken from an Egyptian mummy and started to unwind it.

'No no, Sir,' said the Sergeant and pressed the red panic buttons. Within minutes a doctor and two nurses appeared and started to rewind the bandage and one of the doctors quietly gave me the update on my medical condition.

'You've got severe concussion which has resulted in retrograde amnesia,' he said, then smilingly added: 'That's probably all for the good because it was a pretty dreadful accident. You're very lucky to have been thrown through the driver's side window when the car was turned around 180 degrees; otherwise you wouldn't be here now. There's nothing left of the front of the car; the rest is now a tangled mess under the truck's trailer. Just as well they've not yet introduced seat belt legislation, otherwise there would have been nothing left of you either.'

The young copper was turning a pretty shade of green and excused himself. The Serge shook his head in disbelief: 'Kids today... Should have been in the Blitz, they should.'

'Oh yes...' The doctor paused. 'The good news is you have no head injury apart from the concussion. You do have a dislocated shoulder ... a badly scarred right leg, bruising on your right side ... oh yes, I forgot the little problem under that head bandage ... your jaw is broken in two places and will have to be wired up ... otherwise it would flap open like a swinging gate.' The Serge came over to me to see how I was taking the news.

'Your age ... that jaw should be OK within four to five weeks but you won't be able to eat any solid food for the wired-up period; everything will have to be sucked through a straw.'

Roast beef through a straw ... minced ... you've got to be joking, I thought to myself and shuddered. Which means I've got to drink my pint through a straw ... that would cause jubilation on the messdeck... 'Did you know short-arse Franklin now drinks his pints through a straw ... and that straws are long and thin' ... followed by unspeakable addition to what my reaction would be in the showers including that warning Jim had given to me about picking up the soap. Fortunately, the nurses' kind care and attention had stayed strictly above the bedsheets as, after all, the wired-up mouth would hardly have been a pleasurable experience without a magnet or tin opener.

Good news finally came with the decision that my third and last visit to 'theatre' would be on Tuesday 25th March. All being well, they would release me the next day. The nurse who brought me the news smilingly added: 'As you've been such a good patient, I and two of the nurses wanted to celebrate our hope of a speedy recovery and would like to show our appreciation tonight by sharing a drink with you. Nothing strong, just a glass of beer with your supper.' This was duly delivered to my bedside by Staff. Unfortunately Guinness was not my favourite tipple and I wrinkled my nose.

'Oh ... don't you like it?'

'Not really,' I mumbled through my involuntarily clenched teeth.

'But it's very good for you,' said Staff reassuringly. She noticed my look of disbelief. 'At least, it won't do you any harm.'

One of the nurses told me about how I'd first come into the hospital:

'You were in a terrible state when you were brought in. The inside of your mouth was like a quagmire with little stones in it. The jaw was broken in two places and eight teeth were embedded in your tongue. I was holding the little banana-shaped tin receptacle as Doctor collected them from your mouth with a small pair of tweezers and counted them as they rattled into the tin. "One ...

two ... three," he sang out like the umpire at Wimbledon calling out the latest score "... four, five, six ... we want eight," he added, "to make sure he hasn't swallowed any." '

Apparently I was violent throughout the night and when Staff saw me in the morning she and the morphine had quietened me down and, as talking was almost impossible, handed me a piece of paper and a biro. I did not write a love letter but simply asked: 'Was I violent again and give you a lot of grey hairs?' I have cherished that note until today, but I did not show it to Jamie at Hampton as my grammar was not faultless.

The nurses also gave me a copy of the *Evening Standard* dated 6th March 1953. The two-inch banner headline read: 'STALIN IS DEAD'. The girls had attached a little note with the loving words: 'You were nearly a passenger to hell but got away with it by the skin of your teeth ... all eight of them. Have a safe trip home...'

Tale 22

JOY – GB

Northampton Hospital released me after eighteen days with a letter to 'whom it may concern' regarding the cutting of the wires either at the Middlesex Hospital in London or at RN at Haslar, whichever was more convenient during my convalescence leave. This gave me additional time to tell Uncle Charles of how fate had struck not only 181 Wardour Street but also all the other things that had been happening since I had last seen him.

'You look incredibly fit!' he exclaimed when I walked through the door at No. 779. There were two glasses on the table next to a bottle of Bollinger and, as usual, he had done his 'pre-sell' homework by supplying two straws.

'You never really told me the countdown to the RN.'

So I related my various unsuccessful attempts over the years and when I got to the Ronnie Purcell bit he laughed.

'This is beginning to sound like one of dear Tom's stories that always have a happy ending. What about that sailor friend Jim you mentioned to me. Where does he fit into all this?'

'Don't really know at present, but he's coming up after Easter and his family have asked me to spend some time in Eastbourne...'

Charles interrupted me. 'You'll be able to be up and down those Downs together and, if you both don't like it, throw yourself off Beachy Head.'

'In London later,' he went on, 'come over to No. 779 and we can have a chat and I'll take you both out for a meal.'

I nodded. 'As long as it's not the Czardas or the Épicure. The Captain's Cabin is OK but I don't think Jim's much into the Yorkminster or Fitzroy; he likes a quiet pint. As for other types of entertainment I've not asked him, not yet anyway.'

I was unwired at Middlesex Hospital on 22nd April and felt odd

173

not having used my jaw for three and a half weeks. When Jim came up from RNAS Culham, we went to the Steak House for dinner. I had been dreaming of that juicy steak and its succulent smell since the accident and when it arrived with the crisp chips I just gazed at the feast in front of me. I placed the steak knife on the lightly grilled tender surface and slowly cut it and it went through the soft meat as if were butter. I put the fork into the soft meat, put it in my mouth and ... I couldn't remember what you actually did when you chewed anything in your mouth. Did you move your teeth with the bottom row or up and down with your top row. In desperation I started to cry. Jim looked at me in horror and started to grin.

'Do I have to get you plastered before you remember how to eat? I thought all these things were automatic. I suppose some are,' he added, looking hard at me.

I phoned Charles the next day but he was tied up on Tuesday so we knocked on No. 779's door on the Wednesday. Charles ushered Jim onto the settee and asked him if he wanted anything special and Jim just shook his head.

'I know David is not fussy so I'll give him his regular lager.'

Jim nodded and said, 'That's OK by me.' From that moment Charles and Jim were in a verbal clinch as Charles had done a CV search on Jim, his past and his travels. Although Charles had never been further east than Malta, the *Encyclopaedia Britannica* had been wonderful as a standby for all points beyond Suez.

After finishing *The Times*, the *Financial Times* and the *Drapers Record*, I had exhausted the Charles 'reading room' and they had not even got to Colombo, let alone Singapore, Hong Kong, Japan and the Inland Seas. Jim came over looking very guilty and apologised about monopolising 'dear Charles'.

'No, no, no,' protested Charles. 'I'm really enjoying his company. I've never really met a sailor face to face.' He turned to me, 'You've even met a French sailor, haven't you?' grinning from ear to ear.

'You've not told me about him,' said Jim, raising his eyebrows.

'I'll tell you over dinner or later. Charles knows all my secrets, don't you, Charles? Even the Highland flings ... but let's go ... there's lots of tales to tell!'

And the three of us had one of the most enjoyable non-sexual threesomes I'd ever experienced ... *before* dinner ... *over* dinner or *after* dinner.

174

The next day the Harveys reciprocated the warmth and friendliness that Charles had shown. As soon as the door in Eastbourne's Salehurst Road opened they treated me like a long-lost friend. When I walked into their cosy small sitting room, Uncle Jim got up from a chair, stretched himself to his six-foot height and came towards me, hands outstretched.

'Oh, so you're Jim's "oppo" are you? Look after him well, won't you?' He looked hard at me. 'Or would it be the other way round, Dave?'

I looked at Uncle Jim. 'I suppose it's a bit of both, really, isn't it?'

Jim nodded and permitted himself the smallest of smiles.

When we returned to 'Balcomie' two days later, Madame was in a 'blue sky' mode. 'Her' Jimmy was fitting into her programme like a snug-fitting blue glove, and she immediately made him a member of the 'GB' set. Only there were no PXs at Devonport, HMS *Gamecock* or RNAS Culham, but if anything went wrong which had wires in it – fuses, irons, lamps, toasters, even the electric blanket – Jimmy's GB was put on the urgent list. His Eastbourne Mum and Madame were on totally different circuits, which was just as well as otherwise there would have been a mighty fuse-blow. My Dad always made Jim sit by his side and started to wean Jim on small cigars. He told Jim about the Iron Crosses whereas Jim only had a Defence Medal, Atlantic Star, 1939–1945 World War II medal and was about to receive his Korean medal. As for the weekend, the visitors which were assembled around the table were of the European mixture and later age, and made Jim totally exhausted with all tales stretching back to World War I and the Nazis.

When we walked through the door at 'Balcomie', Madame said that Phil from S.E. Thomas had phoned and had asked me to ring him back. After the crash my insurance were more than correct and the Alliance were pleased that I had survived but mortified that an eighteen-month-old car was a total write-off. They paid up on the nose but asked me if I could recommend an honest dealer whom they could sell the wreck to and agreed that an honest car dealer was a relic of the past and I recommended my Chiswick friend who would be realistically honest. The insurance contacted Phil who then looked at the wreck and gave the insurance a price for it. Phil was very pleased with the deal as they were shipping Citroëns over and assembling them in Chiswick, which filled the gaps in production during holiday time. After telling me all this on the telephone, he asked me over to Chiswick for a drink, at which point I heard him slam his hand against his forehead. 'You've not yet got a hire car at present! I'll come over to Sheen and we can chat there.'

When we had our pint at The Plough, he was astounded that there was not a visible scratch on me. Being a salesman I knew that some kind of deal was in the offing. Young Phil, when in Paris, had heard that that a new Citroën design was on the drawing board but it was too early even to talk about price, and all young Phil could get out of the mechanics was that it was as sensational as the Light 15 had been almost twenty years before and it was going to be named 'DS' – *Déesse* ('Goddess'). The crunch question was 'Are you interested?' and my reply was the oft-used 'How much?' Phil said they were collecting potential customer orders, but as it would be at least eighteen months before delivery times and prices were finalised, our help would be appreciated.

'No rush, mind you, but young Phil is due some leave in the summer. He can give you a ring and if our leave dates fit, he'll buy you a drink.'

As we walked back along Christchurch Road he turned to me and asked if I was squeamish or superstitious and I shook my head.

'I know it's a bit ghoulish but I'm going back to the workshop. If you would like to see what you escaped from, I'll run you over and, if you pass out, give you a brandy before I take you back.'

It was an offer my curiosity could not refuse, so I went upstairs, got my Leica and fifteen minutes later we walked into the workshop. Phil pointed at the rear end of a Citroën Light 15. 'That's it or what's left of it.' We walked around the car which had three doorless gaps in it. There was no windscreen and there was nothing in front of where the windscreen had been. No engine, just a large hole with twisted metal. I just stood there and stared.

'You all right?' he asked.

I nodded and smiled. I took the Leica out and shot about twelve frames. 'Stops me from passing out, doesn't it? You know, it could make me superstitious that there is someone somewhere up there who is looking after me.'

When we got back to 'Balcomie' Jim looked as if to say 'Where the hell did you get to?' but just quietly asked the question and started calculating. 'It's April now ... Six months makes it early

176

autumn. So is he going to give you something until you have a firm date?' I nodded.

In July Phil left a message at 'Balcomie' to ring him back in Chiswick.

'We've got a second-hand Light 15 which may be of interest. It's only eighteen months old and we've done it up and we thought you might like to see it.'

As I walked into the tiny workshop I could see the back-end of a very shiny black Light 15 with highly polished chrome bits shining like so many lighthouses.

'Looks nice...?' quizzed Phil.

I nodded and asked him how many miles it had done and he apologised for having replaced the meter, adding: 'People are always suspicious if there's a low mileage. In any case it has a new engine, but I know the previous owner.' He waved a thick A4 envelope under my nose.

'Want to go for a spin?' he asked, raising his eyebrows. He threw me a key and got in the passenger door.

'In for a penny, in for a franc,' I thought, pushed the key in, switched the ignition on and she rose quietly to her required driving height. I turned right towards Chertsey Bridge and crossed to the other side and shuddered remembering the day when Geoffrey and I had gone over that bridge to see the first V2 in Staveley Road all those years ago.

'You all right? Do you want me to drive?' asked Phil. I shook my head and told him the Geoffrey V2 story.

'Have you seen him lately?'

'Not lately, but he's got himself a lovely cushy number in Vienna and hopes to join the Control Commission and he's also fishing the airwaves to go to BBC Vienna. Still at least he won't have any problems with his perfect German. Last time I saw him he had a broad Viennese accent ... First District ... I remember the first time we met you, when we were haggling a deal for his pre-war wreck. I spoke in German to him so you wouldn't hear what we were saying.'

'He was still at Bletchley then, wasn't he?' asked Phil and I nodded as we circled the roundabout on the other side of the bridge.

'God, she's smooth!' I exclaimed. 'New engine?' and Phil nodded then I asked the usual question, keeping my fingers crossed and on the wheel.

The complete salesman of S.E. Thomas and Co. very quietly said he felt we would come to a satisfactory arrangement, adding 'for both of us', and smiled quietly as we returned to the little workshop.

'I shouldn't say so, Phil, but I think she's terrific.'

'I'll get you the logbook and all the other relevant papers,' said Phil.

He rose and minutes later returned with a fat A4 envelope and showed me its contents. 'Logbook, service certificate and original S.E. Thomas invoice... You're not squeamish, are you?'

I shook my head, just like the time his son had asked the same question. I was puzzled. 'Why do you ask that?'

'Because the car you're looking at is your "JOY 580" with additions, of course, and its black!'

I did not faint but smiled at him, grinned and we agreed on his price and shook hands.

'Easier than with Mr Child ... and we didn't even have to speak German which he spoke morning, noon and night when he was at Bletchley.' Phil pulled out the last contents of the envelope and gave them to me.

'It's the police reports of what you said to the cops in hospital, and the driver of the truck, neither of which threw any light on the accident and time and place of the accident which you don't remember,' and handed the envelope to me. I looked at it and at the bottom of the document it gave the time of the accident which was (estimated 01.15) and the Police District of accident:

'BLETCHLEY.'

'Right,' said Phil and called over one of the mechanics. He came back within minutes with a pair of number plates and handed them to Phil.

'Still OK, are we?' said Phil, turning to me, and I nodded as he screwed the plates on the back and front of the car. He walked back a few steps and looked at them admiringly.

'JOY 580 sets it off well, doesn't it? And here's an additional one for you with my compliments. When you were here that first time with Mr Child you told me your German was so good because you were born in Berlin. So here's a plate especially designed for you:

Stands for "German born",' he grinned as he fixed the 'GB' plate to the car.

Tale 23

Daily Orders – Ashore and Afloat

Six weeks later my jaw was in perfect eating and chewing condition and all the lads on the mess at Victoria Barracks cheered when I threw the straws away. I informed them that I had no problem with chewing anything now and 'Scouse' Murphy asked if he could have that in writing. 'Written by 'im,' he added pointing at me.

During the last week of December, just before Xmas leave, there was great excitement when a list of events for the next year was posted up on the 'Daily Orders' board. However, the volunteers could be counted on the four fingers of one hand. Comments of 'Short-arse Nutty Franklin' were banded around by the eager non-volunteers who could not understand my enthusiasm. The occasional addition to my name was pencilled in above the 'Volunteers Required' with two words 'Arse Crawler'.

It was going to be Coronation Year which meant a name change from 'His Majesty' to 'Her Majesty'. Fortunately this provided the Treasury with no further expense as the cap tallies remained as HM, whatever the monarch's sex. I awaited each date venture with pleasant anticipation and was never disappointed. The only additional personal expenditure was the blanco for our belts, webbings and our caps, which needed it to keep the rain off in case of showers. Unfortunately, the weatherman's forecast proved accurate when 'heavy showers' were announced for all events, as Wolfy seemed to have no control over the weather.

Quite apart from guarding those rice bags, Wolfy was on overtime with the events in my new life. In April, minesweeper No. 1558 was due to pay a goodwill visit to the French ports and, contrary to all the advice given to me by Uncle Charles, Jim and his Uncle Jim never, under any circumstances, volunteer for anything you don't have to, I volunteered to join the trip. In this instance their

179

advice was prophetic, as even they could not have foreseen that the wooden ship made the entire crew of thirty-one men leap for their lives when she caught fire and sank off Ostend in the early hours of 16th April 1954. The survivors were taken aboard by a Dutch coaster and given a good meal on board the Dutch cruiser *Heemskerk*, although there is no record if they were given any hospitality ashore, either liquid or horizontal.

I, however, was not one of those survivors as I caught a heavy cold two days before she sailed; coughing and sneezing over my shipmates in such a confined space would have made the 'arse crawler' even less popular.

I also volunteered to be part of the parade of ratings along the Embankment with the other 1,499 when Her Majesty came aboard HMS *President* on 15th May as part of a Royal pageant. The officers had to wear swords but Wolfy had not supervised the stores, as many were unable to fulfil their true full-dress uniform attire. One of them was quoted in the press on the next day as saying: 'Anyhow, I wouldn't have known what to do with them.' If he had bothered to ask any of the 1,499 ratings, they could have given him the answer.

Almost one month later, Delby Coats was brought back to life with exciting news from the head buyer at Harrods. The company were commissioned to make a rain cape for the Queen. HM was going to take the salute on Horse Guard Parade to review the Golden Jubilee Parade, but the weather forecast for June was decidedly dodgy. Buck House contacted Harrod's to procure attire to keep HM dry for the event. At this time Harrods were buying rubberised rain capes from us and we were asked to make a special cape for the event. 'A cape for the Queen? ... You've got to be joking...' was Delby Coats' response. So all hands were assembled on deck, though Billy didn't have to go to the Palace to measure her bust or hips. Fortunately Prince Phillip had not got any special request for measurements and in any case we did not manufacture ties.

Ten days later the yellow satin cape was delivered to Harrods and all and sundry were glued to their TV sets on 12th June. Wolfy was off-duty when the heavens opened and HM stood on the dais on Horse Guards where two thousand officers and ratings were getting soaked during the hour-long review.

Contrary to the advice of everybody in and out of uniform I

had volunteered again and could see and feel the extra blanco run off my cap, belt and boot garters, making very pretty white streaks down my back and the navy-blue collar which I had taken so much trouble to iron and bang in with the traditional three turns on the collar.

However, I was sorely tempted to ask the Queen to touch it; after all, it was a sailor's prerogative to ask any of the opposite sex to touch his 'Dickey' for luck and I still wish I had.

What may have tempted me to volunteer for this event was the fact that HM, after the short religious service of dedication and remembrance, gave the traditional order of 'splice the mainbrace'. I was not UA and enjoyed the tot more than ever, but this time no sippers were available to anybody.

Those on parade from out of town came up by train and I had phoned Charles the previous evening if there was any possibility to change back into civvies after the event.

'Change back? ... You mean change out of, don't you? ... Will you need Mrs T to help you take your clothes off?' he said, to which I replied, 'I'll see how it goes.' 'OK,' said Charles, 'I'll see if she's free and put her on standby.'

After the parade we all disbursed and most of the lads walked up to Soho from Horse Guards Parade. If they were married, they returned to their dutiful wives, but those who were too far from their loved ones or too far away for the 48-hour pass, made their way back to their bases. Scouse, who had never been 'up the Smoke', came up to me in a dripping state.

'What you goin' to do now?'

This sounded very much like a GB to me. I looked him straight in the eyes, raised my eyebrows. 'We've never been ashore together and you've only told me that you have the wife and two little ones back in Huyton. As you asked the question, I'll ask you one: what would *you* like to do?'

He shrugged his shoulders. 'Dunno.'

'Listen, let's call a spade a bloody shovel!' I said.

A broad grin spread across his face. 'You're from up the Smoke where, me mates have told me, anything goes...'

I nodded. 'Tell you what, have you ever heard of threesomes?'

'Had that in the docks down at Bootle but it was up against the cold ship's side with this bird and a docky smelling of oil, so it was wet and very uncomfortable.'

'Do you fancy it in a nice warm bed with a brilliant lady and me?' He nodded acceptance. 'I'll make a phone call ... but what can I call you now? Is it "Scouse" or "Murphy" or just "Scumbag"?'

He stretched out his hand and gave me a huge grin. 'As I've got me Leading Hand rating, just call me "Hookey" or "Murph".'

Charles had planned everything down to the towels, which he felt were very necessary because 'you must be soaking wet'. I stopped him and told him about Murph and he roared with laughter. 'Better get another set of towels out!'

Grace said it was years since she had been in a *ménage à trois*, but never with two sailors. She laughed: 'It's a bit of a special offer ... two for the price of one.' I could hear Charles protesting in the background: '... Price ... what price? ... All I get is a thank-you.' And I could hear Grace stifle him with lots of kisses.

'Well ... what's happening?' asked Murph, when I came out of the phone box.

'It's all fixed but you'll have to put up with me as well, but as you have always called me "Shortarse", you'll have to find out if it's true.'

He looked horrified. ''Snot you I want to look at, it's 'er.'

'But you don't know what we are going to be doing, or the other way round.'

'Going to find out though, eh ... ?' he replied somewhat reluctantly.

Hours later he could not come up or down fast enough and agreed it was much better in a warm bed with a pint within reach on the night table than in a cold shipyard with a bird and a smelly dockie. Charles was most understanding but agreed that it sometimes pays dividends to be just an enthusiastic if lonely onlooker.

When we went down in the lift the next morning, Murph grabbed my hand, shook it vigorously and thanked me. 'Can I call you Dave from now on? Anyhow the "shortarse" is not true ... I'll give it to you in writing, I'll sign it, you'll have to write it. When's the next Coronation Parade?'

It had not taken me another twenty-five years to move towards Leading Hand rating, and thanks to the preparation of the officer on recruitment day plus the extra training time, I was on my way and could now enjoy the exalted rank of Able Seaman; Grace and Murph confirmed the 'Able' bit anyway. After being paid and given the extra 'splicing of the mainbrace' rum liquid, I really felt that life was very pleasant. Most of the time you did not know what was coming next ... in travel and or in bed.

The rest of the year travel consisted of visiting the Channel Islands, a trip to Hamburg to show the flag, the Kiel Canal and Copenhagen. We were the first three RN ships to enter Hamburg since the end of World War II and were reported in the local press with fanfares.

Pucky, my sister-in-law, had a brother-in-law who worked with Reuters in Hamburg and had told (warned) him of the impending arrival of a long-distance relative and when we came alongside I was 'piped' for and wondered what I had been up, or down, to. Jack was in his mid-twenties, had the overwhelming charm of a reporter wanting to smell the last gram of 'news' out of any story and had come aboard to see his very distant relation in the RN. 'Arse crawler's' stock rose with every step up the ladder to the tiny bridge. 'Cor ... hoo'se 'e then ... What's the photographer doin'?' The final touch of notoriety was when Jack spoke German to me. Murph stood open-mouthed and when he shut it pointed his thumb at me, commenting: ''E speaks foreign!'

The crews were later invited to the town hall and fêted with wine which had been supplied by a local wine merchant who had connections to the vineyards on the Rhine. The favourite for all the lads was a special Rhine wine with the name of 'Kraner Nacktarsch'. It was not so much the flavour of the wine that pleased the tongues of the matelots but the name of the label on the bottles which demonstrated the name by showing a little boy's naked bottom being whipped and slapped by the vintner, the translation of *Nacktarsch* being 'Naked arse'.

Both Murph and I were duty watch for two days but on day three we went ashore. I had asked Jack, the reporter, and he had prepared two lists for me. One was for the ordinary visitors to St Pauli, the red light district, while the second was a special insiders' list which was sheer filth. He didn't even ask which one we were interested in, and went to a place called the 'Grosse Freiheit', which I translated for Murph as 'Big Freedom' to which he started to rub the lower parts of his anatomy. The press always tells the truth and Jack couldn't have been more accurate with the description of this establishment. The two English sailors were hugged and kissed all the way to the bar by the scantily sequined and feathered hostesses. The blurb to the place said it was the 'heart of St Pauli', although I would have thought it was a bit lower down.

We both sat down on the bar stools and two of the girls wrapped themselves around us and drinks were put in front of us on the counter. Murph was much faster off the mark, as his lady appeared to have had previous experience of removing a pair of bells which had a flap held by two buttons and when the flap dropped down had two horizontal overlapping foldovers with buttons to fasten below the flap. Murph had gotten down to the bells being peeled off him. My lady had obviously never had the RN bellbottom experience and, without a copy of *Seamanship Manual Volume 1*, was literally stuck at the first flap. Being of gentlemanly disposition I lowered my head and lent down to assist her and my face touched and brushed against hers. The powder and perfume were very strong, but I was somewhat taken aback by the stubble on *his* cheek. I looked up at Murph, who had a very satisfied look on his face and I felt 'why not?' – in for a penny in for a mark. When we compared notes back on board Murph reluctantly admitted it was quite good but 779 was better.

Kiel was decidedly cool after our liquid and vertical excitement in Hamburg and our passage through the Kiel Canal, if not hair-raising, was within a hair's breadth of scraping other vessels in the narrow canal. In Copenhagen we came alongside the Carlsberg Brewery, and as it was shortly after the war the brewery supplied us with unlimited barrels of their famous brew.

Daily Orders on the first day ashore gave all the details of timing ashore, duty watches and so on and right at the bottom included a hopeful note:

'Remember the Danes were our Allies in the war.'

As most of us were in no way fit to read this, as we had tasted the liquid of our recent Allies, mayhem broke loose after the first liberty men had gone ashore. Any sign not cemented in outside the shops was nicked, but the proudest trophy was the sign from outside the police station, which, under protest, was the only one returned by perpetrators of the crime. The rest were proudly displayed on deck photographed for prosperity.

Copenhagen was highly organised regarding the purchase of the very explicit magazines of the naked male and female body. The market had just lifted all restrictions of photos of the human body and when I told Mike, my gynae friend, about this, he had asked me to bring back a few volumes as in their medical studies they could not obtain as clear photographic images as those available in the Danish porn magazines. Sadly, as they were all passed round the messdeck some got rather dog-eared before they reached the medical world of King's College.

The Tivoli Gardens were almost a religious haven after St Pauli but everything must come to an end which nearly came to the three little Cockleshell minesweepers which had been designed as 'Inshore' but could not withstand a Force 9 gale in the North Sea.

I cannot remember why I did not pass out when at the wheel but all I know is that I was in the company of all the Cockleshell non-heroes or to describe them as accurately as I can: We were all as sick as dogs and where Wolfy could have got to I can't think. Too sick I expect.

When we got ashore in Harwich I phoned central information at 'Balcomie' and Madame was over her blue sky as Hildegarde had arrived to dub her film *The Sinner* into English and all hands were mustered to go to party action stations. I cashed in a few 'sippers' for a day here and a day there and wrote to Jim with the relevant dates. With a few swaps of duty dates and sippers we liaised that he would be here to sample a bit of Hollywood in London. I had hoped that Scouse could have a sample lick, too, but, sadly, he got a draft on our return.

Even my Scottish very Lowlanders had never performed in public and when I informed them that I had now received my ticket as a 'performer' at the Albert Hall on Saturday 7th November 1953 they were a little surprised. 'Twice a day,' I told my Scottish friends 'at 14.30 and 19.00'. The RN had asked for volunteers for the 'Festival of Remembrance' at the Albert Hall in London, I had volunteered to perform covered in blue from head to bells. 'Balcomie' and all our friends were alerted to watch us on TV and Dad was over his Iron Cross moon to see uniformed me on the wide screen from his armchair, cigar in hand.

'Chiefie' Brown who had given me such a friendly welcome on *Chrysanthemum* last September, gathered his flock of twelve eager volunteers, or 'nutters' as he preferred to label them, and bussed us safely to the Albert Hall at 08.00hrs. We practised walking down from the wide stairs into the arena and on the first attempt only I and two others missed a step and were called back to the top by the Chief. On the second attempt only two were casualties, after which the Chief suggested we all picked our bloody feet up and held our heads high. When we tried it to the music of the Marine Band we must have been mesmerised by it as all went well. Chiefie was over his gold buttoned moon and gave us his warming praise.

'Do it like that this afternoon and evening, you'll have fuck all to worry about, but don't let it go to your ... you know where.'

When the stirring music of 'Heart of Oak' by the Marine Band reverberated around the Albert Hall in the afternoon and evening, the loudest cheers came for the Senior Service, but they were always the most popular, which generations of sailors had been able to confirm. Her Majesty, The Queen Mum, and Prince Phillip tried to out-clap each other but we were just glued to that first step down those wide stairs and fortunately could not be affected by the non-tot issue of rum which had been delayed until after the afternoon performance. It was worth every drop as the remarks and comments we received from the other messmates on our return were definitely up to the George Kieffer standard of eight years ago.

Always wanting to try everything everywhere I went to the other end of the social scale and asked Steffie if she would like to accompany me to a black-tie cocktail party at the Ski Club of Great Britain which was being hosted in Eaton Square two weeks later. She looked incredibly elegant and seductive when her and my black-tie picture appeared in the *The Tatler* in 'Jennifer's Journal' on 25th November. I don't think any of my messmates or Chiefie Brown saw it, nor did I tell them about it as I felt they would have told me what to do with the skis.

In the Xmas mail was a large envelope which held a copy of the July *Illustrated London News*. There was a short note from Louis Klemantaski stuck to its cover:

I think you will like the double-page spread of the July copy. Watch the copyright position, as the royalty angle is very dodgy and I can assure you Buck House Press Office would be very reluctant to let you use it bylined with: 'Her Majesty is modelling a Delby Coats cape'. Just buy a few copies and send them to your best clients and attach a note quoting the publication, the date and add: 'As featured in ...' and captioned with:

**'... the Queen wore a yellow cape ...
throughout the parade continuous rain
fell and the Queen wore a yellow cape ...
on parade in the rain ...'**

186

which were the descriptions under the four photographs. You could add a personal note by hand-signing it with: 'Wishing you a Happy and Dry Xmas with a Delby cape ... like HM'.

Louis finished the note off with a suggestion that the next time I'm out in the rain so near his flat off Trafalgar Square he'd 'take some shots himself and get you dried out upstairs with a bottle of Vodka. My neighbour, Hannan Swaffer, can have a séance and, being in the photography game, we'll see what develops. He's always got a few fillies ready to call up with the spirits.'

Jim had also traded some of his leave days with his messmates and our organisational planning worked a treat. Not over Xmas, because they were the days 'traded' with the happy fathers who could then enjoy the actual Xmas days with their little ones. I came back to 'Balcomie' on 29th December and Jim arrived one day later. I had warned Uncle Charles and he was over his moon that two sailors could come and visit him on the 30th. 'Not like the last time when we and all those uniforms were on the floor,' he added with a touch of sarcasm.

Charles welcomed Jim like a long-lost friend and pushed a lager towards him with a smile. 'Now tell me, Jim. Are you still enjoying the wine, women and song that all those sailors join the Navy for?'

Jim raised his eyebrows, looked Uncle Charles in the eyes and took a deep breath. 'David has told me that apart from the daily papers and *Drapers Record* you are a bit of a bookworm, and I'm a little surprised you have swallowed that most misquoted little saying and wondered if you knew how old it is and who said it first all those centuries ago?'

'You're dying to tell me, aren't you, Jim?' said Uncle Charles.

Jim laughed aloud and nodded: 'If I were back on board I'd say "It'll cost you" but seeing you're part of Dave's mishpoche, I'll tell you for free ... well, perhaps sippers...'

'Old Churchill,' he began, 'once quoted Sir Peter Gratton as allegedly having said something about "naval tradition being nothing but rum, sodomy and the lash", but it goes back much further and the actual quote is:

"Who loves not woman, wine and song,
remains a fool his whole life long".

'And the next time Dave's on the Continent he can check it in

187

Warburg in Germany, because the person who said it was none other than Martin Luther.'

Uncle Charles stared at me: 'He's not only a nice fellow but he's a walking edition of the *Encyclopaedia Britannica*. I think you should ask him and yourself what you intend to do after '56 when you both come out.'

'I'm out in '56,' answered Jim, 'and you are out a few months later in '57 but I'll keep a lookout to see what I can find and flog to the natives. Mind you, the Shinto travellers' shrine is pretty but I don't think we'll break any sales records with it. Meanwhile I'll find something to keep me amused and Pucky was dropping some heavy hints about helping her with the garden when they moved into Uplands Close. Dad and I had an allotment and he's taught me to tell the difference between weeds and flowers...' and he pointed a finger at me and grinned all over his face. 'You don't know a weed from a rose, do you, Dave?'

And before I could agree or dispute the sad truth, Charles walked over, put his arm around the two of us and gave a big smile: 'That's settled then. I'll play Tom Avery and put you in touch with my accountant and solicitor. I'll set up a meeting between you two and my shipper who moves all the goods to the UK from Europe because there's all the shipping formalities, duties and other costs which...'

I interrupted him. 'So that's what that Bonwit Teller lady in New York was saying when she mentioned price ... "landed in dollars"?'

Charles was grinning from ear to ear. 'You'll be having to do that, Jim, if you are going to run him and the office.'

And in unison, Charles and I said: 'Look around, boy, and see if there's anything you have missed ... and you've got about eighteen months to find it.'

Tale 24

Dipchicks

The Xmas card I received from Jim had an AA voucher in it. The short note said it was a 'Cheers, mate' from one of his L/EMs that Jim had done a duty watch for when the lad had to rush home to be at the missus's side because junior was two months early. 'Bad timing' was Jim's comment. 'But at least we've got a free AA open booking Dover–Calais because of his holding-hands duty watch with the wife!' Jim's furtive little brain had already mentally put it to good use. 'You can take me to Paris for just the cost of the petrol, we can have a good look around to see what we have missed in the shops in the UK and on the way out we can be at Joyce's wedding in Eastbourne on 9th April. Might even get a look at that new DS Citroën if it's in showrooms on the Champs Elysées. All the best and it's just as well "Old Sparks" is doing some planning for you. In case your Jackspeak has missed it, we call it "Getting your hand in".'

Jim's sister Joyce could have been his twin apart from her looks and being four years younger. She was even quieter than Jim and I don't know how Reg could have heard her 'Yes' when he asked that 'Will you marry me?' question. She sounded like Jim, had the same caustic humour and certainly used one word instead of ten when she could. But Joyce was as sharp as one of those crab shells that Jim's Dad had taught him to catch below Beachy Head. The problem for me was I was not there to pop the question and, in any case, I did not even know her at that point.

Dad had died on 7th February 1954 and eighteen months later the house in Uplands Close was completed and Pucky had to terminate her modelling as the first offspring was on the way. Billy and Pucky's timing had been immaculate and young Peter Franklin saw the first Sheen light of day on 28th January 1956. Madame was over the moon to have confirmation that number two was planned within the foreseeable future.

I now concentrated on climbing up the greasy ladder of promotion and went down to Eastbourne to receive instructions from Uncle Jim whose vast RN experience stretched over twenty-one years. He did not have to instruct me in sail-making as by this time the RN had diesel engines and I had no wish to be sworn at by the lusty stokers from Glasgow, Rosyth and all points north and east. 'Bends and Hitches' still had a place in the *Seamanship Manual*, and every budding seaman had to know those pages backwards. My trade was Seaman, more popularly known as a 'deck ape'. However, it did have the one advantage that, if you wanted to go on deck to get some fresh air, you did not stick out like a sore arm as long as you carried a bucket. But all the most relevant information on that score came not from any book but from Uncle Jim. After all, he had been perfecting that game for twenty-one years. This situation resulted in stories whose contents rivalled those of *Gulliver's Travels*, if not necessarily *One Thousand and One Nights*.

One of the favourite clean ones went back to 1929 when he was aboard '*Royal Oak*' doing his signalling at Gibraltar. 'We were coming in to dock and the skipper was always very fussy about the way his laundry was done. He had this arrangement with a washerwoman ashore who had been a maid in one of those big country houses in Yorkshire. She washed his shirts spotlessly clean and ironed and starched his stiff white dress collars a treat. So when we were about to come alongside, he got me to send her a signal and prepare herself for her imminent collection of the dirty washing.

'Being a "bunting tosser" I knew me Lord Nelson's "England expects" signal backwards, and the famous one he ordered just before he died which SHOULD follow it... "Engage the enemy more closely", but somehow or other I made a big cock-up of this one. The woman always came aboard as soon as we were alongside, so I sent: "Please send Admiral's woman". When the Chief Yeoman heard about it, he did his nut. You should have seen him, runnin' around like a blue-arsed fly he was. And then he came on deck, went to the flag locker, pushed a set of flags into me hand and shouted "send these, chop-chop". You never argue with a Chief, do you, so I sent the signal which referred to the date of the previous signal, its time and group number and added the new message: "Please insert washer between Admiral and woman".'

'Did they?' asked Jim.

'Don't know, but there was a hell of a bollocking for the Chief Yeoman.'

Uncle Jim also extended my own Franklin English Volume I Dictionary whose foundation was laid by 'Jamie' at Hampton Grammar School and the three volumes of William Shakespeare. A few words were added with the help of the Canadian sailor in Chiswick and later some Americanisms from Green and Park Street plus the recent additions from the US of A, Volume II is being constantly abridged with Jackspeak. The word 'diving' is a fairly recent addition as that word to me meant something to do with 'Stukas' diving during World War II or diving with a huge deep-sea dome-like helmet, made of steel or copper.

In my dictionary 'V' did not stand for 'Victory' but 'Volunteer', so when the two words 'Diving Volunteers' appeared on Daily Orders Franklin was there in the queue. Although Jacques Cousteau's brilliant films and TV shows were at that time intoxicating the nation with images of sun-drenched lagoons and warm waters, only three others had volunteered to swim down this dreamy watery road which turned out to be Horsea Island near Portsmouth Harbour on that bleak, grey, freezing morning of 28th February 1956.

The firm but pleasant manner of our Chief reminded me of someone straight out of Noel Coward's wartime naval epics, as we closed up around him on our first day at the RN Diving School by a lake and a wooden watchtower.

'Gather aroun' me,' he said in a lovely 'Ampshire drawl.

'From today, you're moi little dipchicks and if you look at moi sleeve, it says "SW" under a doivin' 'elmet. Nothin' to do with silly wankers, it stands for "Shallow Water' doivin" and moi problem is to always make sure that when you doive you come up again or oi'll have to dip in and get moi chicks out and when you do some serious doivin' remember our three Ss: "stay slim, streamlined and silent".'

I never discovered until later if he was married or not, or had a messdeck of kids, but he certainly deserved them as for the next four weeks he treated us as lovingly as newly laid chick eggs. Our biggest cock-ups were always solved by his saying 'Never moind, little dipchick ... Oi'll sortit out for you,' and he always did.

191

'Rubber suit too big? ... Oi'll get you another ... Too small, don't worry, moi little dipchick ... Oi'll get you a larger one ... Face mask all steamed up ... dip it in the 'oggin...' And the odd part was he never *really* swore at us and the only thing he said every night was 'Go and get pissed but always wrap up well ... if you catch a cold you go to bed ... alone ... or it's your last dip.'

After four weeks he felt all his chicks were ready for dipping and, even though the temperature outside was now –1°C, we dived in. 'Never mind me, little chicks ... keep moving around and keep your hands warm.' This proved very difficult as when you climbed stiff and cold back up the steel ladder, your hands stuck to the steel in a very unhappy marital embrace, leaving a little skin stuck to the metal ladder. All went well at the last test: nose clips tight, mask to face ... perfect ... flippers the right size, oxygen checked AOK. Chiefie waved us off with a 'Best of luck, chicks.' And then I sneezed, blowing the mask off my face. It was the only time I heard Chief curse. 'You've been down 'ere all this time, kept your nose clean and on the last bloody day you catch a bleedin' cold. It's no doive for you tomorrow.' After he dismissed us he called me over.

'Never moind, you can take it again in a couple of months but when we all have a pint tonoight and oi give you all your SW golden badges for your Number Ones, oi'll keep yours when you come down again ... and oi'll promise you oi'll sew it on meself ... the missus will anyhow.'

Eight weeks later his wife did an almost Gieves job of sewing the gold helmeted SW badge onto my Number Ones best uniform and after a few pints he told me about the latest buzz going around Horsea.

Up to World War II shallow water diving was unheard of, as water pressures down to 33 feet were unknown. When the Italian navy started experimenting at this level they found that the use of oxygen overcame this problem with the use of a face mask. During the war they trained and equipped rubber-suited teams, and two-man teams started to attack British shipping underwater, attaching limpet mines to RN ships at anchor. The RN still had the 'Britain rules the waves' complex and at first pooh-poohed the idea, but when RN ships were attacked at anchor in Alexandria and Gibraltar they started to listen to this theory. Among the Brits was Lieutenant Commander 'Buster' Crabb, an eighteenth-century buccaneer type who, if told not to do anything, did it! He got himself a 'wet suit' in Gibraltar and when the ghost Italian swimmers next arrived to fix their limpet mines to RN ships at anchor, he followed the Italians back to their base in Spain. It was the beginning of the SW Diving Branch of the RN.

A major diplomatic row had just been caused when the Russian cruiser *Ordzhonikidze* had paid a 'goodwill visit' to the UK with Nikita Kruschev aboard. The RN knew that the Russians had the latest underwater equipment aboard so both the Russians and the Brits were more alert to the ships being 'looked at' under water at Portsmouth. Lt Cdr Crabb was officially retired but the Chief had had a pint with him before the Russians reported that someone had been trying to spy on their cruiser underwater. The Brits, of course, denied any possible involvement with this. Chiefie said that there were now three buzzes going around; No. 1 was that the Russians had caught Crabb, beheaded him and ditched him back in the water. No. 2 was that they had caught him, paid and settled all his bills and taken him back to Moscow where he 'sang' and told them all about our diving plans. No. 3 was that the Brits had let him do the looking and then chopped his head off as dead men tell no tales.

After Chiefy had told me the story, he added: '... and to date no one has said anything and they have all stayed shtum.' He looked around him in the pub and turned his back to me. 'Can't see him in 'ere tonight. Oi'd recognise him just like that. After all, Buster was a dipchick under me, just like you.'

On 9th June 1957 a headless and handless body was washed up in Chichester Harbour but the only identification was an unusual wetsuit. The official cause of death and identity could not be established.

When I got back the lads all gathered around to admire the golden helmet with the SW below it.

'Bet you did'nee sow that on!' commented Jock from the Gorbals.

'Corse he did'nee,' said his mate from Galashiels.

'I heard the Chief's missus did it for Shortarse...'

Janner interrupted Jock No. 2. 'You know why she did it for 'im? He's a dipchick, int'e but that's not all he dips, I bet.'

The horseplay, albeit verbal, ceased when the PO from the Reg Office appeared with a draft chit and handed it to me.

'Bloody 'ell' was the general consensus, and 'Elephant' from the Old Kent Road said:

'Talk about arse crawling, there ain't no more room up there ...
What is it this time ... then?'

I looked at the chit which told me to report to HMS *Vernon*
after I had finished some sea time at HMS *Hornet* at Gosport. This
would help me at HMS *Vernon* to get my 'hook' as Leading
Seaman.

When I reported all this back to Jim he grinned all over his
face. 'It's about time you did some real work for a change ... You
won't have any spare time once we get going in that firm of ours.
Have you thought of a name for it yet? From your various labels
you have acquired, I don't really think "Arse Crawler (Unlimited)"
would go down well with the Harrods' buyers. As for "shallow
water diver", might keep the rain off but it's more akin to your
Scottish friends' "muff diving".' That was about as rude as I had
ever heard Jim get.

'But do you know anything about *Hornet* at all?'

I shook my head. 'C'mon, tell us and I bet it's nothing to do
with bees.'

He glared at me. 'You know Victoria Barracks backwards and
don't confuse it with Victory Barracks of our Lord Nelson fame.
Across Pompey Harbour is Gosport with a small creek which is
the home to submarines and motor torpedo boats and you should
know that they are the two branches of the Puss where you sail
in boats and not ships. The submariners' cap tallies are "HM
Submarine" and the lads with MTB's cap tallies are "HMMTB"
for "Motor Torpedo Boat". They are berthed alongside each other
like sardines in a can up the Haslar Creek, which gives some
justification to some of the lads, who say they, are literally "up
the creek without a paddle".

'To get to either speedily you walk across a very high and
wobbly wooden bridge which, on a rough day, the lads have
rechristened "Pneumonia Bridge". During World War II the MTBs
from HMS *Hornet* caused havoc with enemy shipping and it was
referred to as the "Hornet Nest". At night, the throb of their engines
was frequently mistaken for the sound of German aircraft attacking
Pompey and Gosport.' Jim came up for air and looked at me. 'You
always romanticise about your days at *Hornet*, why do you think
that is?'

'A mixture of things,' I replied scratching my head. 'It was like
a small family for a start. Only a midi very wet behind the ears

194

and at the mercy of a two or two-and-a-half ringer and, of course the Chief who could eat him for breakfast and wouldn't even burp. The crew were a small band of experts and the "Killick" of the mess ruled them with a rod from a powerful diesel engine which roared like those six Aston Martins setting off for Le Mans. We were on top of each other as space was non-existent. When I came aboard, "Blondie" Haynes, my Killick, welcomed me like a long lost brother, shook his head and his thin blond mane portrayed loving kindness which hid an iron steel firmness which he kept under control unless provoked.

'Not much room aboard for anything and we don't have no cats to swing,' he said and ten minutes later we had completed the "grand" tour and when I asked him where to sling my hammock he grinned: 'Best place for that is Victoria Barracks 'corse there's no room here for that. We've got bunks, problem is the designers of these boats like the subs, always reckon that with "Duty Watches" at night, roughly ten per cent will be on watch so you don't need equal numbers of bunks for the same number of blokes. They plan nine bunks for ten blokes and like the subs, we have what's called "Hot bunking", one empty bunk is always warm as the bloke has just gone on watch. If somebody is in the "rattle", they change the "U" to an "O", so watch it.'

'What did you think of the poster in the "Heads"?' he asked.

'Didn't notice,' I shrugged as he took me back to the single WC. He opened the little cabin door and there was a poster pinned to the inside of the door and it read: 'There's an opening for you in the Navy.'

I was totally baffled and blurted out, 'But that's that recruiting poster that went up all over the place when the Korean War started,' and Blondie nodded his head.

'Yeah, good in'it, they've got two pictures put together. One is a photo of dozens of ships and the other is this matelot looking at all of 'em. He's standing there, clenched fists on his hips and he's lookin' at the fleet, back to the camera and you can see these ships through the wide-apart legs with the "Bells" framing the ships. Then there's the big rainbow shaped message which stretches from the matelots arse right across to his hips, over and across which says:

"There's an opening for you in the Navy" and you can't get hold of one for money or sippers. That's why it's in here safe and sound.'

195

Jim was grinning from ear to ear, 'But apart from that, did you meet with any of the lads from the subs at HMS *Dolphin*?' and I nodded.

'When I came back one night with a "Bunting Tosser" I'd met in the pub he asked me if I'd like to come aboard the sub for sippers, and you know me, I'll try anything once and climbed down the conning tower after him but no thanks, he had to take me back up top straight away and he came aboard our MTB and shared my sippers.

'I'll tell you, Jim, the lack of space doesn't worry me on the Piccadilly Line in London, but the sub claustrophobia is not my ticket. What I did love though was being on that tiny MTB bridge, the wind whistling past your face like skiing downhill at Davos, being told to take her up to 40 knots. It was exciting when she rose majestically out of the water, her sharp bows cut the sea like a band saw cutting wood. The water made a fine spray on both sides of the boat forming a graceful white arc astern over the deep blue sea. And I got paid for it and got a free tot at noon every day.

'We also went out with the radio-controlled little boats (the RCBs) that had a skeleton crew but could and *should* have been controlled by us with a small, black box, aboard the mother ship, but the boffins took three months to sort out the electrics on RCB 8204 before they got their knickers out of the twist.

'Perhaps Ronnie Purcell retired too early. You'll have to ask him when you send him your Xmas card.'

On 27th September I received a letter from the Diving Officer informing me of a vacancy for a permanent L/SEA Diver. Had I been ten years younger and not made plans to dive away permanently from the RN to private life, I would have punched my clenched right fist in the air and shouted, '*Yes*'. My codicil to this acceptance would have been, 'Providing it is in tropical waters and by a sleepy lagoon', but as neither were mentioned I replied: 'Thank you, but no thank you.'

Our trip to Paris had me glued to the shop windows for two days, while Jim, the instigator of this expedition, made detailed notes. What appeared to me to be the governing sales factor was the strong colour scheme of all the merchandise, particularly in French and Italian knitwear. On the last night up in Montmarte we were into our pleasant second bottle of *vin ordinaire*. Jim was collating all the info as if he were tying together the loose ends of one of his wiring circuits. 'Remembering your problems about the weight and quantity of samples, I think it wants to be beautiful strong-coloured knitwear, light in weight with all the colours of a rainbow,' he said, and suddenly I felt as if I were listening to a seasoned buyer at Harrods, not Jim, the seasoned sailor.

'Well, now that's settled,' he went on, 'we can talk about it in length when I take you skiing at Xmas. I've got some money saved up plus the bits in lieu of sippers. We can ask Uncle Charles's shipping friends if they ever get freebies on travel and haggle a deal with 'em to the snowy wastes of Switzerland or Austria. If it works, we can do the shops for a winter range. You've told me that the rag trade works to a summer and winter range so we can kill two birds with one ski stick.'

The Schweizerhof in Kitzbühel was like a picture postcard in a winter wonderland and it was as unreal to me as the Pacific Ocean had been on the beach in California. New Year's Eve at Guido Reisch, with the champagne corks popping, had me clinking glasses with Jim at the bar as we wished each other a 'Prosit Neujahr' for 1957. Jim had bade the RN farewell in the summer of 1956; I was due to leave by the spring of 1957.

Kitzbühel is one of the lower ski resorts and the snow disappeared after three days. This did not disturb Jim one little bit. His orders tumbled down from the room's balcony as if he were back on the flight deck aboard HMS *Unicorn.* 'When you go into the shops and ask about the manufacturer's name, they're bound to think you are a spy working for a competitor ... Wave your passport at them and tell them you want to buy goods for the UK.' It worked like a dream and when we left Kitzbühel, we had the name of two of the suppliers of the Italian knitwear in the shops: Maria Bosco and Avagolf.

Jim's new draft had been to HMS *Balcomie*, where he had obtained a wooden board, placed it on the bed as soon as it was made and put the typewriter and phone on it. This was now his office. The typewriter arrived with Jim and originated in Devonport by kind permission of a Chief who had haggled for the 'Olympia' in Hong Kong and got it for £5. The first letter sent (by two-finger exercise) was to Maria Bosco in the tiny Northern Italian village of Viggiù asking if they wanted a rep in the UK. The answer came in the affirmative but only after their range was ready in the late summer which was just after I would leave the RN.

L/Seaman Franklin changed back into civvies and set off like Columbus on his journey of discovery but this time there was no Rhoda to cheer me on my way.

Tale 25

Anything to Declare?

Billy and Pucky's move made my task of selling 'Balcomie' much easier, although Madame was eventually swayed by the worsening monetary situation at Delby Coats. Sales were disappearing and, although I had put my feelers out by adding knitwear to the range, that had to be paid for as well. There was now only one way to survive and the cost of running 'Balcomie' was horrendous. Jim paid his weekly whack but not threats but only action could persuade Madame that 'Balcomie' should go on the market. This took place, although I neither received the codicil money in lieu of Billy's house, not did I ever receive half of the balance of the sale. Charles shrugged his shoulders and said, 'C'est la vie!' and Jim just added, 'Forget it.' We, with Madame, moved into a very nice two-bedroom apartment at Courtlands on the Upper Richmond Road and Jim set up another office on the bed after I had left in the mornings to sell my new Maria Bosco collection.

There was no room to sling our hammocks as we left them behind anyway. Uncle Charles was our major sheet anchor and we kept in constant touch with him which now brought us into direct contact with his accountants in Ilford, Knight Bland & Co. It was not only their advice but also their follow-up which propelled our midget company into an international trading organisation. We made no move without their expert advice and they were directly responsible for increasing our staff.

When Jim had left the RN he wanted to 'chill out' and he helped Billy and Pucky to get their Uplands Close garden straight. When he had broken the back of this and avoided breaking his own back, he was attracted by an advert in the paper by one of the leading manufacturers of self-assembly office furniture. He was drawn by the wording in the advert, as they were looking for an 'Export

Chaser' and as he had chased so many things in his naval life, he went for the job. It involved making sure that deliveries were shipped on time and got to their intended export customers in one piece.

His immediate boss was looking forward to his retirement and his only remaining objective in life appeared to be to fill his little black notebook, which listed his staff's daily misdemeanours by the hour.

When Jim was called into the man's office after six months, he was treated to a tirade, mainly regarding lateness. But the final straw was a client in Nigeria who complained about the sparse assembly instructions he'd been given. After three tightly typed pages, the lady writing the complaint finished the letter with: '... We are very surprised and disappointed with our goods as we have never had any problems with your erections before.' Jim thought this was an excellent moment to call it a day, asked for his cards and left.

When he told Madame and me this story at suppertime I was horrified, not at his misdemeanour but purely at the prospect of him going on the dole. That morning I had been to see the accountants in Ilford and presented them with a minute description of my working day. As a result, I proved their point that I was spending more time on paperwork which I had created than actually writing orders. Mr Bland took off his horn-rimmed glasses and looked at me sternly but pleasantly and said:

'Fact 1: The goods you are selling are being bought by all the leading customers in your customer file. They must be the right products.

Fact 2: You are spending more than 50 per cent of your possible selling time on paperwork.

Consequence: If you had someone to do the paperwork you would sell at least 25 per cent more goods.

Action 1: Get someone to do the paperwork.

Action 2: Get another salesman to sell your saleable goods.'

'Well,' Jim said, 'I will sort out your office as from 07.30hrs starting tomorrow and I'll look through my diaries to see if there's a name of anyone I can trust whom I can contact c/o Admiralty London.'

He started at 07.30hrs in the morning and also wrote off to an ex-shipmate who was traced by c/o Admiralty to Lossiemouth in

Scotland and he joined the company as a prospective trainee salesman the following year.

Mr Bland of Knight Bland was very pleased with the results of the expansion of the office staff and after six months we recorded an increase of 50 per cent on our sales, the profits started to build up and so did the tax. But then, that was Mr Bland's problem, after all we employed him to reduce our tax liabilities.

Madame still had her 'old ladies' sit-ins' over the weekends and we really wanted to get some fresh air and get away from the flat. Jim suggested we look for a cheap broken-down cottage between London and the South Coast to relax for weekends. Every time I was away within in a radius of seventy-five miles from London I called on estate agents and after a month we received details of broken-down properties in the requested area. We categorised them by price, as all we had in the way of cash was the £250 gratuity which Her Majesty had pressed into Jim's lily-white hands on his departure and completion of fourteen years' service.

After a year's search we eventually found our broken-down seventeenth-century dream cottage with a third of an acre of freehold land, but with just one tap, no main drainage or electricity. But then for £250 haggled down from £500 we couldn't really complain, as it turned out to be the biggest export business puller. Being able to ask our European clients to spend two days at an old English cottage provided us with brownie points vis-à-vis our competitors. Within two years Jim had to start a German, Swiss and Austrian 'Grosse Bitte' file for our clients, to whom 'Killicks' was an 'English must' on visits to purchase British goods.

We were determined to help the Chancellor's cry of 'export or die' and it helped that he had introduced new tax legislation. This made business expenses non-deductible for UK clients but totally tax-deductible for foreign customers. This was brought home to us when we visited a 'press do' just as this legislation had been brought in. We attended the annual exhibition in Harrogate hosted by the Menswear Association of Britain. On the first night the trade press had a huge party and when we signed in they had a long list of expected arrivals. We gave our company name, they ran their finger down the list and looked up at us and smiled: 'Ah yes,' the lady said, 'I think we have you down as coming from Nigeria buying British goods for exports,' and pinned a Nigerian flag onto our lapel which classified us as a 'tax-deductible expenses' export client.

Other measures were also introduced by the Chancellor to stop the flow of the sterling out of the UK, and one of the restrictions imposed to 'save the pound' was the limit on holiday foreign currency everyone was allowed to take out every year. When this reduced down to £25 per annum, the amount drawn on business was listed in your passport and just before Mitch, our new salesman, drove me to the airport, we called in on the bank en route to pick up my limitless business Swiss francs and folded them into my passport. On arrival at Heathrow I walked through Customs and was stopped by a stern-looking water guard with a sort of 'got ya' look.

'Could you step in here, please?' he said, pointing to a cubicle. 'Have you any foreign currency?' He permitted himself a forced smile as I handed him the bulging passport which just held the loose pack of Swiss francs.

He raised his eyebrows, gave a small cough and whispered: 'You are aware, Sir, that there is a currency limit for travellers out of the UK?' I nodded. 'But you have far more here than the permitted legal amount.' He had not even counted the amount.

I gave him the most benevolent of smiles but really wanted to tell him what to do in my best Jackspeak but in my best 'Upper Deck' tone of voice said: 'Oh yes, Officer, if you would care to look at the last page, you will see it is all for business.'

He flicked through the passport to the page of listed items, almost dropping all the loose notes onto the floor.

'Oh,' he said, running his finger down the page. 'Why didn't you tell me you were going out on business?'

And remembering Tom, I gave him a very large smile and said: 'But, Officer, you never asked!'

Tale 26

You Should Be So Lucky

After a year, the knitwear sales from Viggiù rocketed but as they were invoiced to Delby Coats their settlement payments dried up. My patience finally snapped and I said that unless the goods they had received and sent to customers were paid to the Italians, I would resign, take over the outstanding debts to the Italians and reluctantly leave Delby Coats who went into bankruptcy on the 20th May 1960. When I told Charles that night all he said was: 'It's a bit late in the day but at least you are out of it.' I promptly flew off to Italy, where fortunately they listened to my suggestion to repay the debt with commissions I earned in the future and agreed to my proposals. Neither they, Jim nor I ever looked back on this and we traded with them for many more happy years.

When I told the story and it's final outcome, Charles seemed totally relieved, shook my hand, got up, pressed a letter into my hand, and looked at Jim and me.

'You know I told you I was selling high-class ladies couture from Vienna. Preminger's are charming and very reliable people and, because Vienna is pretty small, friends of theirs, who are the best men's shirt manufacturers in Austria, asked Preminger's if they could recommend a good British agent who is selling into the top-end British retail shops, and who do you think I recommended?'

Jim glared: ''Corse, we sell to Harrods, Austin Reed, Hector Powe...'

Charles stopped him. 'That's precisely why I suggested you. It wasn't just because of your pretty faces or your horizontal prowess.'

I grinned at Charles. 'You go to see them twice a year, don't you? Do you think we could as well? Nothing like having a good waltz through the Vienna woods is there?'

'Sorry to spoil your five-finger Viennese waltz,' said Charles, 'but this letter says that the younger brother, Kurt, is coming over next week to have a good sniff at *you*.'

'Does he speak English?' asked Jim.

Charles gave his smooth Maurice Chevalier smile. 'Just a little, I think, he went to college in Brighton and university at Manchester where he met a fellow student whose father invented the drip-dry shirts. Naturally the Schapiras now make them for the European market. Kurt is the younger of the two brothers, is six foot tall and looks a bit like Danny Kaye. The Viennese models who come over to show the Preminger collection for me here in London are always dying to have a ride with him in his blue Alfa Romeo in Vienna.'

When we got back to the flat that night neither Jim nor I could think straight and he didn't even light a cigar.

'Still awake?' I asked in the middle of the night. He turned to me and just said: 'Good ... in't it?' and sat up like a stiff shirt dripping dry, stretched out his hands, opened his palms and said: 'In your best kosher speak, you should be so lucky...' He paused. 'Let's just say ... never worse...'

And before I could even answer, he was fast asleep.

Kurt was the most 'English' of all our Continental friends, his English was perfect and he was the easiest of persons to do business with. We went to the old Army and Navy Club, which was now the Institute of Directors, which Kurt loved.

Kurt kept us in the lounge until after midnight where he put a business proposition to us. I felt then that neither Jim nor I knew we wouldn't get a wink of sleep that night either.

Tale 27

Flower Power

After the family trauma and the resulting zero balance on my personal bank account I thought Wolfy and his brood of pups had finally deserted me. I will never know whether it was the third or fifth litter of little Wolfy's which suddenly knocked on my door.

When we met Schapira for the second time the next day he put his cards face up on the table and told us he was a stand-in for his brother who was recovering from a car accident. Any decision taken by us in London would have to be discussed and ratified in Vienna but the broad outline was as follows:

'We've obviously done a bit of homework in Vienna and everything we've heard about you appears to be quite kosher. Jim, we don't know but we can always have that done later in Vienna...' and Jim stopped him.

'Actually that won't be necessary ... I had to have that kosher bit done after we'd been ashore in Trincomalee. I got a rash and the doctors thought I'd caught the boat up...' and Kurt stopped him and sparked, 'I do know what that is, the boys in Brighton told me when they taught me English slang, but sorry Jim, I stopped you.'

'Well is wasn't that but simply we still wore those very tight and hot bells and the heat and rubbing ... I got a heat rash and the doctors said I would have to get that piece cut off to save further problems and although it was a bit painful at my age, I've lived with it and had it off without any problem...' and Kurt was grinning from ear to ear as the boys in Brighton had also explained what that little phrase meant.

'What Erich and I have discussed is the possibility of you selling SMARTO shirts and pyjamas on a trial basis for about two seasons and then you buy them from us and sell them to your customers, landed with a wholesaler's profit margin which could be anything from 15 to 25 per cent, which is roughly the margin AMC takes' I nodded at the mention of the word 'landed'. 'Your reputation preceded my arrival and as you are a friend, sort of, Preminger and Maria Bosco both speak highly of you. I think our business should increase no end if you sell SMARTO shirts and pyjamas 'landed' to Harrods and the others. You can undercut AMC by at least 10 per cent and still make a nice profit.

'And if you are worried about having no finance, Franz Preminger had told me about your ... family and the financial burden. We'll try the agency bit for six months and if it works, see how much capital you will need and I'll find a backer for you...' He gave me a very benevolent smile. 'OK, is it?' I didn't even have time to ask him for a name for our new trading company.

'Mind you, there will probably be two backers ... You don't mind that, will you?'

In the event I was not really surprised that neither Jim nor I did not sleep a wink for the third night, we had too many Wolfy puppies to count.

SMARTO shirts were beautifully tailored and their fabrics came from all over the world. In fact, selling them was not like selling sand to the Arabs but clean fresh water to their dry throats. They were very flexible in their production and when Carnaby Street and the Beatles arrived in the mid-1960s Kurt came over and we searched the market for 'flower power' cloth.

'Get me these fabrics and you can start another business.' I blinked. Kurt opened his third pack of Lucky Strikes and offered them to Jim and me. I didn't smoke but Dad had weaned Jim on the small Castello cigarillos and Kurt nearly kissed Jim. 'I never know what to bring from the duty free in Schweschacht. Now I know, I'll get a box next time.' And to demonstrate that he had not forgotten all the slang he had acquired in Brighton he added, 'Come to think of it ... I'll buy up all the bloody stock in the shop.'

Kurt and Erich loved British tailoring and hand-made shoes and always spent time buying cashmere blazers and Jermyn Street shirts. When we had finished the 'foundation' idea, Kurt and I wandered down to Jermyn Street and gawped when the shops were full of shirts featuring roll-neck shirts in flower patterns.

'I've got to get back to Vienna tonight but can you do me a

favour and buy a selection of which you think are saleable patterns and styles and send them out by courier. Meanwhile, get on to your friend at Austin Reed. They have far more shops than Harrods and with your sales patter and our roll-neck shirts, offer them GB exclusivity for twelve months in return for mass coverage through their chain of shops.'

At the airport Kurt waved me good-bye but then turned on his heels, grabbed my hand and said: 'You'll have to think of a name and start that West End Office of yours fast. I've got a very simple idea for you and Jim. Just call it David Franklin Ltd, then there's no problem with the goods you sell. They told me at university in Manchester that English companies can trade anything except girls or brothels. You hadn't planned to go down that road just now, had you?'

I shook my head. 'I'd rather go down Jermyn Street tomorrow and buy those shirts from Turnbull and Asser, get them to you by courier, receive your made-up flower ones with a roll-neck collar and ring Claude Leaver at Austin Reed. I think he'll like the "exclusive to Austin Reed" bit quite a lot.'

In the event he did, thank you very much, and the only change he haggled was that the exclusive period was increased to twenty-four months in return for an increase of price by 5 per cent. The customers were delighted, Claude was very happy, British Commercial Transport (BCT) in Blackfriars shipped them over, filling their half-full trucks, and our company's new account at Barclays Bank grew.

The Schaps were pleased with the trading name and we became their official buying agents in the UK, and BCT phoned Jim the next day asking for an appointment regarding our apparently larger amounts of business.

I was out of the flat when Jack Palmer from BCT introduced himself after asking where the 'heads' were. Jim tackled him about the 'heads', followed closely by 'What were you in then?' 'Destroyers,' was the answer, and when I returned two hours later, they were still knee-deep in the Med, on their way to all points east in carriers, destroyers, chasers and liberty boats. Tom Avery's 'services bond' was in full swing and from that moment onwards Jim was always one step ahead of any competitor, who found his freight docs and custom entry forms now placed below ours.

By the beginning of 1963, it was blatantly obvious, especially to Jim, that the wooden board on top of the bed was getting to breaking point, and when I met Mr Bland, our accountant, and mentioned the name change and office problem, he was over the accountancy moon.

'Location should be somewhere equidistant from Harrods and Austin Reed, our two largest accounts,' I hinted.

'Strange you should mention that because I rent two rooms in Great Marlborough Street for my West End clients but I only use them a day or two a week. Shall we share the cost because we don't run a knocking shop by the hour?'

'Sorry about that,' he added very apologetically and I suddenly remembered my horizontal adventures that I had never apologised for to anyone, let alone a certified accountant with a long string of letters behind his name.

Tale 28

Wolfy's Viennese Waltz

Just before Xmas 1958, Kurt phoned from Vienna and asked if I could come to Vienna and meet Erich to finalise *the* deal discussed in London. When Jim told me, he was tempted to ask Kurt if he was joking nor did he suggest my schedule was too heavy during that time. All he really asked Kurt were the suggested dates and whether he could come to Schweschacht to collect me. Kurt replied, 'Tell him to bring an overcoat *and* scarf ... it's bloody cold here.'

When AUA landed it was dark and snowing and the lights in the terminal shone like little candles on an Xmas tree. We walked into the warm main building and Kurt said: 'Where's your bloody fur hat? ... And don't give me all that shit about being a macho type ... You, a macho type? Don't make me laugh...' But we did laugh a lot during my five days in the very hospitable arms of the Schapiras.

Erich was a few centimetres taller than Kurt but powerfully built. He could have been on the cover of *Business Today* as 'European Businessman of the Year'. Kurt's blue little Alfa Romeo was the little brother to Erich's big blue BMW which now moved silently over snow-covered streets into Vienna City. The trees were dripping with new snow and the whole scene matched my mood of euphoria mixed with disbelief.

Kurt smiled benignly and after ten minutes quietly said: 'You seem to be enjoying it.' I nodded. 'Well, you'll have to bring Jim next time and we haven't even sampled the schnitzels yet.' I just nodded again.

And I didn't stop nodding ... and from then onwards I was in my own Schapira winter wonderland.

In the early evening we met at the bar of the InterContinental Bar. I was given a massive kick into my non-exploratory Viennese five finger exercise.

The InterContinental has a massively high hall with large circular pillars holding up the ceiling. A few steps up on one side is the bar and anyone coming in through the entrance door could be looked down on from the bar. I arrived a few minutes before the appointed hour of seven and saw the be-furred and fur-booted clients come into the hotel; most single males were turning towards the entrance to spot or devour any female arrivals. Like watching the tennis balls at Wimbledon, all male eyes were suddenly turning towards the lady coming through the front door and into the lobby. She half removed the mink and draped it casually over her shoulders, just lightly trailing it over the marble floor. All male eyes were now glued to her and I fully expected the umpire to call 'love all', but I just kept staring at this stunning lady who could have been Jackie Kennedy's younger sister.

Her jet-black hair was beautifully groomed, flowing around her sculptured face like a liquid halo, and as she ascended the few steps up to the bar, smiled at me, tugged the mink a little closer to her alluring body and just planted the most fleeting of kisses on my cheek. I was just speechless and did not even have time to decide whether it was the alluring scent of Schiaparelli or Christian Dior that enveloped me. 'David,' she said with a deep sigh, 'Erich described you down to a tee...' I was dumbfounded. All I knew was that it was cruelty to have something so alluring near me with that large 'don't touch label' firmly stuck to every part of her visible body. I couldn't even begin to think about the invisible parts.

Olly was born in Vienna, where her Dad was one of the largest furriers in Middle Europe with branches in Brussels and Paris. She went to finishing school in Switzerland but her homes were hotels based in many of Europe's capitals. As we sat eating in a Viennese restaurant, I couldn't keep my eyes off her. I had to pinch myself to remember that not so many months before I had been sleeping with twenty sweating, burping, farting sailors who were hard put to keep their hands to themselves in the mornings even if they were hard.

The two Schaps and I met at the factory the next morning, had a *Jause* (a bit like a late lunch cum afternoon tea) at Café Demel, that most famous of all coffee houses in Vienna. I could hardly think whilst all this was going on, but Jim had prepared a 'potential' sales sheet for the new company, expected payment rosta and estimated income and expenditures for six months' trading. Erich and Kurt mulled this over and ten minutes later looked at me.

'He's been very thorough, hasn't he?' I nodded. 'Was Jim in the accounts department in the Navy?'

I grinned. 'Accounts ... Not really, but he always had to account for what he was doing. But what about the figure you asked him to estimate for six months' trading?'

There was a little huddle between the brothers and then Kurt got out a little notebook and wrote the date and a sum and then looked at me.

'Who do you want the cheque made out to?'

I blinked. Then I blinked a second time, pointing to the figure. 'But this is 25 per cent more than Jim's figure.'

Kurt grinned all over his face. 'As the lads told me at Brighton, there's always cock-ups, so it's much safer to have more; saves all those phone calls when you run out of cash, doesn't it?' He got up. 'There's not much point in having a contract; they are there to be broken.' He handed me the cheque. 'I'll send you an official letter on company notepaper which you must give to your accountants. They'll need that for the tax inspectors, who assume everyone is a crook, so one of my university friends told me. He knows because his Dad is in the Inland Revenue and every time they see a non-Brit address they immediately assume it's the Mafia laundering the accounts ... I only wish! As to the repayment of the loan, I suggest ... "as funds permit" completion within five years. As I'm younger than you or Jim, if there's still something owing, it'll come out of your estates, which proves I didn't get my English law degree for nothing.'

Erich got up and held out his hand and a large smile stretched across his face. 'You'll phone when you want some more. We have a list of types of cloths we want you to buy for us in the UK. And it's not Viyella; we're buying that already...'

Kurt cut in. 'You'll have to get off your little arse and get some new business...' He looked me hard in the face. 'But I don't think you are one of those. Preminger's have been told by Uncle Charles that you've had enough of being treated like a shyster so, c'mon, let's have a look at what you can do!'

Jim phoned at an appointed hour every afternoon and he thought I had drunk too much of the fresh white wine up at Grinzing. 'Are you sure you're not pissed? All I can add from this end is we're still in business. Mitch is selling as if there's no tomorrow and he wants to see the Vienna woods as well but, as I told him, we'll see.'

The next afternoon I told Jim that I had been given a sales training day by their sales manager Herr Wurmhöringer. Jim interrupted to see if it was really a worm turning and I told him, 'It'll turn even better when he gets your stamp doubles which you keep on ordering.'

'He collects stamps, does he? What kind? Mint or used, what country ... old issues or new ... any covers?...' and I was totally lost in Jim's worldwide knowledge of philately.

'Tell me tomorrow afternoon and I'll see if we can oil the business arrangement in London's favour...' Just before I left Vienna I was able to hand Mr W. a big parcel courtesy of Jim. He was shattered. 'How did you know I wanted all these?' he cried, throwing his arms around me.

I didn't mind, but I would much rather they had been Olga Schapira's but, then, she didn't collect stamps. She only licked them, occasionally.

The end of the tale is that whenever Jim wanted anything in the way of info, he got it. I reported to him that one of our big SMARTO selling points was that we could offer nine neck sizes because UK shirts were sold by the inch and Europeans sold them by the centimetres which gave three more neck sizes. QED. And dear Mr Wurm even included a mock-up inch/centimetres sketch proving the QED or as Jim commented to me on my return, 'Not many people know that there are 2.6 centimetres to the inch, do they?'

Wurm also taught me how to fold shirts because new customers always unpin new shirts to see the fit, so every time I wrote an order I had to refold or iron the unpinned samples. Or as Jim acidly observed: 'Just proves it's always better to have a dry run.' And as usual he was spot on, especially with the drip-drys.

In a very short time, we had come from tiny flat with a wooden worktop bed to 39 Great Marlborough Street, which looked out on the explosive honeypot of Carnaby Street and the industries that were springing up around it. The day before Kurt Schapira had gone back to Vienna, Jim had heard us talk about 'flower' cloth patterns. When I got back from Heathrow he asked if all had gone smoothly, which I had confirmed with Kurt. I was standing by

Jim's window and when I had finished my report he asked me to turn around 180 degrees pointing to the side window of Liberty & Co.

'And apart from Carnaby Street,' he said, 'what can you see in the Liberty window? ... And don't say cloth; What *sort* of cloth? I'm not in the rag trade but my little eyes spotted some cloth that might be just right ... and it's all with Liberty prints ... I think ... I'm not an expert like you are, Dave!'

I smiled at him and walked over to the phone and picked it up.

'Don't bother, Dave,' Jim interrupted, 'I've phoned them ... got the wholesale cloth department ... and they don't have an Austrian agent and they'll be here in our flash offices at 08.30hrs tomorrow and I'll bet you it won't be a minute before 09.30hrs without a flash.'

Exclusive sale rights followed and the SMARTO shirt/pullover style in exclusive Liberty prints was a sensation with all SMARTO sales persons in Austria, Germany and Switzerland as well as, of course, exclusively at Austin Reed.

Swiss gnomes withstanding and the pound in our pocket made us grow by leaps and bounds. With Theo's expertise and wise advice, our company's progress was almost meteoric and my movements were now on the basis of 'if it's Tuesday, it must be Zurich' and that was much better than Plummer Roddis in Hastings, and so was the food and wine.

Tale 29

'*HMS* Vilomi'

David Franklin Ltd was born on 30th March 1960 and initially operated from a very modern block of flats which did not look like an office. The first person to comment on this was a very pleasant raincoat-wearing minute officer from HM Customs and Excise (Purchase Tax Division), who must have been the prototype figure for the twenty-first century 'Hector, the tax inspector'.

He rang the front-door bell and was somewhat taken aback by me answering the door wearing a sweater and jeans. I opened it and asked him in and he thrust his station card in my face, withdrew it quickly and apologised for disturbing me. He looked around, straightened his hair in the mirror and asked:

'This *is* David Franklin Ltd?' I nodded courteously. I did not want to disturb Jim in the bedroom-cum-office because I knew he would be knee-deep in invoices and currency tables.

I ushered the gent into the lounge and he looked around in amazement and its contents seemed to suggest that we were not running an office but a Bovril. Not that I thought for a moment that he would want to partake but he gave me a very suspicious sort of sideways look. He opened a file which reminded me somewhat of Chiswick all those years ago.

'It says here you are importers and exporters of general goods...' I nodded.

'Where are they?' He swung his head around the room and looked at the pictures on the wall. I felt like saying 'in transit' and Jim could have tracked them down, centimetre by centimetre, from Bosco or Schaps, Jack Palmer at BCT, down to the bloody truck number en route to the Austin Reed receiving dock at Thirsk. Jim was like that, everything by the book, down to the last line, and woe to anybody who dared challenge him or made a cock-up.

At that moment Jim himself appeared. With a very pleasant smile Jim turned to me: 'Would the gentleman like a cup of tea and biscuits?'

Hector cheered up visibly when the 'biscuit' bit was mentioned. 'Now that is kind of you,' he said and took a sip of tea out of the Augarten Viennese cup.

'Ah yes...' There was a long pause. 'BCT have contacted us to arrange a purchase tax number to facilitate speedier expediting of goods through customs ... but looking around me there appears to be a small problem. This beautiful flat really cannot qualify for an office and although you are a limited company there is no name plate either outside this flat or even outside by the listed tenants. Although I appreciate what you are doing is totally legal, but to issue a PT number I must file a report that the premises are visibly an office and/or a trading company. Consequently, to issue a purchase tax number now is out of the question. I suggest you try again when you have an office with name plates on the door and on the front door.'

He rose and handed the cup to Jim with a smile, commenting, 'Thank you so much ... was it Indian or China?' If Jim had answered his question it would have qualified for the lowest of the Lower-Deck Jackspeak, from India or China!

We moved into Great Marlborough Street on the 25th February 1963 and the following day Hector threw his six-footer striped scarf through the opened door like a lasso and shouted: 'Congratulations ... you've made it. Your name is downstairs on the floor-by-floor listing of tenants and you've got it on the bloody front door as well. I'll bring you the PT certificate next week. Any tea going?'

When the PT certificate was in Jim's hands he phoned Jack Palmer at BCT in Blackfriars Road.

'Great ... that means faster clearances through customs and less work for you, Jim.'

Jim stopped him right there, 'So if it's less work for me, you will have less as well. How much less are your charges going to be?'

Jim snapped the trap shut but before it closed he added: 'You may not know it but I was koshered out in the east and I know that Dave was at birth so, how much less?'

Once for him, and once for this semi-koshered bloke or as we both used to say: 'It'll cost you or I'll have you,' and being Jim, he scrutinised the next 'invoice PT entry form' and Jack knew that Jim would do so. In the event, that last threat was never exercised.

However, what Jack did tell Jim was that he had a little Swiss gent in the office whose company was the largest manufacturer of men's clothing in Switzerland and apart from their manufacturing plant in Zurich they also had twenty retail shops throughout Switzerland.

'Lovely little man that Mr Steinmann. Always brings me a bottle of Flümli, that plum brandy, and he's selling PKZ to a small number of retailers in the UK but he's looking for an agent who deals with all the best shops ... Do you know anyone, Jim?'

'OK, Jack, you win ... but if you are not careful with those charges I won't let you bend over for me in the showers, it'll cost you much more but ... cheers a lot ... where is your little gnome now?' And the next thing Jim knew was our dear little Hans Steinmann was at Great Marlborough Street.

The boss of PKZ had friends in Winchelsea, which was four miles from our cottage, and Walter Burger was greatly impressed by the cottage, its age and the Killick occupants. So impressed that a request came from Zurich for an addition to the marble plate outside 39 Great Marlborough Street: 'Burger Kehl & Cie. Head Office Zurich. London Office 2nd Floor'. We did not have to have a long board meeting to see if all the directors agreed and we did not tell him: 'It'll cost you!'

The activities of the company were now exploding and when Jim had sent that letter to his ex-shipmate, c/o Admiralty, London, it finally caught up with Mitch in Lossiemouth in the north of Scotland. On one of my Scottish sales trip I tore myself away from the *ménage* in Edinburgh and diverted to Lossie to have a good look at Mitch, who seemed as keen as mustard to join as a salesman. When his RN service terminated he did not want to return to his home town of Kendal in the Lake District but, like many of his mates, was attracted by the bright lights of 'the Smoke'.

As he had nowhere to kip and no job, Jim and I decided Mitch could 'sling his hook' with us and we put up another divan in our bedroom at Arundel House. Before deciding on a salesman job with us he went to the Singer sewing machine company as a salesman trainee at a starvation rate of pay.

They got points for the sales of sewing machines to private

householders who had phoned the shop because their machines had broken down. The sales patter always gave the housewife a new machine before the old one had been 'repaired'. Mitch waited about two weeks and returned with the 'repaired' sewing machine, but by this time the careful owner had got used to the new one and was very pleased with Mitch's attentive service, which did not count for the points system.

Payment in kind was very pleasant but did not pay his food and lodging and all his personal attention to the housewives produced no extra money. He taught them how to thread up the cotton, licking it into a fine brushlike point and inserting it into the hole of the needle but ... no extra money. At the end of the first year he showed the manager that he had produced maximum points on the shop sales but as the manager was of the very old school it was 'last in' equals lowest rewards. Mitch asked for his cards. This was the precise moment when 'David Franklin's' activities exploded and instead of an opening for him in the Navy, it turned out to be at David Franklin Ltd.

When the company was finally registered, Jim and I had wracked our brains for a 'telegram' address and tried anagrams of all complexions but, one evening at The Plough in Christchurch Road, Jim did a 'eureka'. He had even sourced his *Quotations Dictionary* but finally, after the third thimble full of Navy Rum, came up with: 'We trade with the Schapiras in VIenna, we are in LOndon and all that Italian knitwear comes through MIlan ... It's quite simple really: our telegram address should be VI-LO-MI!'

Within one year VILOMI proved too short a name but we decided not to add the other companies who wanted us to sell their top-class goods in the UK. There was simply no room on the entrance door to 39 Great Marlborough Street.

TUSA cotton knitwear were the leaders of cotton velour sweaters and pullovers in the European market. They were founded in 1868 and Theo and Silvia Tuchschmid were descendants of the founder Gottlieb Tuchschmid. Although they were brother and sister everyone in the village of Amriswil near Lake Constance addressed them as 'Mr & Mrs'. Gottlieb was a typical nineteenth-century entrepeneur who founded the factory next to the new railway line from east to west through Switzerland and prudently built it next to the new railway station. He was a wise and honest businessman in total contrast to some British politicians who peddled the image of the

Swiss being mythical little gnomes who were robbing the Brits of the pound sterling. Being an honest entrepreneur, Gottlieb and his descendants carried on enlarging the business. Theo and Silvia were single and childless and were always helping other families who had not been quite as fortunate financially as the Tuchschmids.

Silvia had a friend who had two sons and Theo arranged for the two boys to have a good education. The eldest went to the finest engineering college in Switzerland and from there climbed the steel ladder in the United States, finishing as president at Aluisuiss back in Switzerland. Jörg Tschopp, the younger of the two, had textiles in his blood and studied at St Gallen, the top of the Swiss knitted bobbins. From there, Theo Tuchschmid sent him to London to learn British retail trading at Harrods and Jaeger and then to the US to complete his total knowledge of the entire retail and wholesale knitwear scene. After two years he returned to Theo's company in Switzerland and they started exporting their knitted velour sweaters from Theo's factory in Amriswil. This Swiss/English/American charm-oozing salesman found no bridge he could not cross.

At this point I was visiting PKZ in Zurich and on looking through their own Zurich shops was struck by the colourful cotton velour sweaters. PKZ's buyer was delighted to give me TUSA and Jörg's phone number. I suddenly felt that Tom and Wolfy's presence were almost getting too much for my shoulders but nevertheless decided to phone Jim from Zurich to find out from BCT who their shipping correspondents in Switzerland were. 'I'll ring you at 20.00hrs tonight, London time and I'll give you all the answers,' said Jim quietly. At 19.55hrs I was sitting by the phone in my hotel and watched the second hand creep to 21.00hrs Zurich time. Seconds later the phone rang, I answered it and heard Jim's voice ask for Mr Franklin.

'It's me ... Jim ... not adrift?'

'Me, adrift? ... You must be joking ... Do you or don't you want the info? Jack's oppo in Zurich is Italestero and their firm is doing a bit of business with Harrods and Jaeger through AMC, but nothing else. Your direct contact at TUSA is a Mr Tschopp who speaks brilliant English... Anything else or shall I get some help from Bletchley for you?'

'Not at the moment, Jim. Thanks for all the info.'

I could see Jim give his little chuckle, put the notes into the out-tray and get the next job from the in-tray.

Jorg Tschopp oozed American-style friendly chat combined with Swiss–Brit efficiency. He collected me from Kloten Airport and then gave me a whirlwind Cook's tour of eastern Switzerland; the Santis was breathtakingly beautiful with its small snowy cap. We then drove down to Lake Constance and had a delicious meal of the local fish, the *egli*, pan-fried in butter and washed down with a very dry white wine, the *Féchy*. After that feast I was ready for a snooze but we went on to Amriswil and TUSA, the home of Theo and Silvia Tuchschmid, and he was a Swiss version of Uncle Charles with banking connections. All my knowledge in that area was acquired with the patient and very knowledgeable help of Theo, who became our best friend and private banking advisor as he, like many of his other business friends, was also on the board of a small Swiss private bank. I think if he had been an advisor to the Downing Street politicians instead of the two Hungarian wizards, Kaldor and Balogh, whom the UK press had dubbed Mr Buda and Mr Pest, Britain's finances would have been like Switzerland's – solvent.

The TUSA range added a certain exclusive air to the David Franklin collections and was the finishing touch to our range of men's raincoats, overcoats, anoraks, jackets, trousers, shirts and knitwear and we had to expand our offices on the second floor by taking the additional rooms to house our ranges. Mitch couldn't put a foot wrong apart from being badgered to come back to Kendal and get married and start a family.

'In Kendal? You've got to be joking!' he loved the 'international' sales executive label far too much and much preferred to stay at 'HMS *Vilomi*.'

Tale 30

Gerry and Vicky at The Bell, Iden

Our one escape valve was the cottage and we tried to go to 'Killicks' Friday nights, business permitting. If I wasn't back by the Friday night, Jim and Mitch drove up from the cottage and collected me from Heathrow or Appledore station on the Saturday. What none of us had either expected or realised was that an entire new world had opened to us in Kent.

Just after we had agreed the purchase of the cottage in October 1957, Jim and I made our way to Rye to get some lunch. It was only three years after food rationing had ended and even restaurants in London hardly had any variety of food on their menus. Rye was five miles from Wittersham and neither Jim nor I expected to find anything apart from soggy *News of the World*-wrapped fish and chips; if we were lucky.

Halfway to Rye is the village of Iden and at the top of the hill is a T-junction. On it is The Bell Inn which that day had a black-board outside with a simple message chalked on it saying 'Luncheons being served'. 'Go on, you try it,' said Jim, grabbing my arm as I pulled into the carless car park. Next to the door marked 'Saloon Bar' was a small door marked 'Dining Room', which I pushed open and entered a storybook, Xmas-card cosy room reeking of hospitable comfort. On one side was an inglenook oak-beamed fireplace with a roaring wood fire; opposite was a hatch into the bar where I saw a small rotund white-jacketed, black-trousered barman who turned around to look at me, raising his black eyebrows. The jet-black Eton crop hair was flattened down and the open-necked white shirt showed the paisley silk cravat off to perfection.

I asked if they were serving lunch and Vicky growled, 'Bloody well read, can't you?' Without another word she handed me a menu which would have done any leading restaurant proud. I looked

220

and gulped when I saw the day's special, lobster thermidor and the special sweet of the day, savoyard. Stunned by this selection available in a village pub in the depths of the East Sussex–Kent border in October, I asked if all these dishes were on. Vicky exploded. 'What the hell is the matter with you?' she thundered. 'Wouldn't bloody well be on there if we were not offering them to the punters, would they? First you can't read the blackboard and now you've got a problem with the menu? Are you a nutcase or something, or didn't they teach you anything but to shoot and kill people in the Army?'

Which broke the ice when I replied: 'Well ... actually, dear, it's the Navy...'

Her face broke into a huge smile. 'Bloody hell, you're not a bleedin' sailor, are you?' She turned around, pushed the door open into the kitchen and shouted to her friend. 'Gerry, darling, the fleet is in town. There's not a bed made and the town's full of sailors.'

Turning back to me with a grin, she asked, 'How many of you are there?' Not out of disrespect, I showed her two fingers. 'Ah well,' said Vicky, 'we'll have to play eeny meeny miny moe to see who pulls the short straw, or whatever you like pulling.'

'Go on then,' she finally urged me. 'Bring it in, whatever it is!' So I went to the car but left Jim to figure out what he had to expect.

His face was a picture when Vicky embraced him with a very wet and impassioned hug. She disentangled herself, stepped back, turned to me and asked: 'Where on earth did you find this lovely bit of seaweed, not at the Fitzroy I'm sure... Ah well, those were the days when you could fish for anything in the bar and get it for a pint ... well, perhaps two!' Jim gave a grin as I had never seen him give before.

'To business!' said Vicky, grabbing the menu out of my hand, 'and it is all on...' she turned around and screamed into the kitchen: 'Gerry darling, I've got two sailors here wanting to eat your lovely bits of stuff ... and I think one of them is actually quite dishy.'

We had a brilliant thick home-made mushroom soup and, after the lobster, Gerry appeared from the kitchen complete with blue butcher's apron carrying her Campari, gave us both her famous 'hugs and kisses' and trilled 'hello daaaahrlings!' She returned to the kitchen after more hugs and kisses. 'See you in a jiffy after I've tossed myself off...'

221

We were into our second bottle of Beaujolais and *beau* it was, when we heard strange whirring noises coming from the kitchen and Vicky saw us look towards the kitchen. 'Don't take any notice of the old girl in the kitchen, she's just getting your sweet ready and whisking herself into buggery.'

Minutes later she reappeared with two large glasses filled to the brim with the smooth-as-silk savoyard and smiled. 'My special treat for my darling sailors. Enjoy and here's a little ditty my father used to sing to me when I stroked the family cat:

> My pussy is prettier than yours,
> Got no whiskers, never shows its claws,
> I never give it meat, cos I want to keep it small,
> My little pussy is the prettiest of all.

Over the following year Jim and I undertook the repair and renovation of the cottage. It was a challenge. Even the Royal Navy provided hot water, showers and WCs but 'Killicks' had one cold tap, no kitchen, no heating and a ladder as a staircase. The WC was a thunderbox at the end of the garden and as there was no gas or electricity, the Bell became our dinner, bed and breakfast for the following twelve months. On Saturday mornings, Gerry appeared in our bedroom with an enormous hearty breakfast on a tray and proclaimed: 'Something eggy on a plate for my two darlings.' In return for the royal treatment, I helped Vicky in the bar when they got busy whilst Jim assisted Gerry to chef brilliantly in the kitchen.

At weekends, around nine in the evening the curtain went up, Gerry entered 'centre stage rear' and the customers were entertained to the most amusing show which lasted well past closing time. When the stories got too outrageous, Vicky shook her gin goblet at us mumbling: 'Don't take any notice of the old girl ... she's at it again ... Act 3 Scene 2 ... Line 4...' But very entertaining and amusing all her stories were but only when we asked her friends the pre-1956 background did we discover some of the reality.

She had lived with her parents at 44 Orchard Street, St Margarets, and during World War I was a typist at the Whitehead aircraft factory near Kingston (Gerry's mother, 'Mummy', gave us some cutlery stamped with the company's name). After the war Gerry relished the roaring 1920s and '30s, leading to an 'ambisextrous' existence in London's West End. She briefly married Leslie Billings, who worked in a bank, and Mummy adored him, hoping he would provide Gerry with a stable family life. Although the marriage quickly ended in divorce, Mummy had Leslie's photograph in an large frame hanging on the wall beside her until the day she died at the age of ninety-four at Highfield Nursing Home, Hythe.

In the 1930s Gerry met Lucien Gow, one in the large circle of friends she moved in and out of. Lou, as she was known, and Gerry remained firm friends for more than thirty-five years. Her family were purveyors of fine game, meat and fish and had a chain of shops and oyster bars in London. Lou did not join the family business but became an architect whilst her brother practised law. She drifted in and out of Gerry's life until Vicky, who could have been her double, reappeared on the scene in the 1950s. However, Lou used to pop over to The Bell after she had moved from Chelsea to Tenterden in the 1960s.

After the divorce, Gerry and a girlfriend ran a coffee and sandwich bar in Marylebone High Street and lived in a block of flats at Grove End Gardens near Lord's Cricket Ground. Other residents included a family Covington: mother, son 'Buster' and his brother. Frank Ducker, who was a manager at Coutts, the bankers, also had a flat there and so did Nell Gielgud, Sir John's sister. The Gielgud family stretched back to Ellen Terry, England's greatest actress of the 1890s and 1900s, and all the talk was of actors and the stage, which Gerry loved. Nell married Frank Ducker who sadly died after eighteen months.

The bar at Grove End Gardens was presided over by Vicky Leech, and soon Gerry was running the restaurant *and* Vicky. However, Buster won the battle of the sexes and Gerry moved around with him when he joined the RAF during World War II. After demob, he and Gerry ran the Stoner Arms near Woodchurch but sadly, he took to drink. Gerry left him and ran the restaurant at the Woolpack in Tenterden in the early 1950s and became friendly with the Kerrs, who ran the hotel. Their son Graham achieved early TV fame as the 'Galloping Gourmet' and was the first 'Naked Chef', which made the media flock to Tenterden and Gerry glow with theatrical pride. That is, until the day when Vicky, who had been in the Land Army in Sussex, walked into the Woolpack, saw Gerry, conquered and, as they say, the rest is history.

They opened the Yew Tree, a tearoom opposite Ellen Terry's

home in the Old Harbourmaster's House at Smallhythe. In 1956 Mrs Geraldine Covington obtained a licence to run The Bell at Iden, three miles inland from the old Cinque Port of Rye, which dates back to the fourteenth century but which is no longer a port as the mouth of the Rother is nearly two miles away. Mermaid Street, the steep cobblestoned narrow street, is lined with the eighteenth-century red brick and weatherboarded beamed houses and is a must-see tourist attraction to visitors from all over the world. From Durham to Düsseldorf, Delft to Denver, they all buy Rye pottery and gaze at the Mermaid Inn, an original oak-beamed hotel with a long smuggling pedigree.

Off Mermaid Street is Lamb House, an eighteenth-century brick-fronted house which is rented out by the National Trust to sitting tenants. It was the home of Henry James from 1898 to 1916, and when Gerry and Vicky were at The Bell, Rumer Godden lived there and one of her many books, *The Greengage Summer*, was made into a successful film. She often visited The Bell, where we had the pleasure of meeting her. Elizabeth Taylor, not *the* Liz Taylor, helped in researching her book material and became friendly with Gerry and Vicky as well.

Rye and Romney Marsh still is a magnet to the literary, film and music world and as The Bell not only served gourmet food but also provided first-class entertainment from the bar, it shone like a beacon across the Kent–East Sussex border. In fact, Gerry and Vicky made The Bell a mixture of The Ivy and The Old Vic rolled into one. The public bar served Iden locals including the fireman's wife Madge who 'did' for Vicky and Gerry. But the private bar and restaurant not only attracted customers from Rye and its immediate surroundings but many of the music, media and entertainment world who flocked to Iden to eat the finest gourmet food and see 'the show' afterwards.

'Daps', Lady Daphne Russell, the late sister of the Duke of Bedford, motored over from Beckley in her open Lagonda. Peter Katin, the famous pianist, spent the weekend with 'Les Girls'. Marion Davies, the Geraldo and Ted Heath dance-band singer of the 50s and 60s came over from Tenterden. Douggie Byng, the great pantomime dame, called into The Bell and many of Noel Coward's entourage were regulars. Gladys Calthrop became a well-wisher and Gerry treasured a picture of a parrot she had received from her.

Laurie, the real South American grey parrot, greeted everyone entering the tiny private bar with 'Hello, my darlings' which was a brilliant echo of Vicky's greeting and many first-time visitors were startled to hear this from inside a cage which was perched at the far end of an empty bar. Bertha, the enormous St Bernard, Tuti, the Pekinese, and Fanny, an elderly shaggy mongrel dog and two goats in the garden completed the animal members of the family.

Vicky owned 'Stephen', a battered 1940-vintage beige Buick and once a week took Gerry and Bertha on a shopping expedition. Trying to push Bertha into the car was a hazardous operation as she was slightly bigger than the width of the car. Vicky pulling her in on the off side of the car, and Gerry pushing her in on the on side was like a Max Sennett film. Once inside, her head stuck out of the off-side open window, tongue flapping and breathing heavily and out of the on-side window, the tail was wooshing like an enormous feather duster.

Stephen, the Buick, once turned into an ambulance when I had gone for a swim in the Rother on a hot summer's day. I had swallowed some water and within hours was delirious. Jim phoned Vicky in a panic and she was there, complete with first-aid kit, brandy and stomach pumps within twenty minutes. She pushed Jim aside like Hatty Jacques in a 'Carry On' film and administered her first aid. Before Jim could even say thank you, she had jumped into Stephen and was off in a flash.

Apart from all the auxiliary members of The Bell menagerie, there were not many blood relations on either Vicky or Gerry's side. Vicky had a distant cousin who never visited The Bell and apart from Mummy, the only other family visitor was Mummy's sister, Mrs Mason from Hungerford, who occasionally had a quick wet bite and sometimes stayed in The Bell.

When we were in the bar in the early 1960s, Vicky had a phone call from Buster Covington's landlady who told her that he had committed suicide. Vicky called Gerry into the bar, comfortingly put her arm around Gerry's shoulder and said: 'Sorry, old girl ... I've just heard that Buster has killed himself.' Taking a large gulp of gin out of her enormous crystal glass, she poured a brandy for Gerry and consolingly put her arm around Gerry's shoulder. 'Ah well,' she sighed, 'c'est la vie.' Gerry did not reply, although she occasionally claimed to speak French fluently. She had a penchant for make-believe. She once told us she had to swim for her life when the aircraft they were travelling in to visit her relations in the Emerald Isle had come down in the North Sea. Her stories about her parents cutting short her US piano concert tour are pure Noel Coward as she had neither ever been to the States nor could she play a note on the piano. Mummy once cut her short when Gerry informed a customer in the bar that she could not have children because of her genital problems. Mummy angrily thumped the bar exclaiming: 'Don't be so silly, Gladys. All you ever wanted was a good time.'

In 1963 Vicky and Gerry bought 'Paynes', a cottage about fifty metres from our cottage, and Mummy sold the house in St Margarets and moved into 'Paynes' with Gerry and Vicky, who became very ill and died in 1963. We had just bought a house in Lambeth and suggested Gerry move into our downstairs flat in London after Mummy had gone to a retirement home in Hythe. Whenever she felt lonely, Gerry popped upstairs to be with us and this closeness helped her to find her feet again.

Our business necessitated extensive European travel and she came with us on our next car trip to Germany and Austria and was quite taken by the thousand-mile drive through breathtaking mountain forest and lakeland scenery. She had been noting all the foreign signposts with interest and after driving on the autobahn in Germany, turned to me and exclaimed, 'Darling, isn't it strange that all towns are called "Ausfahrt"!' We explained that they were the 'exit' signs and without a twitch of an eyebrow she quipped: 'Now, darling, that's given me a wonderful idea for the name of my next dog. I'll call him Ausfahrt ... or farty for short.'

In Vienna she played Marie Antoinette to perfection, and when the steaming hot coffee and hot rolls were brought to her in bed for breakfast, she rested back against the huge down pillow and stretched her legs below the enormous down duvet that rested on her like a mountainous balloon. She stroked it gently and smiled. 'Darling ... I think these Viennese muffins are gorgeous.' After the trip with the three of us in the car, we christened her '004', with apologies to Ian Fleming whose films and books were breaking all records at the box office and in the bookshops.

She settled happily into Oakden Street and started working part-time at an estate agents and at Hammond's, in Knightsbridge. Customers flocked to speak and listen to her amusing stories and not many left without having purchased or ordered some of the company's goodies. However, Liz Taylor suggested she move to Folkestone and open a restaurant with her. The Hacienda opened in September 1967 and although Gerry tried hard to make it into another 'Bell', Liz would not follow Gerry's advice to serve high-class dinners. Liz would only serve 'teas' and luncheons which hardly proved a rip-roaring financial success and the Hacienda closed in February 1968. Gerry bought a flat with Nell in Folkestone and moved to Clifton Crescent in 1978 and then bought 37a Ormonde Road in Hythe.

We sold our cottage in the same year, moving our home and offices to 121 Kennington Road, a large 1774 Georgian building, 500 metres from Westminster Bridge and the Houses of Parliament. It became a perfect company headquarters building for our European operation and Gerry added the corporate entertainment touch whenever we had important UK and European clients for lunch and dinner. She played the perfect hostess, staying and chefing for us for three or four days at a time and they all loved her. As all the clients came from the four corners of Europe, she used to joke about 'the Mafia days at one-two-one'.

Gerry 'Daaaahrling' died at the age of 102 and there is no finer epitath than the Bard's: 'All the world's a stage and all the men and women merely players...' And Gerry certainly was a player and although her feet never touched the 'boards', she lived her life as she liked it.

The Horrors of War

The Schapira business increased by leaps and bounds in Austria and they were very conscious of the looming presence of the European Economic Community. At present they were a large fish in a small pond but realised that in the not too distant future they would be a small fish in a very large EEC pond. They bought a lot of cloth in the United States and the cloth manufacturers put them in touch with one of the largest manufacturers of shirts in the US. They joined forces and became an 'under licencee' manufacturer of 'Manhattan' and 'Lady Manhattan' and we followed as UK sidekicks.

As they were a worldwide licencee operation we had many 'visiting firemen' and amongst them was the New Zealand licencee sales director. After discussing business aspects I asked him to dinner and suggested the very British Simpson's, possibly in 'a small box'. We met at around eight-thirty but both Jim and Mitch were tied up and after ordering a typically 'Brit' meal he asked me if the war had knocked at my door.

'Come to think of it,' I said, 'not really because I was at school during the Blitz and didn't see anything gruesome. And when it was all over, I was a peacetime pissy-arsed matelot...'

He stopped me right there, his face dropping at the 'matelot' word. 'I know you invited me to dinner but I would like to buy a bottle of brandy so I can try to get over the worst naval event of my life.' He beckoned over the sommelier.

'When I joined the company in 1948,' he began, 'they were buying all their fabrics from Lancashire because the firm's founder came from Accrington. After the war, and especially during the last two years, our sales have dropped and keep on dropping and when I had an inquest with the boss, he paused to ask me what the major reason was for the drop in sales. "All our competitors are now using Japanese cloths because they are newer fabrics and designs and the logistics to get them from Japan to us makes them faster and much cheaper than from Lancashire," I replied. The boss looked at me and said: "That's no problem, get a Japan flight and buy the goddam cloth there. We've around 150 employees and unless we act fast within six months, we'll have to pay them all off." '

He looked around for the brandy which just arrived at our table, grabbed the bottle, drank about a quarter and refilled the glass whilst the sommelier looked stunned. He looked up at me pleadingly and mumbled: 'Dave ... Your name is Dave, isn't it?' and I nodded. 'I had just turned eighteen after Pearl Harbor and joined the NZ Navy. My best mate was eight months younger but told them he was the same age as me. We were in a NZ destroyer when the Japs got us and three Aussie destroyers at Java. I just remember drowning when my mate swam along with a lifeboat and pulled me in alongside him.

'In the morning the Japs picked us and another ten mates up and paired us off, especially as we were buddies. We got to a prison camp which had been a school with a games pitch beside it. We were made to watch what they did to our mates and they picked four of the youngest from the twelve and tied their arms in front of them, arms extended forwards. The four jeeps came along and the four lads were pushed towards the rear of the jeeps, the loose ropes holding the tied knuckles were tied to the rear seat of the jeeps. When they were taut, the jeeps moved slowly forward until the ropes were as stiff as a wire.

'They slowly revved up the engines and the four lads started a slow trot behind the jeeps and as the speed increased to around 5mph the lads just about managed to run behind them. The Japs revved up the jeeps and the legs just gave way and the screaming and crunching of the bodies were worse than seeing your buddies disintegrating by inches. The ground beneath them was just running in blood and I'll never forget my buddy looking back at me before he was torn to pieces.

'When the carnage was over, an immaculate Jap officer appeared in a spotless uniform complete with sword and walked towards the tail end of the jeeps which still had the remains of the tied wrists attached to the rear seat. He looked at the bloody stumps, unsheathed

229

his sword and with one clean sword whoosh cut the rope holding the smashed wrists. He picked up the bloody remains of my mate's wrists and walked slowly towards me gingerly holding what was left in his gloved hand. When he was inches away from me, he threw them contemptuously at my feet and spat at them, and I'll never forget that look of hatred in his cobra-like slit eyes.

'When I arrived at Tokyo airport last month, I looked at all those slit-eyed Japs and couldn't even cry...' He broke down and held my arm. 'Sorry, Dave, I had to tell someone, I'm sorry it's you...' He grabbed his napkin and just cried and cried.

I suddenly thought to my myself how lucky I was not to have witnessed that sort of nightmare. At least I didn't even know what the gas ovens looked like into which my two aunts had been pushed all those years ago.

'Sorry, Dave,' he kept on sobbing. At last he clutched my hand and pressed it hard and just said, 'Thanks for listening ... I haven't told anyone except the shrink after the war.' He suddenly sat up and slowly, very slowly his face broke into a very small smile. 'You said you were an ex-matelot as well? Did you also say, "Cheers, mate"?' I nodded and tried to smile back. 'Right then...' and he lifted his glass. 'Cheers, mate.'

When I got home Jim and Mitch were fast asleep and the minute my head hit the pillow so was I. When I awoke in the morning they had both gone and Jim had left a short note: 'Hope you're OK. You mumbled in the night but I thought we'd let you sleep. See you, J.' When I got to the office they asked me about the evening and I just gave them a bare outline and, when I had finished, Jim picked up a letter with Deutsche Bundespost on it and handed it to me. It was from one of the largest manufacturers of trousers in Germany, who wanted us to represent them in the UK.

I glanced at it and both Mitch and Jim said in unison: 'You're the boss, Dave... We're going to stay shtum but logically, if they were fifteen when the war finished, they'd be in their fifties now ... but it's up to you, of course.'

I shook my head. 'Well, I don't really see any problem with anyone under that age. After all, are the sons going to be made responsible for the crimes of their fathers?'

Good old honest and practical Jim gave a small smile. 'Well, if they're over sixty, Mitch can always tell them to crawl back into that bunker in Berlin and wrap the 3,000-pair-a-day production around their little Nazi necks. But changing countries for a moment, I had that Mr Burger from PKZ in Zurich on the phone. I thought it was a bit odd for the big chief himself to phone me. You remember him, don't you? He was over with friends in Winchelsea and they all came to the cottage for tea. Didn't see a lot of him once Mitch did his "garden tour" and proudly showed off his roses and clematis and how Mitch had gotten to know Christopher Lloyd at Dixter, and Waltie Burger was all over Mitch as Burger's gardener was trying to develop some clematis. The upshot is a very large GB, not in the rag trade but flowers/garden/info/planting and soil details. Well, it'll please Mitch, he'll have to fly over to Zurich to do a hand delivery. Walty is sending over soil samples next week so Mitch can nip over to Dixter to get all the info first hand. Mitch was already on the mental garden trail.'

'... Oh yes, I was going over to have a chat with Chris anyway about the ...'

Jim gave a very satisfied smirk and I asked if they chatted about anything apart from blossom time.

'Oh yes...' Jim added, 'I nearly forgot ... they want you to go over there to view the factory with that lovely little Hansi Steinmann, the one who was our original BCT contact and gushes cracked English like a tumbling waterfall and Waltie Burger thanked me for getting the marble PKZ plate fixed on the front door at No. 39. Could Mr Franklin arrange to have it photographed and bring the photo with him? They want it to be widely circulated that PKZ now have a London office. I wasn't sure whether that was a good moment to ask him for a discount or royalties but, Dave, you're better at haggling than I am.'

I just looked at Jim and felt like adding the word 'bastard' but as he had already been so busy that morning I just glared at him. He grinned at me adding, 'It'll cost you ... and I'm counting and adding it all up...' He shook his head sideways and a great big smile appeared. '...Just watch it ... wings or bash will 'ave you!' I didn't know where to wing myself to.

Tale 32

Suisse Biz

A month later Mitch had done his clematis research, I had a photograph of the PKZ London office marble plate and a Swissair open return to Zurich was on my desk. I got on that plane and looked forward to Hansi Steinmann welcoming me with a 'Huullooo, Day-weed...' at Kloten, along with a very wet kiss and embrace.

Jim had all the Daily Orders typed out for me and all I had to do was follow instructions: lunch with Hansi at the Moevenpick in downtown Zurich complete with two day working schedule including clematis handover with WB.

When we got to the Parade Platz luncheon I was overwhelmed with hugs by Hansi's wife, Clara, who could have stepped off the southern plains of Reggio di Calabria. Five foot five, jet-black hair with matching fiery eyes; I was certainly not her glass of *rosso* but Hansi's Italian gardener or Mitch's green fingers could certainly have pruned her roses. As it was lunchtime she knew the bill would be picked up by 'the company' but Hansi had not briefed her about the level of expenses allowed.

PKZ stood for the founder's name Paul Kehl Zurich but the employees felt it also stood for '*Papa kann zahlen*' – 'Papa can pay' – and Clara asked Hansi the question if it was the big boss who was paying or just the sales department. Hansi confirmed the former and Clara immediately switched her attention to the à la carte section and gushed over the wonderful extras she was going to have. After the two menus and one à la carte meal Hansi and I made our way to the factory which was only a kilometre from the Parade Platz and I got a smoochy farewell kiss from Clara. Hansi also gave me a kiss adding, 'When you the next time come you eat with us. Clara will cook you well.'

Daily Orders stated 'PM—Walter Burger' and the gardening

arrangements were duly handed over and I felt any future matters in that area should be handled by Mitch; after all he could also trim Clara's roses for her and possibly his satisfaction could be guaranteed without the smallest rose prick.

Daily Orders – Day 2 was a meeting with cloth buyer E. Zinniker, which passed off peacefully. He showed me the latest cloths he had selected for the Spring range and all went as smoothly as the new soft mohairs from Zegna's Italian mills. I asked Hansi to meet with the accounts department people as we would be buying PKZ goods in the future and we would have to calculate a 'landed' price when we offered the goods in sterling to our customers. They were about as helpful as Wardour Street had been when I had mentioned the subject after my return from the States. 'Just add on 5 per cent for the freight' was about as nonsensical as 'think of a number'. Five per cent of the value of a Jaguar was different from 5 per cent of the value of a shirt and I made a note to consult Theo, Kurt and Jörg Tschopp on that specialist subject.

For the final farewell, WB wished me a pleasant trip and asked me to ventilate the possibility of getting a stand at the next MAB exhibition in the UK, either at Harrogate or Brighton. 'We'll pay half,' he added reassuringly. I didn't push my luck to discover whether payment was going to be per invoice, cash or in Swiss francs, as I wanted to test the validity of the existence of the Swiss gnomes.

When I got back to the hotel there was a signal from the Bridge of 'HMS *Vilomi*': 'Will phone you 22.00hrs ZURICH time', which Jim did precisely to the minute.

'Sorry to disturb you but Bosco want you to come to Viggiù. I have checked with Jack Palmer about the open return ticket and if you nip into Italestero tomorrow they'll give you a ticket to Milan and you can get a bus or cab from there up to the Swiss border and Viggiù, which is where Bosco are. All I can say to an old deck-ape when he casts off to sail away: 'Let go fo'rrad ... let go aft ... I think that's what you used to do ... but watch it ... I haven't a clue if they have showers in the winter wonderland. They do in the Far East, showers *and* deck-apes. Have a good trip!'

'Don't bother,' he added, 'to ring Bosco. I will say ETA is around 11.30 ... OK?'

The train trip from Zurich to Milan was breathtaking and, as we left the city behind us, the train climbed slowly southwards and after about an hour reached Andermatt at the northern end of the St Gotthard Tunnel. The approach to it had been quite bleak but once the train emerged from the tunnel on the southern end, everything was green, the sun was shining, the birds were singing and it was as if we were on the set of *The Sound of Music*. I had been so engrossed that I had not noticed a mid-thirties gent wearing the uniform of the typical European businessman: dark suit, white shirt, Hermes silk tie and Crockett & Jones shoes. My copy of the *Financial Times* had slipped off my lap, but the *Zürcher Zeitung* remained, confusing him as to my nationality, so his opening gambit was in German.

He was fishing as to my profession or business and when the word 'textiles' cropped up, he was away as if the starting wires had been lifted at Ascot. He was the MD of a specialist knitted cotton company who manufactured very fine mercerised cotton sweaters. He wondered whether there was a market for this type of merchandise and opened his crocodile briefcase and showed me some beautiful samples which I thought were silk. By the time we got to Milan, we had exchanged cards and he gave me samples, swatches and prices and for the next three years we quite literally swept the British market with his Ochieppo Superiore knitted-cotton T-shirts. I also asked him to send samples to SMARTO, as they made no knitted goods, and they also had tremendous success with the addition to their range.

As per the orders from the Bridge of the 'HMS *Vilomi*', I caught a bus from Milan to Varese and then a sort of a cab to Viggiù. I'm sure it had seen better days on the set of *Bicycle Thieves*, almost ten years before but I just sat back, closed my eyes and thought of my own 'bi' adventures I had experienced in all those years.

But I just could not drop off and wrinkled my nose. That smell ... it was a very pleasant smell ... sort of perfumed rose ... but where was such a sweet aroma coming from an old decrepit scrapyard-ready clapped-out taxi like this? I looked at the cabbie and he certainly wasn't chewing rose-smelling chewing gum nor the usual Italian-based chewed garlic pong. Nor did he really fit the tough ruthless Mafioso ready-to-shoot-your-head off type but he eyed me suspiciously and asked if I was looking for anything in particular. I nodded and searched my very limited Italian. All I could remember was that most important question of 'How much?'

in Italian, which was 'Quanta costa?' Of course ... I kicked myself ... perfume ... *profumo*, which scored an instant hit with the swarthy cabbie and he pointed to a little flat green cardboard tree about five inches long hanging on the rear-view mirror.

'No Italian,' he explained in his broken English and pointed ahead of the cab through the windscreen. 'In Svizzera.'

I asked him to sell it to me.

After a lot of protestations and a few extra 500-lira notes he handed me the tree which, below the 'Magic Tree' product name, had an address of 'Watertown, NY, USA' on it.

Battered and bruised we arrived safely in Viggiù and I was welcomed like royalty by the Crosettis. My menu Italian was decidedly limited but it did include one of my favourite spring European delicacies: white asparagus. I wasn't sure whether the Italian version was green or white but when Bosco asked me if I would like to taste *asparagi* I was certainly up for it. I was not aware that five kilometres away was one of the best areas for this delicious veg and I was over the moon when we arrived at a local farm which had wooden tables and tressles outside and the bottles of Frascati on the tables were nudging each other ready to be emptied into the green long-stemmed white-wine glasses.

We started with the freshest of Parma ham and melon and then large oblong plates were put in front of us. There were six asparagus spears pointing towards the middle of the plate and on top were two poached eggs nudging the tips of the asparagus. A large bowl of freshly ground Parmesan cheese sprinkled over the eggs completed the feast and I was too much of a pig not to refuse second helpings. Signor Crosetti and his Mum were somewhat taken aback by my attack on the food and Mum kept on urging me on but I did not need much pushing.

When we got to the sweet I declined and gave up as I was eager to find out the reason for asking me to visit them and over the second *cappuccino* he revealed the subject in a somewhat shy manner. He pulled a letter out of his hip pocket which originated from AMC Milan and which related to the Bosco goods delivered by them to us. AMC had exclusive delivery rights for all goods supplied from non-British companies because they received a 25 per cent sales commission and therefore quite clearly we should not be involved.

When Signor Crosetti had spoken with Jim he had asked him

how much we were invoicing Bosco style numbers 2423, 2356 and 2379 and when Jim had told him on the phone he could not believe that our landed prices were so much cheaper. When I had shown those style numbers to Harrods they nearly swooned, and as AMC/Bosco business collapsed, ours grew. Bosco had now received a very strong letter to stop supplying us with these style numbers because it was against AMC's contractual agreement.

Signor Crosetti nipped off to the British Chamber of Commerce in Milan who explained that Bosco had no problem as their contractual arrangements were not being infringed because they were supplying their goods to a British company who were then selling to another British company – that is, Harrods – so there was no case to answer. When Bosco had the screws turned on them they coolly answered that that would not present a problem to them as they would contact all the customers worldwide, as long as they were Brits, which resulted in more business for Bosco. We then clinked glasses with the contents of the third bottle of Frascati. Signora Crosetti kissed and showered me with incomprehensible Italian and he just raised his glass, looked at me and smiled:

'You help me with the money problem ... I help you now ... But if we make much more business, what about the taxes in England?' I could hardly really explain to him that this might be a problem for the future but he persisted and asked me how many sets of books we kept for our company and I innocently replied by putting one finger up and he was speechless. 'One?' he queried. 'We have three in Italy: one for the taxman, one for me and the third for my partner.' Which was my first introduction to the Italian solution to paying taxes.

I thanked them again for the delicious meal and the settling of the problem and he asked if there were any more customers who wanted exclusivity and I promised to listen around. 'If they like Italian food you can always bring them over and we will do something *speciale* for them. Are you going back from Milano, or shall I run you the three kilometres into Switzerland and you can get a direct train from Lugano to Zurich?'

I plumped for the latter; even in May there was always fog at Linate or Malpensa. We had a beautiful drive along Lake Lugano and Mama gave me another kiss and said, 'Don't forget ... bring customers ... we have good food and wine. *Arrivideric*i...'

When I got to Zurich I went straight to the Swissair desk in the station and got a standby for the 20.00hrs flight to London. I went on a 'see what you can find' trip and found a pack of 'Magic Trees' on the concourse, caught the coach to Kloten at 18.00hrs, went straight to the international telephone desk and ten minutes later was talking to Jim.

'Busy day was it?' I could see him smirking. 'Anything special?' I could feel him raising his eyebrows questioningly. 'Too much to tell ... This phone call will cost us ... but what I can categorically say is that I really don't think it can get much better!'

'Good ... So you think it will mean the new DS Citroën?'

'Could be! We'll see. I'll phone you when I get to Thiefrow.'

There was no hold-up at HM Customs and the only raised eyebrows materialised when I opened my briefcase and showed the waterguard the 'Magic Trees' I had bought in Zurich.

'What on earth are they...?' he asked.

'Air fresheners and I bought a few for myself and my friends.'

He looked me straight in the eyes and out of sheer curiosity asked, 'Air fresheners for what...?'

'Well...' I shrugged, 'in the car...'

He shook his head. 'I don't smoke.'

'What about Saturday nights when you've had a few pints with the lads?'

'Could be...' he admitted with a small smile very reluctantly.

As he gathered the trees up and returned them to me, I handed one to him and grinned and in my best Jackspeak said: 'Go on, mate, it won't bite you and you can always stick it ... in the loo.' He picked it up and said, 'Cheers, mate, but if I like it where can I buy another?' If I had known the answer to that one, I could have told him, but I couldn't say 'back in Zurich, mate', could I?

If it was that hard to give one away, I wondered what the reaction would be to prospective buyers in the UK but when I got back to Oaken Street that night, the 'Tree' was the last item in my account of my Swiss–Italian adventures of the last few days. When we discussed things in the morning, and Jim had noted everything down, he turned to me: 'I'll get a letter off to Watertown, USA, and see if they'd like a UK agent...'

I stopped him. 'I haven't got a spare moment. I know nothing about that trade and nor does Mitch, so we'll have to advertise for agents...'

Then Jim stopped me. 'But I haven't even written the letter, sent it off, had a reply or a yes or no. So let's hang on and we'll find out.'

We all nodded and that was a typical example of our communist method of operating. But only the three of us shared the profits, those anyway that the Chancellor allowed us to keep.

Tale 33

ED

Geoffrey Child had finally returned to London and joined Decca International part-time which entailed constant European travel to many of their European offices. The minute he heard of Iden's 'Bell' – 'Les girls', his bells rang and he came down with us at weekends. On his daily trip to Decca he had seen the shell of a bombed house being rebuilt in Kennington Road and discovered it was owned by a local charity who were keen to let it, which he was not at all averse to. On one of his trips to the cottage he asked us if we were interested in buying property in the area as he had heard that we had moved the business to Great Marlborough Street and the daily travel from Richmond, times three, twice a day, meant there was hardly any time left for work.

The estate contacted us and we moved to Oakden Street just after family Morbin moved next to us into a Victorian terraced house. I used to carry the eighteen-month-old Greg up and down the tortuous spiral cement staircase and his Mum was most grateful to have some not so burly ex-sailors help her with the little bundle of joy.

Although the move from Richmond to Oakden Street in Kennington changed my closeness to Madame the final break was the business. I was kept up to date in October '58 with the addition of young Michael to Billy's family but otherwise Uncle Charles was my only link to the past, and now, when I was away such a lot, Jim became the sheet anchor in that area as both Charles and May were like old family friends and neighbours.

Charles was now in his mid-seventies and winding down business, pleasure-wise. May Corne was born and bred in Chelsea and her Dad owned three greengrocers in that part of town. She had moved into Chelsea Closets in the forties and she and Charles had a kind of open relationship. They had their own flat on different floors and liked their own company. They were the best of friends and spent most weekends and holidays together. It was a very practical arrangement in every sense of the word and they happily accepted that situation.

When I was away, Jim phoned Charles every week to report on the progress of the company and May also showed a great interest in business as she had been apprenticed to a hairdresser and his wife who ran and owned a ladies' hairdresser's in Sloane Square. They had no children and as they got older had three girl assistants in the shop. As the girls left or died, the remaining shares went to those remaining. After the death of the couple, the other two girls and May inherited the shop and freehold in Sloane Square.

Charles had worked all his life and, together, he and May were comfortably off as May eventually was the only survivor in the shop. May and Charles both glowed when they saw the progress Jim and I had made and loved the expansion of our company as if they were running it. Both of them were closer to Jim and me than any other member of our respective families.

The arranged marriage between Uncle Ernest and Auntie Henny from Amsterdam was working out well but now they were all in their late seventies as well and had slowed down to a quieter life. Henny's three sons were all married with children and two lived in the United States, and ED and Henny, Charles and May came down to our cottage at Wittersham and loved it and admired Mitch's show garden.

Jim had picked up a lot of culinary skills from Gerry at The Bell and amazed our visitors with the combination of a luxurious show garden mixed with four-star cordon-bleu cuisine. Jim and Mitch always said that I did nothing else but talk which, very reluctantly, I had to agree with.

Charles and May had been down to the cottage at Easter and when I returned from my Swiss trip Jim broke the bad news that ED was not at all well and Henny was totally distraught. I phoned her on that first Monday and she suggested I go and see ED in Isleworth Hospital. When I saw him he asked me to come over and sit by his side.

'Come and sit here,' he said, patting the bed.

'Goodness me!' he said. 'You look so much older than when I last saw you.' They were the last words he spoke to me and I could hardly speak when I told Jim and Mitch that evening. When the three of us spoke about ED that night Jim remarked that I had never really known him and I agreed.

Jim added his down-to-earth comment: 'Well, at least you never had a fight, did you?' and I nodded.

'C'mon, let's have a drink,' and we all drank to ED, a lost good friend.

Tale 34

Swiss Gnomes and Devalued Pounds

When Mitch and I were over in Switzerland just before Xmas 1964, Mitch was going over the collection with Jörg at TUSA when Theo asked me into his office.

'Sit down, David,' he beckoned. 'I hope you are pleased with our service. Jörg always pulls out all the stops for you and makes sure all the deliveries are on time and Jim has never phoned to ask why we have not delivered...' I nodded.

'When we started and talked about "landed" prices I gave you all the info you requested but with a change of your government we ought to have a chat about the rate of exchange between the pound and the Swiss franc...'

I stopped him. 'I'm pleased you brought it up because we've had some problems in Italy regarding our landed prices and the difference to the price Harrods pay through AMC. You know perfectly well that I'm not a bad salesman and we pay our invoices to you, but I would appreciate it if you could sit down with me and do a thorough search on the landed costing regarding freight costs...'

This time Theo interrupted me. A big broad smile stretched across his massive face and he opened a desk drawer and handed me a sheet with freight costings for sweaters, boxed weights and quantity discounts. 'Jörg had been telling me you were dropping hints about whether we could give this to you but he felt you were a bit shy about asking so we've done it in advance.' He handed me the details and costs. He looked up and smiled, got out two brandy glasses and poured 'gulpers' into them. 'Much better than at the Lake with a bottle of Féchy?'

I nodded, lifted the glass and we clinked and before I could thank him he put up his open hand, lifted it towards me and gave one of his warm smiles.

'Don't thank me; it'll mean more business for you and us ... Cheers!' and we had another sip.

Theo went on: 'Jörg has checked with Danzas and Italestero and they have agreed on the freight charges being identical. If they're not, Jörg will just tell them to get knitted.' He smiled. 'I learnt that in London just after World War I.

'But seriously, you've had the Nazi experience yourself and know what havoc politicians can create, and when you're a businessman you are caught in between them. You have just had a change of government and politicians have all the theoretical answers which sometimes work but are mostly the brainchild of some eminent professors who *think* and believe they have all the answers.

'Your Mr Wilson has just appointed two eminent economic advisors and I believe the appointments have sent shudders through the City of London...'

He handed me a copy of *The Times* dated 30th October 1964. I read the first few lines:

> *'The Government has now chosen its economic*
> *advisers: Dr Thomas Balogh for the Prime*
> *Minister and Mr Nicholas Kaldor for the*
> *Chancellor. He has also advised governments*
> *from India and Ceylon to Ghana, Mexico and*
> *British Guiana on budgetary policies.*
> *In Guiana and Ceylon attempts to put this advice*
> *into practice were followed by riots.'*

'I don't think you will have any riots,' Theo continued, 'but I think you ought to prepare yourself for any eventuality starting with invoices in foreign currency. We are delighted to note you pay all your bills promptly, but there are invoices out for payment, not due, all the time.' I nodded.

'To save any currency loss, pay them immediately and haggle out an extra discount. If you don't have the money I'm sure we could help you.

'But the biggest danger is that you have ordered goods for delivery months ahead so you could get caught this way and the two gents could alter the exchange rate overnight and thus devalue the pound. They would do this over a weekend because of the world timezone difference, so always make sure you owe no foreign currency before the banks close on Friday night.

243

'As for future business between us the Swiss franc vis-à-vis the pound, phone me the minute you hear something as I will certainly act at this end. In any case, I could always stop one of Mr Wilson's gnomes in the Bahnhof Strasse and ask him or her, whichever sex they are.'

He raised his eyebrows and asked if all this was too much in one go but I had been hanging on to his words as if they had come out of Steff's mouth all those years ago at Hampton Grammar.

'When you are away I think Jim is always in touch, so brief him when you get back, but whatever you do, don't wait, because it won't go away!' He offered me some more Grand Marnier, which I sipped willingly.

Almost to the day, three years later on, in '67 the pound *was* devalued. Fortunately we had followed Theo's advice and the problem was only on goods that had been ordered but not yet delivered. Yet the Prime Minister, Mr Harold Wilson, had assured TV viewers on the 19th November that 'devaluation does not mean that the pound in your pocket, nor in your bank, has been devalued'.

As the devaluation was 14.4 per cent and was effected on a Friday night, our weekend phone lines between Austria, Italy and Switzerland were smouldering.

On Monday morning I went to our bank and asked for the manager, who was not altogether surprised to see me. After all the niceties had been dispensed with I asked him straight out: 'Why didn't you tell me that the pound was going to be devalued?'

He leant back in his chair, took off his glasses and quietly said, 'My dear Mr Franklin, if I had known that last Friday, I would be sitting in the Bahamas right now. But seeing you fought your way out of the Delby Coats' disaster all those years ago, your best bet really is ... and I should not be saying it ... Head Office won't like it ... the amount of foreign currency business you are now doing, you should find a small merchant bank to do that for you and don't ask me who...' He opened a drawer in his desk, handed me a sheet with three typed names on it and I looked and gasped at one name on the list: Leopold Joseph and Sons Ltd was the bank that ED had worked in just after World War I.

When I got back to No. 39 I didn't even say hello to Jim but grabbed the phone, rang the number on the sheet and asked if there was anyone there who would have known ED's friend Mr Worthing prior to World War II and the lady on the phone said:

'Oh, I knew Mr Worthing but I think our Mr Ruge would have as well. Would you like to speak with him?' I nodded, even forgetting to say 'yes'.

Karl Ruge was just about to retire but he felt that this was too good a coincidence to pass by and Leo J. became our bankers for all the following years. When I explained the problem of guaranteeing foreign currency prices six months ahead, all he said was:

'What problem? We can buy the currency forward and hold it for you until the exact day you have bought it forward for, although there is one small snag. Sadly, I don't know you from Adam or, in your case, Mr Worthing.'

I asked if a Swiss guarantor would do.

'You have contacts to Swiss banks ... ?' and I felt what he really wanted to say in Jackspeak would have been: 'So what the hell are you asking us for when you have a Swiss bank.' But it was all getting a little too complicated as Theo was not a Swiss bank but a Swiss banker.

Theo was delighted with the arrangement; our competitors were asking us how we could guarantee prices six months ahead when the pound was dropping like a stone by the minute. This started to trickle through the trade and to the MAB, of whom we were members. The final problem to be solved was the 14 per cent price devaluation of cost to our customers for outstanding orders. We made a few phone calls and told them to vote Conservative next time around and would they accept a price increase of half the devaluation of 7 per cent. We would carry the $3^1/2$ per cent loss and so would the supplier, and they all jumped at it and didn't ask or threaten the age-old Jackspeak of 'It'll cost you'. Anyway I wasn't quite sure how this could work out in non-Jackspeak.

Bert Failes from the MAB phoned me regarding any info on the devaluation problems and we agreed to have a pint as their offices in Argyll House were literally across the road from us in Great Marlborough Street. Many of the UK men's retailers were MAB members and Bert suggested we went down the Annual Exhibition road and booked a stand. I nearly threw up the remains of the pint as we had been bending over backwards to try and get a stand for more than two years. It wasn't even a question of dear old Tom Avery's backscratching, someone had to propose you and I didn't bother to explain to him that I had had a number of those over the years but I never mixed business with pleasure. However,

Bert came to the point, which wasn't actually the 'currency' info bit but that the largest textile conglomerate in Europe had contacted him with a view to a MAB delegation visiting their factory in Italy.

GFT is the largest vertical manufacturer in Europe supplying every menswear outlet in the UK from Marks & Spencer to Harrods and a group visit by MAB members would cement relationships between them and the UK. Gruppo Financiaro Tessili made all types of clothing and the MAB were not only going to see their Turin set-up but their mills on their Italian trip as well.

We were into our second pint when I asked Bert to come across the road as he hadn't seen our premises. As we walked into the office Jim made us most welcome. I excused myself just in case I was in the way but when I returned they were knee-deep in conversation. Bert was just intrigued by the smallness of our 'three-room set-up' when so many of his members were talking about us. Finally Bert said he had an interesting chat with Jim and the idea of Jim's to stop off in Zurich and visit some of PKZ's shops and the factories would be quite interesting. SIDI are the largest in Europe and PKZ being a smaller, family-type business would give them a good picture over the whole spectrum.

'What a good idea,' I added, turning to Bert and keeping my fingers firmly crossed behind my back.

Bert turned to me and, pointing at Jim, added, 'Jim's idea of you and I doing a dummy run in advance in Switzerland, fixing exact stopwatch visiting times and then adding a time-sheet plan for all members is great. Will it take you long to organise?'

Jim looked at him and pointed at me. 'If you can get him out of the office, I'll phone Switzerland and have it all wrapped for you by 17.30hrs.'

Bert blinked and turned towards Jim. 'You weren't in the Puss were you?'

Tale 35

Trade Unions and Political Correctness

Bert's and my dummy run to Zurich went like a happy dream. Waltie Burger promised to supply a most spectacular exhibit for the next MAB show and I blinked when we were taken to the basement of PKZ's factory in Zurich. His grandfather had started the company and in the nineteenth century they used an enormous horse-drawn wooden sleigh to deliver their goods to other shops. It was beautifully carved and had ornate gold leafing on the side and was now used as a centrepiece for exhibitions. I just stood there and gazed and Bert felt it was perfect for the centrepiece for the next MAB Exhibition in 1968 at Brighton and I thought I was hearing things.

I don't know if Tom would have classified this as 'backscratching' but I was really only interested in the clinking of all those silver one-franc pieces which would drop off the sleigh, snow or no snow, or in the Bahnhof Strasse in Zurich.

When I reported back to Jim on those two nights in Zurich he knew I was not pissed, especially when I had to describe the special packaging for the sleigh and Danzas had to make a special trip to view it, package it and insure it for the trip and the additional insurance for the time on the MAB stand. Still the good bit was that, as we were sharing the cost of the stand with PKZ and they paid for getting the wooden museum piece to and from Brighton, the whole operation had been a terrific success and the resulting spin-offs were impossible to calculate in pounds or Swiss francs.

The mid-1960s were just when the unions were getting muscle power and all working hands preparing the stands were 100 per cent closed-shop unionised. If you lifted as much as a screwdriver or hammer on your own stand everybody 'came out' on strike, which was particularly annoying if you wanted to move any electrical gear or tighten a screw on a plug.

Jim was helping us prepare the stand and was busily fixing wires and lamps when he was told to stop as he was not a member of the union. Fortunately this was on the very first preparation day, which resulted in him going back to the office and making complete sets of wiring and banks of plugs which only required non-unionised bare hands to push the plugs into and they lasted throughout the following seven MAB yearly shows. He wondered about patenting his ideas and flogging them to exhibitors at all UK shows throughout the year, but he already had his hands full with the jobs at Great Marlborough and we spoke about this and how busy we were to our friends the 'Pee-Gees' (Phillip and Georgie) whom we met a lot at The Bell at Iden.

They had a farm at Beckley which was just across the River Rother and we used to meet socially either at their farm or at 'Killicks'. Just before the Brighton show we were talking to them at The Bell as Vicky was releasing Phillip from an armlock when they were messing around behind the bar. As we walked in she was holding him from behind his back with one hand and the other was clutching his new bushy sideburns which were at least seven inches long.

'Better than an armlock,' said Vicky. 'He's grown them especially long for me, haven't you, darling?' she said, grabbing hold of both of them by the side of Phillip's face.

'They are my special bugger grips, aren't they?' she trumpeted through the whole bar, 'or yours dear?'

'Shut up,' said Phillip and asked us if we were still busy and Jim nearly passed out. 'Tell you what, Georgie's got a god-daughter who wants to 'temp' in the West End. Would you like to see her in your office? I think she is in-between-bosses at the moment.'

And indeed she was. Di became Jim's heart of gold and when he asked her about times of working she replied: half-time please, and when Jim asked which hours half-time Di shook her head and replied: 'Well, actually it's Mondays, Tuesdays and Fridays. The other days I go hunting down in Sussex and I have to look after the horses and there is the Mini-Cooper to keep clean and the flat in town.'

Di fitted into our completely mad set-up, proving that the lunatics had finally taken over the asylum, and stayed with us until she married ten years later. She spoke two other languages fluently and could write letters in those languages as well. Jim was sorely tempted to find out if she could write French letters but she would have put him firmly down with a very strong 'Jiiiiiim!'

One or two shows a year, six trips abroad to Austria, Germany, Italy and Switzerland, a house in London and a cottage in the country. It was no wonder we saw little of our families and close friends, except Uncle Charles and May with whom Jim had regular telephone contacts. Jim had a very fixed routine which, like the routine in the RN, was divided into his own 'watches'. Breakfast was at 07.30, if the post had arrived; view post; if not, WC for an hour. This enabled him to study the *Daily Telegraph* and *Financial Times* in total peace without phone calls. After that, off to the office and bedlam, and if he broke this routine it was 'action stations' which he did in December 1967.

The loo door opened and he shouted at me: 'Dave ... you'll never believe it, but our solicitor had been struck off for taking clients' money. He doesn't have any of our deposits!' As usual, Jim was right but my immediate thought was how do I get another one.

'Go and ask the bank manager. He was very helpful with that city bank!'

When I got to the office Jim pointed me in the direction of Wardour Street and I walked into the office of the person Jim had just made an appointment with.

'Oh do sit down ... Everything all right with Leo J.?' He gave me a very pleasant smile.

'Many thanks again; I felt it was better not to write an official letter to the bank,' I said and the manager turned a definite paler shade of white.

'It's just that you know so many people. This morning Mr Harvey saw in the paper that the company's solicitor had been struck off. No, no fortunately he holds no funds of ours but we wondered if you could recommend any solicitor who handles small companies like ours?'

'Oh, Mr Franklin, you are too modest. Of course with the loss of the foreign-ex business, but we still value you as an old customer.' He opened an address book and ran his finger down a lined page. 'I do believe I have just the right person for you. He's on the City–West End borderline, is very efficient and as sharp as a razor.' He wrote Freddy's name, address and phone number on a piece of paper.

'Glad to have been of help and tell me how you get on. Splendidly I think, he's roughly your age.' He rose, gave me the piece of paper, walked to the door with me and opened it. I shook his hand, thanked him again and he stopped me.

'I'm sorry, but with all this political correctness around, I hope you have no colour, sex or race prejudices...' I shook my head and looked at him.

'Well, that's all right then; you see, Freddy is Jewish.'

Tale 36

The Doctor from Zurich

On 15th April 1950 Admiral Patrick Brind, Commander-in-Chief Far East Station had issued a Special Order of the Day which stated that: 'During flying operations on 4th February 1950 a Seafire aircraft crashed on the deck of HMS *Triumph* and burst into flames.' Jim was not one of these physically involved but had seen the accident. He had shown me the photograph of the pilot in the burning plane when I had visited in Eastbourne and when he told me the story of that living inferno which he had witnessed at first hand, his face went as white as a death mask.

When I came down for breakfast on the next Monday morning after the 'new' solicitor episode Jim had the same death mask look on his face.

'Anything wrong?' I quipped and he just growled about Mitch having had to rush off to Bentall's in Kingston to see Mr Head whom he had been trying to get hold of for months.

'Nothing else?' I persisted and Jim eventually snapped and burst out: 'I just don't understand you, Dave. I try and keep everything in order and worry myself silly every time you fly off. And when you get into that car of yours, I always tell you to be careful, we don't want a repeat of that "Kill-JOY" affair of five years ago. I thought you would have told me if you had any health problems. So why did you go and see a doctor in Zurich? Have you caught the boat up after a cheap flight with those pretty Swissair maidens or perhaps a quick tussle with an Alitalia steward in the heads?'

I just stared at him and shook my head.

'I haven't a clue what you're talking about. I know no doctor in Zurich and wouldn't even know where to find one.'

Jim thrust a letter under my nose with a Zurich postmark and on the back of the envelope was the name and address of the sender: 'Dr Julius Saemann, 43 Klosbachstrasse Zurich'.

'Go on...' he urged, 'you open it, it's your problem.' He handed me a letter opener. I sliced the letter open, grinned and turned to Jim handing him the letter.

'I think it's going to be your problem as it'll be more work for you and you've never had to do any Customs entry forms for US goods before have you?'

He read the letter and burst out laughing, collected himself and just uttered: 'Good, in'it?'

Dr Saemann was the owner of the registered trademark 'Magic Tree', which was manufactured by his company, the Car Freshener Corporation of America in Watertown, NY, USA and they had forwarded our letter to him. After all, they felt London was in Europe and so were we ... so that's all right then! His letter gave us his phone number in Zurich and as Jim was dialling the Zurich number, he handed the letter and receiver back to me.

When Mitch returned with an order from Bentall's, he was much happier and when we told him about our chat with the doctor from Zurich. He was already on his sleigh ride to the Swiss mountains, though not on the antique PKZ nineteenth-century sleigh. We all adjourned to the 'our' local in the kitchen with three bottles of lager and Jim did not take any 'company' notes re the new company's activities but just made a 'plan of action'.

Details of this tale over the next three years could fill the flight deck of HMS *Triumph* but the 'magical' doctor came to see us and we signed an agency agreement with the possibility of buying Magic Tree from them and wholesaling them with ... surprise, surprise ... a 'landed' margin. The response from most prospective customers was totally negative, as when you had finally explained what an air freshener was, the 'smelly' trail had evaporated. Another board meeting was convened and it was decided we needed specialist salesmen who had to be recruited.

That morning Jim had his usual 'duty watch' in the loo and appeared triumphantly waving the *Daily Telegraph*. Wolfy must have caught up with us because an agent in the automotive trade in Scotland wanted a fast-selling line to implement his range. We couldn't really pretend to Jim Shannon that it was fast-selling but we felt it had good sales potential. He was over his smelly haggis and sold 'Magic Trees' as if there were no kilts to be pinned or unpinned in the future.

I remembered the rise of the supermarkets that I had witnessed in the USA and started banging on a few supermarket group doors. At that point in time, ASDA was the fastest-growing company in the UK supermarket field, and I knocked on their door every month, month after month, year after year. As I was younger than the buyer and never took no for an answer, Robin in Leeds couldn't resist an offer I made him: 'We will supply you with "Magic Tree" on "sale-or-return" for three months, and if the profit on the goods is higher percentage-wise than your other goods you place it on order throughout the group.'

After three months he very happily agreed that the percentage-wise profits they were making were higher than the other goods, even food, which was number one. The other supermarket groups did not want to miss out on this either. After five years we had propelled MT into the market-leader position. Or as dear Uncle Charles had told me years ago, if at first you don't succeed, try, try and try again. Only he had put it a little more graphically by using the 'sex' element in his equation and exact location.

I met with the Swiss doctor frequently and when our sales reached large volumes, he pointed out that importing the product was great but we would never break the market unless we started to manufacture it under licence in the UK with UK packaging. Freddy Fishburn put us on the road to a trademark lawyer and we now acquired that trademark legal knowledge which was not only complicated but extremely expensive. Once we had acquired the trademark we now had to rent premises to manufacture the product and found a factory site close to Kennington at Battersea. It was at this point everything now became almost spooky.

When we moved to Oaken Street from the flat in Richmond, our new neighbours were the Morbins, whom I had helped with the little bundle of joy up and down the tortuous cement spiral staircase. Young Greg's birthday was the same as Billy's, my brother, but his Dad's birthday was identical to mine, which much later caused Jackspeak comments like 'So he's your father then – tell us another!' which I did not pass on to Maureen, his heart-of-gold Mum. I think if I had, she would have hit me with a frying pan and Dad would have joined in with another. Greg, the original bundle of joy, was now turning into an object of Lambeth female's lust. Six foot two inches out of his socks and around fifteen stone, he continually won trophies on and off the football field in his local football club colours, with his shorts on and off. His Mum came around to us just as Greg had turned seventeen, as she had heard that we were starting a factory in Battersea and were looking for staff. I did not say 'That's a silly question to ask' – Maureen was much too nice a person for that – but her retired Mum and Dad started as part-timers. Later she asked if there was an opening for a trainee as well. We assured her there was, not in the RN but at 'HMS *Vilomi*'.

In the event, Greg started with two of his mates, one of whom had been a lifelong friend and one who did not believe in work, on principle. When I asked him about not turning up for one whole day in the first week I put it to him in the nicest possible way that we all had to work to earn some money. He looked at me in utter disbelief: 'No we don't,' he replied, 'I can go on the social.' And we really had no answer for that.

Having once invested our money in the factory we simply had to try and recoup it and decided to sell the 'Magic Tree' directly to the buying public and the only two options were blanket national advertising and/or an exhibition to the public. The 'Ideal Home Exhibiton' is held at Earls Court once a year and it was cheaper than blanket national advertising, so we took the plunge and raided the bank account to finance it. We asked the Americans to help with the finance of this operation, to which they said: 'It's your show ... you'll have to pay for it. You're making all the money selling it.' We just had to grin and pay for it. However, it turned out to be a colossal eye-opener to deal directly with the buying public.

'Air freshener, what's that then?'

'Makes your house smell nice.'

'Are you trying to tell me it's dirty?'

In the final resort you mentioned that there was one place in the house where there was a permanent pong, and you either got them dissolving into giggles or offended that you had spoken 'dirty' to them.

However, Mitch got first prize for my new 'Tree-Speak' dictionary. Two charming ladies in their early seventies watched Mitch with his expert spiel of cutting the cellophane bag open, shaking the 'Tree' forward, pulling the little loop which held the 'Tree' slightly out of the bag and, very gently, waving it under the noses of the two ladies.

'Oh, it IS a lovely smell!'

Mitch was already counting the sale of definitely one if not two 'Trees' and turned to the potential customers to ask if they wanted two whilst they were at it.

'Perhaps...' replied one. 'But does it kill moths?'

Mitch gave her one of his long-tried 'Singer' smiles adding: 'Of course ... if you hit them with it. Did you want two or an economy pack of four for the price of three?'

The lady was so taken aback that she bought two packs and Mitch was tempted to ask if she had a moth farm.

The sales-stand people were not unionised, which was just as well as it was a twelve-hour day in shifts, seven days a week for four weeks. None of us had ever seen so much cash and the bank bags were rolled out on trolleys every night and the bank-robbing fraternity was definitely fast asleep as the nightly haul from the companies on the first-floor balcony ran into tens of thousands of pounds every night.

The TV Jamie Oliver of the sixties was the chef Philip Harben and he had tied up with the first manufacturer of non-stick frying pans and pots. Their stand was opposite ours on the other side of the gangway and he had four demonstrators doing hourly shifts, which represented about 20 sales per quarter of an hour; twelve hours a day equals 960 a day; 6,720 per week; 27,000 for the four weeks; at £5 per pan that was around £135,000 cash for the show. The Krays were murdering people for less cash in the East End barely five miles away and this was legal. In today's value this would represent about £2 million for four weeks' work, less wages and stand cost.

We were deliriously happy but very exhausted. I had contacted Louis Klemantaski to introduce me to a press cuttings company who had monitored the press for mentions of 'Magic Tree' during the show, and at the end of the four weeks they presented us with a sack full of cuttings. We had these reproduced and next month sent a mailshot, along with samples and prices, to every major retail outlet in Britain and the letter box was jammed on most weekdays for the next month.

We were contented and the bank was very happy, but all the powers-that-be in Watertown said was: 'Is that all? We want far more from that market because your population is 52 million, and we always estimate sales to be 10 per cent of the population.' I

255

pointed out that this could be very misleading and when I asked Watertown how many they were selling in China and Russia, they changed the subject.

From Berlin to Bletchley

I was born in Berlin but nearly died in a car crash in 1953 near Bletchley. Ironically, the success of the Government Code and Cypher School at Bletchley during World War II laid the foundations for the success of our company from the 1970s.

According to the well-known author Robert Harris, the cracking of the German Enigma codes was the weapon that won the war, and George Steiner, a fellow of Churchill College, Cambridge, maintains that '. . . the work done at Bletchley Park was . . . the greatest achievement of Britain during World War II.'

Alan Turing, the brilliant Cambridge mathematician, played the crucial part in breaking the Enigma code which helped to read communications between Berlin and all units on the German fronts. He and Tommy Flowers built a prototype machine at the Post Office Research Station Dollis Hill and within ten months Collosus lived up to its name. It was a gigantic metal fixture, was valve operated and stood eight feet high and twelve feet long.

Just before the war in the summer of 1939 sixteen cryptoanalysts arrived at Bletchley to try and break the Enigma Code. At the end of the war there were 10,000 working around the clock to crack all the codes with ten Collosus computers and they included Geoffrey Child, academics, eccentrics, classicists, historians, chess players and musicians. But I am not sure which category Geoffrey was employed in but it is on record that a man who had won the *Daily Telegraph* crossword competition was recruited and spent the last two years at Bletchley Park. The German Enigma machine was like a large typewriter with vertical thin wheels which were rotated after each letter had been typed and had proved impossible to decode.

On 9th May 1941 the 3rd Escort Group went to convoy OB-318 in the Atlantic and was attacked by U-110 commanded by the notable U-boat ace *Kapitän Leutnant* Julius Lemp, the man who had sunk the liner *Athenia* on the first evening of the war. The U-boat was depth-charged to the surface and her crew poured out of the conning tower abandoning ship. A boarding party led by Sub-Lieutenant David Balme of HMS *Bulldog* went aboard U-110, recovered binoculars, sextants, books, logs, charts, diaries, tools, instruments and two large packing cases including U-110's Enigma cipher machine with its settings for 9th May on its rotors. The visitors from Bletchley who went to Scapa Flow could not believe their eyes and the rest is history. Many believe that the capture of the U-110 shortened the war by two years, saving hundreds of thousands of lives.

The cracking of the Enigma Code of a possible 150 trillion settings by the Collosus machines laid the foundations for a large-scale program-controlled computer and as such was the forerunner of all post-war digital computers. Had the latter not appeared on the commercial market in the 1970s our company could not have functioned. I was amazed that Jim had not gone on strike. The amount of work increased and having to convert four shillings and eleven pence per yard into Swiss francs, Deutsche marks or Austrian schillings per metre without a machine would have been an impossibility even for dear Old Steffs at Hampton. At this point our accountant Mr Bland in Ilford decided to sell his business to the largest firm of accountants in Essex and Mr Elliott fitted our bill like a smooth twentieth-century quill pen. He put us in touch with a company who could handle our computer requirements and I visited them with a view to purchasing a computer that could handle that sort of software. As expected, however, there was no such currency conversion software available off the shelf. 'We do, however, supply a "programming handbook" which will enable you to write that sort of program yourself, *if* you can handle "figures".'

When the large cardbox containing the computer arrived it was a bit like undoing a Xmas present without a bow and I could not get the unwrapping done fast enough. Everything was beautifully wrapped, except there was one small problem: there was no programming book and Jim and Mitch had to tie me down as they thought I was about to explode. Jim picked up the phone and handed me over to the sales manager who had drooled over me, especially about the 'programming book'. 'Humble apologies, Mr Franklin; I'll get on to Nuremberg immediately and call you back.'

Fifteen minutes later, oozing oily apologies, he confirmed that the bloody computers did *not* have a programming book. Jim tried to hold me down as I explained to him that I had been given a beautiful full-colour four-page booklet saying just that. Had he been near me I would have rammed the leaflet ... in my best Jackspeak ... up his posterior. Just to prove my anger was not unfounded, I mentioned something about the Trade Descriptions Act. Local Trading Standards Officer ... etc ... etc ...

He phoned back fifteen minutes later and apologised again. He had spoken to Germany again and, under the circumstances, they were only too happy to give me a crash course in programming. When Jim asked me 'how much' I grinned back and said, 'It'll cost them ... not us!'

Exhausted but not deliriously happy, we now had to contact our VAT office regarding invoicing in foreign currency as VAT was only applicable to sterling. Three visits from the various echelons of VAT visited us and it had to go to the 'Board' as to the converted invoice Swiss franc value in sterling. After three months VAT decided that the value in sterling should be at the day's rate of exchange in the *Financial Times*, with the cutting attached to the invoice.

As sterling was as volatile as HMS *Triumph* in a hurricane, Leopold Joseph, our bank, had advised us to work directly with local banks in the three countries we were selling to. Permission from the Bank of England had to be requested and confirmed and as the spin doctors were still peddling the Swiss gnome myth, every customer that came to our showroom tried to wind us up and mockingly said: 'Ha-ha! ... I suppose you have one of these black Swiss bank accounts?' To which we always replied with a small smile: 'Of course we have ... and in Germany, too,' adding, 'but with Bank of England permission of course! And they are both whiter than white.'

I don't know to this day whether they were impressed or jealous or just wanted to use it as well. But in any case they increased the size of the orders. In sterling.

When the new bank transactions had been completed, Mr Elliott was delighted with the ease and legality of the operation and added a further suggestion. 'I suggest you try and increase your export sales because if your export sales equate with your imports, you don't have to worry about buying currencies forward; one will balance out the other and you save some money.' Jim must have had this in mind because when he had his official 'stand easy' coffee break at 10.30 the next day he looked out into Carnaby Street and pointed down into it: 'Do you remember Hector from the Revenue who was so helpful with the VAT/PT number?' I nodded.

'Look at all the kids in Carnaby Street; they're wearing the usual clobber but now they've got those six-footer scarves wound around their necks ... around and around ... just like Hector. I've been on to Bert at the MAB, he's given me two firms in Nottingham and they are sending off samples and prices. Mind you, they thought I was mad when I said "Export"; "for English university scarves? You're joking."'

This tale is short, very positive and lucrative.

We got the samples and dear little Hansi Steinmann in Zurich sent his 'Jiiiiim' a list of German stores they sold PKZ to, and when I phoned the first one he gave me the name of ABZ in Essen who were the central buying group for German stores for 'sundries'. As they represented almost 120 stores, the manufacturer in Nottingham was surprised that the Krauts wanted so many English university and school scarves. 'You can't have a chap from Berlin University wearing a Rugby school scarf!' he protested, and I almost felt like telling him I agreed that it wasn't really 'cricket' but that the Krauts didn't play that game anyway.

Three days later I was with the buyer in Essen and he couldn't understand why we had only just contacted him now. Beatles clobber was everywhere but no one had offered him six-footer scarves. He couldn't thank me enough and could I get him samples for each store.

'I'll get them to you as soon as I'm back in London,' I said.

'Why wait? Phone them now...' I gawped at him as he pointed at a large glass cubicle with a lady in it and said: 'Tell her to get London for you and she'll connect you, and if it works get your colleague to telex us back with the answer.'

Before I could protest and confess my ignorance, he was gone. My German was perfect but my knowledge of German business efficiency was as barren as the Sahara. The girl was most helpful and seconds later I was speaking to the Bridge on HMS *Vilomi*.

'This is an unscheduled call' protested Jim. 'Anyway, you're OK I hope? What can I do for you?' and I told him in non-Jackspeak.

On my return to London I rang Leo J., our bankers, to get filled in about telex, the new telephonic contraption, and Jim said they'd not had telex on HMS *Unicorn* either, which was not really surprising as it only used land lines. The switchboard girl confirmed that my call had been booked to Herr Schmidt and also gave me their telex number, which started to receive my delivery details from our newly found friends in Nottingham.

The new Telex machine was like a gigantic noisy typewriter on a huge desk and punched holes into a two-centimetre-wide tape which one tore off, dialled up the required telex number and fed the tape through. The machine rattled the telex through but it was impossible to hold a conversation in the room when it was sending the tape. It was Jim's object of love and he always used any excuse to leave the room when it was clattering away, which it started to do when the order came through from Essen. The spewed-out sheets were like those Andrex toilet rolls that the TV puppy held in its little jaw and the very first order just kept on rattling for ten minutes. When Jim pulled it off the roller, he looked at it, turned to me and just uttered seven words:

'Good God ... and that's only the start!' After that, we were the bright boys for Mr Schmidt and every time the group wanted something special, we got it for them.

Jim was still holding the floor trailing telex in his hand and handed it over to me. 'Excuse me a minute,' he said and left the room. Ten minutes later he returned holding a copy of *Time* magazine in his hand and pushed it at me.

'I saw this on the news-stand and it's all about "Swinging London"' He hummed a little ditty which was always being played on the radio and TV: 'London swings like a pendulum do...'

'Why don't we,' he continued, 'mailshot all the leading stores in Germany and Switzerland and you, Dave, can organise a haggle with *Time* to get 200 copies to put in the mailshot and do a German letter with it. For France we'll have to do a French one...' I stopped him before the conversation got out of or into someone's hand.

I picked up the phone and spoke to Louis Klemantaski, told him our plan but he knew no one at *Time*. Then he gave a little chuckle and said: 'But, Dave, *you've* been to the States and heard all that "marketing bullshit". Wrack your brains and start flattering them first and see how it goes ... circulation telephone number figures, market leader ... brilliant layout... If you talk massive number of copies ... more than a wholesaler would take ... and maybe that was last month's copy, so thousands are now gathering dust on their shelves? Tell me how you get on and bring me up to date how Civvy Street is treating you.'

Jim pushed the *Time* phone number into my hand and I got a very junior marketing executive fresh out of college to talk to me. I felt it was somewhat unfair for the lad to have been let loose on me but all I was interested in was to screw him down to the lowest price they wouldn't fire him for. It was the previous print-run number which put him on the defensive for a start but as it was our hard-earned cash I had no pangs of conscience. After all, Uncle Charles had always told me that we learn by experience, especially when it comes to money, and it's your own.

Schap and Hansi Steinmann now gave us a top-up of the German, Austrian and Swiss retailer lists. We had our German letter duplicated and only had to wait for the response to the *Time* cover and our letter from the three countries and the first one came by phone three days later. I was glued to it for the next fortnight and Jim helpfully suggested I sling a hammock but there were no hooks for the three ex-hookys. However, Jim insisted on having an extra phone line put in as our ordinary line was being burnt up by the sizzling Cowbellers, Sauerkrauters and Schnitzlers.

Mitch and I started in Hamburg and worked our way south into Switzerland and at the end of the second week visited the annual menswear exhibition in Cologne. When we had tasted the first 'export' blood last year we were eager to find a UK cashmere sweater manufacturer who was not already selling into Austria, Germany and Switzerland. The cream of the trade like Braemar or Lyle & Scott had been represented for years but we spoke to one of the Derby suppliers of cashmere to M&S who were not represented. We mentioned we had contacts who could buy similar volumes to M&S and they were all ears.

'Good,' said Freddy, our solicitor, and we made an exclusive sales contract with them. When he prepared the contract Freddy queried the content regarding exclusivity and penalties if terms were not adhered to. Due to our trading-terms clauses, which were based on the info from the Schaps, we got Freddy to insert 'as per standard German penalty clauses'.

Freddy protested with: 'I bet they don't know what they are. They'll never sign that...' Using Uncle Charles's old methods, I replied: 'If you don't ask, you don't get!'

They returned the contract duly signed, including the 'exclusivity' clause and vast damages based on two years sales into that market which is something they were obviously not aware of.

When we got to the fair at Cologne we made straight for the bar and ran into the buyers from ABZ and it was like 'a run ashore' from bygone days. Amongst all the banter one of the buyers said he had admired *our* stand and Mitch and I blinked. 'What stand?' we asked.

'Oh the cashmere knitwear stand with the goods you sold us last year.' Mitch had to hold me to stop me from passing out.

We bade them good-bye and Mitch told me to hang on whilst he went to see our friends from Derby.

'Hello, Mitch, what are you doing here?'

Mitch glared at them. 'More to the point, what are *you* doing here?'

'Selling our cashmere! You opened up the market so nicely for us. Come and have a drink.'

In his mildest form of Jackspeak Mitch pointed out that they had signed an exclusivity contract with us.

'Oh that doesn't matter,' said Dad, and Junior nodded his head.

'It does to Dave. I'll guarantee you that when you get back to Derby there will be a letter from our solicitors explaining the facts of life to you. Dave is a very nice bloke but if someone tries to piss on him, he blows it back with the help of a large blowtorch and it will be a Mr Fishburn from London.' He waved them good-bye.

When Mitch returned he was grinning from ear to ear and told me the sordid details. 'Freddy is going to love this, it's like going clay-pigeon shooting with all the targets glued to the branch.'

When we went to see Freddy on our return he could not believe his luck and really enjoyed himself with their solicitor. He asked him why they had not checked on the 'standard German penalty clauses' but the answer was a shrug of the shoulders which resulted in five-figure cash damages. This was spread over two years and coincided with the Derby's company bankruptcy.

When we took Freddy out to dinner after having cashed the last cheque, we clinked glasses and he said: 'I'll give you some advice. Never let anything get to court if you can possibly avoid it. The only people who benefit are the two lawyers.' He gave a big grin and added: 'But this was almost the exception but you really put it on a bloody plate for me with that "German trading terms". Just goes to show that someone without an Oxford law degree can also teach you something. Any other stupid suppliers you know?'

The telex also helped us get over the national postal strike which started in 1971. However, the prospect of no letters, orders or cheques in the post demanded immediate DC and all Jack Palmer said to Jim when he mentioned this were two words: 'No problem'. Jim thought he had misheard and before Jim could protest, Jack said: 'I'll sort it out for you. All our docs for the shipped goods from the UK have to be aboard the ferries in Felixstowe or Harwich before 20.00hrs every night before they sail. We send a car or truck down from here so if you get a "Vilomi" sack to us here in Blackfriars Road by 17.00hrs we add it to our lot and if there's any mail coming from Europe, get your suppliers to mail it to our office in The Hook or Rotterdam and they "sack" it the same way to us here. What the hell are oppos for, eh Jim?'

He awaited Jim's response but before he could reply Jack added: 'It'll cost you...' Jack couldn't see Jim's grin or tongue.

The following week Mitch was tied up and unable to make the BCT run down to Blackfriars Road in the afternoon and I went to see Jack. In his office was a youngster of around fifteen who was sorting envelopes and Jack turned to me and introduced him.

'This is Ron's son, Cliff, from upstairs. He comes here every afternoon after leaving Archbishop Tenison's School at the Oval and does a postal bike run for us. Earns him a few quid and we have a much better service than the bloody striking postal non-workers. The lad noticed it last week when we wanted some mail delivered in Greater London, and Cliff now has a little postal gaggle with two of his mates who bike all the mail for us.

'When we checked with our solicitors regarding the money, NIC and tax they asked us if we could do the "law" runs for them as well, which solves their exchange of contracts delay for them. The only problem now is that we must get some more bikers from the school to do all the courier work. If it gets too much we'll have to form a subsidiary to BCT; I think we'll call it "Courier Bikers" or "Corkers" for short.'

When the strike finished seven weeks later an entirely new courier bike industry had been created which is still flourishing today.

Tale 38

West One

Almost nine years after the war ended rationing finally came to an end in 1954. Four years later National Service finished and these two events reshaped the lives of all sections of the community. The kids of the nation broke loose from their parents' apron strings and now everybody wanted to do their own thing. The girls went into mini-skirts and the boys did not consider purple shirts or flower patterns to be the trademarks of queers or poofters and an explosion in fashion and unorthodox behaviour started in Carnaby Street in London W1.

Banking and insurance, the two traditional bastions of respectability, were founded and remained in the City of London but business of all kinds moved 'West' into the 'West One' postal district. Wolfy must have kept his nose very close to the ground when our accountants suggested we share offices with them in an office at Great Marlborough Street. It was a bone's throw from Regent Street, while at its side was Carnaby Street, the youth's Jerusalem. Our office on the second floor overlooked the Magistrates' Court which provided an almost continual monthly display of misdemeanours by Cabinet ministers who had been frolicking with young ladies of leisure.

The ladies' liaison with John Profumo, who was Minister for War, and a Russian naval officer broke the Tory government and we saw the story unfold from our second-floor windows. Sadly, they did not overlook the pool at Cliveden, where the frolicking took place.

How Jim managed to put one finger to the typewriter I can't think, but perhaps he was more interested in the comings and goings from and to the stage entrance of the Palladium. Budding stars and starlets provided a steady stream of hangers-on and autograph hunters for a glimpse of Cilla (White) Black or gap-toothed Jimmy Tarbuck. His car was there all day when he was on stage and immunity from parking fines was provided by an ample supply of free tickets to the matinee performance. In case the coppers were not sure which car not to ticket, his number plate was an unforgettable: 'COMIC 1'.

Richmond, Surrey, was a very genteel and solid flat address but we wanted to be neither of these two so the 'W1' address now gave a certain cachet to the organisation.

As Freddy, our solicitor, had always told me: 'It doesn't really matter what you were doing at Oxford ... as long as you can say you've been there ... dustman, pimp. You don't have to mention a college or law degree, do you?' and he gave one of his heavy guffaws.

I don't think anyone of the three of us were aware that it was going to be a battle of monetary survival but the possibilities of success seemed to be endless.

What we were not expecting were incredibly obstructive regulations by ignorant and bigoted politicians which all turned out to be useless, expensive and time-consuming.

We had survived the 14.9 per cent devaluation of the Pound Sterling due to some excellent advice from our friend Theo in Amriswil but in 1968 HM Government introduced a 'temporary charge on all imports of 15 per cent, (TCI) repaid after six months without interest to the person who deposited the TCI with Customs'.

The economic illiteracy of ministers was beyond belief as an entirely new trade was created by this idiotic measure which did nothing to stop imports but simply started a new business.

Daily adverts appeared in the major papers advertising 'TCI-financed' and the cost of this was promptly added to the cost of the goods. The people financing it had documents which were better than many IOU documents as 'HM Customs promise to repay £... on demand on "A" day.' The day after the introduction of the TCI, BCT told me they had just got the DM12 million cheque which was needed by HM Customs for a container of machinery. Naturally, it had been deposited by the manufacturer of the goods in Germany who simply added the interest cost to the goods.

HMS *Vilomi* was sailing peacefully when I returned from Switzerland and Jim sat me down. He handed me a letter from the landlords at 39 Great Marlborough Street: all tenants had leases which expired in 1979 and they had all been handed 'notice to quit' because of compulsory acquisition. The property had been sold to a large developer who planned to rebuild the entire block. Freddy later explained that the developer who had got their teeth into this very desirable property in London's West One was one of the leading property companies.

'They've done their homework... They've got the top planners and a firm of leading architects in the City, with a matching lawyer...' I was waiting for the punchline.

'The bad news is there's nothing you can do except find new premises. Planning permission has been approved by the GLC and Westminster, finance had been arranged and it's in the high seven figures. The builders are standing by to pull the place down to commence the work and...'

I stopped him. 'That's the bad news ... and the good news, Freddy?'

He threw back his head and gave one of his massive chortles. 'Why do you think I charge so much? The good news is ... as Jim would say ... it'll cost them ... and I reckon it will be around a round five figure. You must look for new premises immediately but when you depart, leave a desk, a chair and a phone so you are 'in occupancy'. Most of the tenants are already out of the building but if one remains, the builders can't come in, but the interest charges start from day one. The longer the delay, the more it's going to cost them.'

My penny was beginning to drop. 'How long can we delay it?'

'Oh months ... There's the post for a start ... solicitors take ages, but remember every day interest charges on a few mill is not funny and you can virtually work it out to the day when the compensation they agree to pay you to get out is more than if you delay your stay there...' He handed me a sheet which demonstrated that if we could delay the builders by coming into the building by four months it would be cheaper for them to cough up the compensation.

Mitch got up and said, 'When I parked the car in Poland Street Garage this morning there was a sign opposite in that modern block with a "To Let" sign up; I'll get a leaflet...'

Freddy had calculated the last landlord 'sweating' day to the day and they threw the towel in on the last day. We moved into

Poland Street in 1974 and a large cheque paid for the move *and* the new furniture. Freddy was very happy with the knowledge he had not only acquired at Oxford but in the muddy profitable waters of the legal profession.

Jim was deliriously happy with 12/13 Poland Street as the telex was tucked into a small corner surrounded by three large soundproof panels. The slight hitch was the furniture which by now looked somewhat tatty. Not having large funds we had stretched ourselves when we had first moved into Great Marlborough Street and bought the 'latest' vogue desks and chairs from Ryman's. Full of enthusiasm I telephoned them and a very keen young salesman arrived in our very splendid-looking airy offices in a gleaming chrome-and-concrete building. He looked around and was obviously impressed by the affluence and the splendour of the room. 'It's so light and airy... What were you looking for?' I pointed him in the direction of the eleven-year-old Danish items we had purchased from them. The catalogue was most impressive and he was already drooling over the pieces that would fit beautifully in many parts of the room. When we got down to the brass tacks I finally shot the question:

'All the pieces you see here came from Ryman's in '63. You will do a part exchange, won't you?' and if the floor under him could have opened he would have disappeared down to the ground floor.

His mouth opened, and there wasn't a sound coming from it. He just gazed at me and stuttered: 'I'm terribly sorry, Sir, but the Danish scene is a little passé, well before my time ... I'm terribly sorry, but will you still require the attractive pieces you selected?'

I felt like answering, 'I'm terribly sorry, sonny, but I'll let you know,' but just shook my head. He parted with his tail between his legs and the certainty of the wrath of the sales manager which would engulf him on his return.

When we told the sad salesman's tale to Gerry and Vicky at the weekend at The Bell, Vicky brought out a sales catalogue from Vidler's in Rye, or Fidler's as she called them.

'But daaarling, you mustn't buy your furniture retail. We don't! We go to local auctions and this time of the year they are dirt cheap.' She leafed through the catalogue:

'Look, daaaarlings ... everything from tables to chairs ... even Victorian pisspots ... they are quite good for plants, Mitch ... look!'

Mitch and I became regular auction vultures, especially as we were particularly short of tables or desks to display our expensive clothing and cloth to our buyers. When there was a 'tables' auction on at Geering and Collyer in Rye, it was like the cheese to us mice. They had posted the catalogue to us and on the drive down I scrutinised the catalogue as to the age and type of tables available. As there were in excess of 150 on offer, Mitch slowed and calmed me down and assured me that if we couldn't get Lot 5, there would be plenty more later on.

Filing into the auction hall down in Rye there were many familiar faces, including the usual sprinkling of 'the ring', who had earmarked certain pieces between them and not 'run each other up on price'. At the end of the sales they would divide the spoil between them and have their own little sale at a cheaper price and settle it for a pint or two at The Woolpack in Tenterden. Mitch and I sat about twenty rows down and Lot 5, a square mahogany table, started at £5. I bid it up to £6 and was shocked to hear the auctioneer 'hammer' it to someone behind me with 'Sold to Mr Thompson'. I exploded.

'Shut up!' said Mitch. 'There's plenty more fish in the sea.'

This repeated itself twenty numbers down and again I was frustrated by 'Mr Thompson' behind me.

When it happened a third time I protested to the auctioneer, fuming:

'This is the third time I have been forestalled by Mr Thompson when quite clearly I bid for it.'

The auctioneer looked stunned. 'But you are Mr Thompson, aren't you? I've hammered all the three tables down to you.'

Mitch was smirking and chuckled.

'Oh, that's good then, isn't it? I'll have my own table for the mohairs, the pure wool and one for the mixtures, too!'

The three tables looked splendid when we had them waxed and polished and the total auction cost had been £18, though that was back in 1975. The one William & Mary table with the square pedestal and square mahogany top sold for £750 when we moved to Lerpiniere House in 1978, so at that point we could have easily started up our own second-hand mid-Victorian furniture business.

However this had no bearing on the visitors who presented their station cards to us on our return from the summer break in 1975. We used to close the office for a month but all the mail was forwarded down to us and any visitors left their cards with our neighbours, the Waites. Mitch and I always returned to the office on the first Monday to go through any mail that had slipped through the net, and as it was a pretty messy job, Mitch and I opened all the letters on the floor. We were suitably attired for the dirty job by wearing our oldest jeans and tatty shirts. Mitch was busily slicing open the letters and odd parcels which the Waites had taken in for us when the door was pushed open and we looked up at two navy-suited gents with their Samsonite briefcases who thrust their station cards into our faces.

We looked up at them as if we were gazing at the Statue of Liberty without the torch, as they said: 'Customs & Excise – Investigation Branch'.

I rose to my full five-foot-six height and quietly asked if I could help them.

Totally ignoring my polite question one of them brushed it aside like squatting a bluebottle. 'Is there anyone in charge here?' Mitch rose to his six feet in his very tatty knee-holed jeans. They clearly could not decide which tramp they should talk to and demanded to see a director to which we both nodded and in unison said: 'We both are!' They clearly thought that that statement was not only an impertinence but obviously a lie and I couldn't resist a 'Tom-type' comment. 'Of course, Officer … had we known you were coming, we would have been dressed to our station in the company, but actually, we are both directors and I am also chairman of the company.'

'Very well then,' said the junior of the two. 'Can we come in and look at some files?'

I was tempted to say something in Jackspeak but Mitch gave me a kick to shut me up.

Instead, we showed them into the room where he repeated the 'file' request. We had a metal upright filing cabinet with eight rows of twenty hanging files and I walked towards it and Mitch pressed a release button and the horizontal spring loaded pull-down cover shot up to the top with a loud bang. Junior gazed at the row of files and uttered one word: 'Invoices'.

I was beginning to enjoy this. 'Which invoices?' This made the officer bristle with anger.

'We have a great many: purchases … sales … UK suppliers, non-UK suppliers,' I said, waving my hand across the rows. Junior appeared not to have grasped my question, so wishing to be helpful I pulled out the 'MISC – UK Purchases' and handed them to him.

He flicked through them, walked back to the table, opened his sandwich-packed Samsonite briefcase, removed a pre-printed C&E pad and wrote on it: '1) File marked "MISC" – UK Purchases' removed from the premises...'

I stopped him in the nicest possible way. 'You are not removing the file, are you, Officer?'

At this point he exploded and turned to his colleague. 'You've witnessed the gentlemen refusing permission to remove vital evidence to an HM Customs officer...'

I went ice cold and moved into total 'Tom' overdrive. 'Officer, I have done nothing of the sort and I have a co-director as a witness. Would you please show me your station card again so I can take this whole matter up with your superior officer. Please show me your card, and *your* name is...?' I looked up at him and raised my eyebrows to which he just shook his head.

I looked at him very hard. 'There is a phone number on your station card and I'll just phone your switchboard and ask for the SEO.'

'You wouldn't, would you, Sir?'

I walked over to the phone and lifted the receiver. Junior closed the briefcase with our file in it, tore off the C&E chit and handed it to me. 'You'll be hearing from us,' he said and they walked out.

Minutes later I was speaking to a senior officer off Fleet Street to register a serious complaint and had a very pleasant 'what appears to be the trouble' gent calming me down. Mitch was grinning from ear to ear.

'You see, Sir ... and I'm not trying to excuse the manner of my officers ... but we teach them to treat everyone as if they're guilty and then they make a mistake ... I'm sorry if the officer appeared to be overbearing...' There was a long pause. 'You're in the West End, aren't you? I have to make a call there next Tuesday around 10.30hrs. If by any chance you were free perhaps you would join me in a pint?' And when I did join him in a pint, he asked where the 'heads' were ... and we both entered the unrarified land of Jackspeak.

The file was returned by Junior the following week with a very forced smile and he nodded to his colleague with the words: 'I think Mr Franklin has been most helpful but we were looking for some foreign invoices which could have been paid twice into some black Swiss account.' I nearly had to kick Mitch not to get the fire extinguisher.

Our collection of mid-Victorian antiques grew and every time the Schapiras came to London they asked me to get them some similar items. Jim and I had managed to get a restored Victorian Partners desk which was ideal for two people facing each other in the course of business. Kurt loved it because it was a typical piece of attractive Victoriana. We went to our friends Jewell's in the City, who specialised in making 'antiques' from genuine old wood, and they produced an almost identical 'Partners desk' for Kurt and Erich.

Tale 39

Deesse – DS – Goddess

There was something odd about that Monday morning at 5 Oakden Street. Mitch was not on his way to Birmingham, and as it was Monday I really should have been in Milan and the only stalwart was the secure sheet anchor of HMS *Vilomi* who was now mustering the crew.

As it was not yet 'stand easy'. Jim was listening out for the postman and heard the two white West Highland terriers bark at No. seven. The now rather tall eleven-year-old bundle of joy was helping Maureen get his little brother Dean, ready for school and when that was done Greg had his morning swing on our iron gate as Dad was already on his way to Covent Garden. Otherwise a mighty 'Get off that gate!' would have thundered down Oakden Street.

Barny continued to bark, Greg got off the squeaking gate and Postie walked up to No. 5 and pushed the letters through our letter box, whilst Wellington waited to snap at Postie's heels. Mitch had been watching the proceedings through the window and collected the bundle of letters off the mat and brought them into the house. He was slicing the envelopes open, removing their contents and handing them either to me or Jim.

He paused, grimaced and handed one to me, commenting: 'A bit flash this ... just down your street ... or should it be "*rue*"?'

It was a beautiful red/white/blue/gold-edged rounded-corner invitation card from Phil Thomas in Chiswick with the usual flowery marketing speak of 'It gives us great pleasure and honour...' Mitch did pause for a moment when he came to the bits at the bottom: 'Moët champagne ... *pâté de fois gras* ... three hostesses from the Folies Bergère...' His tongue started to wet his lips and I wasn't sure whether it was for the champers or the afters.

Jim wanted to get down to the reason for the bash and urged Mitch to tell us what all this was for and he glared at him.

'Launch of the new DS, isn't it?' said Mitch.

Jim looked at me and smiled, adding: 'You're going, aren't you?' and both Mitch and I in unison nodded. We were the automobile version of the Entente Cordiale after all.

It was a brilliantly choreographed evening presentation with a truly Gallic flavour, although the three girls from the Folies Bergère were definitely of the 'for display only – do not touch' variety. Phil was circulating, talking to his clients in turn, and when the lights dimmed at dusk the showroom was thrown into total darkness and a hush descended. Suddenly the 'Marseillaise' trumpeted through the showroom, the spotlight shone towards the rear of the room and slowly ... very slowly ... three red, white and blue gleaming new DSs appeared like bulbous spacecraft to loud applause. All I could think of was 'how much' and before I could say it Mitch did. 'Franklin thinking of the shekels again?' I punched him on his shoulder, commenting, 'Right first time.' I couldn't reach any higher anyway.

After all the 'ooos' and 'aaahs', Phil handed out the full-colour leaflets and when he came to us there was a small silence as he knew what I was going to say. 'Lovely "do", Phil, but what's the bottom line?'

I felt like following that up with Jackspeak but there were too many ladies around in their refineries.

'Pop in tomorrow and I can give you the gen around eleven. I should have all the details from Paris.'

He, Mitch and I were sitting comfortably, which was just as well as the ladies were no longer there to revive us if we passed out. Mitch put all the leaflets and prices into his briefcase and rose. I followed suit and turned to Phil. 'We're off to Germany on Thursday; there's never much to do on weekends, so we'll pop into a showroom in Rheine and compare prices. You never know, perhaps Citroëns are cheaper in Germany...' I honestly meant it to be without sarcasm.

Phil's face dropped as if he had been hit by the rear end of the new DS.

'Actually, Dave, you could be right, as Paris sets the prices in the UK market and they are always inflated.'

'Are you serious, Phil?' I stared at him incredulously.

275

'Oh yes!' nodded Phil. 'Higher-priced cars in the UK are either bought by people who have more money than sense and the rest are company cars approved of by the accountants who never check prices and just allow percentage increases from the previous year's purchase costs. There's nothing I can do about it or I'll lose my franchise.' He turned to Mitch, grinning. 'Just as well we don't have many kosher customers like him,' he said, thrusting his thumb at me.

'Thanks, Phil.' I grabbed his hand and pressed it hard.

'I'll promise that if the price is the same in Germany, France or Israel, we'll buy it from you.' I just looked at him and almost expected a 'Cheers, mate' in return but then, Phil had been in the RAF and not the RN.

The company we were visiting in Rheine were specialist raincoat and blouson manufacturers and ironically were the first Germans whom I had to put to the age/Nazi test. Mr Stratman was around my own age and had been a German POW in Russia since Stalingrad. He never asked me why my German was so good and I did not ask any Hitler Youth questions. However, we were on the same wavelength commercially and when he asked me to get the best-selling raincoat in the UK there was only one answer: Burberry. In fact, they now produced a better-class make than the British version and the only thing they could not do was to copy the check lining. But then, when the garment was on window display, you couldn't see it and the punters were not all that bothered as it was half the price of the 'real thing'. So much for the power of advertising!

We never mentioned the 'B' word to a prospective client as we had learned a lot about trade marks and the danger of 'passing off' a competitive product. We sold them by the thousand and it was a manufacturer's production dream as it was always the same model.

After the war the British Army of the Rhine had made Hannover, Minden, Münster-Osnabrück and Rheine a 'BAOR' mini-Aldershot and when the squaddies' tour of duty came to an end many signed on, as booze, birds and bonking were available around the 24 hour clock every day including Sundays. Many preferred to look for the '3 Bs' in jeans and T-shirts and when Mitch and I entered the rather elegant Citroën showroom near Hannover, the salesman assumed our attire to mirror that of two BAOR off-duty squaddies and addressed us in excellent English.

'Have you seen the new DS?' the eager young salesman asked, leading us to the cheapest version of the car. Citroëns were not usually the flavour of the month with squaddies but there was no harm in trying. Whilst Mitch was rummaging through the vehicle I asked the salesman for a brochure. He looked at me with a puzzled expression and handed me a sterling price list, right-hand drive, delivered to Tilbury, inclusive of VAT.

Mitch poked his head out of the car and grabbed the price list. 'Tilbury? ... I don't have a customer there ... Why Tilbury?' Mitch's English required the assistance of the sales manager who had appeared as back-up.

Oozing sales patter, he smiled at me, and to confuse him I broke into German. I would have loved it to have been Jackspeak but felt it would be wasted one hundred miles from the sea in landlocked Rheine.

However, the sales manager was now totally at sea. Two Englishmen ... one of whom spoke perfect German ... who wanted a Deutsche mark price *without* VAT, collected from Rheine, right-hand drive ... paid by cheque from the Deutsche Bank in Stuttgart ... and neither of the Brits looked like a mafioso with a bank account in Messina.

The poor man was now totally up the Messina Creek without a paddle and in desperation he asked me if we required the CDH discount? When Mitch, with a smile, replied 'Natürlich' – 'of course' – we nearly had to catch the poor man as he looked set to sink beneath the waves without a trace.

We had joined the CDH after the Derby disaster at Cologne, at the recommendation of the German buying group, ABZ. They explained to us that CDH was a blanket organisation of all professional salespersons in Germany. They had branches in all the German *Länder* (counties) and each one had their own staff of lawyers. ABZ explained they preferred to work with this highly organised and efficient legal organisation in case of any disputes with their suppliers, and after Freddy had collected the last cheque we became members.

Having a huge salespersons membership, their discount offers with many leading companies are without parallel. From hotel groups to petrol chains, from the German railways (the Bundesbahn) to car companies, there are hardly any sections of the retail industry that do not grant discounts on their products or services, Citroëns were one of them.

277

Mitch and I returned to the hotel (with CDH discount) and sourced out a CDH Citroën supplier and honed in on one very close to Rheine. Six months later the telex spewed out the news that the new DS 19 was ready for collection, and they would collect us from Hannover. The hotel, the car and the petrol were all discounted with our CDH card, and although the VAT had finally been sorted out by my friend near Fleet Street he could not have been more helpful. 'VAT on own car imports? I remember you have a VAT number and whether your company imports raincoats, cars or durexes you only pay the VAT when you invoice the goods out to your customers. What's the problem? And you can buy me a pint, eh?'

Our accountants were somewhat dubious but you don't argue with a SEO from Customs & Excise, do you?

Sadly for Phil Thomas the price worked out almost 15 per cent cheaper than his price and we were thinking of buying the Citroëns in Germany for sale to S.E. Thomas but Paris would not have loved that one little bit. However, *we* did, and continued our purchases of the DS 19, 20, 21 and 24 over the next years in Germany, but both Mitch and I were too old to even see the possible introduction of the DS 69.

The additional financial bonus rather shook our accountants when we told them. When we paid for the hotel in Rheine with the CDH discount, the receptionist deducted it without a murmur, smiled and handed me the receipted bill.

'Will you need a second copy?' she asked, and had the word been 'triplicate' I would have wondered if we were in Italy.

'Second copy? For what?' I queried.

She looked at me as if I had arrived on a spacecraft.

'For the MWST [VAT] people, of course. Your passport and company are British and you have just paid the bill inclusive of MWST; you are entitled to reclaim that from the German tax authorities. Restaurants, petrol, gifts and even if you needed a new crocodile briefcase for the business, you can reclaim all MWST items. How long do you keep your books in England?'

'Seven years,' I replied in a somewhat dazed state and felt a phone call to the Bridge of HMS *Vilomi* was totally justified.

'Seven years?' quizzed Jim. 'You're joking. I might have to go down to the dungeon. Be worth every penny though ... or should it be mark? Be a nice Xmas bonus with that and the discount on

278

the car! ... Will you be sending a bill to the accountants for all this info?' He paused. 'At a very rough guess I make that around ten grand ... It'll buy a baby Citroën for Greg.'

Tale 40

Georgian Splendour

The move from Great Marlborough Street to Poland Street had been trouble-free and thanks to Freddy's legal skills turned out to be very profitable. After all, that was what he and we were supposed to be in business for.

Mitch was on one of his Scottish 'runs' which he always combined with a weekend visit to Kendal and his Mum, who was still hoping and scouring high and low for a suitable wife. Mitch went up north in the new 'Goddess' and Jim and I decided to walk to Lambeth North Tube and train up to Oxford Circus. Walking along Kennington Road Jim spotted a board which read 'Commercial/Residential property to let'.

The mixture intrigued us and when we got to Poland Street I phoned the agents in Kennington asking them to explain the mixture in detail. There was a long pause, the voice was cleared and the gent recovered his composure. 'Explain the tenancy mixture, Sir...? It says exactly what it is. Of course, Sir, we'd like to meet you, but it will have to be in daylight as much of the property hasn't been touched for a hundred years.' I felt like asking if we needed candles to find our way up the original staircase.

Daniel Lerpiniere was one of the leading engravers of the eighteenth century. He was of Huguenot stock and his ancestors had come over to England during the seventeenth century. Lerpiniere House was built in 1774 by him at 121 Kennington Road and is a perfect example of late Georgian architecture with an imposing two-pillar portico and a typical Georgian rectangular layout: on the symmetrical ground floor, front door and four windows and five windows on the first floor balance five smaller windows on the top floor.

There was one WC complete with pull chain, one washbasin

and one sink in the so-called kitchen – those were all the amenities though they would have been luxuries in the mid-1880s, which was the last time the building had had a lick of paint or been modernised in any shape or degree. Jim discovered that it was in the *Survey of London*, which increased conversion costs, as everything had to be restored to its former eighteenth-century glory.

However, once the conversion was complete, it became a perfect Central London company headquarters, which our clients and friends dubbed 'One-Two-One'. As many of our contacts were now in the Europe, every penny spent on it by the company was worth its weight in Swiss francs, Deutsche marks and Austrian schillings, as well as US dollars and there were not many buildings of that age in the US of A. It was furnished with antiques from the cottage, Oakden and Poland streets, which gave the finishing 'museum' touch to One-Two-One.

As the building was 'Within the Division Bell', and many MPs lived within the bell's ring, we used to host meetings with our trade organisation members to meet the locals. Jim always asked if it did any good and after many years I had to reluctantly agree that the only thing it did was no harm, but it did wonders for one's ego and name dropping when you had just had a word with a DTI minister... 'Not that it made the slightest difference,' as Jim used to add acidly. But it did start me on the *FT* letter-writing circuit, which resulted in an invitation to St George's House at Windsor.

The only comment was from Mitch, who looked at the envelope and me, shook his head and murmured: 'Oh gawd ... it's Dave, he's at it again, arse-crawling for a cuppa with "Brenda" at Windsor Castle.' He wasn't altogether wrong because I became a member of St George's House at Windsor. I went to their annual bashes, which always have a guest speaker – from the clergy, politics, science or the arts – and was normally introduced by Prince Philip.

One of the most interesting was the late Katharine Graham, the proprietor of the *Washington Post*. She was the guest speaker to an audience of around 600 inside St George's Chapel in 1982. Commenting on the Watergate scandal of ten years before she recalled she had been upstate in New York when her editor had phoned her to agree on the cover story for the Monday edition of the *Post*. There were two rather odd stories being prepared by the reporters. One was about a driver who had lost control of his car, after which it had crashed into a house, passed through a drawing room where two people were amorously engaged, out the far side, right through the wall. The other story involved five comic-opera-type burglars dressed in surgical gloves and walkie-talkies who had been caught in mid robbery at the Headquarters of the Democratic Party in the Watergate Building. 'Well,' said Katherine Graham, 'is there any serious news?' adding, 'Print the first one.'

The proceedings in the Chapel were always followed by sherry, served by the Guardsmen outside or, if wet, in the Cloisters. If a visiting European client happened to be on hand, the white-gloved Guardsmen would just set off the business proceedings serving Harvey's sweet or dry sherry off the oval silver trays.

On leaving the car park, my foreign visitor would insist on me peeling off the special windscreen sticker with 'Castle Hill Car Park' printed on it, which somehow cemented the London buying trip.

Next door to us lived the Rev Richard Craig and his wife, and when he accompanied me to Windsor he was delighted to meet many of his contemporaries. Bishops, Archbishops or just plain Reverends like Richard enjoyed the rarified atmosphere and we were all dutifully name-tagged with plastic stickers. There was a minor hitch with the non-clerical Jewish boy, so instead of my neighbour's tag of 'The Rev. Richard Craig – Lambeth', mine simply had 'David Franklin Lambeth' on the plasticised tag without any indication of status. A gentleman in splendid purple regalia chatted pleasantly with Richard and turned to me and noted my rankless description but mentally registered the Lambeth location. 'How nice to meet you, Mr Franklin. How is the Archbishop these days? Well, I hope?' And before I could recover he had moved on to much higher planes.

The One-Two-One project was escalating daily with the conversion costs and we all three agreed not to borrow the money but to sell the cottage. Mitch would get his third-of-an-acre garden to develop, though it was not ideal clematis soil, but he made a find of a peach tree tucked in the sheltered corner by the house. Jim could have his gourmet kitchen with all the essential items as suggested by *the* chef at The Bell in Iden and I had an office with all the latest connections to our European clients. A Board meeting agreed that if the cottage were sold on time the proceeds should go towards the new luxury establishment at Kennington and there was no opposition to the motion which was passed three to none in favour. The only ones who were sadly disappointed were the bank, who had agreed overdraft facilities. But you can't please all the people all of the time, especially bankers.

Just before Xmas 1977 Mitch and I had returned from a European sales trip and Jim was already at the cottage to pack for storage and final removal of furniture. We drove straight from Dover to the cottage, and I then dropped Mitch at Ashford to train to London. Jim and I awaited the removal people at the cottage and we bade 'Killicks' farewell. Little did we know the name would become part and parcel of the company.

Uncle Charles and the Schapiras

The prophecy that Wolfy was going to be my guardian for life had turned out to be chillingly accurate. He had not lifted a paw for me to join the disastrous family involvements but instead had watched over me with the help of so many people of different backgrounds and nationalities.

Uncle Charles was more than a father in my adolescence and introduced me to the pleasures of growing into a man. After that he pointed me in the right business direction and made sure I chose the right partners in life. Through Preminger's in Vienna, he had made my first contact with the Schapiras, and Olly, Erich and Kurt were as much a part of me as any family could be. It was turning out to be much better than a blood relationship, which sadly, in my own experience, had turned out to be a bloody family relationship. Kurt Schapira was younger than I but had also had an excellent English education at public school and university that was certainly superior to mine. However, I had been very fortunate to have sampled the enjoyable rigours of the Lower Deck which had rubbed off all the corners of me ... not 'arf it hadn't ... and I wouldn't have missed the steel-wire rub for anything. In fact, when Kurt was with us in London or we were together in Vienna, we seemed to be cloned mentally, although next to him physically I looked a little David to this massively handsome Goliath.

When Kurt phoned me in March 1976 to tell me about how great the desk looked he mentioned his worries about Erich, who had to go to hospital to have a heart bypass operation: 'It's over the holidays. We could spend a few hours together and drink the new wine up at Grinzing and not talk business ... although knowing you, that'll be difficult.' When I reported this to Jim he was all over my white wine. 'Go on, Dave ... Do you good to get away from all those calculations...' And the next day he pressed the AUA return Vienna ticket into my hand and Mitch took me to the airport.

It was boiling when I got to Schweschacht and I took my jacket off. Kurt was in light-cotton trousers and wore an open-neck polo shirt.

'Bloody warm, isn't it. What's it like in London?'

'About the same,' I said, rubbing the sweat off my face.

'Do you want a shower at the hotel or straight up to Grinzing?' he asked

'Might as well go up there now. If I shower I'll only sweat even more' and hopped beside him into the little blue open Alfa.

The breeze up to Grinzing was like liquid oxygen and I was now in my own, slightly tipsy summer wonderland. We sat outside at a wooden garden table and the waiter brought a carafe of wine in a litre jug and poured it into two crystal glasses. Kurt lifted it, pushed one towards me and gave one of those big embracing smiles of his. 'Here's to absent friends ... which covers a lot of sins...' he said and threw back his head, roaring with laughter.

'You never talk about your family, Dave. Preminger hinted that you don't exactly kiss each other, but is it really that bad?'

I nodded. 'Uncle Charles told Preminger's and they probably filled you in?'

'They did, but if you'd rather not speak about it, that's OK.' He pushed his massive palm towards me and I grabbed it with relief.

'Tell you what, Kurt; I only know you went to Brighton and to Manchester University. What about the rest or is that "out of bounds", like my lot?' Kurt shook his head vigorously.

'When Hitler marched into Vienna in March '38, Dad was immediately taken away by the Gestapo and sent to Dachau, one of the worst KZs and from there to another at Buchenwald. Meanwhile the firm was nicked without any compensation because Dr Goebbels had to cleanse the polluted Jewish atmosphere and new non-Jewish owners were given the company. The good doctor even created a new word for this process which was *arisiert*, or "Aryanised".

'Dad was released in January 1939 provided he left the country and we left Vienna in August '39, seven days before the start of World War II.'

'That was cutting it a bit fine?' I added, and Kurt gave one of his massive roars.

'Had no bloody choice, did we? We went to Palestine via Trieste. I don't know how good your "history" was at school but you might know that it did not become Israel until 1948 when the Brits left one of their colonies, but sadly there was no peace ever after... They're still bashing their brains out... Politicians! ... They should all be drowned in the Red Sea.' He refilled our glasses. 'In '46 Dad went back to Vienna and Erich had to do his National Israeli Military service for two and a half years and joined the family in Vienna in 1950 to start in the "returned" SMARTO shirt company. Meanwhile, I was perfecting my English slang verbally and horizontally but, sadly, my father died in 1966 and I returned to Vienna to run the factory with Erich.

'My mother hates me driving fast cars and always says I'll get killed one day and I always tell her that it's more likely to be the wine, women and the "Blue Danube" waltz.'

After three hours he cruised me back to the Ahrenberg Pension and the minute I hit the pillow I was corked back into that tall green bottle of delicious white wine.

The three days went like minutes and I had never known Kurt so relaxed and at ease, except for his concern for Erich. On the last evening I spoke to Olly on the phone and wished her all the best and we had a little smooch on the phone and she promised to ring me in London as soon as she had some news about Erich.

When I walked through the door at Oakden Street two nights later the phone rang and Jim gave it to me. Olly was totally distraught and sobbing continuously and I tried to calm her down. Eventually I asked when the funeral was and amid sobs she blurted out, 'Erich is just arranging it...' I stopped her.

'Erich you said ... but I thought...'

'No, no, no ... it's not Erich who has died, it's Kurt. He walked you back to the Ahrenberg on Monday night and because it was so hot he decided to go the air-conditioned all-night movie house on the Ring and came out in a daze around three in the morning. You know it's a one-way road and he automatically looked for the traffic from the right and the tram which goes against the one-way system killed him outright. I'll ring you tomorrow.'

Five days later I flew back to Vienna and it was even hotter than before.

'Will it be a real kosher funeral?' asked Jim.

'I think so, the Schaps are not strictly kosher but I'll certainly have to take a head cover, black suit, white shirt and black tie.'

Mitch added, 'Sorry to be the bearer of sad tidings, but it's going to get hotter and I've just heard on the news it's over 35°C in Vienna.'

I could have kicked him. 'You're going instead of me?' I glared at him and he just shook his head. 'He was your mate and anyhow, I'd have to be koshered first ... not at my age.' Jim remained diplomatically silent.

I phoned Heathrow on the morning of the flight to Vienna and all the cheerful lady on the phone could come up with was: 'Oh ... it's a glorious day today ... it's going to be the hottest of the year.' It was all so depressing that even my Jackspeak had dried up.

'What are you going to wear in the plane, Dave?' asked Jim and I wasn't sure whether it was interest or sheer curiosity.

'Shorts, sandals and a very large T-shirt and lots of Kleenex, but I better go and pack my clobber for the funeral.'

'Rather you than me,' said Mitch at the airport. I nodded ... had no bloody choice, did I?

I checked in at Heathrow and every step I took left dripping sweat marks at the end of my trouser legs. When I finally shuffled up to the very cool-looking AUA stewardess to check in, she smiled at me, took a deep breath, cleared her throat, took on a sorrowful look and apologised profusely: 'I'm dreadfully sorry, Sir, but there has been a small problem on the Vienna plane. We are flying you direct to Zurich and will give you a first-class dinner at Kloten. Then transfer by Swissair to Vienna and that should get you to the Schweschacht around 22.00hrs.'

She gave me one of those maxi smiles that kill any possible objection and pressed the tickets into my hand, complete with Swissair dinner vouchers for Zurich.

You can shout, you can scream or curse, but as you are totally at their mercy all you can do is fume ... and in that bloody heat. I was steaming.

There were no mishaps to or at Zurich and as I had arranged that Olly should not bother about transport in Vienna I had no one to inform as to the change of ETA in Vienna. The dinner was delicious but in that heat, I would have rather had just an ice cream. Right on time at 22.00hrs the Swissair connection landed in Vienna and not wanting to sweat too much I walked slowly to the luggage gondola which was spewing out the passengers' luggage in the arrival lounge. I waited ... and waited ... and waited ... and saw no one in the luggage hall, which was now totally deserted. The Swissair stewardess from the plane came up and asked me a perfectly logical question:

'Are you waiting for anybody, Sir?'

'No, dear ... not somebody ... just my small suitcase,' I grumpily replied.

'Oh,' she said cheerily, 'I'll go and look for you.'

She returned ten steaming minutes later with a male helper and smiled at me. 'You know you had to switch planes in Zurich? The case was not transferred to this plane but we'll get it over from Zurich tomorrow morning and taxi it over to the InterConti hotel first thing. Should be no later than midday.

Before she could even attempt to wipe the smile off her face I exploded. 'Look at me ... I'm wringing wet in my clothes. My change of clothes is in that case and the funeral I have to attend is at ten ... I'll look good in this ... I'm not fit to go to a wedding in this clobber let alone fit for a bloody funeral...' At this point I was close to tears.

When I phoned Erich from the hotel, the news broke the spell. Both he and Kurt had a wonderful sardonic sense of humour and Erich, who was six foot tall and built like a golf pro chuckled. 'I'll lend you a black suit though it could fit Jim *and* you...' Reception at the InterContinental were somewhat taken back by my attire and helpfully asked if the luggage was on the way. I explained.

'Don't worry, Sir, we can get you a razor, shaving cream and anything else you may require in the night.' I thanked them profusely and took the lift up to the sixth floor. The shower was an absolute godsend and after that I crawled naked under a single bed sheet and dropped off immediately and slept like a popped cork straight out of that white wine bottle.

The cold shower in the morning was very welcome and I let the power jet hit my back like thousands of tiny steel needles. Then I heard this odd buzzing noise. I switched off the shower and just grabbed a towel, not bothering to wrap it around tightly, and walked towards the buzz and door. The buzzer went again and

I just pulled the door open and there, in front of me, was a perfect copy of the grinning San Francisco bellhop. I was so startled, I let go of the towel and gawped at him. At this hour in the morning ... in this first-class hotel ... you've got to be joking.

He gave me the friendliest of smiles, bent down and said: 'I have this for you.'

Before I could ask what 'this' was, he lifted up my battered piece of luggage and thrust it into my hands, turned around and disappeared down the corridor before I could be arrested for attempting to rape a minor.

Apart from the actual sad service, my tales kept everyone from crying too much and I could see Kurt chuckling away in his sardonic way, running his hand through that massive head of hair and grinning at me. 'You are in shtook ... never mind ... thanks for coming ... I appreciate it ... regards to Jim.'

All the way back to London in the plane I could not get that Fred Astaire/Ginger Rogers song out of my brain – 'The way you hold your head ... you can't take that way from me...' – and I was still humming it when we landed at Heathrow. I gave Jim a quick 'We've landed' and he immediately asked how it had gone and he seemed quite relieved. Two hours later I walked through the door and he seemed more under the weather than I felt.

'You OK, Jim?'

'So-so! Charles always said problems coming together are problems halved but May is distraught as Charles has been taken to Gordon's Hospital. She wanted you to go of course, but when I told her you were coming back from Vienna, all she said was, "You'll tell him please".'

Half an hour later Matron phoned and asked us to come immediately and I grabbed a cab and picked up May. On arrival, Matron was waiting in the entrance lobby. May was about twenty years older than I and Matron assumed her to be his wife and I the son and she walked towards me.

'Could you follow me please,' she said, and May urged me to go on alone.

I followed her into her small office, and she beckoned me to sit and in her best long-practised sympathetic tone of voice and said: 'I'm terribly sorry to tell you that your father passed away a few moments ago...'

I just stared at her and suppressed a small sniff. After a few seconds I had recovered sufficiently to inform her that, although I was his closest friend, I was not his son, at which point I nearly had to comfort her.

'Well,' she said very firmly. 'We'd better tell his widow!' I could almost see Charles chuckling away somewhere up there shaking his shoulders, just like Maurice Chevalier. I went outside to comfort May, who just held my hands. She was a very down-to-earth lady. She looked up at me and gave a tiny smile.

'You know, he was very fond of you...' I nodded and gave her a little kiss.

'You will arrange everything won't you, David ... I just couldn't face it ... Jim will help you, won't he? He loved him just as much as you...' and she burst into tears.

I returned to Matron and asked her to assist me in the funeral arrangements, explaining that although Charles officially was of Jewish faith he was not practising.

'Oh,' said Matron in a very workmanlike manner. 'That's no problem any longer as even for cremations Golders Green do one when this sort of situation arises. Just leave it to me and I'll instruct the clergyman accordingly. Short and sweet is the motto...' She rose, shook my hand and ushered us out to a taxi and we were back at Chelsea Cloisters within fifteen minutes.

'Would you like me to come up with you?' I asked May and she nodded.

When we got to her flat she was quite composed and handed me the keys to No. 779. I opened the door, looked in and paused and suddenly my entire life over the past years engulfed me. No. 779 without Charles ... it just wasn't possible! I walked towards his small drop-flap desk and opened it. There was a buff envelope just marked 'David' standing upright in front and I opened it. Inside was a note asking me to write a letter to all the ladies on an enclosed list: there were sixteen of them dotted all over the UK and America.

And there was Charles standing behind me chuckling away with that wicked Chevalier guffaw...

Right behind the envelope was another which held the latest Ann Summers catalogue. (Charles was in his eighties!)

The will listed May as a total beneficiary, bank accounts and details of 779 contents and everything was neatly in place and just a little note to me and Jim:

Thanks for your friendship. Please help May if she needs it. She is a very determined lady but her sight and hearing are failing. I am sure that you and/or Jim will give her any assistance she may require.
Look after yourselves.
Charles.

The arrangements for the cremation proceeded smoothly and when Jim and I were at the crematorium up at Golders Green we were the only males there, except a very young Church of England clergyman. The music started and we all awaited the final bars before Charles went on his last journey and the C of E youth stepped forward to say the last few words. Jim and I froze.

He went rambling on about Jesus and the Holy Ghost and went on and on and I felt like throwing the Holy Sacrament at him, in triplicate. Jim's grin turned into anger, but finally, after many more amens he finished and the body slowly moved out of the chapel towards cremation.

Extremely self-satisfied and oozing condolences, the young man wished everyone a pleasant good-bye. A very small lady in her late seventies came up to me and asked:

'Excuse me...' Deep pause. '...Are you David?' I nodded.

'Tell me ... did you arrange the funeral?' I nodded again silently.

'You did know that Charles was Jewish?' I confirmed this with another nod.

'I did wonder,' she continued. 'I was a bit late, I couldn't get a taxi and came in the middle of the Holy Ghost bit and I thought to myself ... I must have come to the wrong funeral.'

Tale 42

Good Accountants and Architects

Geoffrey Child and Tom Avery were as different as West One is to Cliftonville but in one area they seemed to be cloned. Ask either of them for information on almost any subject and they would press their own green button and the answers would come out as fast as the telex rolls off the printer.

In 1964 Geoffrey had put us in touch with the property at Oakden Street and as it was in a totally derelict state we asked him if he knew an architect who could survey it and/or supervise the renovation. 'Reg Grainge from Hood, Huggins & York in Covent Garden' was Geoffrey's instant reply, and he fitted into our plans as smoothly as Maria Callas singing *Tosca* on stage at the Royal Opera House, which was only a note's sing away from Hood, Huggins and York in Endell Street.

Three months after we had moved into Oakden Street the landlords who had sold us the property asked if we would be interested in a similar property in the street parallel to Oakden Street. It was going very cheap because a bomb had fallen near it during the Blitz and damaged some of the sewer. Reg came around and asked ... surprise ... surprise... 'How much?' No. 8 Wincott Street was one floor smaller than Oakden Street and Reg asked if we had made any retirement plans as he felt the location and size were perfect for that phase of life. As far as the property buying public was concerned in the 1960s, Lambeth was a slum and property totally worthless, so in the end we felt almost guilty to offer them low four figures. When Reg Grainge discovered that the drains from the house had been destroyed by the bomb, the purchase price almost disappeared down the new drain.

Reg had done some research before gutting the inside and replanning the interior and found that St Thomas's Hospital was always looking for accommodation for their doctors and senior staff and the house was only ten minutes' walking distance from St Thomas's. Reg suggested we split the accommodation into two self-contained flatlets which could, on retirement, be pulled back into one dwelling. Without much consultation and with a mortgage rate of $2^1/2$ per cent from Lambeth Council, we took the plunge and tested the new drains. Tommie's was delirious when we informed them of this new accommodation within walking distance and immediately asked, 'Have you any more?' We started looking but even Wolfy could not sniff out any more bargains.

When the 'project' at One-Two-One started, Reg was consulted from day one, which was just as well because the actual property had not been touched for almost a century. Along with Jim, he took care of everything, including doing some research at the British Museum. When they found that the house had been built by Daniel Lerpiniere, Jim asked the Print Room at the BM if they had any of his prints and they rang back within the hour.

'Oh yes, Sir ... How nice to speak to you, but what is your interest in that engraver?' And when we told him we had just moved into Lerpiniere House he almost collapsed. The result was that I went over to the British Museum Print Room where he showed me the eleven prints they had in the museum.

'It's very difficult to get hold of any these days, but if you would like me to give you a list of known prints, you can look around for them.'

'Where do you suggest looking?' I asked, hoping for a name of one or two second-hand shops.

He returned a few minutes later and pressed a list of the prints and London shops into my hands and added: 'I'm sure you will be able to find one or two, but I can tell you where you *can't* buy any.'

'Oh dear,' I said, 'where's that?'

Giving a very benevolent smile he replied: '*Here* ... Good hunting.'

We photocopied the lists and Mitch and I always carried them on us, whether in Kendal, Kingcussie, Edinburgh or Eastbourne. After one year we rivalled the number of Lerpinieres at the British Museum: BM = 11 *Vilomi* = 16. And we never finished looking or buying. Wolfy was in total command when Mitch came back one day and triumphantly held a huge print of *London – Looking*

North from Greenwich high in the air and said: 'Bingo.' I could not believe my eyes because that very morning I had found *London – Looking South from Hampstead Heath*, which was the other half of Mitch's pair.

Reg was quite amused by our searches and findings and when it came to the interior decorations he came over to One-Two-One regarding the colour scheme. He turned to me and permitted himself a very small smile: 'David, you in the rag trade *should* have an eye for colour ... The Georgians did as well because the walls had to show the wooden furniture off to perfection. The three of you should pop down to Bath for the weekend. Look at 'The Baths' by all means but what you should do is go to Bath's most famous Crescent and visit 1 The Crescent. They have a number of rooms with Georgian furniture and the walls have the original colourings. Buy a guidebook which has the colour photos of the walls, bring it back and we'll give it to Morrell's to copy for the wall colours here. Might as well do the job properly so when you eventually get out, you never know, some idiot might give you a fortune for the lease.'

Reg Grainge could have been a clone of Jim. Everything was documented down to the colourings of the walls and woodwork and had to be initialled 'OK' by us before a lick of paint was put on it. The comments by the local lads who did the paintwork rivalled those of days gone by when we were all 'painting the ship's side'.

'Ere, Bert ... you seen this bleedin' red ... reminds me of the missus on one of 'er off months!' To which his mate would add a rather colourful description of the terracotta on the stairs, which he labelled as 'shit brown'. However, they both agreed to the azure blue in the sitting room being perfect for a brothel. 'Has Graingy told ya if it's going to be a knocking shop ... At this address, we can't afford it anyow...'

Reg had had a meeting with the accountants before the job started because they did not want any arguments with the Revenue regarding the dividing line of 'business' and 'private work'. Nothing was touched without the accountants' approval. Ian McFarlane at the accountants was very happy after completion when the Revenue just asked for the itemised 36-page book of works. No questions were asked and the renovations were accepted to the last penny.

There was no bathroom before conversion so Reg had planned

a rather splendid bath, shower, WC, bidet and two matching washbasins.

'Go to the "Ideal Home" on the first day and select a luxury suite,' he advised. 'Haggle an "end of show" price because with a bit of luck, the gold taps will be a little tatty and there will be a number of scratches after four weeks of careless visitors...' His advice was perfect. Visitors to One-Two-One were usually overwhelmed by this impressive addition of luxury to the eighteenth-century splendour.

We enjoyed every minute living in this luxury to which none of us had been accustomed and the last hurdle to be surmounted by Ian McFarlane was the 'benefit to the "living-in" directors of the company' for Revenue purposes. It was difficult to find similar accommodation in the area so we collected leaflets of vaguely similar make-up. However, Ian had done his Revenue homework and the stark facts were that there were three grown males sharing the living accommodation, had only one kitchen for three people and only one bathroom for three which was almost down to the messdeck level of the RN. I think Wolfy must have supplied an eye bandage to the Revenue because there was no argument as to the value of the benefit to the directors, as they all had to use "basic" standards of *shared* accommodation. After all, there were three Killicks who had to share one WC, one shower, one bath, so it really was not very different to Victoria Barracks in Southsea: 'A benefit in kind', divided by three, and you do not argue with your accountant.

We had many happy and profitable years at Lerpiniere House and with the amount of foreign-currency dealings that flowed through the office we could have started our own Foreign Exchange Department for all those orders that were written in the rather splendid Georgian surroundings.

As Gerry observed so correctly: 'The mafia days at "One-Two-One".'

Tale 43

Don't Ask the Price, It's a Penny

This was the slogan which appeared on the board over Michael Marks's open stall in Leeds Market in 1884. He had arrived in Leeds from Poland via London, was penniless and hardly spoke any English. The nearest was Yiddish which brought him into contact with the firm of J.J. Dewhirst who were wholesale merchants. They sold to peddlers like young Michael who borrowed £5 from Mr Dewhirst with which he paid his first purchases from Dewhirst's.

Tom Spencer was Dewhirst's cashier who was greatly impressed by young Marks and the business progress he was making, and when Michael asked him to form a business partnership with him, Marks & Spencer were born. On the 28th September 1894 Tom Spencer paid £300 for half the share in the business and Michael Marks put his own capital in the business which stood at £450.

When we first encountered M&S they had gone from one open 'penny' stall in Leeds Market to 264 UK stores and their pre-tax profits were £265.3 million. Compared to M&S HMS *Vilomi* was not even a rivet in the keel of the ship, let alone the golden rivet (available in the 'glossary' of Jackspeak; price one double tot).

When Schaps production in Vienna started to rocket because of the increase of EU sales, their US production guru advised them to drop anything which was slowing down the production of shirts and the answer was: pyjamas. The advice was 'Drop 'em' ... not just the pants but also the jackets ... and when Kurt mentioned that they were thinking of this, he asked whether I could suggest a possible UK pyjama replacement. On my return Jim and I sourced the market for a British company, but they all replied 'Terribly sorry, but all our spare production is taken up by M&S'.

Using Uncle Charles's old method of not taking no for an answer, we telephoned M&S and asked to be put through to 'Exports'.

'Which country?' asked a very pleasant gent and I had to search Tom's appendix but it wasn't much help so I tried his well-tried method of 'If in doubt, ask for the top man or woman', which I proceeded to do.

'Can I help?' to which I would have loved to reply with a 'Not 'arf, mate' in my worst Jackspeak, but Jim would not have approved, nor would Jamie at Hampton Grammar.

'I wonder if you could... We are a buying agent for a number of European companies who market British goods and we have been in contact with our correspondents in Germany, Switzerland and France and they have informed us the M&S is well represented through retail stores. On checking with our friends in Austria, however, you do not appear to be in that market...' I paused and waited.

All I got after a few deep breaths was a fuddled waffle. 'How interesting of you and your colleagues to mention that particular market...'

I cut him off brutally but nicely. 'Ah well, if you are already at negotiating point, there is no point in continuing this conversation...'

At which point he clutched at a lifebelt as he was sinking below the waves of the blue Danube.

'Oh no, Sir ... the negotiations have not been finalised ... but who are your people in Austria?'

Jackspeak told me to say 'None of your f—ing business,' but Jim was watching me and put his left arm out, crooked an imaginary violin on it and with his right hand grabbed a non-existent violin bow and started to bow it across the mystery violin. I don't know if Jim was playing *Tales of the Vienna Woods* but I was now on my best Upper-Deck Jackspeak and started to talk down to him on the Lower Deck.

'Actually ... our people are one of the largest textile firms in Austria and would like someone who is well established in the entire retail scene in that market; we'd love to meet you ASAP.'

I could almost hear him turn the pages in his leather-bound diary with the gold M&S lettering embossed on the green cover.

'How would next Thursday around eleven suit you? We could have a bite of lunch in the executive suite. I'm sorry to ask but are you kosher? Because of the catering.'

Jim put two fingers up.

'Oh thank you ... that's very kind of you; I'll have some of those frozen giant prawns you sell off the shelf in your food department...' I must have hit the right note as he seemed dead keen to go out to Iceland to catch some more for me.

I just loved the meeting. It was textbook fishing, not for prawns, but for the name of our company in Vienna.

He knew it and I knew he wanted to get the name but the prawns were excellent and he promised to let me know after he had consulted the Board – Export Division. This meant himself as he was the chairman of that Board. After two more conversations he asked me to meet with him again, with the result that they gave us samples, prices, delivery times and agreed to our sales exclusivity conditions and I wondered which branch of CDH they were members of.

They delivered on the day, we paid one day before the due date and when he got our cheque he phoned to thank me for the prompt payment and added his surprise as to the name of our bankers. I could not help gloating with my comment that 'of course they don't go back to 1894 but Leo J. were established in 1919, which is long before we were in the "schmattes game".' This, I imagine, produced a small smirk.

Kurt and Erich were very pleased with the smooth operation and when they repeated, with much larger orders, Kurt phoned me.

'Tell me, Dave, are you a betting man?'

He seemed surprised at my 'No'.

'But all the boys at Brighton went to the bookies once a week to place their bets. Why didn't you?'

'A very simple answer, Kurt. I bet once and lost everything and when I was older I lost everything in the family raffle.'

Kurt just said, 'I'm sorry about that, David...'

I cut him off.

'But we're changing that now, aren't we? Jim and I are quite happy and hope you and Erich are as well.'

''Course we are,' he said firmly, 'I was just winding you up, which proves I've not forgotten some of the slang. But talking about betting, what are your odds about the M&S chap contacting us direct? You know that there are no secrets between shippers. The M&S–Schapira goods have been in the shops around three months now. Their Swiss bloke can nip across the border at Constance, go in to any shop where the pyjamas are, do a bit of digging *à la Jim* at BCT and Bingo ... you have the answer. I'll bet you ... in Swiss francs ... SF500 ... I'll be getting a phone call from Baker Street by the end of the month. Are you on?'

'No way,' I replied, 'I'm no good at betting but this is not a bet and, if I may say so, for you it's a bloody certainty.'

And we were both right. He got the phone call from Baker Street and I had not taken the bet on.

Kurt told me the contents of the London conversation and Jim was listening to it on the extension phone. 'First the pussy-footing around ... then the direct approach ... if you buy direct from us you will save his percentage...' and Jim was accompanying it with hand gestures of thumbs-up, open palms or two fingers up and I think he was enjoying it as much as I and Kurt. However, Kurt had the last laugh because the chap did decide to come to Vienna 'just to have a chat'. 'If you want to, I can't stop you but it will be a waste of time ... for you and for me... There are only two of us here and you do have staff.'

When he did get there Kurt let him wait for twenty minutes and then ushered him into the office. Basically it was a repeat of the telephone conversation which Kurt terminated after fifteen minutes with a beautifully polished Manchester University accent: 'I'm dreadfully sorry but I did warn you...'

The only reply was: 'But I've come all this way to see you.'

Kurt slaughtered him: 'I never asked you to come. Do enjoy the Wiener Schnitzel and the wine is delicious up at Grinzing. Have a great time. Good flight home!'

Business continued until the market changed but I still follow the profit motive motto which Michael Marks's son put so eloquently many years later:

'I learned my social philosophy from Michael Marks and not Karl Marx.'

Tale 44

Family Trust

Uncle Charles had told me many years ago that there were three very pleasant things in life which were food, drink and sex and that they lasted longest in that order. Throughout my life I had tested and sampled all of them and the older I got the more I agreed with every word and the order Charles put them in. The physical experiences with the 'Lady from the Holy Land' also confirmed these findings and I had come to the conclusion that our last contact in London would bring the curtain down on this rather complicated but very pleasant physical affair.

Over the years, every time the word Inge was mentioned by me, Jim would stand up, lift his arms, cross himself, bow from the waist down and give a very large grin. When he opened the letter with a Haifa postmark he didn't stand up but just read and handed it to me. Manny was updating us on their latest movements and 'it was such a pity we hadn't met for so long etc. etc...' There was a phone number on the letter and before I had picked up the phone, matter-of-fact, honest Jim raised his eyebrows and before I could say anything he said very quietly: 'I know that you told me she was one of the best sex experiences you have had but ... that's *years* ago and she and you are both much older now...'

Before we both got into rough sex water I grinned at him. 'Well ... we never did find out if semi-Arabic Manny practised what many Arabs do.'

All Jim said was: 'It's all yours, mate... Dig out...'

I shook my head. 'No, Jim, I was only trying to wind you up ... but seriously, as the peace offering is from him, why don't you ring and see if they still combine their travel with the UK or places you visit.'

Jim shook his head negatively. 'Go on, you phone him. You never know the Lady from the Holy Land might be on the phone.'

In fact she wasn't. Manny was over the moon and thanked me and I told him that Jim was the instigator of the call.

I asked Manny if they were still gypsies, flying everywhere on the European map, and he said, 'Yes, but mainly Zurich ... for obvious reasons ... shekels... You know that, David, don't you?' He promised to telex me dates and places over the next three months and if one of the dates coincided with the arrival of the new DS21 in Rheine we could meet up. When Manny heard this he was over his half-Arabic moon and got me to promise to liaise in Zurich.

I had been keeping Jim informed of the content of the conversation and his only reaction to the proposed meeting in Zurich after the collection of the new Citroën was a very definite thumbs-up pushed towards the half-kosher sky. The question of date and liaise in Zurich went telexing backwards and forwards and when the definite delivery of DS21 was finalised, the Bridge of HMS *Vilomi* went to action stations.

Jim and I flew to Greven and were met by a car from the CDH dealer who had received the new DS21. They bought us a very pleasant dinner of *Kalbshaxe* and Jim really enjoyed the steamed knuckle of veal and sauerkraut which was washed down liberally with two litres of Hamburg beer. The garage's car collected us at nine o'clock in the morning and the duplicate hotel bill was supplied without any problems. After all, nothing could have been more tax-kosher than a trip to purchase a company car.

The only disappointment with the shining graceful car was that it had a local number plate which bore no relation to my beloved 'JOY', but as dear Charles used to say 'everything in life has it's price', although in this case it was much less than in the UK. The only complaint from the sellers of the DS was that our company had not ordered more cars per year.

The trip down to Basle on the autobahn was breathtaking. I had told Jim about Gerry being intrigued by all the 'Ausfahrt' signs, but he did not request an explanation. His only comment was: 'I'm not surprised Gerry liked the scenery, it really is stunning with or without "Farty".'

Zurich was basking in sunshine and the reflection off the lake was like a sparkling diamond. Jim lit another cigarello and leant back contentedly. 'Now I know why Mitch makes all these sacrifices to come with you on the Continental jaunts. Back-breaking, isn't it?'

Jim's typed-out itinerary matched the note which awaited us at the Seidenhof Hotel and Manny had concurred about dinner at the Kronenhalle, a comfortable lofty typically Swiss noshery. Jim was loving it. The hotels and restaurants, the food, the efficiency … his only comment was, 'Good, in'it?'

When Inge and Manny joined us for dinner, neither party commented on the sad fact that we were all older and tactfully did not mention that we looked it. In fact, so much water had passed under all our bridges that the early part of the conversation seemed much easier. Manny was intrigued how much our business had increased but being born in the Middle East could not understand that it had all happened legally without a backhander or even a 'front-giver'. Inge added that I had not been on my own in achieving this and that 'David has been so lucky to have had Jim to help him.' This signalled a peace-offering to show that the four of us were now one happy family, and Jim suddenly glowed with relief and satisfaction. This was reinforced by the rösti and pork schnitzels which were fatter and juicier than their Austrian veal counterparts. Two hours later we all agreed to continue our update exchanges on the Bauer-au-Lac terrace the next day.

Hugs and kisses all round were perfunctory and Inge started off by telling us that they had stopped coming to London because it was too embarrassing. They had always been invited to stay with Billy and Pucky as guests but had always reciprocated the hospitality by taking them to the latest restaurants and clubs. Manny did not mind but when he found the cost of the clubs and nightspots were three times that of having a double room at the Dorchester, he called a spade a bloody shovel. Things came to a crunch when Billy suggested that as there were two spare rooms and en-suite bathroom at their newly moved-into apartment at the mews in Eaton Place Inge and Manny were always welcome to stay there when in London. Manny thought this was a great idea but after two visits Billy suggested that perhaps Manny would like to buy the two rooms off Billy so he could have a pied-à-terre in London. Manny was a little wary of the size and shape of the handshake, and suggested an exchange of lease documents. Billy asked him, 'Why? Don't you trust me?' and eventually got Manny to part with the money without a contract, promising that they would talk about the contract in Zurich: 'Pucky and I will finalise everything with you there and we can all stay at that little hotel, off the Bahnhof Strasse, which David usually stays at.'

'We all had a pleasant evening there,' Manny related, 'but we did not even get to the "C" of the contract nor on the Saturday. On Sunday morning there was no Billy and Pucky but just a note from Billy at breakfast:

'Sorry about today. There was a panic on at Eaton Place Mews but it was great seeing you. Love to Inge.'

When Inge and Manny left later on Sunday, he paid the bill and was given four bills. One was Inge and Manny's and a copy, and the other two were handed to Manny with a large smile by the clerk. 'Mr Franklin asked me to give this to you. I've made a copy for you as usual.'

Manny finished his tale: 'The last time we were in London and asked for the return of the money, Billy just said "What money? Have another drink!"'

Manny turned to me: 'What about you, David? Have you been caught?'

Jim blurted out: 'David has the dubious distinction of having been the first one in the money-knicking queue!'

Manny had to have another Grand Marnier. He recovered first, raised his glass and clinked with me: 'Cheers, partner.'

I Love the Sound of the Horn

So said Alfred de Vigny in 1826 but Jim loved it whenever Stan Wilkinson from Horne Bros came on the phone to him.

Throughout the 1960s and 70s large groups in the retail menswear field were beginning to purchase different types of European clothing and, like Austin Reed, came to us to see if we could offer them fabric and design exclusivity. Moss Bros, Leonard Lyle, Cecil Gee and Horne Bros were all on that particular path and if we kept cloth and styling exclusive, our manufacturers in Europe were happy as long as these were bulk orders.

Our first success was the SMARTO roll-neck flower-power shirt with Austin Reed, and as everything had fitted snugly into the roll collar we continued to work more closely with them. Although neither Jack Shorter nor Claude Cleaver of AR were of the 'navy-blue' blood connection we got on splendidly with them. The success of the roll-neck flower-power shirt now rolled down to our Italian knitwear, as we fulfilled Sigor Crosetti's wish to bring them 'more customer and eat asparagi'.

When Jack Shorter had told Jim that he and his wife were going on a cruise from Genoa and were spending a week with Claude in Lugano, he asked: 'Is your Italian factory anywhere in the north of Italy so we could visit them?'

'No problem,' replied Jim. 'They are just across the border near Lake Lugano. Dave can pick you up from there because the three of us are out there with the car to visit the Milan Fair.'

'Brilliant,' said Jack, 'I'll liaise with you on dates,' and the meeting in Viggiù resulted in an exclusive knitted jacket for AR's Xmas catalogue; there weren't enough asparagus in the fields near Viggiù to match all the jacket orders.

This 'dummy' run with Britain's leading group of menswear

shops paved the path for others who wanted exclusivity, which our people in Austria, Germany, Italy and Switzerland were all able to supply. Horne Brothers were a well-established family business with a chain of shops throughout the UK, and although we had made contact with them, Stan Wilkinson, their buyer, did not buy much clothing outside of their own factory in North London. However, they had tried a sample order of trousers with our people in Germany, who were one of six of the best-equipped specialist trouser manufacturers in Germany. Everything in the manufacturing process was automated including the side seam of the trousers and the accuracy and 'clean' look of the trousers, and the price could not be matched by Horne's own factory.

'When are they off to Germany again?' asked Stan when he spoke to Jim. 'I'll give you my dates and perhaps they could collect me from my last call in Germany, take me to Westrich and give me a lift home.'

'You've got a passenger from Ramstein,' said Jim, giving me the message from Stan, lifting the phone, dialling the Westrich number and handing the phone to me.

'We'll put the flags out in Ramstein,' said the Germans and there weren't enough flags to match the zeros on the unit numbers of the trousers placed on order and we had a splendid meal in Ramstein at the Italian–German *ristorante* which catered to the GIs whose air-force base was in the town.

We set off the next morning after shaking off too much red wine and the plentiful spaghetti. After joining the autobahn half an hour later, Mitch wound up the DS21 which was cruising effortlessly at around 140mph on the unrestricted-speed limit motorway and the Goddess was flying like a holy bird.

'Any music going, Mitch?' asked Stan, pointing to the car radio and Mitch pressed the 'overseas services' button and we just caught the tail end of the London news: '... and it has been confirmed that Lord Louis Mountbatten and some members of his family are missing believed killed by the IRA'. Mitch switched the radio off. There was complete silence between the three of us and Stan broke the spell: 'Well, if I remember nothing else about this trip it will be that on the 27th August 1979 I heard that Lord Louis Mountbatten had been blown up on his boat *Shadow V* off Mullaghmore.'

He changed the subject and told us that before going to the previous supplier he had been to Paris to sign an exclusive tie-up for Hornes to retail the entire Jacques Fath range of ties and clothing.

We got to London safely and he thanked us again for the taxi service after we had dropped him at Tottenham and returned to the office.

'Anything special since we spoke on the phone, Jim?'

'Nothing really,' he replied shaking his head, '....except one thing. You won't believe it but I had your darling brother on the phone ... three times ... saying it was urgent... He had to speak to you personally. So I crossed myself three times, locked the cheque book up and asked if I could help but he refused ... thankfully...'

I made sure that the cheque book in the drawer was definitely under lock and key.

'Would you like to speak to him, Dave?'

'"Like to" is the overstatement of the year but perhaps Madame is ill or something.'

When I spoke to him he was gushing: '... Most wonderful collection ... you, Dave, know all the leading menswear retailers... It's an opportunity not to be missed, fantastic collectionn... When could you pop over?' I said I'd let him know.

Dear old practical Jim snorted: 'For goodness' sake, Dave, it's only across Oxford Street. Go over there now and get it over with. Mitch can sort all the trip bits out with me. Be less for you to do!' Mitch threw his hands up in horror.

Fifteen minutes later I was in Billy's office which was packed with a brilliant collection of all kinds of menswear. I started to look through it and froze. Every tie, every shirt, every jacket, suit or overcoat had the very elegant label of Jacques Fath sewn into it.

'Nice stuff?' asked an expectant Billy.

I shook my head. 'It's pirated ... from Taiwan, I expect. You want *me* to sell it? You're joking, of course. I've just come back with the buyer of a British company who now have the legal rights to sell "JF" wear exclusively in the UK ... You must be out of your little mind. I wouldn't touch it with a barge pole, Thames or River Kwai.'

'But it's beautiful stuff, David. Nobody will know.' I thought that not even a sledgehammer could have pounded it into him and left the office.

Jim and Mitch were all ears and all Mitch commented was: 'He wants you to sell pirated clobber? What would Stan say?'

'I won't even give you one guess, Mitch, but I'm going to warn him because of the "Franklin" name bit.'

Stan was still on the 'many thanks' bit and then switched to the four paper notes on his desk: 'From a Mister Franklin. I knew it couldn't be you because Jim would not just leave vague notes like that and in any case you were with me all the time.'

'Forget it, Stan. Probably some nutter using my name to get you to sign my life away. Tell them on the switchboard to cut off. If he is persistent, tell them to cut *it* off.'

'Thanks for the trip,' said Stan, 'I did enjoy it and thank Westrich again for their hostility ... I mean hospitality...' Suddenly I thought: 'You never know, do you, old man Adams? He's fifty-plus, could have been in those KZs, couldn't he?'

Stan was right, of course, but we were both too tired to argue.

Jim had flown straight back after the Milan Fair whilst Mitch and I had manned the 'taxi' service to and from Lugano and Ramstein. We were both pleasantly knackered and after dinner Mitch went upstairs to a well-deserved rest. 'Schnäppsli?' asked Jim; it was his German code word for 'sippers'. Schnapps is a rough German brandy and the '*li*' is the diminutive version of 'small' so it should really have been 'sippers'.

I nodded and gulped it down. Jim turned to me and asked: 'You don't think your dear brother has gone off his rocker?'

I shook my head negatively. 'I think "gone" is the wrong word. You remember in '66 when Madame phoned us in Great Marlborough Street and asked to speak to me urgently? Madame was on her maxi GB tack: "A word in your ear, David ... Billy has a small problem... You will help him, won't you? It's Pucky." I had visions of her having had it off with some young artisan from the builder's but I couldn't have been more wrong.'

I continued to remind Jim of the story, which went something like this. Madame started to half sob and blurted out, 'You'll see Billy has been in a little trouble but you will take his side, won't you?' As I had always been quite ready to take any side I asked her to be a little more forthcoming.

'You know they have a German au pair from Berlin... Her mother runs a brothel there and she received a letter from the au pair at Pucky's saying that she was getting on wonderfully with Billy and things might work out...'

I was getting slightly confused at this point and stopped Madame. 'Where did you get all this information from, Madame?' I asked.

'Pucky phoned me and said it was all in this letter from the mother to her daughter, the au pair.'

'But how did Pucky get hold of a letter to the au pair?'

'Oh,' said Madame, 'Pucky opened the letter and then gave it to the au pair.'

This was getting like a top-shelf Boon & Porter paperback gone rough at the edges and I urged Madame to put me out of my misery and tell me the rest.

'Pucky is terribly upset about hearing that Billy had been unfaithful...' which really should not have surprised anyone in Sheen because the bush telegraph had been informed by the United Dairies milkman that when he tried to deliver the milk to put it on top of the table, he had found them on the kitchen table and "at it".'

'So what do you want *me* to do about it?'

'You will take *Billy*'s side, won't you?' and I wasn't quite sure whether she wanted me to take the sex baton and continue on the kitchen table so I said:

'Which side do you want me to be on?'

'Billy's ... of course...' she answered decisively and I just scratched my head.

'Go and see Pucky first,' Madame urged. 'She has swallowed a bottle of aspirins...'

The phone call ended in more sobs, and I was at Pucky's side within the hour. She almost looked like death and vaguely like the painting of Lord Nelson dying in the cockpit of the *Victory* without an English or French sailor in sight.

'Thank you for coming ... I don't know what to do...' she wailed.

Trying to shorten the conversation as quickly as possible and knowing there was no DC available in any shape or form, I sat beside her on the bed, held her hand and tried to calm her down.

'Look, Pucky...' I was pleased to see that the mental DC seemed to be OK. '...You can't put the clock back but it's no good pretending it's not happened. You can only do one of two things: 1) Get a divorce ... You've got enough grounds to take him to the cleaners but the problem is that when you win and are awarded costs and maintenance there is no money to pay those. I should imagine the house is mortgaged up to the eyeballs so that's a no-go. 2) You can decide to forgive and forget and keep your fingers and his legs crossed, seal the zip up. I'd advise the second option.'

She thought for a moment, grabbed my hand, gave me a little kiss and murmured softly into my ear: 'I knew you'd come up with the right solution. You're lucky you don't have these problems.'

Pucky took the second option and on the 22nd November 1966 Lizzy Franklin was born.

Tale 46

There are Three Kinds of Lies: Lies, Damned Lies and Statistics

Our own statistics were living proof of this saying by Benjamin Disraeli. Jim and I had started the company and after two years increased the staff by the addition of Mitch. The increase was a statistical increase of 50 per cent, which was not a lie but living proof of the misleading nature of statistics as an increase of staff was no guarantee of an increase in profits. When we moved to Lerpiniere House and the factory in Battersea the number of staff had grown from three to eight, the latest addition being Kit Wadman, the loving lady with the Hoover, mop and wax-polishing cloth. Yet HMS *Vilomi* did not sink under the additional financial burden but fortunately sailed majestically towards further rich islands of fortune.

At the factory Greg and Mitch had a brilliant 'Boy Seaman' working under them and Greg's grandad and grandma kept a watching brief over the young crew. Greg was now firmly attached to his boyhood sweetheart and signs of a wedding were obviously on the horizon.

We had always kept our car in a garage which was behind Geoffrey's house in Kennington Road and was paid for by us but also housed Geoffrey's Vespa, which was a backscratch from days long gone bye at 'Balcomie'. Just before we moved into Lerpiniere House the estate offered us a garage to the rear of the house which did not have direct access into the garage from the garden. Consequently the morning nods with other garage occupants turned into longer 'chats'. Our direct garage neighbour was a London 'black cab' taxi driver who turned out to have been an RN captain's steward and I was beginning to think that the entire male population of London was ex-RN. The 'hellos' turned to the weather and about two weeks before our move into Lerpiniere House Charley popped the question regarding the new occupants of the house.

Weekdays Charley bought his *Sun* at Mr Hing's on the corner of Wincott Street. On Sundays, he switched to the *News of the World* to see what his dodgy mates had been doing to the lonely cabbies' wives and what they had got for doing it. Mr Hing had told Charley that we had changed our paper-round delivery address to Kennington Road. It did not require much digging or Bletchley to locate who the new occupants were going to be so, instead of 'Hello, good morning...' Charley suggested we had a chat regarding the move and possible 'standby' of any small 'transfers at sea' from the house in Oakden Street and Poland Street to the new house. When he popped into Poland Street and saw casual male clothing samples, off came his jacket, out came my tape measure, and any garments which were not available from us we ordered up from the manufacturers. He was a normal '42 long' and we did not even have to measure his inside leg measurements for any ties.

Every night Jim 'made a list' for items to be collected from the two addresses and Charley was given keys to collect the items at his leisure, which got over possible parking problems. Black cabs have 'immune from parking fines' written all over them and Charley could also have the luxury of using the three house loos instead of the smelly WC rent-boy pickups in Great Marlborough Street and Kennington Lane. Apart from the 'wanted item list' Jim kept a price addition total and when Charley discovered that we also sold suits to Martin Green in Marylebone Street, they lost out and Charley got them direct from us, price depending on Jim's list; in any case it was less than the wholesale price.

On one of Charley's collection delivery trips to One-Two-One, he went all mysterious, forgot himself and said: 'Mr Harvey...' Deep Captain's Steward pause... 'I'm sorry to be so nosey but who's going to do the cleaning for you in that big place?'

Jim felt like saying, 'Dunno, mate', but they were not yet on such intimate terms and Jim was much too busy to chat anyway and advised Charley to tackle me on the subject. This he did that night as we were both parking in the garage complex behind One-Two-One.

'Sorry to trouble you, Sir, but I was talking to your colleague in the office when I was doing a run for you from Poland Street.'

Deep pause and he wasn't quite sure whether he should continue in Upper Deck vein or not. 'It's a beautiful house you're moving into and I wondered if you need any help in keeping it clean...' He looked up at me with a sort of 'I wonder what the gaffer is going to say' look and raised his eyebrows.

'Actually, MrWadman, we've not made any arrangements as yet, but what had you in mind?' As I couldn't really see him getting down on his hands and knees to scrub the deck. Stewards don't ... deck-apes do.

'Well ...' he said, diving in at the deep end, anchor-depth, 'the wife does a bit of cleaning and I wondered if you would like to have her services...'

I cut him off. 'Great, send her round tomorrow and she can have a chat with Jim.' Charley suddenly dropped his guard and said, 'Cheers, mate.'

When we got home that night Jim informed Mitch and me that the staff total now numbered nine. The latest addition, 'Kit', duly came for a visit and asked to be called by that name.

'Sorry, love,' she added, turning to Jim, 'I can't start for a month, I'm just off to Spain with me mates. Not a problem is it I 'ope?' Jim felt that this time he would be able to cope without her. Had no bloody alternative did 'e?

Tale 47

Sunrise – Sunset

Contrary to everything I was taught at Hampton Grammar School, the Japanese Order of the Rising Sun and the Far East were not only the places where in the mid 1970s the sun set but it also rose in their commercial and industrial worlds.

Everything, from cars to velour sweaters were being produced in the Far East with modern machinery and cheap labour and Jörg Tschopp was seeing his markets dwindle. But he was not alone, as all our European suppliers had identical problems. I met him on a stopover from New York back to Zurich and we had lunch at Thiefrow, which was 'between planes'. His market in the US had disappeared and even his sales in Europe, including Switzerland and the UK, were disappearing. The 'golden' 60s were now but a happy memory and the reality had to be faced that sooner or later TUSA would have to close. He was very depressed because Theo's ancestor, Gottlieb Tuchschmid, had founded the business in 1868 and Jörg felt it his moral duty to guide the company to a successful bicentenary in the year 2068.

I did not join him in a schâppsli at Thiefrow as I was driving back to Lerpiniere House (orders from the Bridge on departure: 'Be careful, Dave!') but just had a lager. Jörg opened his heart: their plan for the future of TUSA was brutally realistic and logical. Theo was pumping his entire savings into the company and it was literally bleeding to death. He had eventually been able to persuade Theo and Silvia to sell up and they were slowly planning to do this. They managed to find jobs for all their 185 employees and also sold their machinery over the next months. This left the original factory building, which he converted into offices, design studios and a kindergarten.

However, the final crunch did not materialise until 1980/1 because Theo's eightieth birthday was due and Jörg wanted to give him a big farewell do as Theo was one of the bastions of Amriswil society. Apart from TUSA, Theo was the director of a bank, was one of the leading lights in the community and was well known in local politics, which have a much higher standing in Switzerland than in the UK, as MPs receive no salary but only expenses. In fact Jörg was planning this to be Amriswil's event of the year, or as it would have translated in Jackspeak 'a bloody big bash'. Jörg planned this venue at the medieval castle of Hagenwil, which dates back to 1275 in a tax return. (Gnomes please note – Tax return? You must be joking but it is true!)

The castle nestles peacefully in the valley on the northern edge of the village of the same name. It is the only moated castle still standing in the German-speaking part of Switzerland and it has an old drawbridge which gives access to the castle. At its entrance is a small statue of the Madonna. Its main hall with its high beamed ceiling had been turned into a sumptuous dining room, which was to be the venue for the lavish party.

When he was telling me all this over the not-so-lavish airport lunch, he asked me to send Theo a card for the celebration. 'A card?' exclaimed Jim when I told him. 'He must be out of his Swiss mind. Theo has been one of the three greats in your life: Uncle Charles was the one who launched you; Kurt pushed the ship along and Theo was the anchor that held everything together. Not to put too fine a point on it, he's the only one still alive to tell all your tales ... well not quite all but almost...'

When I had the Zurich–London ticket on my desk I phoned Jörg to tell him. He was nearly speechless.

'You're coming especially for Theo?' There was a deadly hush for a minute. 'What a wonderful idea!' I stopped him. 'Well, actually, it was Jim's...'

'Put him on, will you, Dave?' It was the only time I had ever seen Jim blush.

Orders from the Bridge were AOK and when I got to Kloten and walked out of Customs, Theo was there with his big Maurice Chevalier smile. He grabbed my shoulders and embraced me.

'Thank you for coming,' he said, suppressing a small tear. 'Silvia and I have prepared a small guest room for you.' Jörg told me later that they had *never* put anybody up for the night before. The 'Grand' pub had always been on standby with Frau Schneider fussing around her Englanders.

I was now on top of my Swiss wonderland roller coaster which came down with a bump at the 'Pflug' when they served 'crepe suzette' with a double Grand Marnier... Later Jörg gave me a rundown of the operation for next day's celebrations.

'Seeing you have made a special trip, I have placed you next to Theo on the top table and left your speech to last. Unfortunately, you will have to say it in German as most of the visitors don't speak or understand English.' I almost died.

My German was fluent, but as it had not been updated since well before World War II, a speech was not on the agenda of a pissy-arsed German speaking ex-matelot in Switzerland to the cream of the top-notch assembly of bankers, businessman and local dignitaries. I couldn't even get Jim to throw me a life belt; all *he* could say in German was 'Ja' and 'Nein'. Then I suddenly thought that there are many words which work in both languages: toilet, garage, football, foul, and the one word which the Germans and Swiss revered, which they still regard with awe and great respect.

To them it still represents English honesty and integrity and that word was 'gentleman' ... and I wrote it down on a pad next to the bed and went fast asleep.

The next morning Jörg collected me after breakfast with Silvia and if Theo had asked if I had slept well and he would have understood if I had added 'like a log'. I couldn't tell him that I was now sweating 'Neaters' which was Jackspeak for the sweat pouring off you as a result of too many undiluted 'neat' tots. Consequently, sweating like the proverbial pig.

At the party, the oak-beamed dining room was packed. Theo sat in the middle of the top table and Jörg and I were on either side of him. Speech after speech sang Theo's praises and when it came to my turn to stand up Jörg introduced me as '*our* good friend and customer from England'. The clapping and banging of the wooden tables ebbed and as I got up I nearly wet my pants. However, after a few sentences I soon got into my stride and found the company vociferous in its approval. I felt it almost seemed like the proverbial 'piss-up ashore with your mates'. I held my hand up for quiet – it was the important part of my speech:

'...Over all these years it has been an honour and pleasure to work with Theo, who has been a great help to us. I do not know anyone as pleasant or as correct as Theo Tuchschmid...' I paused, '...In fact he has been *the perfect gentleman*.' I used the English

315

word, knowing that it was one that the German-speaking world still revered.

I sat down and the place erupted in hand-clapping and the banging of wooden tables. I looked at Theo, smiled and sat down.

As the dining room emptied, Theo said 'thank you' and put his arms around me. For a second I felt as if he were my father and I was his son.

Tale 48

Computer Literate

TUSA was the first of our suppliers to close, followed by the Swiss PKZ and AFW. Westrich in Germany moved their production to Tunisia and Erich Schapira sold his factory in Vienna to a German company. However, vigilant as ever since 1933, Wolfy had been very aware of events and his scent had picked up the fact that the more we created what the marketing boys labelled 'product awareness' for 'Magic Tree', the more we sold. As a result, the loss of the textile business coincided with an expansion on the air-freshener side. Staff numbers incrased at the factory in Battersea, where Mitch was now spending most of his time during and outside working hours.

Greg married his sweetheart from Lambeth and moved into a flat almost next door to where he was born in 1961. At the factory as the number of units invoiced increased in disproportionate numbers to the diminishing number of textile units, ALFY, our micro-computer, was doing overtime and Jim came to hate it even more than the telex.

'I know you've written all the programs, including the currency conversions, PAYE and the VAT, but, to put it bluntly ... and if I were the Chairman of this company ... which ... thankfully I am not ... you are a little too expensive to sit in front of ALFY all day and type out invoices. I think I'll put an advert in the *Telegraph* and see what happens.' As usual I agreed.

There was a 'eureka' next morning from the loo.

'I've got it,' Jim cried *à la* Professor Higgins.

'What have you got, Jim?' I called back.

'I was looking for a word in "qwerty computer" speak for someone who can bang away at that silly keyboard and press buttons who is cheaper than you.' Emerging from the loo, he thrust the *Telegraph* crossword into my hands and pointed to '5 across, 8 letters – can handle computer. 'The eureka word is "LITERATE",' he said.

I looked at him as if he was speaking Chinese, not that I would have known if he had actually done that.

'Let's put in an advert for "young girl wanted..." ' He grinned from ear to ear.

'Just winding you up ... I'll put in "white" as well, so they can lock us up ... race relations ... equal opportunity ... and, of course, ... the trump card "sexist",' and he was really enjoying himself.

'You put in whatever you want,' I added helpfully.

'Cheers, mate,' he added emphatically, 'I usually did!' I felt like adding 'Bastard!'

But the ad had no response whatsoever so we contacted all the local schools' 'careers masters', which had the identical result: zilch.

'We'll have a go next term,' said Jim, and we did.

In April 1983 I had a phone call from Archbishop Tenison School near the Oval.

'Mr Franklin? I'm the careers master and I believe you were looking for an non-sex-specific person. I think I have a boy here...'

And I thought for a moment he had misunderstood our requirements to be sex oriented, but as I had told Uncle Charles years ago, dogs, animals and underage males or females weren't really my tot wants, unless you could swap them for double tots instead.

The careers master asked if I was still on the phone to which I said: 'Yes.'

'I've got a boy here for you...' I felt like telling him that a school with such high academic standards should rephrase that. 'He's only fifteen...' I thought, we're off again, and waited.

'He lives very near you, so he doesn't have far to come,' I felt that for a school with such high standards of English he should be more selective with his words.

However, the outcome was that when Mark Notton pushed back our squeaking iron gate at Lerpiniere House, Jim and I rushed to the window. Jim exclaimed:

'Good heavens, he looks like Chocballs's twin.'

Mark pressed the bell, and Jim opened the door, grinned and smirked. 'It IS Chocballs but without the smell and black bags under the eyes. It looks as if he has raided the bank and bought

318

himself a suit for the interview. We should send him to Leopold Joseph, they are always looking for trainees in their investment department and this lad has invested everything he or his Dad have and bought a new suit.'

At his interview with Jim it turned out that, unlike Chocballs, Mark had a father and had been scrubbed spotlessly clean by Mum. Dad did not rape him Friday nights coming home from 'The Print' and Mum did not go to any bottle, let alone a bottle of meths. In fact Dad took him to the 'Blue's' home every Saturday to follow the team's fortune which rose and fell like the tide on London's Thames in Fulham. If they played 'away' Dad went with him to Tottenham when they played the 'Yids' up at White Hart Lane in North London. Especially if Gary Lineker, the Queen Mum of English football, was scoring against them.

But whether 'Home' or 'Away', he and his mates donned blue and white baseball caps, worn backwards and tied their striped blue scarves around their necks which were the blue badges of courage of all Chelsea fans.

Four weeks on, when he got hot, Mark asked if Jim objected to him wearing a blue and white CFC T shirt to which Jim replied he could come starkers if Kit didn't mind although she would have been deeply shocked if her new 'love' Mark – 'wiv a K' had been so common.

During the interview, Mark looked around the room and said that the main reason for coming and 'having a look' was that we had a computer.

'If you turn 180 degrees, it's in the corner,' said Jim. Mark turned, saw the chair in front of the computer, sat down on it and started to tap away on the keyboard. Jim was horrified. 'I told you where the computer is but I didn't say you could use it!' Despite this, Jim gave Mark the job and always had the highest praise for him. This turned out to be quite prophetic, as Mark was made a director and joined the Board of David Franklin Limited in December 2003.

Tale 49

Hurricane at Lerpiniere House

Mitch was away up north, and Jim and I were watching the BBC news before retiring with our schnäppsli. After the news on 16th October 1987 Michael Fish gave the weather forecast for the following day, adding a little footnote about a phone call from a lady regarding the possibility of gale-force or stronger winds in the south. 'Nothing to worry about,' he added reassuringly as neither the BBC script nor the newspapers in Dad's shop in the Downs at Eastbourne had made any mention of any impending disasters.

Schnäppsli number two had made us sufficiently mellow and we went upstairs around eleven o'clock. 'Cheers mate,' was the last thing I remembered until I heard this whooshing noise in the night. I sat up and heard a tinkle of leaves coming down like heavy confetti at a wedding. I got up and walked to the window, peeped through the curtain and saw a submarine-like object lying across the front wall. The iron gate was like a conning tower sticking through it, which I now recognised as the forty-foot tree which had been standing there by the gate for generations.

Jim turned on the light and asked me what was going on and I couldn't really explain it or put it into words and all he commented was 'Good heavens... The tree has fallen down... You'd better ring the police... It might hurt somebody if it topples over more...' I went downstairs to the office/switchboard and rang the local nick. It was permanently engaged and when I got a ringing tone after half an hour I got a rather weary, 'Can I help you?'

'I wanted to report a tree which seems to have fallen down...' No doubt he really wanted to tell me in Jackspeak not to be so idiotic as every tree in Kennington Road had been brought down as if a giant bulldozer had come down the road and chopped down

320

every tree in sight, on both sides of the road. He immediately switched to practical 'Tom speak' and asked if there had been any actual damage to any person or persons, and I was happy to report in the negative.

'Can you get in or out of your house?' I had another look and reluctantly had to admit that I could possibly manage to climb over the tree for exits or entries. After all we had three loos so we needed no tree to relieve ourselves against and in any case that was against the law … in public that is.

'I'll send someone along in the morning when he looks at all the damage in the street. Do you have the name of a tree surgeon?' asked the copper.

I knew that the doctors at St Thomas had many titles but what on earth was a tree surgeon, and when I asked him he patiently explained to me that their function was to chop, trim and cut down trees which needed attending to.

Five years at Hampton Grammar, many more at the University of Life at No.779 Chelsea Closets, four months in the US and five years in the RN and I had never even heard of this occupation. Nor had many in southern England until that terrible night when tree specialists were required by the victims of the millions of trees cut down by the hurricane.

Our long residency at the cottage in Kent provided a valuable lead in this direction and within two weeks two very keen English lumberjacks arrived and scratched their combined heads. 'Be easier if we chopped it into two-foot-wide lumps.' As they were four foot in diameter we needed a crane to lift them out and over the smashed gate. The problem was getting a crane into the front garden. After a lot of discussion and trial and error the job was completed in two days. However, I was very cross with myself because I could smell some very tasty wood dust mixed with pound notes.

Britain was not a country which had many tree surgeons and it was therefore obvious that there were few electric saws in use in Britain. I found out that the most used electric chainsaw manufacturer in Germany was STIHL and I could already see the sawn-off trees turning into lovely rolled-up bundles of Deutsche marks.

'So sorry, Sir', said a director in Germany with perfect English, 'but there is so much business there now, we have sent a sales group over to the UK and they can't cut down enough trees to write down on paper all the saws we are selling in Britain right now. Better luck next time. Bye-bye...' And he hung up.'

What the hell was he talking about ... next time?

'What's next then?' asked the ever-practical Jim. I wanted to practice my Jackspeak regarding the removal of the tree trunks which resembled an English timberyard in the front garden.

I now thought of the actual wood itself, much of which still graced our front garden. We contacted our antique furniture friends, Jewell's, who put us in touch with a specialist company who wanted 150-year-old oak which we had a few ounces of. The resulting haggle over removal costs versus wood value proved a textbook exercise in bartering.

One year later a gentlemen of 'Hector' calibre walked through the hole of what had been the iron gate to No.121. He thought for a moment, paused and sucked his pencil. Minutes later he proceeded to the front door and rang the bell.

'Could I see the owner please?' raising his bushy eyebrows.

'I'm sorry but the owner is the Walcot Estate; they're a few doors away.' I pointed him along Kennington Road.

'But you reside here; you must be the owner,' he insisted.

I really did not have the time to pass on my ownership legal knowledge which had cost us so much to acquire at Freddie's.

'We're only tenants to the estate,' I insisted, thinking this free information would be appreciated. He totally disregarded my helpful info and continued: 'As the owner, it's your responsibility to look after, repair or replace any trees, and we don't appear to have received a request or permission in my department to remove a tree from this property. I'm the Tree Preservation Officer of the Borough of Lambeth and as such you have contravened the relevant order and you will be notified of the contravention and the immediate action you must undertake to replace the item that was removed without permission. Did you apply for or receive permission in writing to remove the tree?'

I felt that the only way I could resolve the impasse was to be brutally factual and with the best of smiles I could muster I said: 'That will be a little difficult as the tree came from India almost two hundred years ago. The person who removed it was...' I pointed at the heavens above us.

'Sarcasm will not solve this problem,' he pointed out acidly, turned on his heels and departed. Halfway towards the smashed gate I called out to him: 'Excuse me, but there was another tree in the back garden. Are you interested in that as well?' But he had disappeared as fast as those STIHL saws could slice through tree trunks.

Tale 50

Lambeth Elks

'Elk' – large, four-legged animal, deer-kind found in Northern Europe (*Oxford Concise Dictionary*). Not found in South London's Lambeth, it ain't, which Jim confirmed when he heard the iron gate squeak and looked out of the window.

'Oh god, you haven't parked somewhere dodgy, have you, Dave? It's a copper coming to the front door.' Before I could answer him, the front-door bell rang and I opened the door to a two-legged blue-uniformed PC.

'Sorry to disturb you, Sir, I hope it's not too inconvenient, but can I come in for a minute?' Before I could answer, he crossed the doorstep and stepped into the lobby. He looked a chubby, baby-faced thirty-year-old Dixon of Dock Green type, with starting signs of a beer belly. I pointed him towards my office and before sitting down he looked around the room admiringly. 'Beautiful, isn't it? I've passed this place for years. It was almost derelict before, wasn't it?' I nodded. 'Sorry to digress...'

Before sitting himself down on the other side of the partners desk, he placed his hands to the sides of his helmet, lifted it off and apologetically said, 'I hope you don't mind, Sir?' and placed it on the floor next to his chair.

As his head came up I looked at it and froze. It was as snow-white as his newly washed Persil-white shirt and he noticed my stare.

'I'm sorry ... I shouldn't stare...' I said, but he cut me off with a wave of his hand.

'I got a bigger shock when I came off duty sixteen months ago and found a 'Dear John' letter on the mantelpiece: the wife had done a runner with the local doctor...' Much to my surprise he grinned all over his face. 'The shock turned it white overnight,' he said, running his five fingers through the mass of white hair.

'Well, at least it's all over now and I think that there will soon be another missus to keep the bed warm ... but I've not really come to tell you my life story, have I? What I've come about is to introduce myself ... I'm your local beat officer.'

I hadn't a clue what that was because the only beaters I'd ever heard of were the gentlemen who beat the heather to disturb the birds at a shoot up in Scotland. My only previous knowledge of the Metropolitan Police had been the two coppers who had taken Dad and Billy away to be interned in 1940; PC Charles Wing, who had detained me for my seven-minute lateness at Richmond station in 1941, and the two coppers at the foot of my bed at Northampton General after the car crash in 1953, even then, those two were not from the Met.

My visitor explained to me that many houses in Kennington Road had now been converted – 'Not as nicely as this one, if I may say so!' – and the local Nick had now allocated a squad to watch for the 'regulars' and 'casual kids' who were 'doing' the nice houses. 'Next door to you No.123, the tea importers, were done last week; must have been kids, they only nicked the 'petty cash' which was by the open window...'

He handed a card to Jim and me: 'Ring on the direct line and ask for Robin if it's panic stations.' Jim smirked. 'That's the talk I picked up from a bloke who has joined us from the RN.'

Now Jim was grinning from ear to ear. 'The heads are up top if you want them,' he said and Robin turned on his heels and proceeded up our fine old staircase to the loo.

Looking visibly relieved he returned a few minutes later.

'It is a beautiful house, isn't it? Charlie had told me a lot about it. He and his cab are in the garage complex behind here and the *South London Press* tells me everything that goes on in this little corner of Lambeth. The Elks know when anybody coughs...' I stared at him. 'That's why we have these,' he explained. He touched the epaulettes on his shoulders and his finger pointed to the two letters preceding his number. 'It says "LK", doesn't it? Stands for LK division or "Elk" for short. But we don't have any antlers...' This he proved by running his hand through his thick white hair.

Even if they had grown antlers, they would not have been much use from Friday 10th April until Monday 13th April 1981. A Methodist minister called the events that unfolded for seventy-two hours in April 1981 in Brixton 'a firewall of anger'.

On the afternoon of Friday 10th April a police patrol spotted a young black man with a stab wound in his back wandering along Railton Road. With the intent of taking him to hospital, an ambulance was called and when the police were bandaging the teenager in the car a group of black youths attacked it. When the ambulance arrived and the teenager was taken to hospital a second police car arrived, bottles were thrown through the police vehicle windscreens and mayhem started, exploding into a build up of police strength and 'Swamp 81'. The police action plan was one of the reasons which set the match to an explosive situation which neither they or anyone else had ever experienced before or since.

It engulfed black and white, male and female, young and old and was the worst example of multiculturism and multi sexism working together towards the complete destruction of society as we know it. Cars and houses were burned; ambulances, fire engines and police cars were destroyed and torched. The George and Windsor Castle public houses were petrol-bombed and razed to the ground. Post offices, and shops were looted and burned to the ground and anarchy reigned for those days in one of the leading capitals of the Western world.

When it was all over and in excess of £7 million of damage had been done, the inquests started, but one of the unifying strands was the hope that it would never happen again and the local communities combined to try and find a way to put a constructive plan into action. Robin, my local beat officer, came around a month later and reported the sad details of the events in Brixton and asked for volunteers to help in rebuilding the community. He had seen Jim and I run a tight 'ship', which impressed him, and he asked us if we could help set up organisational office work as LK was stretched to the limit in that particular area. I promised to help out and met with Robin and one of his mates on a project to try and keep kids off the streets during the school holidays.

We leafleted local firms for donations and set up a committee to explore ways and means to keep the kids occupied. A derelict site near Kennington Road seemed the ideal place to rebuild and employ young labour during the holidays. The idea, it seemed, was eventually to open a Community shop. This blossomed into the Kennington Summer Project and was up but not quite running when I was asked to join the committee. In my personal experience in the UK and Europe, I had always found that the smaller a

Committee, the sooner one had a decision and if you asked four people you usually received four different answers and I was not the ideal person on a committee of six persons.

At the very first meeting I asked what the local project was going to achieve apart from the kids on the site being occupied instead of nicking and stealing cars and their contents. A building firm had put their architect and works manager on a 'free availability' list and also freely allocated a foreman and two staff to show the kids how to handle and use the building tools.

At the end of the first day the craftsmen, who used their own tools, discovered that the best ones had been nicked by the kids they were teaching and I also asked the committee what the shop they were building was going to sell and the answer was 'goods'.

There were blank looks and when I explained that my experience over many years meant one had to plan and examine the 'feasibility' of the goods one was going to sell. 'What sort of goods *are* we going to sell?' I asked and they replied that the 'ladies' could bake some cakes and they could be sold in the shop. 'How many are you going to bake if you don't know what the customer flow is? And what are you going to do with the unsold ones?' To all of which which I just got more blank stares.

However, we all continued to collect money for the project and funds, which had now reached five figures, were being spent on raw materials for rebuilding and renovating the shop. This was a former gatehouse to a Victorian almshouse, down a side street off Kennington Lane – not exactly a prime location for a shop near the Elephant and Castle Shopping Centre. This had already proved to be the biggest White Elephant of any retailing venture in SE1 since World War II. Eventually we did not exactly come to blows but it was suggested to me, in the nicest possible way, that they would be grateful if we parted company. A royal visitor opened the shop on 30th September 1992 with great fanfares. Three months later it closed due to a lack of customers. All the voluntary work, time and money spent on it went down the drain to the Thames and out to the open sea.

All Jim said was: 'Told you so... Volunteer? Never again, ... Dave!'

Tale 51

Gizza Ballott

Having recovered from my fruitless efforts to help and rebuild some of the local community, I took Jim's advice and concentrated on enlarging the air-freshener side of the business. European textiles were being replaced by Far Eastern and Eastern European merchandise and many high class suppliers closed down.

Mitch was totally tied up in the factory in Battersea and the 'Bundle of Joy' had transformed from a teenager into a husband in his twenties. He followed Maureen and Roy to the new development in Surrey Quays. This was just as well as not only my personal 'South London Press', but the newly found coppers were telling me that the bottom end of Oakden Street was becoming decidedly 'dodgy' with an influx of 'villains'. I never did find out which sector of villainry they specialised in as the only response I got when I asked was a 'shaking of the head' accompanied by a sucking of teeth which sounded like the woosh from a soda fountain.

This silence was also the hallmark of Greg, the late bundle of Joy from Oakden Street. He would have been the ideal occupant of Bletchley, as it was quite impossible to get anything out of him even if one were to have tried to squeeze him. Oyster wasn't in it. He almost gave an answer if asked and 'under duress' wasn't in it. I somehow felt that he had so many female balls in the air at one time it was natural for him not to say anything ... just yes or no. But he oozed charm which all the ladies I had seen with him confirmed prior to that ring being attached on the third finger of his left hand.

He and Mitch seemed to divide the duties at the factory but, as the textiles had almost died and I was spending all my time at Lerpiniere House or with the major supermarkets, the only time I

328

saw six foot tall, jet-black haired smiling Greg was either on occasional mornings to collect the air-freshener mail or to collect the evening mail to be posted. His smile was as infectious as his efficiency and at times it seemed as if Mitch was more isolated at the factory than either Jim or I could have known.

Two years into the new lifestyle and on a Saturday morning in the spring of 1984, Jim and I were knee-deep in the papers. Jim had his pen ready to mark any items of interest to me, or which would be guaranteed to wind me up. Suddenly he sat up, turned the paper back on itself and read something that seemed to surprise and shake him.

'I don't know if this should be marked with a cross...' He stopped himself and stared at me. 'It's an item about the miners' strike. Since it started in March all the news had been reported as the "democratic" wishes of the NUM being quashed by the marauding brutal Police force of Mrs Thatcher's bully boys. I think you ought to read this, though it may bring back some bad memories and your Wolfy saga by the Wannsee in Berlin all those years ago.' Jim handed the paper over to me. I started to read what was an English version of an article taken from one of the leading newspapers in Germany, the *Frankfurter Allgemeine Zeitung*:

MR SCARGILL DOESN'T EVEN ANSWER OUR LETTER
A GROUP OF WORKING MINERS FIGHT ARTHUR
SCARGILL

London 23 October

To someone who has lived here for decades but can remember his youth, the sight of battling picket lines and working miners being intimidated is sending shivers down the spine, recalling the street battles and saloon brawls of the Weimar Republic. Nearly 8,000 miners have been arrested, some for minor offences, some for arson and some for attempted murder, including the attempted decapitation of a motorcyclist by a wire being stretched across a road in his path and the forcing off the road of a car containing four members of a working miner's family.

More than 800 policeman have been injured, 65 seriously; two miners have committed suicide and two were seriously injured on the picket line and later died. The National Working Miners Committee, an action group of nine miners from various areas, has compiled a catalogue of violence, insults, threats and attacks on homes which have been committed day by day. The variance of insults continues and recently even children of working miners have been shouted at and attacked as 'scabs'. The nine members are under constant threat of violence themselves and the local police has installed 'a panic alarm button' in their homes to protect them and their families.

Letter from a working miner's wife in Stoke-on-Trent, 15.10.84:

> 109 Newlands Street
> Shelton
> Stoke on Trent
> Staffs S14 2RS

On 14th May 1984 someone entered our home (uninvited I may add). They then decided they would pour a tin of paint over our children's pets, their toys and our one-year-old's pushchair. Since then we have exhausted ourselves trying endless ways to replace not only the toys but the security the children have lost. I nearly forgot to mention that the word 'Scab' was daubed over both front and back doors and windows and our van was also 'kicked in'. We have nightly visitors who take delight in banging on the doors and our children are called 'scabs' etc. A neighbour has even been stabbed – the police treated it as mistaken identity believing my husband was the intended victim. Our son, who is six, had his brakes meddled with and ended up under a bus. We contacted the NUM for compensation but no reply came. Our local MP told us Neil was wrong to work and should join the strike!

I suddenly remembered those stormtroopers ... and Wolfy jumping over the fence with blood everywhere ... it was like a film going backwards with the spool unwinding. Jim asked if I was OK. I sort of mumbled 'yes', knocking over the coffee cup and spilling it over the half-eaten bacon and egg.
'You sure you're all right?' he asked again in a very concerned tone of voice. I stared at him. He forced himself to give a little

grin and adding, 'Bet you want to do something to help, don't you,' I nodded.

'Can't blame you! What will you do?'

'Well it's Saturday. But on Monday I'll ring this bloke and dig something out...'

At eleven thirty on Monday I spoke to the filer of the story and expressed surprise that there was no mention of it in any other paper or on radio or TV.

'Simple,' came the reply. 'For one thing, it's a very small story against the media avalanche that Arthur Scargill has mounted since the strike began at the beginning of the year. And for another, not putting too fine a point on it, many NUJ members are slightly left of Beijing, even the ones at the *FT*. But what's your interest in it and what do you want me to do?' he asked.

'My interest in the story is that I was part of it in line one of your copy and as for what you can do to help, put me in touch with the Working Miners Committee to see if I can help them in any way.'

He seemed to have no objection to that and gave me the direct line to a pithead that John Blessington worked in. When John answered the phone he was very cagey, thinking I was a Scargill spy. Only when I told him my background and offered my help did he begin to thaw out. When I told him I knew a number of London journalists the only thing that stopped him from kissing me was the telephone. 'We'd like to meet you... Do you mind?'

Two days later three of them arrived at Lerpiniere House and I thought I had walked into a film studio that was auditioning for a mining movie. They had a mix of Nottingham and Staffs accents between them and had never been further south than Rugeley. Kit was on hand to serve coffee and tea and the air was thick with 'Oh, aren't they lovely boys?' They stayed until The Ship opened, to which we adjourned with pads and pencils.

I rang every journalist I had ever spoken to, or handed a story to, without my byline or name, which reminded me of collecting 'sippers' or 'gulpers' in days gone by. One of them knew Jochen Rudolph who was the London correspondent of the *Frankfurter Allgemeine Zeitung*, which was *The Times* of Germany. He suggested we organise a meeting of journalists and foreign TV crews at the Foreign Press Club in Pall Mall, and by the end of the month the packed meeting had lift-off. Six members of the Working Miners

331

Committee were the specially invited guests and I felt that Cecil B. De Mille would have been proud of us. Except of course, there were no members of the Folies Bergères present, but then, you can't have everything. Dear Charles would have commented 'Why not?' But surely not in Pall Mall at the Foreign Press Club.

The burly blokes from the Midlands were delirious and British journalists started to take notice of the working miners' press releases and the mass of coverage in the European press and I was shit-scared as my name and address was on all the press mentions. However, Wolfy must have mustered his own flying pickets as none penetrated the security of Lerpiniere House. Perhaps the self-adhesive posters of the working miners stuck on all the doors and windows of cars helped. They just had two words on them which was 'Gizza Ballot' which was the reason for them not joining the strike. Arthur Scargill had flagrantly broken the Union Rule 43 by not having a ballot before calling the strike.

In October Mrs Thatcher and the entire Cabinet were staying at the Metropole Hotel in Brighton to attend the Conservative Party Conference. On the 12th the entire hotel was torn apart by a bomb, which maimed many but not Mrs Thatcher, as she was in the bathroom when the bomb had exploded.

Just before Xmas we had some money to give to the working Miners' kids whose toys had been destroyed by Scargill's storm troopers and some of the Working Miners Committee came to Lerpiniere House. They had booked tickets with the same bus companies who were transporting striking miners to demonstrate their protest outside Mrs Thatcher's hotel. On checking the booking sheets for the striking miner buses they found that the buses had been cancelled for the day they had been booked for and the pages for the bookings had been removed on the day the bomb exploded.

No-one has ever reported this nor were Wolfy or his puppies ever able to pick up the scent of the mysterious disappearances of the booking sheets with cancellation of the buses. Nor was there an explanation why they were cancelled at the last moment.

Adolf Hitler served his term of imprisonment in Landsberg jail from 11 November 1923 – 20th December 1924. He wrote 'Mein Kampf' (my 'Struggle') which became the Nazi blueprint which many ignored.

In an interview with 'New Left Review' in 1975 Arthur Scargill clearly set out what his blueprint aims were:

'The issue is a very simple one: it is THEM and it is US.
I will never accept anything else because it is a class battle,
it is a class war.
While it is them and us, my position is perfectly clear:
I want to take FROM them FOR us. In other words I want
to take into common ownership everything in Britain.'

Tale 52

Cordon Bleu – Chez Winco

When Inge and Emanuel received our 'change of address' card in 1988, he was on the phone like a steely flash from the Mossad. 'Why the change?' he urged me to tell him. 'I know we haven't seen you since Zurich but to cut a long story very short, we're in London next month and would love to see you. Don't worry, we'll book our double at the Dorchester. How far is Wincott Street from Kennington Road?'

'It's literally around the corner, and I can pick you up by car,' I replied.

'You are still driving, David? But please don't bother, we'll get a cab. Lunch or dinner?'

'Whichever suits you better...'

'Constance Spry', and all her neighbours on Jim's Cordon Bleu bookshelf, were summoned on the Saturday prior to the Holy Land nosh. I always felt the preparation was the bit he really loved to organise, going to the market in Brewer Street and a few select locations in Lambeth like Bob White's for the fish.

Jim had a collection of memo pads which listed every dinner party at One-Two-One with visitors' names and menu details. This way, he avoided the indignity of serving the same dishes twice. Inge and Emmanuel had not featured in any booklet going back to the pre-Lerpiniere days, so Jim had a free hand. Had it been a little later in the day he would have lit a cigar but instead he had another cup of tea, got out his biro and started to plan: 'Manny has agreed to shellfish and a non-kosher meal so I think...' short Pause '...I'll order up some giant prawns from Bob White's ... six each. No, I'll order thirty-six so we can have some for lunch the next day, just as we had them in Malta when I took you there last year. Mushrooms chopped fine, tossed in butter and fresh

334

parsley and two cloves of garlic crushed and served from the pan after the prawns have been tossed in. A little rice on the side and I can smell it now ... yum ... yum. Slaters can cut us a piece of veal for roasting... Get three pounds so we can have it for another meal...

'Sweet is dead easy ... I'll do them Gerry's favourite, orange fool, which she used to swear came from Boodles but to be honest, I couldn't care less if it came from down the Old Kent Road...' He put his pen back on the table, folded up the little notebook, handed it to me and ordered: 'You take the shopping list for the menu ... or I'll have ya, wings!'

I just nodded. After all, you don't argue with a Killick.

The day of the dinner soon came. 'They're here,' shouted Jim from the first-floor lounge and I rushed to the door to welcome them. We had a very narrow hall, which they now proceeded to squeeze through. Inge's Chanel filled the air. Jim appeared at the top of the stairs and Inge threw her arms around him as if they were re-enacting Rodin's *Lovers*. As she entered the lounge her hands came up to her face and she gasped. 'When I saw the small street and the terraced houses I was quite taken aback because of the down-market appearance against One-Two-One, but this is fantastic... It's a complete replica of a small One-Two-One...'

'...And it looks just as cosy,' added Manny, appearing in the doorway behind her.

When it came to exchanging news, I didn't really know where to begin. Manny pushed me along helpfully: 'You brought us up to date in Zurich, so what's happened since then?'

I took a deep breath: 'The textile scene collapsed and then, in '88, we discovered that Mitch seemed to be suffering from the male menopause. He was having it off with an Italian widow with two grown-up sons who was working part-time in the factory. She decided to ensure full and night time employment and when we asked Mitch why, he replied that if he didn't look after her, she would throw herself off her council-flat balcony and Mitch would be responsible for her death. To bring home her threat, one day, when Mitch and I came out of the factory, she stood in front of me, stamped her foot on the pavement and screamed at me: "Don't you touch me or him ... HE'S MINE!"'

'If he had been a sixteen-year-old boy seamen I would have tried to talk to him but he was a 54-year-old ex-Killick who should have told her when she threatened to jump off the balcony: 'Go ahead, love, there's the balcony'... But sadly he didn't and went off to live with her in her council flat.'

Inge just stared and Manny, under his breath, murmured something about his being a certain fornicating Jackspeak illegitimate child.

'This, plus the fact that One-Two-One had been fabulous as a monument but without a business was now "surplus to requirements". We had bought this house just after moving into Oakden Street and always let it out to nurses and doctors from St Thomas's. We reached a friendly agreement for them to leave and also put the One-Two-One lease up for sale. It did not take long before the "Desirable eighteenth-century company headquarters within the sound of the Division Bell" went on and off the market...'

At this point Manny stopped me. 'What about the factory? What happened to the "Tree" business and the staff?'

Jim smiled benevolently. 'They say that all koshers are lucky!' He pointed his thumb at me. 'Dave certainly is and the night Mitch left to find his new life, Dave and I asked Greg out to dinner as we felt that we had to close the factory because Mitch had left. Over a very nice local Italian dinner, we put our cards on the table and told him straight that as Mitch was running the factory we would have to close as there was no one to run the place.'

I took up the story: 'Placid, oyster-like, voiceless Greg exploded and in his best local vernacular spluttered: "No one to run it...? Who do you think has been running the factory all of last year... He's been at Candida's flat all day and *I've* been running it!"

'After another litre of rosso later we had heard the whole sordid tale, so when Greg ran out of breath and thirst Jim got practical. "Look you know you can run the place but we don't know that. You don't know if you can put up with us ... and don't take that literally ... you know old sailors' tales... If after six months there are no problems between us, you take over," and he pushed his hand toward Greg.

'He grabbed it, searched for mine and a big grin spread across his face. "So we've got a deal?" I felt he thought it was easier than scoring goals from penalties.'

As personally-imported cars were still cheaper than buying identical vehicles in the UK we had continued on the own personal-importation path. At the beginning of '88 we had ordered another Citroën and when the dealer in Germany sent us a fax that the new XM Citroën was ready for collection Jim told me that as I was now officially of retirement age there was no way I was going to get the car and drive it across Europe on my own. 'Ask Greg if he wants to join the gravy train and co-drive the new XM with you to London,' he suggested. Not surprisingly Greg uttered two words only. After all, that was an effort because it was 100% more than just that one word: 'yes' and the two words were 'why not?' and I don't know how many words that satisfied grin that accompanied the two words would have qualified for.

'Are you going to do anything apart from the collection?' Greg asked me adding coyly, 'Bet you've got something else planned.' and I grinned for a change.

'Clever little bastard!' I replied.

A big smile spread across his face. 'Wrong on two counts, Dave.' I raised my eyebrows. 'I don't know about clever, but Mum and Dad wouldn't like it if you said I was a bastard. As for little, that's not what me mates usually comment on in the showers after the game.'

'Boasting again?' I grinned at Greg and he just shrugged his shoulders and crawled back into his oyster shell.

The car went like a dream and Greg wound it up once we were on the autobahn. At Greven I shuddered for a moment and told Greg about that time we had heard about Mountbatten being blown up in his boat all those years ago. We called on Ford of Germany in Cologne to see if there was a chance to make an air-freshener for them and then turned back towards the motorway and the coast. After twenty minutes Greg turned to me and raised his eyebrows. It was simpler than talking but as I hadn't a clue what he wanted, I asked him.

'Fancy a "change of driver" stop? I'll take the next exit coffee place and you can try the XM if you like. Sorry, but she's only got four wheels... Be all right for the two of us ... two of each,' and he pulled into a motorway rest-stop. He switched off the engine, handed me the keys and said, 'Your turn...?'

I thought I could imitate him and just nodded and said nothing. 'Fancy a bite to eat apart from the coffee?' I queried and he actually uttered a sentence. 'I'll have what you have.'

I deliberately did not choose *Kalbshaxe*, as I thought this would upset the delicate veal wagon, so we had two enormous Bratwurst which got the full-sentence treatment of 'Great'.

After the second cup of coffee I thought I'd be daring and asked him a question: 'Listen Greg, that trial period is over for us and you...' I waited and got a small smile and nod. 'How do you feel about taking over the factory?' I nearly died awaiting the answer. He looked at me and gave me a smile which turned into a very large grin.

'Dave, I thought you were joking when you said it originally. Yes, I think I could handle it but what about Jim; is it all right with him?' and a large look of relief came over Greg when I nodded as he sat back contentedly.

'But seriously, once you've run the factory, what do you really want to do apart from that?' I looked straight into those questioning brown eyes of his.

'Do you really want to know, Dave?' I was all ears and nodded.

Uncharacteristically he suddenly thawed and looked me straight in the eyes and very quietly said, 'I want your job of course,' and jabbed his thumb at me as if wanting to stab me with it. His grin was spreading from his face across the autobahn and all the way to Wincott Street in London and he looked as happy as if he had finally won the last match of the season and was carrying the 'Vets' cup in his left arm, raised his right arm, clenched his fist and shouted: 'YEEEES.'

Tale 53

The Doctor and GP Son from Zurich

When I met Dr Saemann in Zurich thirty years ago I discovered that his doctorate was in the chemical field. I also met his wife, his little son and daughter. It is ironic that his daughter married a GP. The son, Ronald, qualified as one and worked as a locum for his brother-in-law.

However, after a number of years, Ronald decided to emigrate to Canada just across the border to run their factory in Watertown. The 'Magic Tree' business exploded worldwide and ours did as well. However, what Ronald did not appreciate was the fact that we had opened up a market which had zero sales when we started. We were continually increasing sales and pumping more money into the manufacturing side by updating machinery annually.

He came to London in November 1990 and we met for lunch on Armistice Day at the Strand Palace Hotel. This, like President Roosevelt's famous remark on 8th December 1941, turned out to be a 'day of infamy'. I gave him a royalty cheque which was 15 per cent higher than the previous highest sales total and got the usual 'Is that all?' comment.

Our salesmen were hearing stories that 'Magic Tree' was going to be sold on 1st January 1991 by a competitor which Ronald dismissed like brushing a bagged Tree off the dining room table and when we had finished the main course he produced a lined A4 pad and started writing. As I am not very good at reading handwriting upside down, I asked him about the contents of his literary effort.

When we had made preparations to start manufacturing, Freddy had strongly advised us to get a specialist lawyer as 'under licence' manufacturing was a minefield of very costly proportions. Roger Losely was one of the top trademark lawyers in London and had made a waterproof contract which specified cancellation dates and penalties of large proportions. I was still awaiting the contents of Ronald's writing and, not having a direct line to Bletchley, I was tempted to ask 'What's all this then?' in Jackspeak but waited until he had finished the bottom of the tightly-written three pages.

'Oh that?' he said with a gracious wave of hand. 'Your sales are totally insufficient for your market and these here are the guaranteed minimum required or we finish tomorrow.'

I tried to point out to him that we had a contract which would expire in eighteen months as he had missed the last possible cancellation date last month. 'Rubbish' was his only comment which made me sarcastically point out that the contractual cancellation clause specifically required it. 'I don't know about that' was his firm reply, which really left me no option but to reply with 'But I do.'

We were getting nowhere very fast and he finally smiled and paused. 'If you were to agree to stop now...' (I was tempted to point out that it was Sunday.) '...I would offer you substantial compensation for the goodwill, your stock and any raw materials; I am prepared to be very generous...' He smiled a hyena-type grin.

Remembering all my previous experiences in other fields I smiled back at him and asked if he could put a figure to his generosity.

'Oh yes' ... he announced, as if he were opening the vault of the Bank of England. 'Ten thousand pounds for everything.'

If Jim had been there, he would have propped me up as he had recently increased our machinery insurance to £150,000.

I smiled benevolently at him, took a deep breath and slowly replied in 'Tom-speak'. 'If you were to make a reasonable offer ... of course our Board would consider it. Why don't you do that when you get back to Watertown and send it to us. Thank you for the lunch and have a good flight back.'

On Monday I met with Roger who laughed like a running drain. 'Silly man! Doesn't he read contracts...' He suddenly stopped. 'Do you want me to write the rest of the scenario?' He grinned all over his face. 'Are you a betting man?'

I shook my head but Roger can't have been joking.

'You make all the Trees here, don't you?' I nodded. 'But you have to buy the perfume from him? I'll ask you again, David... Do you want to take a bet that he'll stop the liquid supplies?'

'What do we do then?' I asked.

A very benevolent smile now stretched over Roger's face. 'Why do you think that there are always so many noughts on our bills? I'll bet you he is not aware that if he has accepted an order and doesn't deliver the goods, you can sue him for damages for loss of profits and if you want to know how you are going to get the damages money out of him, you stop paying the royalties...' Roger looked rather pleased with himself.

In the event we had a letter from the Doctor confirming what Roger had anticipated, including the sad fact that, due to a disaster in the factory, the liquid was not deliverable. Roger's only comment was 'Bollocks... Pay the damages or no royalties.' Meanwhile, our agents selling Magic Tree had already heard that another company had the goods from Watertown as from January 1991, so we held an emergency meeting.

As Greg was now a director, Jim and I called a spade a bloody shovel and asked him very quietly what he suggested we do. We had a factory and staff but no product to sell. We could fight and try to establish a new product in the marketplace but this would take time and money.

'Fight the bastard' was Greg's short but very much to-the-point reply. He looked at Jim and I, raised his jet-black eyebrows and frowned.

'There's just one thing; it's your money you are both risking.' He gave a large grin, 'I can always go and drive a bus but you're a bit too old for that, Dave.'

Jim looked hard at Greg. 'So you want to have a go and fight them at their own game: Magic Tree against a product we don't even have a name for?'

'Why not?' He smiled at Jim, who stretched out his hand.

Greg grabbed it and turned very serious.

'But, Jim, I have manufactured around 50 million units since I've been here so I do know a little about making air-fresheners. All we need now is a name which is well known...'

Jim cut him off. 'I don't think Roger would agree to Durex, would he?'

Before we continued on that slippery path. Greg had recovered his composure. He turned to me and asked, 'When are we seeing Roger?'

Just before Xmas Greg broke his leg. He swore black and blue

341

it was the Border terriers who had got entangled with the leads and made him slip, but Jim and I felt he had got as pissed as a newt to celebrate the new nameless product. However, many name-searching and solicitor-visiting days later produced the answer to that searching question and our own trademarked air-fresheners were presented to the market. Much to our delight, business took off like a rocket.

'Mighty Oak' could not have sounded more British and 'Pongo' could mean 'pon-go' or could be just a name, which was internationally flexible. The thing that surprised us was the total American silence on the introduction of our air-freshener, although Roger had been meticulous in his avoidance of us being open to accusations of 'passing off'. The silence grew less ominous with the years but four years later Watertown did, in fact, sue us for that very reason and we were apprehensive as to the outcome. Roger and Council were convinced the dear Doctor was up a very greasy pole, but we weren't so confident, which was underlined by the fact we could lose and have to pay six-figure damages and be closed down.

The hearing was fixed in the High Court and then we discovered the reason for Roger's confidence. In English law, in case judgment is given against a foreign company, it must deposit a sum in the court prior to the hearing to assure payment to the British company in case they lose. In the event, the Doctor dropped his bandages the day before the hearing and instead of a smiling nurse looking at him, he was looking at a very large lawyer's bill. Roger was delighted. After all, the deposit the Doctor had to make was wiped out by our and Roger's bill. Greg punched his right fist in the air; I had a double schnäppsli and Jim just said: 'Good, in'it?'

Tale 54

Not Grimm's But Dave's Tales

From trainee to company director and eventually chairman of the company had taken the 'Bundle of Joy' less than the combined life span of Barney and Wellington, Greg's two Border terriers.

Inge and Manny had been listening spellbound but as Uncle Charles had told me years ago that the romantic belief in boy meets girl, get married, have kids and live happily ever after, hardly ever happens. Like hurricanes, subsequent problems arise and Greg's life ran into rough waters when he and his wife split because she had mental problems. Fortunately there were no kids so everything was settled quite peacefully. Maureen and Roy persuaded Greg to go on holiday with them, which he jumped at, and they and Greg's mate warmed themselves in the sunny glow of Lanzarote.

Mum and Dad must have been psychic as Greg and his mate not only found sand, sea and sex, but on their return Greg got married to the sex side of his treasure hunt whom he had found in the warm climate of the Atlantic Ocean. When dear Kit, our home heart of gold, heard this, there was only one comment from her – 'Loooooooovely' – which was repeated again and again when the new marriage produced two little Morbins within the next three years.

'Are we going to eat anything today?' queried Jim acidly and pushed us downstairs, seating us around our mahogany circular table in the dining room.

'I remember this from One-Two-One,' said Inge admiringly. 'Gerry and Vicky gave it to you when you moved into Oakden Street and, of course, the beautiful set of eight chairs complement the picture. The two together must be worth a fortune now.'

Jim nodded but beckoned her and Manny to sit down on them. 'They are worth a lot and are over a hundred years old, Inge, but

343

quite honestly I'm not interested in the price now. Dave and I have made a pact that if one of us can't manage these thirty-seven tortuous stairs any longer, we'll sell the furniture, the house and hopefully enjoy whatever we have left of our lives and retire gracefully.'

Manny coughed. 'Not to put too fine a point on it, that'll be after us, won't it, dear.' Inge smiled benignly at him.

The prawns were served to 'yums' and 'ahahs' and I continued to fill the glasses. The veal was duly approved of and when Jim brought in the Boodle's special, Inge and Manny were over their non-kosher moon. Inge leant over the table to Jim and gave him a kiss. 'You should have opened a restaurant, Jim; you would have made a lot of money.'

Jim was grinning from ear to ear and stretched out his hands, palms upwards, and looked hard at her. 'Who's complaining?'

Manny smiled benevolently. 'You've done very well, haven't you? But both of you worked hard for it.'

Jim looked at me and we both joined in nodding agreement.

'You two did not even start from scratch ... you had to scratch to repay all those debts. Did you ever get any money back at all?'

'You're joking...' was Jim's instant response. 'I bet you didn't either, did you?'

A large grin spread across Manny's face and he chortled. 'What money? So it would seem that you are not on kissing terms with any of them, are you? But I can't remember you ever talking about your Dad either. It's always Uncle Charles this and Uncle Charles that but never anybody else.'

'That's true,' I replied, 'I had no affection for my Dad and I always had the impression that he hated me.'

Inge brought her hands together and gave a small clap.

'There you are, Manny; I told you that when I was in Berlin with the family, Billy was always referred to as "Little Lord Fauntleroy" and David was never mentioned. It was a pretty small circle of friends way back in the 20s and they all swore black and blue that David was not Richard's son.'

I gasped. 'Well, who the hell was my father?' Inge brushed this aside as if she were flicking Sachertorte chocolate crumbs off the white tablecloth.

'Uncle Ernest, of course! Didn't you know?'

Jim was listening transfixed and recovered before me.

'Well,' he said, 'At least you never had a row with ED, did you?'

I just sat there and Manny grinned at me. 'I knew that Billy and you were not brothers. It wasn't even like chalk and cheese ... well, perhaps Jim's chalk from Beachy Head and very ripe Camembert from France. Still there's one good thing, Uncle Charles really was your Uncle because Inge always thought he may have secretly "fancied" you...'

I burst out laughing. 'Not at all, that was sorted out years ago when he told me straight after my first ambisextrous adventures in Soho. Still, it now makes me feel much better and somehow explains his wanting me to look after May and her affairs... Well, at least that has sorted that out, but I wonder if all this explains the Franklin mania for not calling people by their real name...'

Inge chipped in: 'You're absolutely right. Take this habit of calling Billy by that name. He was named Heinz Martin Fraenkel and after his enforced Army name change became Harold Martin Franklin. I know where "Billy" came from. The German for boy is 'Bub' and the diminutive form is "Büble",' and Jim looked as blank as we all felt.

'Büble just became "Billy" for short...' she explained in desperation.

Jim put on his superior smile adding: 'We used to call that "arse over tit" or "as clear as bloody mud" ... Sorry Inge,' and Manny joined my grin.

'What about Pucky?' I asked. 'When she arrived at "Balcomie" I asked Billy why "Pucky" when her name is Elizabeth,' and he waved his hand at me.

'Because,' Inge explained, 'she acted in a Shakespeare play when at school and played Puck. As she was born in 1926 and was thirteen when the war broke out, the *Midsummer Night's Dream* must have turned into a fairy tale.'

'Some of the name changes were bizarre though,' I said, 'and all our families were glued to the Bakelite radios in the 40s when there was nothing but doom and gloom on the wireless. Doctor Goebbels had got this British bloke to broadcast for the German radio. He had this terrible nasal twang of "Jairminny calling", which became as familiar to all the Brits as Alvar Liddell reading the news. When the German bombers returned from their nightly raids on the British cities this bloke, William Joyce, would tell the terrified listeners things like: "Last night, German bombers destroyed Terminus Road in Eastbourne and 250 women and children died." Some poor lonely soldier from Eastbourne hearing this in a rathole in the Western Desert would worry himself sick because of his wife and the little ones off the Terminus Road.

'This was probably the most morale-destroying weapon used with terrible effect on British listeners. It poisoned people's minds throughout the war and William Joyce and his wife continued on this treacherous path for five years. They stayed in Berlin until the very end and made their escape westwards to the German–Danish border.

'There they parted company and on 29th May 1945 he was walking alone in a forest when he came across two British soldiers who were looking for wood. One was Captain Bertie Lickerish and the other Lieutenant Geoffrey Perry. When Joyce spoke to them in English in that nasal twang they immediately recognised the "Jairminny calling" Nazi radio call sign. They arrested him and he was eventually tried for treason, found guilty and hanged on 3rd January 1946. The irony of the whole event is here was a Jew-baiting British traitor surrendering to Lieutenant Geoffrey Perry whose real name was Horst Pinschewer, a "Jewish refugee from Nazi persecution" and had escaped to Britain at the same time as I but had not yet been naturalised.'

'I bet Jim dug all that up for you, David. Sounds just like him,' said Manny.

'Yes, he gave me the book last Xmas. It's by Mary Kenny and is called *A Personal Biography of William Joyce, Lord Haw Haw*.'

Inge looked hard at Jim. 'With all this knowledge and the cordon-bleu noshing, have you never wanted to get married and have kids?'

Before he could answer, Manny became very edgy. 'My dear Inge, I think going down the "kids'" road is a bit of a "No Entry".'

Trying another road she opened a second front and smiled at Jim. 'You know, when I met David in the 50s he loved to dance...' Manny coughed loudly. Totally ignoring Manny's unease, Inge shot another question at Jim with a broad smile: 'Tell me Jim, did you like dancing?'

'I just loved it, especially with the sailors,' replied Jim, glowing with pride.

'You didn't, Jim?' gasped Inge, who appeared to be in deep shock.

Like Greg's West Highland terriers, Jim would not let go and smiled very broadly adding: 'I used to love to run my hand over the rounded bottoms and then run my hand up and down ... well mainly down ... and then clasp them more tightly and they loved it.'

Inge was still in shock when Jim added: 'Sometimes they wore bell-bottoms but mostly the WRNS wore skirts.'

'You were asking for that, weren't you, darling?' said Manny and smacked a large kiss on Inge's cheek.

Armistice seemed to have been declared and Jim followed with a kiss and gently stroked Inge's cheek with the open palm of his left hand and Manny grabbed it tightly. 'Now I remember where I have seen you before.' He struck his forehead with the open palm of his left hand. Manny held the four fingers of Jim's hand up and came to rest on the small finger which had a ring with a tiny black stone in it. 'You told us that you were out east in carriers, but you must have gone through the Suez Canal via Malta. That was around the 50s?' and Jim nodded.

'Israel was created in 1948 and we stopped fighting the Brits and got quite friendly with them. After my adventures in the Irgun Zwei Leumi I joined Mossad and exchanged a lot of info with your lot. Colonel Nasser wanted to finish us off so anything we could buy in the way of arms we bought to protect ourselves.

'Your lot, Jim, were experimenting with some very small boats which could be radio-controlled from a mother boat without a crew...'

I stopped Manny. 'You mean the RCBs, don't you, Manny?'

His eyes boggled.

'That's the ones we used to muck around with down at *Hornet*.'

I cut in. 'The little red Radio Control Boats had a total mind of their own...' It was getting like a rugby scrum gone berserk at Twickenham.

'We took four of them out aboard HMS *Perseus* to Sliema to test for service in Malta,' added Jim.

Manny was grinning from ear to ear like a happy sailor who had just 'scored' down the 'Gut' in Valetta.

'Those were happy secretive days... We, your lot and the French were aware that Colonel Nasser was going to have another go at us, sooner or later, so the three of us pooled all our intelligence info and, as you know, Nasser later nationalised the Suez Canal which started the Suez War in '56. We contacted the RN as we thought those little RCBs would be the answer to us having a go at him at Alexandria. When we heard that four of the little RCBs were coming to Malta we asked if we could have a look at them.

'The RN told us OK but the electrics were still dodgy. Down at Gosport, one had gone out of control and rammed the stern of the mother MTB. A hurried signal from the mother boat warned them that if they touched them there again, they'd scream ... and not just blue murder... Mate ... just bloody Jackspeak.

'When the four had been safely hoisted from *Perseus*, the RN hinted that if we went aboard the little bastards, we'd be sure to find someone in "Electrics" who could sort those out for us and suggested a *Perseus* bloke who loved challenges. He had got rid of all those electrical hiccups on the Seafires and also had experience from Boscombe Down where they experimented and tested all those new gadgets. "Buy the Sparks Chief a pint or two, he'll point you in the right direction which will be a little cabouche that the bloke works from aboard *Perseus*. He's brilliant at fixing anything with wires and is a nutter when it comes to mending watches. Almost all the ship's company line up to have their watches repaired and he charges per rank; the Commander pays more for the job than the Marine Bandsman!!"' suggested Manny.

'In the event, he did love the challenge and I remember Sparks held the black control box in his right hand like handling a raw egg while his left hand caressed it like a long-lost lover. So obviously he was a left-hander and he had a very small ring on the little finger of the left hand...' Manny grabbed Jim's left hand and turned the small ringed finger around for all to see. 'And that's the bloody ring I remember...' He punched Jim in the chest.

After a few minutes of silence Jim seemed to recover and turned to Inge with a warm smile: 'Well ... Inge ... that sort of squares the circle, doesn't it? It was in the 50s when Manny held my hand and Dave held yours on all those trips to London.'

We all collapsed with laughter. Manny was the first to recover and changed the subject.

'Inge and I are older than you two and we are both looking forward to retiring gracefully to an OAP home and then, in ten years' time, you can join us. We'll play bingo, dominoes, musical chairs and snakes and ladders and eventually, when we have lost the use of our tongues and hands, we can go back to that oldest of OAP games...' He turned to the three of us in turn. 'Give me your hands...' He grabbed Inge's right palm and flattened it down on the table, fingers stretched out like an open fan. Turning to me, he urged, 'Now give me your hand and put it on top, fan fashion. And now you, Jim!' He placed Jim's on top of the slowly rising hand pyramid.

Finally he put his own hand on top and urged all of us to pull the hands out slowly from the bottom up and then replacing them slowly on top of each other. After a few minutes of the pull-out and upwards movement, he looked around the table at every one of us, giving the warmest of half-Arab and half-Kosher smiles, and then commented: 'I do hope we will be able to continue this into a very ripe old age. After all, it's the oldest of games and is called:

"Group sex in an OAP Home".'